SGML und XML

W0257278

Springer
Berlin
Heidelberg
New York
Barcelona
Hongkong
London
Mailand
Paris
Singapur
Tokio

Wiebke Möhr   Ingrid Schmidt (Hrsg.)

SGML und XML

Anwendungen und Perspektiven

Mit 79 Abbildungen

Springer

Dr. Wiebke Möhr
GMD-IPSI
Dolivostraße 15
D-64203 Darmstadt

Ingrid Schmidt
Parkstraße 7
D-69126 Heidelberg

ISBN-13: 978-3-540-65543-5   e-ISBN-13: 978-3-642-46881-0
DOI: 10.1007/ 978-3-642-46881-0

Die Deutsche Bibliothek – CIP-Einheitsaufnahme
SGML und XML. Anwendungen und Perspektiven / Hrsg.: Wiebke Möhr; Ingrid
Schmidt. – Berlin; Heidelberg; New York; Barcelona; Hongkong; London; Mailand;
Paris; Singapur; Tokio: Springer, 1999

Dieses Werk ist urheberrechtlich geschützt. Die dadurch begründeten Rechte, insbesondere die der Übersetzung, des Nachdrucks, des Vortrags, der Entnahme von Abbildungen und Tabellen, der Funksendung, der Mikroverfilmung oder der Vervielfältigung auf anderen Wegen und der Speicherung in Datenverarbeitungsanlagen, bleiben,
auch bei nur auszugsweiser Verwertung, vorbehalten. Eine Vervielfältigung dieses
Werkes oder von Teilen dieses Werkes ist auch im Einzelfall nur in den Grenzen der
gesetzlichen Bestimmungen des Urheberrechtsgesetzes der Bundesrepublik Deutschland vom 9. September 1965 in der jeweils geltenden Fassung zulässig. Sie ist grundsätzlich vergütungspflichtig. Zuwiderhandlungen unterliegen den Strafbestimmungen
des Urheberrechtsgesetzes.

© Springer-Verlag Berlin Heidelberg 1999

Die Wiedergabe von Gebrauchsnamen, Handelsnamen, Warenbezeichnungen usw. in
diesem Werk berechtigt auch ohne besondere Kennzeichnung nicht zu der Annahme,
daß solche Namen im Sinne der Warenzeichen- und Markenschutz-Gesetzgebung als
frei zu betrachten wären und daher von jedermann benutzt werden dürften.

Umschlaggestaltung: Künkel + Lopka, Heidelberg
Satz: Reproduktionsfertige Vorlage von den Herausgeberinnen
SPIN: 10703731   33/3142 – 543210 – Gedruckt auf säurefreiem Papier

Vorwort

SGML, die Standard Generalized Markup Language, setzt sich weltweit immer mehr durch: Bücher, Artikel und SGML-Web-Sites,
Konferenzen, Anwender- und Arbeitsgruppen sowie der zunehmen-
de praktische Einsatz bei Informationsanbietern und Industrieunternehmen haben SGML zu einer wichtigen Technologie für das
Dokumenten- und Informationsmanagement gemacht. Die Konzepte, auf denen SGML basiert, haben überzeugt, und die SGML-
spezifischen Werkzeuge werden leistungsfähiger. Dazu kommt die
bemerkenswerte Entwicklung der SGML-Sprößlinge HTML und
XML.

XML, die Extensible Markup Language, wird das Publizieren im
Internet ein gutes Stück voranbringen. Sie wird dies tun, weil große
Softwarehersteller wie Microsoft, Netscape und Sun an der Entwicklung des Standards mitarbeiten und weil sie daran interessiert
sind, XML-unterstützende Werkzeuge auf den Markt zu bringen.
„Smarte" Dokumente im Netz versprechen eine erhöhte Geschwin-
digkeit bei der Informationspräsentation, mehr Kontrolle über das
Ergebnis und bessere Zugangsmöglichkeiten. XML erlaubt den Nut-
zern, eigene Dokumenttypdefinitionen zu schreiben und damit die
Einschränkung durch die feste HTML-DTD zu überwinden. XML
wird aber vor allem erfolgreich sein, weil es ein Subset von SGML ist.
SGML hat als internationale Norm eine relativ lange, stabile Ge-
schichte. Das Know-how für die Entwicklung generischer Markup-
Sprachen und die Erfahrungen der täglichen Praxis fließen von
SGML zu XML – immer noch ein „moving target".

SGML ist in Deutschland durchaus etabliert und wird beispielsweise für die technische Dokumentation verschiedener Industriezweige wie der Automobilindustrie, der pharmazeutischen Industrie
und der Luftfahrt angewendet. Verlage, die strukturierte und langfristig wertvolle Substanzen in unterschiedlichen Medien publizieren
und für die Zukunft sichern wollen, benutzen ebenso SGML wie

Nachrichtenanbieter, die zunehmend auf Cross-Media-Publishing setzen. Dennoch hat SGML die breite Öffentlichkeit nicht erreicht.

In diesem Buch haben wir Beiträge aus der Praxis zusammengestellt, die einen Einblick in das Spektrum unterschiedlicher SGML/XML-Anwendungen und -Erfahrungen bieten. Ausgehend von den technischen und ökonomischen Herausforderungen der Informationsgesellschaft wollten wir herausfinden, inwieweit SGML zum wirtschaftlichen Umgang mit der Ressource Information beiträgt. Darüber hinaus interessierte uns auch der kreative Umgang mit den Informationsinhalten, der zu innovativen Geschäftsideen und neuartigen Produkten führt. Indem die Anwender selbst über ihre Erfahrungen berichten, ergibt sich ein Bild des praktischen SGML/XML-Einsatzes in unterschiedlichen Bereichen. Es war dabei nicht beabsichtigt – und auch nicht möglich –, eine streng repräsentative Auswahl aus den vielen SGML/XML-Projekten zu treffen. Wir haben uns leiten lassen von dem, was uns im weiteren Umkreis unserer eigenen Arbeit an eingeführten und innovativen SGML/XML-Anwendungen bekannt war, und wir meinen, einen interessanten Querschnitt zu bieten.

Drei Beiträge mit dem Blick zurück und nach vorn haben wir unter dem Titel *Standortbestimmung* zusammengefaßt. Charles Goldfarb und Pamela Gennusa waren international maßgeblich an der Konzeption, der Entwicklung, der Verbreitung und Umsetzung generischer Markupsprachen, insbesondere natürlich von SGML, beteiligt und wirken weiterhin in wichtiger Funktion an der Realisierung von XML mit. Manfred Krüger hat als Pionier die SGML-Geschichte in Deutschland angestoßen.

Der Teil *Praxis – heute* vereinigt Beiträge über den SGML/XML-Einsatz in unterschiedlichen Anwendungsbereichen wie der Nachrichtenindustrie, der Terminologiearbeit, bei Nachschlagewerken und Fachzeitschriften sowie in der technischen Dokumentation der Automobilindustrie.

Praxis – morgen widmet sich Pilotprojekten und eröffnet Perspektiven auf das Potential, das bei richtiger Organisation und mit entsprechenden Werkzeugen durch die Anwendung von SGML/XML ausgeschöpft werden kann.

Wir danken all unseren Autoren. Wir wissen ihren Beitrag – den sie neben ihrer laufenden Arbeit fertigstellen mußten – zu schätzen und wünschen unserem Buch, daß es viele interessierte Leser findet.

Wiebke Möhr und Ingrid Schmidt im Dezember 1998

Inhalt

Praxis – morgen

Anhang

Standortbestimmung

Future Directions in SGML/XML

Charles F. Goldfarb

Abstract

SGML is unique among information representations for its ability to preserve the abstract data content of arbitrarily complex document structures. That capability has led, over the past ten years, to the near-universal adoption of SGML for large-scale document processing. Now XML – the streamlined subset of SGML for the World Wide Web – is applying generalized markup to a vastly different class of applications, ranging from data interchange to self-describing software.

In this paper, Dr. Goldfarb, inventor of SGML and co-author of *The XML Handbook* (Goldfarb/Prescod 1998), explains the profound implications of this major shift in computing technology (as an *InfoWorld* editorial called it). He describes how the SGML family of International Standards has already been revised to accommodate these new applications, and other changes that can be expected in the near future.

Copyright ©1998 Charles F. Goldfarb. All rights reserved.

1   SGML, HTML, and XML

SGML is one of the world's most widely-used but little-known technologies. It is no exaggeration to say that our most complex and important social and technological systems are utterly dependent on SGML. Mission-critical, large-scale documentation is maintained in SGML by governments, aerospace, defense, automotive, telecommunications, and computing, to name only a few.

The most powerful information system in history, the World Wide Web, is driven by the best-known SGML application – HTML. Yet HTML, unlike other SGML applications, is used mainly for very short documents. And the fact that HTML is SGML is rarely known, even to the people using it.

The latest excitement surrounding SGML is over XML – a streamlined subset for the World Wide Web that isn't focused on document processing at all, large-scale or small. It is intended chiefly for data interchange. And once again, the fact that it is the same SGML that is used for documenting nuclear power plants and offshore oil rigs is hardly known.

How can SGML do such diverse things, on such a grand scale, and yet remain nearly invisible to the world at large? The answer isn't simple – if it were, SGML would be much better known and understood. For a first step toward that answer, we should examine the excitement over XML.

2   Why Is XML So Exciting?

Although XML and HTML are both based on SGML, there is a substantial difference between them. Consider how the markup for a comparative shopping guide for computers might look.


```
<p>P200 Laptop
<br>Friendly Computer Shop
<br>$1438
<p>P200 Laptop
<br>Discount Computer Warehouse
<br>$1299
```

```
<product>
<model>P200 Laptop</model>
<dealer>Friendly Computer Shop</dealer>
<price>$1438</price></product>
<product><model>P200 Laptop</model>
<dealer>Discount Computer Warehouse</dealer>
<price>$1299</price>
</product>
```

Both of these may appear the same in your browser, but the XML data is smart data. HTML tells how the data should look, but XML tells you what it means. With XML, your browser knows there is a product, and it knows the model, dealer, and price. From a group of these it can show you the cheapest product or closest dealer without going back to the server.

Unlike HTML, with XML you create your own tags, so they describe exactly what you need to know. Because of that, your client-side applications can access data sources anywhere on the Web, in any format. New *middle-tier* application servers sit between the data sources and the client, translating everything into your own task-specific XML.

But XML data isn't just smart data, it's also a smart document. That means when you display the information, the model name can be a different font from the dealer name, and the lowest price can be highlighted in red. Unlike HTML, where text is just text to be rendered in a uniform way, with XML text is smart, so it can control the rendition. And you don't have to decide whether your information is data or documents; in XML, it is always both at once. You can do data processing or document processing or both at the same time.

But XML can do even more. In a recent editorial, *InfoWorld* called XML "a major shift in computing technology". It said that XML could:

- End the browser wars: create once, distribute everywhere;

- Provide a data-neutral file format for Internet-commerce;

- Bridge transaction processing architecture models (Enterprise JavaBeans, Windows NT);

- Speed Web performance with more efficient data interchange.

To return to our question: How is it that one technology – SGML and its derivatives – can be used successfully for such a wide range of purposes? It is because SGML is not a processing technology; it is a document representation technology. SGML is unique among information representations for its ability to preserve the abstract data content of arbitrarily complex information structures. To appreciate the implications of this fact, let us take a closer look at the way documents are represented in computers.

3 Document Representation

Document representation can be a complex issue, combining as it does the concepts of presentability, document notation, data object notation, and character sets. Even storage methods – such as files, databases, and document management systems – are involved, because they can change a representation in subtle or undocumented ways. The relationship of all these concepts is illustrated in Figure 1.

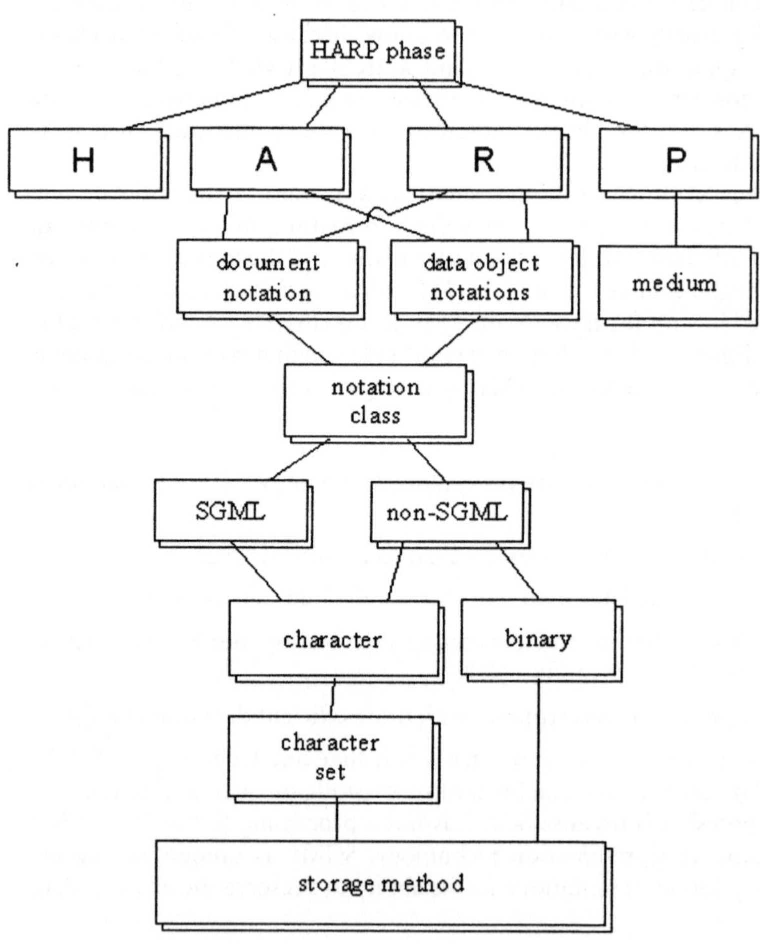

Figure 1
Document Representation Components

Of all the components of document representation, it is presentability that is the most important for understanding SGML and its future direction.

All of these document representation issues are discussed at length, with extensive tutorials, in my book, the *SGML Buyer's Guide* (Goldfarb/Pepper/Ensign 1997).

Presentability is a trait of a document that describes the document's readiness for presentation. A document can either be rendered (presentable) or abstract (unpresentable), in either the physical world or in the computer. The combinations yield four phases of presentability – Human thoughts, Abstraction, Rendition, and Presentation – derived as follows:

	Physical world	Computer
Unrendered	(H)uman thoughts	(A)bstraction
Rendered	(P)resentation	(R)endition

We call presentability the "HARP" trait, because of the initials of the four phases (and because "presentability" is such a mouthful). It could also have been called the "usability" trait, for reasons that will be described.

The concept of presentability is perhaps best grasped by considering the flow of document information among humans, with and without computer assistance.

Without a computer: A human thinks, then presents a rendition of his thoughts in a physical medium – like voice or paper – so it can be perceived by other humans. A rendition has a "style" – a set of artistic characteristics. The style helps the rendition communicate to a specific audience in the most effective and appealing way.

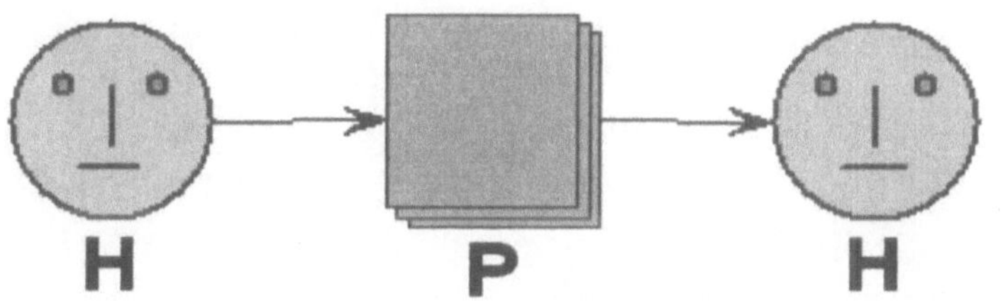

Figure 2
*Information Flow
without a
Computer*

With a computer and a word processor: A human thinks, then captures a rendition of his thoughts in computer storage. The rendition can later be presented in a physical medium – like a computer screen or printout – so it can be perceived by humans.

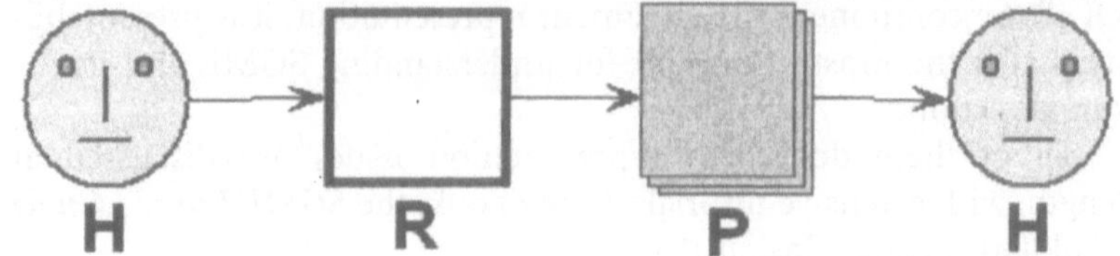

Figure 3
Information Flow
with a Computer
and a Word
Processor

With a computer and SGML: A human's thoughts are captured as abstract thoughts in computer storage. The abstract thoughts can be rendered many times within the computer, each rendition in a different style for a different audience. The multiple renditions can be presented in different physical media, so they can be perceived by humans under a variety of conditions.

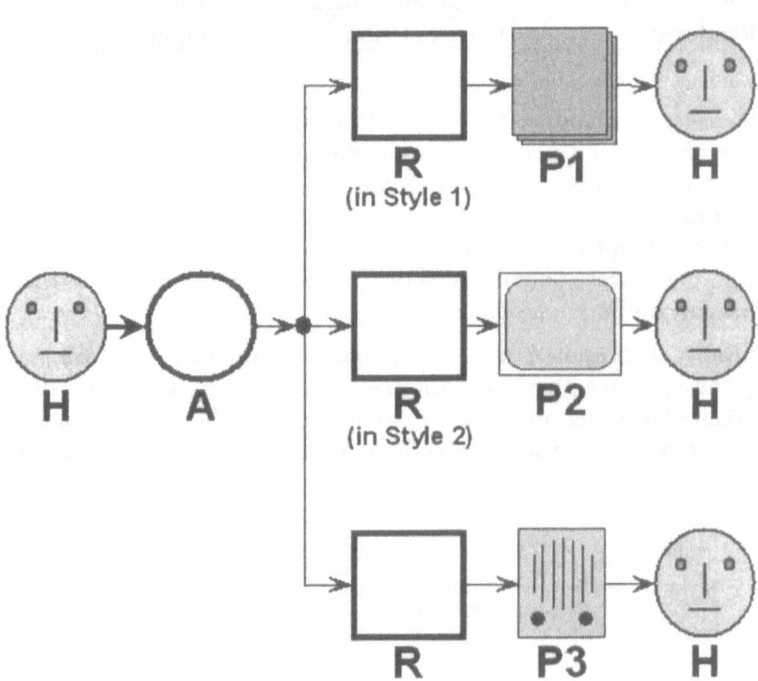

Figure 4
Information Flow
with a Computer
and SGML

The vital point about presentability is that there are more potential uses for an unpresentable (that is, abstract) document than for a presentable (that is, rendered) one. That makes the abstract phase the best choice for a document archive with long life expectancy and lots of expected reuse. Lord Chesterfield said "Style is the dress of thoughts", and naked abstractions can always be dressed as needed to

Future Directions in SGML/XML

fit the situation. On the other hand, there may be greater value (or at least, greater expense) associated with a rendition, especially if it was created by an interactive process.

The complement of presentability, then, is usability. A document in the abstract phase is maximally reusable, since multiple renditions and alternative abstractions can be created from it. However, only a rendition is ready to be presented to a human.

In summary: Thoughts are abstractions that exist in the real world, in a human mind. Presentations are renditions that exist in the real world, where humans can perceive them. A rendition has style; an abstraction does not.

a rendition has style;
an abstraction does not

Abstractions and renditions can also exist as data files in a computer. It is possible to create multiple renditions of the same abstraction by applying different styles. SGML experts frequently call abstractions "structured information". That is technically accurate, but insufficient to distinguish abstractions from renditions, which also have structure.

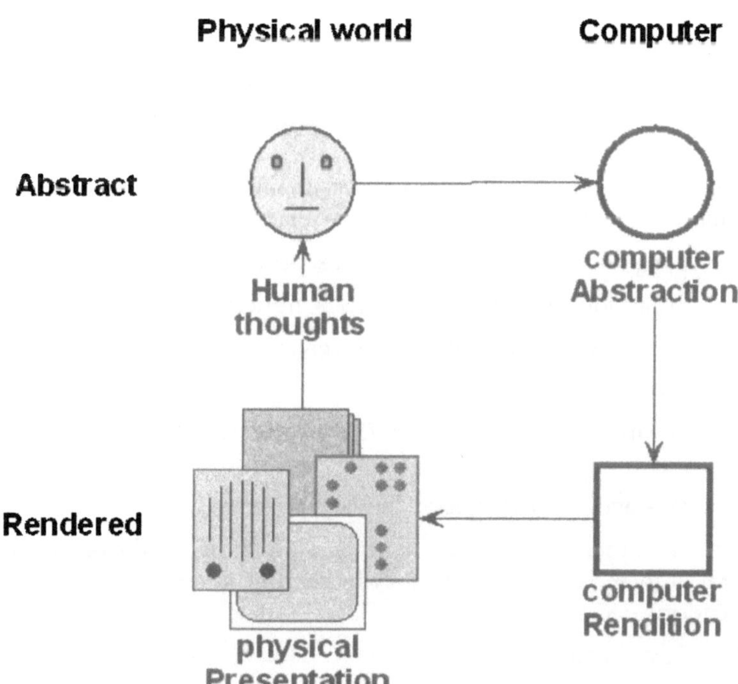

Figure 5
Summary of HARP Phases

4 The Role of XML

The power of SGML is that it can represent abstractions of any structural complexity; anything, for example, that can be represented in a relational, or object-oriented, or hybrid database. But SGML can do so without relying on proprietary database formats or software.

XML retains this power, but with much less parsing overhead. That is because it eliminates almost all of SGML's syntactic customization and options, while retaining the ability to create your own document types, element types, attributes, and hyperlinks.

XML scales down so well that it can be used efficiently for the smallest pieces of data. And it has the added benefit of enabling that data to be processed both as data and as a document.

4.1 Is XML for documents or for data?

What is a document?

My dictionary says:

> Something written, inscribed, engraved, etc., which provides evidence or information or serves as a record:

Documents come in all shapes and sizes and media, as you can see in Figure 6. Here are some you may have encountered:

- Long documents: books, manuals, product specifications
- Broadsides: catalog sheets, posters, notices
- Forms: registration, application, etc.
- Letters: email, memos
- Records: "Acme Co., Part# 732, reverse widget, $32.50, 5323 in stock"
- Messages: "job complete", "update accepted"

An e-commerce transaction, such as a purchase, might involve several of these. A buyer could start by sending several documents to a vendor:

- Covering note: a letter
- Purchase order: a form
- Attached product specification: a long document

The vendor might respond with several more documents:

- Formal acknowledgment: a message
- Thank you note: a letter
- Invoice: a form

The beauty of XML is that the same software can process all of this diversity. Whatever you can do with one kind of document you can do with all the others. The only time you need additional tools is when you want to do different kinds of things – not when you want to work with different kinds of documents.

the beauty of XML ...

And there are lots of things that you can do.

4.2 XML – An endless spectrum of application opportunities

Sorry about that, we've been reading too many marketing brochures. But it's true, nevertheless.

At one end of the spectrum we have the grand old man of generalized markup: POP – Presentation-Oriented Publishing.

You can see him in Figure 7.

Figure 7
POP Application

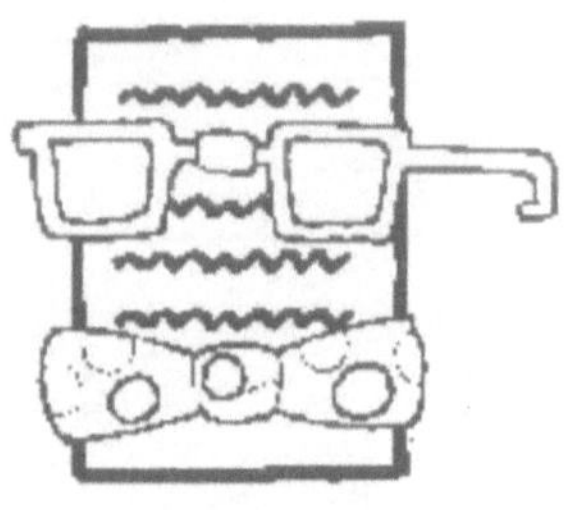

At the other end of the spectrum is that darling of the data processors, MOM – Message-Oriented Middleware. She smiles radiantly from Figure 8.

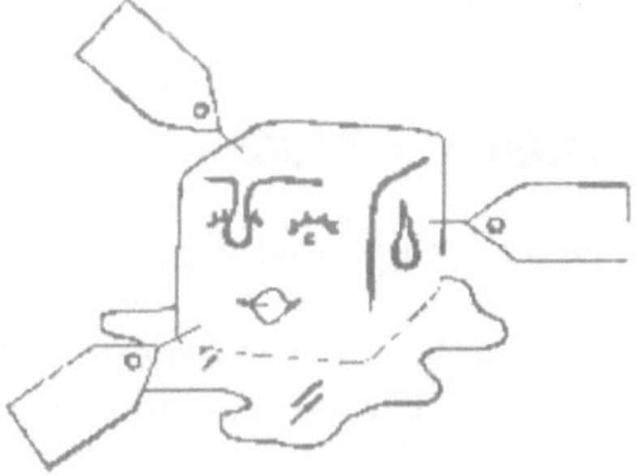

Figure 8
MOM Application

Let's take a closer look at both of them.

4.2.1 Presentation-oriented publishing (POP)

POP was the original killer app for SGML, XML's parent, because it saves so much money for enterprises with Web-sized document collections.

POP was the original killer app for SGML

POP documents are chiefly written by humans for other humans to read.

Instead of creating formatted renditions, as in word processors or desktop publishing programs, XML POP users create unformatted abstractions. That means the document file captures what is in the document, but not how it is supposed to look.

To get the desired look, the POP user creates a stylesheet, a set of commands that tell a program how to format (and/or otherwise process) the document. The power of XML in this regard is that you don't need to choose just one look – you can have a separate stylesheet for every purpose. We know that all office suites have some degree of stylesheet support today, but the SGML languages did it first, and are still the only way to do it cleanly. At a minimum, you might want one for print, one for CD-ROM, and another for a Web site.

POP documents tend to be (but needn't be) long-lived, large, and with complex structures. When delivered in electronic media, they may be interactive. How they will be rendered is of great importance, but, because XML is used, the rendition information can be – and is – kept distinct from the abstract data.

4.2.2 Message-oriented middleware (MOM)

MOM is the killer app – actually, a technology that drives lots of killer apps – for XML on the Web.

Middleware, as you might suspect from the name, is software that comes between two other programs. It acts like your interpreter or guide might if you were to visit someplace where you couldn't speak the language and had no idea of the local customs. It talks in the native tongue, using the native customs, and translates the native replies – the messages – into your language.

MOM documents are chiefly generated by programs for other programs to read.

Instead of writing specialized programs (clients) to access particular databases or other data sources (servers), XML MOM users break the old two-tier client/server model. They introduce a third tier, the *middle tier*, that acts as a data integrator. The middle-tier application server does all the talking to the data sources and sends their messages in XML to the client.

That means the client can read data from anywhere, but only has to understand data that is in XML documents. The XML markup provides information about the data (i.e., metadata) that was in the original data source schema, like the database table name and field names (also called *cell* or *column* names).

The MOM user typically doesn't care much about rendition. He does care, though, about extracting the original data accurately and making use of the metadata. His client software, instead of having a specialized module for each data source, has a single "XML parser" module. The parser is the program that separates the markup from the data, just as it does in POP applications.

And just like POP applications, there can be a stylesheet, a set of commands that tell a program how to process the document. It may not look much like a POP stylesheet – it might look more like a script or program – but it performs the same function. And, as with POP stylesheets, there can be different MOM stylesheets for different document types, or to do different things with message documents of a single document type.

There is an extra benefit to XML three-tier MOM applications in a networked environment. For many applications, the middle-tier server can collect all of the relevant data at once and send it in a single document to the client. Further querying, sorting, and other processing can then take place solely on the client system. That not only cuts down Web traffic and overhead, as *InfoWorld* observed, but it vastly improves the end-user's perceived performance and his satisfaction with the experience.

MOM documents tend to be (but needn't be) short-lived, non-interactive, small, and with simple structures.

4.2.3 Opposites are attracted

To XML, that is!

How is it that XML can be optimal for two such apparently extreme opposites as MOM and POP? The answer is, the two are not really different where it counts.

In both cases, we start with abstract information. For POP, it comes from a human author's head. For MOM, it comes from a database. But either way, the abstract data is marked up with tags and becomes a document.

But XML documents are special. An application can do three kinds of processing with one:

- *Parse it*, in order to extract the original data. This can be done without information loss because XML represents both metadata and data, and it lets you keep the abstractions distinct from rendition information.

- *Render it*, so it can be presented in a physical medium that a human can perceive. It can be rendered in many different ways, for delivery in multiple media such as screen displays, print, Braille, spoken word, and so on.

- *Hack it*, meaning "process it as plain text without parsing". Hacking might involve cutting and pasting into other XML documents, or scanning the markup to get some information from it without doing a real parse.

The real revelation here is that data and documents aren't opposites. Far from it – they are actually two states of the same information.

The real difference between the two is that when data is in a database, the metadata about its structure and meaning (the schema) is stored according to the proprietary architecture of the database. When the data becomes a document, the metadata is stored as markup.

A mixture of markup and data must be governed by the rules of some notation. XML and SGML are notations, as are RTF and Word file format. The rules of the notation determine how a parser will interpret the document text to separate the data from the markup.

Take another look at Figure 1.

Notations are not just for complete documents. There are also data object notations, such as GIF, TIFF, and EPS, that are used to represent such things as graphics, video (e.g., MPEG), and audio (e.g., AVI). Document notations usually allow their documents to contain data objects, such as pictures, that are in the objects' own data object notations.

Data object notations are usually (not always) in binary; that is, they are built-up from low-level ones and zeros. Document notations, however, are frequently character-based. XML is character-based, which is why it can be hacked.

In fact, a design objective of XML was to support the "desperate Perl hacker" – someone who needs to write a program in a hurry, using a scripting language like Perl, and who doesn't use a real XML parser. Instead, his program scans the XML document as though it were plain text. The program might search for markup strings, but can also search for data.

Since databases and documents are really the same, and MOM and POP applications both use XML documents, there are lots of opportunities for synergy.

4.2.4 MOM and POP – They're so great together!

Classically, MOM and POP were radically different kinds of applications, each doing things its own way with different technologies and mental models. But POP applications frequently need to include database data in their document content – think of an automotive maintenance manual that has to get the accurate part numbers from a database.

Similarly, MOM applications need to include human-written components. When the dealer asks for price and availability of the automotive parts you need, the display might include a description as well.

With the advent of generalized markup, the barriers to doing MOM-like things in POP applications began to disappear. Some of the POP-like SGML applications that have been in use for many years appear to have invented the middle tier on their own. And now, with the advent of XML, MOM applications can easily incorporate POP functionality as well.

In fact, we'd go so far as to say there is no longer a difference in kind between the two, only a difference in degree. There really is "an endless spectrum of application opportunities". It is a multi-dimensional spectrum where applications need not be implemented differently just because they process different document types. The real differentiators are other document characteristics, like persistency, size, interactivity, structural complexity, percentage of human-written content, and the importance of eventual presentation to humans.

no more a difference in kind between MOM and POP

At the extremes, some applications may call for specialized (or optimized) techniques, but the broad central universe of applications can all be implemented similarly. Much of the knowledge that POP application developers have acquired over the years is now applicable to MOM applications, and vice versa.

You can find detailed descriptions of dozens of XML applications – MOM, POP, and hybrid – in my book, *The XML Handbook* (Goldfarb/Prescod 1998).

5   Revising the SGML Standard

The original clients for SGML were large enterprises using POP applications in controlled and robust mainframe environments. In contrast, the new users of XML are predominantly using MOM applications in open and relatively unreliable networked environments.

As you might expect, these new uses created a need for changes to ISO 8879 in order for XML to be a proper subset of SGML. Fortunately, a revision process was already under way when XML arrived on the scene in 1996.

a need for changes to ISO 8879

SGML and its related standards have been developed in the *International Organization for Standardization (ISO)* under the same group of leaders for the past twenty years. During that time, the development committee has changed names several times. Most recently it was promoted to a full-fledged technical subcommittee: ISO/IEC JTC1/SC34. For clarity, I will refer to it only by that name.

5.1 Revision History and Policy

In May, 1990, in the light of five years of user experience with SGML, SC34 directed me, as Project Editor, to lead a complete review of ISO 8879. The idea was to see whether user requirements or technology had changed sufficiently to justify revisions to the standard.

guaranteeing backward compatibility   We developed a policy document, N1289: Future development of ISO 8879, that would protect existing users of SGML by guaranteeing backward compatibility. It says:

> Any document that is a conforming SGML document according to the current standard shall continue to be a conforming document under the provisions of future versions of the standard.

5.2 SGML Extended Facilities

We took our time with the review, for several reasons. One was the importance of building user confidence in the standard by maintaining its stability. Another was the desire to be thorough.

A third reason was the realization that we lacked something essential. We had no adequate formal definition of the output of an SGML parser: the structure and other properties of a document that are described by the SGML language.

a specification for property sets and groves   Our response to that problem was to develop a specification for property sets and groves in general.

Groves are collections of trees, the structure of a parsed document, and the SGML property set in particular. The latter became the basis for navigation and querying in DSSSL and in HyTime, and has influenced the XML DOM and XLink work.

Both specifications are currently published in the *SGML Extended Facilities,* Annex A of ISO/IEC 10744 HyTime 2d Edition. SC34 has voted to move the extended facilities to the SGML standard when it is republished.

Annex A also includes, among other things, definition requirements for:

- Lexical Types (LTDR)

- Architectural Forms (AFDR)

- Formal System Identifiers (FSIDR)

A document can use any or all of these facilities modularly.

For a reader's guide and the text of the extended facilities, see (HyTime Users' Group 1998).

5.3 Extended Naming Rules

The first change in nine years was made to the SGML standard itself at the request of the Japanese delegation to SC34. In 1997, SC34 approved Annex J to ISO 8879, the *Extended Naming Rules*.

Annex J allows changes to the SGML declaration that make it easier to specify large character sets. It also makes it easier to specify name characters for languages that have no concept of upper- and lower-case. These changes enhance the usability of SGML with Asian languages.

5.4 WebSGML Adaptations

SC34 originally intended to produce the revised version of SGML all at once. However, the XML development activity presented clear user requirements for certain changes, and we decided to give them priority. Accordingly, on December 5, 1997, SC34 approved the *WebSGML Adaptations*, consisting of new Annexes K and L to ISO 8879.

priority to XML user requirements

WebSGML offers many new capabilities, including some that SGML users have requested for a long time. Some of the favorites include:

- SGML declaration reference
- White space handling: KEEPALL
- Optional quantities and capacities
- Hex character references
- Empty elements can have end-tags
- SHORTTAG unbundled
- Multiple and universal ATTLIST
- Duplicate nmtoken values permitted
- Domain names as public text owners
- Element type declaration

There are too many even to mention them all here, let alone supply all the details, but you can read about them at my Web site.

As a result of WebSGML, all XML documents – whether valid or merely well-formed – are also conforming SGML documents.

5.5 DTD-less Parsing

One of the original objectives for SGML was the ability to validate a document when editing, then to process the document without validating it again. That is why ISO 8879 conformance allows both validating and non-validating systems. It was intended that a non-validating system would not have to access a DTD.

Unfortunately, some aspects of markup minimization prevented DTD-less parsing, but these have now been remedied. Prior to WebSGML, a conforming SGML document required an explicit DTD association, and the instance had to conform to the DTD. Such a document is said to be *type-valid*.

In WebSGML, type-validity is optional. In this respect, it is similar to XML. But WebSGML goes a step further in allowing partial type-validity: it is permissible for DTD declarations to be omitted, but the instance must still conform to any DTD declarations that are present.

Also, XML requires all document instances to be what WebSGML calls *fully-tagged*. That is, there must be a start- and end-tag for each element, and attributes cannot be defaulted.

XML's so-called *empty-element tag* conforms to this rule. In SGML terms it is actually a start-tag followed by a null end-tag.

For DTD-less parsing, WebSGML also allows markup minimization that does not require access to the DTD. For example, the end-tag of an element can end any open children of that element.

5.6 Entity Constraints

Another innovation in WebSGML is the ability to constrain the use of entity references. They can be prohibited, limited to internal entities, or used freely as has always been permitted in SGML.

A further possibility – one that is used by XML – is to require that entities be *integrally-stored*. That is, elements and markup strings must end in the same entity in which they begin.

5.7 Datatypes

A facility that is new to WebSGML – and not yet available in XML – is strong datatyping for attributes. You can use any form of modeling notation, such as regular expressions, to define a datatype for an attribute value.

In the following example, `regexp` is defined as a notation. It requires a `model` and a `max` (maximum length) to be specified when expressing a datatype. The date attribute of chapter is defined using the `regexp` notation. The model is "[0-9]+-[0-9]+]" and the maximum length of a value is 7 characters.

```
<!NOTATION regexp SYSTEM "url of regexp handler">
<!ATTLIST #NOTATION regexp
   model CDATA #IMPLIED
   max NMTOKEN "128">

<!ELEMENT chapter (%chapter-stuff;)>
<!ATTLIST chapter
   date DATA regexp [model=" [0-9]+-[0-9]+] "
max="7"] #IMPLIED>

<chapter date="12-97">
```

When the date attribute is parsed, the value is passed to the `regexp` handler identified in the notation declaration, along with the `model` and `max` parameters from the definition of `date`. The `regexp` handler can then tell the parser whether the date value conforms to the datatype.

5.8 DTD Data Entities (DTD Schemas)

A DTD performs the same role in SGML and XML as a schema does in a database management system (DBMS). Originally, SGML only allowed DTDs to be expressed using markup declarations. Nevertheless, many SGML products also used optimized proprietary notations for DTDs.

And recently, several proposals have been made for using XML documents to express DTD schemas. These schemas would express not only the standardized DTD properties that can be expressed by markup declarations, but additional ones as well (such as inheritance, synonyms, etc.).

In response to these requirements, SC34 is in the process of finalizing an enhancement to WebSGML that would allow alternative notations for DTD schemas. From the standpoint of SGML, they would be safe to use under the same conditions in which WebSGML allows the DTD to be ignored.

Here is how you might declare that such a notation is used in the external subset of the document type declaration:

```
<!DOCTYPE mydoc SYSTEM "location of external subset"
       CDATA some-schema-notation [
<!NOTATION some-schema-notation
       SYSTEM "location of schema interpreter>
] >
```

The *schema interpreter* must communicate the standardized DTD properties to the SGML parser, which will use them as if they had been expressed by markup declarations.

Similar declarations are possible for external parameter entities, and different DTD schemas can be used in each case.

5.9 Completing the Revision

A number of activities remain before a complete revised edition of ISO 8879 can be published. There are many corrections, clarifications, and minor design changes, most of which have been documented in the reports of meetings of SC34 (see website: SGMLsource).

development of modularized DTDs

One of the most interesting design efforts is the development of modularized DTDs. Modules would allow a robust method of combining components of multiple DTDs with duplicate object names, while preserving the context of the original namespaces. The original proposal was made by the Japanese delegation to SC34, and Japan continues to lead the development effort.

Also under consideration is the possibility of clarifying the presentation of the standard by replacing much of the normative text with formal notations.

6 The Future of SGML

the tail that wagged the dog

When the World Wide Web became a phenomenon, just five short years ago, HTML suddenly became the tail that wagged the dog. A vastly larger number of people knew about it and used it than had ever used its parent, SGML. And SGML users found themselves in the position of having to convert their documents from their own DTDs to HTML in order to display them in Web browsers.

Lots of SGML users disliked HTML because it was rendition-oriented, but some experts embraced it. We heard speakers at GCA conferences claiming that "HTML is all the markup we'll ever need."

Well, it isn't, and we eventually found that out. In fact, XML is, in part, the Web community's response to the shortcomings of HTML.

Now we are hearing the same things about XML that we heard about HTML. Only now they are much louder, they have much more support from the SGML community, and they are much more justified – but still just as wrong. As with HTML, there are two sides to the argument.

XML and SGML don't even compete

Some claim that XML will replace SGML because there will be so much free and low-cost software. Others assert that XML users, like HTML users before them, will discover that they need more of SGML and will eventually migrate to the full standard.

Both assertions are nonsense ... XML and SGML don't even compete.

XML is a simplified subset of SGML. The subsetting was optimized for the Web environment, which implies data-processing-oriented (rather than publishing-oriented), short life-span (in fact, usually dynamically-generated) information. The vast majority of XML documents will be created by computer programs and processed by other programs, then destroyed. Humans will never see them.

XML: simplified subset of SGML optimized for the Web

Eliot Kimber, a member of both the XML and SGML standards committees, says:

> There are certain use domains for which XML is simply not sufficient and where you need the additional features of SGML. These applications tend to be very large scale and of long term; e.g., aircraft maintenance information, government regulations, power plant documentation, etc.
>
> Any one of them might involve a larger volume of information than the entire use of XML on the Web. A single model of commercial aircraft, for example, requires some four million unique pages of documentation that must be revised and republished quarterly. Multiply that by the number of models produced by companies like Airbus and Boeing and you get a feel for the scale involved.

for certain use domains XML is simply not sufficient

I agree wholeheartedly with Eliot.

I invented SGML, I'm proud of it, and I'm awed that such a staggering volume of the world's mission-critical information is represented in it.

I'm also proud of HTML. I'm delighted that Tim Berners-Lee created it and used it in the World Wide Web. And I'm gratified that he based so much of it on the original element types that Ed Mosher and I created for GML – SGML's precursor – over 25 years ago.

And I'm thrilled with XML. I'm proud of my friend Jon Bosak who made it happen, and I'm excited that the World Wide Web is becoming XML-based.

Consider the two "handbooks" that I've written. *The SGML Handbook* (Goldfarb 1990) has been in print since 1990 and continues to sell well. But *The XML Handbook* (Goldfarb/Prescod 1998) sold more copies in its first eight weeks than *The SGML Handbook* had sold in eight years!

Clearly, the world needs SGML and HTML and XML.

The major producers of documents will always need SGML – nothing else can do the job. It provides the enormous flexibility needed. It is stable in a way that nothing but an honestly ISO-developed International Standard can be. And any other representation – such as HTML or XML – can be generated from SGML automatically.

So the SGML standard will continue to respond to the broad demanding needs of the large user, and will continue to be a source from which XML can draw future enhancements. But it will carry on doing so in its current relative obscurity.

As with HTML, the public attention and excitement will belong to the child, not the parent. XML will have an order of magnitude more users, who will revolutionize the world's business and financial relations by exchanging commercial data over the World Wide Web.

But the unimaginably large SGML repository of long-lived intellectual property will continue to grow. There will always be vastly more persistent information in SGML than in HTML and XML combined.

Acknowledgments

I am grateful to Fujitsu Network Communications for supporting the development of this paper. I would also like to thank Chet Ensign, Steve Pepper, and Paul Prescod, the co-authors with whom I wrote the books from which parts of this paper are derived.

References

(Goldfarb 1990)
> Goldfarb, Charles F.: The SGML Handbook. Oxford: Oxford University Press, 1990

(Goldfarb et al. 1997)
> Goldfarb, Charles F.; Pepper, Steve; Ensign, Chet: SGML Buyer's Guide. Upper Saddle River, N.J.: Prentice Hall, 1997

(Goldfarb/Prescod 1998)
   Goldfarb, Charles F.; Prescod, Paul: The XML Handbook. Upper Saddle
   River, N.J.: Prentice Hall, 1998

(HyTime Users' Group 1998)
   HyTime Users' Group: HyTime Users' Group Home Page. o.O., September
   1998. Information on the SGML Extended Facilities and HyTime. Available
   from Internet: http://www.hytime.org

(SGML Source Home Page 1997)
   Charles F. Goldfarb's SGML Source Home Page. o.O., December 1997.
   Information on the SGML revision. Available from Internet:
   http://www.SGMLsource.com

Evolution and use of generic markup languages

Pamela L. Gennusa

1 Introduction

This article will provide:

- a brief overview of the key concepts of generic markup languages used for structured documents;

- an introduction to the two most prominent languages in use, SGML and XML, and their respective families of related standards; and

- reflections on the impact of the use of these languages to structure documents in the real world.

I hope this article will provide an understanding of why generic markup languages were created, why their details are so energetically debated, how they will contribute to the next generation of document processing technologies, and how their use can help companies better realize business goals.

1.1 The challenge for publishers

Corporate and commercial publishers have long been held captive by publishing software and hardware vendors. If a publisher had thousands of pages encoded in a single vendor's proprietary markup language, it was very time consuming and costly for the publisher to move to the use of another vendor's software or to re-purpose the

In the beginning

information. The markup embedded in the documents was typically format oriented, describing how the text should be laid out on the page. Each typesetting vendor used a different set of commands to achieve the same result, thus making interchange of documents between typesetting systems very difficult. When the only output was printed documents, this situation was minimally tolerable. However, when publishers wanted to produce their documents on multiple media, the publishers' tolerance level quickly fell. The use of an internationally agreed generic markup language meant that publishers could create information once and automate its reuse multiple ways, saving time and effort.

1.2 Key concepts of generic markup languages

content vs. formatting markup

The use of a single, internationally agreed syntax was not the only reason why a generic markup language was the appropriate solution for publishers that wanted to publish to multiple media. A fundamental concept in the use of generic markup languages is a move from formatting markup to content markup.

For example, in early typesetting systems, a date at the top of a letter might be encoded as a 10 point type on 12 points of leading, using the Times Roman font, and set with a 20 pica indent quad left on the line. Later systems allowed the use of macros, so the above set of micro formatting instructions might be referenced as a whole by a macro named `indent-head`. The same macro might be used for the signature line in the letter as well. Using a generic markup language, the date would be identified as a *date*. Additionally, the components of the date might be further identified as *day*, *month*, and *year*. The signature line might be identified as `signature-block` and further decomposed into *signer* and *position*.

One advantage of the use of content markup is the ability to delimit components of documents into named structures and, thus, to be able to find and use specific pieces of content. In the example above, a query could be given to a database to find all letters written after 6 August 1997 and signed by the Comptroller. Without content markup, letters that reference a later date or the Comptroller in the body of the document would also satisfy the search.

Evolution and use of generic markup languages

2 The rise of generic markup languages

2.1 GenCode®, GML, and SGML

As long ago as 1967 (for the source of this information, see *A brief History of the Development of SGML*, SGML Users' Group 1989), Mr. William Tunnicliffe, chairman of the *Graphic Communications Association (GCA)* Composition Committee, made a presentation to a meeting of the *Canadian Government Printing Office* on the topic of the separation of content from format. Coincidentally, during the late 1960s, Stanley Rice, a book designer, proposed the idea of a universal catalogue of parameterized 'editorial structure' tags.

Understanding the significance of these proposals, the GCA established a generic coding project in their Composition Committee. The committee, recognizing that different generic codes were needed for different kinds of documents and that smaller documents could be incorporated as elements of larger ones, developed the 'GenCode concept' and registered the *GenCode* trademark. This project later evolved into the GenCode Committee.

Generic Coding project

In 1969, Charles Goldfarb, together with Edward Mosher and Raymond Lorie, invented the *Generalized Markup Language (GML)* at IBM. GML was created to allow text editing, formatting, and information retrieval systems to share documents. Following the initial development of GML, Goldfarb continued his research into document structures and defined additional concepts in generic markup.

Generalized Markup Language (GML)

In 1978, Goldfarb was asked to join the *American National Standards Institute (ANSI)* Computer Languages for the Processing of Text committee and to lead a project for a text description language standard based on GML. The GCA's GenCode committee members became the foundation of the membership of this ANSI committee. The first working draft was published in 1980. By 1983, the GCA was able to publish the sixth working draft as an industry standard (GCA 101-1983), which was adopted by the *Internal Revenue Service (IRS)* and the *US Department of Defense (DOD)*.

ANSI project for a text description language

The project was also authorized by the *International Organization for Standardization (ISO)*. In early 1985, the draft proposal for an ISO standard was published and, by October 1985, the draft international standard was ready for balloting. Following a year of review, comment resolution, and production, *ISO 8879 Standard Generalized Markup Language (SGML)* was published on 15 October 1986,

publication of ISO 8879

using an SGML system at the *European Particle Physics Laboratory (CERN)*.

SGML is a meta-language

So, how can we define SGML? Primarily, SGML is a meta-language, that is, a language for creating markup languages. It has an internationally recognized syntax that is human-readable and machine processible. The syntax is used to define document classes and to mark up individual instances of a class. Although SGML didn't become an international standard until 1986, from the preceding history, it can be seen that the need for SGML and the concept of generic markup had been apparent for a number of years. By the time SGML became an ISO standard, there were applications running in conformance with the Draft International Standard and even earlier versions because this was a standard that many industries were anxious to use.

2.2 HyTime

The advent of electronic delivery of documents opened the door on the use of highly internally and externally referenced content. The market need grew quickly and a number of vendors created proprietary products to address that need. Again, the user was faced with using interesting technology, but being tied to a single vendor.

publication of ISO 10744

The SGML standard provided only the most basic support for the embedding of cross-references. In response to the burgeoning need in the hypertext marketplace, ISO created *ISO 10744 Hypermedia/Time-based Structuring Language (HyTime)* in 1992 to provide a standard syntax for the description of such linkages. The second edition of HyTime was published in 1997.

2.3 DSSSL

Because SGML is typically only used to describe the content and not the format of documents, users were also interested in a way to interchange vendor-independent style specifications. ISO responded with the creation of *ISO 10179 Document Style Semantics and Specification Language (DSSSL)* in 1996. Using a DSSSL specification, it is possible to specify the intent of formatting for each element-in-context within an SGML document as well as the general pagination rules.

  ■ *Evolution and use of generic markup languages*

Work on DSSSL began in the mid-1980s. In the early 1990s, it was balloted and approved as an International Standard. However, the ISO Working Group was not satisfied that the standard had met its goals. They continued work on the standard until it was again balloted in late 1995. DSSSL is considered a sound and comprehensive standard, albeit a complex one.

publication of ISO 10179

2.4 CALS

In 1983, the *US Department of Defense* adopted the use of the GCA's industry standard built on the sixth working draft of SGML. However, this was just a placeholder until SGML was published as an ISO standard. In September 1985, a full year before SGML achieved the status of an ISO standard, it was cited for use in a major US DOD initiative regarding electronic data. CALS (originally for Computer Aided Logistic Support, see References) endorsed the use of standards for the encoding of text, graphics, product data, logistic information, etc. The principal standards initially recommended for use were *ISO 8879 Standard Generalized Markup Language (SGML)*, *ISO 8632 Computer Graphics Metafile (CGM)*, and *ASME/ANSI Y14.26M Initial Graphics Exchange Specification (IGES)*.

The adoption of SGML by the DOD was probably one of the greatest contributions to its growth. The US DOD is often referred to as the 800-pound gorilla. The joke goes: 'What do you give an 800-pound gorilla? ... Whatever it wants.' The DOD's decision to make SGML part of its CALS initiative gave rise to a generation of vendors who believed that there would be a market if they were to develop new products or redesign their current products to use SGML.

the 800-pound (363.63-kg) gorilla

2.5 OS/FOSIs

Due to the protracted development period of DSSSL (approximately 10 years), the CALS project office was not prepared to wait until DSSSL was ready to be able to non-proprietarily specify the intent of formatting. Therefore, the CALS project office approved the development of an interim style specification called an *Output Specification (OS)*. The OS defined the (DOD's) universe of technical documentation formatting parameters available for application to any DTD. A Formatting Output Specification Instance (FOSI) was an instance of the OS, applied to a specific DTD. A small number of

an interim style specification

commercial products implemented the FOSI in editorial and paper output environments. It was a step in the right direction, but the OS/FOSI suffered from the early rush in its development. There were certain formatting characteristics that could not be expressed in the language. Thus, for the sake of expediency, the OS/FOSI standard permitted some of the formatting specification to be provided in a non-standardized way. Though well intentioned, such trap doors left the user again with a non-portable formatting specification.

2.6 Interactive Electronic Technical Manuals

an electronic delivery model

The US DOD was also working on a number of electronic delivery models. Proposals for a DOD-wide standard were created in both the Air Force and the Navy. A tri-service committee ultimately developed a set of three standards defining a database structure for the underlying content, a formatting style for the user interface, and a quality assurance specification. This type of delivery is known as an *Interactive Electronic Technical Manual (IETM)*. The IETM specifications broke new ground by incorporating a holistic view of a set of documentation, using HyTime constructs to model relationships, and by modeling the interactions that might be used with the documentation. For example, a procedure says to test a voltage and then, based on the voltage, cross-references other places in the information set. This interaction might take place between the documentation and the maintenance engineer. Alternatively, it might take place between the documentation and a piece of automated test equipment. IETMs have been adapted for use across nations. For example, in the UK, *Def Stan 00-60* cites the use of *Interactive Electronic Technical Publications (IETPs)*, referencing a UK version of the US IETM specifications.

3   Advent of the Web

But that was yesterday

In the early 1990s, the Internet was gaining users. To make the Internet easier to access, the concept of the World-Wide Web was born. The WWW project, started by Tim Berners-Lee while at CERN, seeks to build a 'distributed hypermedia system'.

Early on, the *HyperText Markup Language (HTML)* was developed for use on the Web. The first version of HTML was not strictly SGML, although it tried to 'look' like SGML through the use of tags.

Evolution and use of generic markup languages

Due to the efforts of a number of SGML proponents, most notably, Yuri Rubinsky, HTML was 'SGMLized' by the time HTML 2.0 came out. The development of the HTML DTD made it possible to programmatically ensure that HTML documents did in fact conform to a common definition.

However, most browsers accept less than perfect HTML, or perhaps it is more accurate to say, they accept more than a widely accepted definition of HTML. Each browser vendor developed proprietary extensions, allowing 'tags' that were not in the then current definition of HTML.

3.1 Pressure for less than SGML, more than HTML

Although SGML has been a stable standard since 1986, it was created at a time when information technology for text processing was in a state of immaturity. For example, at the beginning of the development of SGML, there were not even word processors that used programmable keystrokes, nor was the concept of SGML editing software established (i.e., that software would enter all of the markup commands). During that period, standard working practice was to have text keyboarded by a typesetting company or typing pool that charged by the keystroke. Thus, parts of the SGML standard were written to address the ability to 'minimize' the markup through various conventions.

The use of minimization and other complex features made the SGML standard difficult and time-consuming to implement. With hindsight, and knowledge of today's available software support, it is acknowledged that many of the more complex parts of SGML may not be needed by all users. Further, a more streamlined version of the standard would mean that more software companies could create products for a lower start-up cost, thus increasing the number of more affordable text processing software.

complex features made the SGML standard difficult

The advent of the Web and its global popularity also had an impact. The markup language of the Web, *HyperText Markup Language (HTML)* is an application of SGML. It is a single tag set based on the HTML Document Type Definition. Although very useful for the presentation of a wide variety of document classes, it suffers from the use of formatting over content markup. Even if a corporation's text databases were encoded in SGML, they had to be transformed into HTML, losing the richness and processibility of the content markup in the process. This has meant that client-side processing has been

HTML is an application of SGML

constrained due to the 'sameness' of information once it is encoded in HTML and that most processing has to take place on the server site, resulting in poor performance and long wait times. As noted above, an alarming and negative consequence was the proliferation of proprietary extensions to the HTML tagging set by individual browser vendors, flinging users of the Web back a decade or two to an age when documents were 'stuck' within a vendor's product.

3.2 The role of the World-Wide Web Consortium (W3C)

request for a 'slimmer' version of SGML

The above conditions led to an initiative by a number of SGML experts to create a 'slimmer' version of SGML. Many of these SGML experts were also involved with the World-Wide Web Consortium (W3C). The strong impetus to cut down SGML for use on the Web became a good reason to house this work within a W3C committee. Led by Jon Bosak and others, the W3C approved the creation of a Working Group to develop an extensible language for use on the Web. The SGML background of those involved meant that they would produce a streamlined version of SGML to achieve this goal. The result of an 18-month effort was a highly successful, well-received, cut-down version of SGML called the *Extensible Markup Language* or *XML*.

3.3 Enter XML

XML = leaner, meaner SGML

XML has all of the characteristics of SGML that made it a strong choice for returning business benefits, such as the use of an internationally agreed syntax; the ability to create well-defined and well-structured documents; and the use of generic, content-based markup. XML has been called both a 'kinder, gentler SGML' and a 'leaner, meaner SGML'. Both are true. For someone just moving to generic markup languages, it is easier to learn and to use. For developers of software and systems, it gets the job done with reduced complexity and lower risk.

Current users of SGML are in an advantageous position in that the majority of their SGML documents may already be very close to XML conformant. A complete transition to XML is far less time-

Evolution and use of generic markup languages

consuming and costly than the initial adoption of a generic, content-based markup language.

3.4 ... and XLink

Following immediately on to the start of the creation of XML, the
Working Group determined that they should also create an *Extensible Linking Language (XLink)*. XLink, originally known as XML-link
and then as XLL, is an encompassing term for XML hyperlinking
(linking and addressing). It has two major components: XLink
(proper) and XPointer. XLink is more robust than the unidirectional
cross-referencing in SGML and less complex than the range of facilities in HyTime. XLink (proper), released as a working draft (March
1998), 'specifies constructs that may be inserted into XML resources
to describe links between objects'. (A link in this context may be
unidirectional as well as multi-ended and typed.)

XPointer, also released as a working draft (March 1998), defines
'constructs that support addressing into the internal structures of
XML documents. In particular, it provides for specific reference to
elements, character strings, and other parts of XML documents,
whether or not they bear an explicit ID attribute.'

XML linking language

3.5 ... and XSL

DSSSL is a large and comprehensive specification that took a number of years to complete. It is generally acknowledged to be too much
for the Web at some levels (complex pagination) and not enough for
the Web (interface behavior) at others. HTML, being a fixed set of
tags, was relatively easy to format without further information. The
HTML tags had associated formatting characteristics that could be
changed on a per instance basis. The use of XML on the Web introduces the concept of markup tags that are unknown to the rendering
device. In order for XML to be accepted on the Web, it was necessary
to address the issue of how a document creator could specify the
formatting to be applied to a set of tags and a browser could interpret that formatting specification.

To address the need to specify formatting for an XML application,
the W3C approved another work item called *Extensible Style Language* or *XSL*. The XSL Working Group released a requirements
document in May 1998. Even as the specification is being drafted,

XML style language

vendors are experimenting with and prototyping the output of the
Working Group.

3.6 ISO's Web SGML

SGML for Web applications

The creators of XML were all experienced in the use of SGML. They
understood the role that an ISO standard plays and the importance
of compliance with SGML. Specifically, they knew that the existing
SGML community would not be able to easily transition between
SGML and XML if the two were not compatible ... and they were all
users of SGML. They knew also, that dedicated SGML users wanted
to be able to use SGML on the Web and wanted a wider choice of
products. Thus, compatibility with SGML became an important
design criterion. To ensure that end, communications between the
W3C XML Working Group and the ISO SGML Working Group
were frequent and extensive.

concept of well-formedness and other differences

Perhaps the most significant difference between XML and traditional SGML was the optionality of the *DOCTYPE Declaration*.
Whereas, an SGML document is not complete without it, an XML
document may or may not have one. XML brought forth the concept of *well-formedness*. A well-formed document is one in which the
structure can be completely determined from the instance. To make
this possible, the XML Working Group determined that there would
be no tag omission, except in the case of empty elements, where the
end tag would be omitted. However, without a DTD, it was not possible to know that an element was empty unless the start tag 'looked'
different from other start tags. Thus, it was necessary to introduce
the special construct known as the *Empty-Element Tag*
(`<tag_name/>`).

SGML/XML compatability

A few other differences also became necessary, such as the use of
predefined character entities, the ability to use only a specific subset
of the SHORTTAG feature and absolutely disallow other parts, and
the ability to have an optional or partial DTD. To ensure that 'what
was XML, was SGML', the ISO SGML Working Group set about
creating two annexes (K [normative] and L [informative]) to the
SGML standard. These two annexes, extended SGML to encompass
those aspects of XML that were initially outside the scope of SGML.

Today, with the addition of these annexes, XML truly is a subset
of SGML, as per its design objectives. Further, SGML processors, if
they support Annex K, can be said to support XML and SGML.

Evolution and use of generic markup languages

3.7 A thought about SGML Mark II

In his closing keynote speech at SGML Europe '96, Tim Bray, *Textuality, Inc.*, called for a streamlined version of SGML, one that would be easier to implement and understand. Shortly thereafter, the XML Working Group was formed within the W3C.

However, sometimes I wonder what SGML would have been like if it had been created now, with a dozen years experience with a standard generalized markup language available to users; with computing systems in their current state of evolution; with the web as the next publishing frontier. My guess is that it would have looked very much like XML does today. For example, take the SGML features of RANK and DATATAG. These were never really used, and the ISO Working Group, had they thought it would have been permissible, probably would have dropped them from the International Standard after the balloting of the Draft back in 1986. Further, today, with cheap memory, fast processors, advances in editorial software, and fairly inexpensive bandwidth, I don't think that the developers would have perceived the need for minimized markup.

SGML was the right standard in 1986 for its audience. It has stood the test of time and become the foundation for a more streamlined version of itself. Its stability over the first 10 years of its life meant that developers could concentrate on developing most of its features without fearing that the Standard would change. The trade-off was stability against dynamism. It has probably worked out well. If the SGML standard had been a moving object, the level of implementation would have been lower, perhaps making it possible to miss its importance.

4   SGML, XML, and the marketplace

4.1 Industry acceptance

The effect of SGML on industry has been extensive. When the DOD adopted SGML, they made it financially viable for their suppliers to use SGML not only for their military products, but also for their commercial counterparts. The most obvious area where this progression took place was in the commercial aerospace marketplace.

Airframe manufacturers eventually promoted the use of SGML to the *Air Transport Association (ATA)*, which amended its ATA100 specification (now ATA 2100) to use SGML. After all, if airframe suppliers had to retool to provide SGML deliverables to their military customer, why not also use SGML for their commercial customers, thus providing a greater business case for the conversion to being an 'SGML shop'.

At the same time that the DOD was moving toward SGML, so were commercial publishers. The *Association of American Publishers (AAP)* published its *Electronic Manuscript Project* in 1986 just before the final Standard was published. Scientific publishers were particularly interested in SGML to help in the areas of tabular and mathematical data.

Throughout the late 1980s and early 1990s, more and more industries moved toward SGML including automotive, semi-conductor, and telecommunications. The volume of information in SGML has grown steadily. Industry has seen SGML as an industrial-strength solution to an industrial-strength problem.

Just as SGML made significant inroads into various industries, XML has also attracted many industries. Some of these industries had individuals or small numbers of users who had promoted the use of SGML. The visibility of XML, together with its perceived simplicity, has broadened the attractiveness of a generic markup language to more members of an industry and more industries in general. Some examples include:

- financial

- classified ads for newspapers

- speech synthesis

- real estate

- mobile phone interface design

- graphics

- electronic commerce (EDI and retail trade)

- translation memory

- scripting for new broadcasts

- ontology

- astronomy

- genealogical data

4.2 Product marketplace

Companies that embarked on the development of SGML products had a lot of work ahead of them. ISO 8879 was written by publishing professionals, not all of whom were computer scientists. Many of the rules of SGML, while seemingly sensible for a publisher, were counter-intuitive to a computer scientist. The development of parsers, editors, databases, transformation utilities, and browsers was a long, expensive process. Although the numbers of vendors has grown over the years, the rate of growth has not been extraordinary.

The DOD's acceptance of SGML provided the necessary 'carrot' to entice software developers to the market. Yet, even after 12 years, the vendor community has not grown to the extent envisioned. There are still only about 3 or 4 editorial tools, 2 or 3 transformation tools, 2 or 3 databases, and 3 or 4 browsers, widely in use today. SGML tools, despite the wide acceptance by industry, is still considered a 'hard' market to break into.

not an extra-ordinary growth rate of vendors

5 Market impact

So, let's face it, SGML is not considered a 'sexy' standard. It is viewed by those who have not come to love it, as a dry, hard-to-read, idiosyncratic and harder-to-implement standard that appeals to a very niche market. Everyday, people who think SGML is old and boring ride on planes, drive cars, use semi-conductors and computers, and talk on telephones that have been documented in SGML; they look up words in dictionaries and encyclopædias and surf pages on the Web that have all been encoded in SGML. Yet for all its acceptance under the covers, SGML is not something people tend to admit using in public. Why? Probably perception.

SGML is not a sexy standard

Over the years we've heard: it's too hard; too confusing; too expensive. Yet, as each ardent opponent is converted to an ardent supporter, those who have been promoting and using SGML since the beginning have looked for the magic words needed to make that conversion in perception easier, faster. And what has been found? Nothing ... there are no magic words beyond how using SGML makes good sense for a business because it protects the business' information assets.

SGML – too hard, too confusing, too expensive?

*XML – preaching
exactly the same
gospel has
become hot*

Imagine how much more amazing it then seems, that in less than two years, XML, by preaching exactly the same gospel regarding ownership of data assets and the need to move away from proprietary markup has become, well, 'hot'. XML is SGML, just without the lacy frills. It has been reconstituted without the ability to change the delimiter set and without the 'features'. It has been spruced up to take more notice of accepted computer science practice.

So, what will be XML's market impact? So far, XML has proved to be a marketing star. No matter which angle the media photograph it from, they deem it to look pretty good.

*user demand will
fuel product
development*

XML already boasts a growing army of vendors and individuals who are investing in the development of XML tools or the adaptation of SGML tools. Although hard to qualify at this early stage, the indication seems to be that the number of product choices will grow considerably. As in all thriving industries, user demand will fuel product development, and product innovation will excite and attract more users. This cycle repeats and magnifies throughout the growth stage of a market. The XML market is right at the beginning of its lifecycle. I'm sure that we will see an ever-increasing spiral of product innovation and increased use of the XML recommendation over the coming years.

6 Evolution toward more sophisticated information processing

6.1 Component vs document publishing

Many interesting developments have occurred over the past decade or two in publishing. These developments challenge how we think about documents and other information containers. Perhaps the most compelling of these developments is the movement from documents to components.

*a new view on
documents*

In traditional publishing, the document was a single entity. It was complete in and of itself. And, typically, it was opaque. The structures within the document were not explicitly defined in the encoding of the document. SGML, of course, changed all that. Through the use of structure-based and content-based markup, portions of documents could be delimited. Although before SGML it may have been typical for publishers to keep documents divided into chapters, there was usually not any further decomposition of the information.

SGML helped to change this view of the document from two perspectives. First, there is the inward looking perspective. What was a document, through the use of SGML markup, could be decomposed into several layers. Information that occurred more than once could be aggregated to a single instance that is pointed two multiple times.

Second, from the outward perspective, each component of what used to be a single document, was now available to be part of an unlimited number of other documents. Further, such use of components in myriad combinations could be static or dynamic. A document could exist for years or for moments, depending on the needs of the user.

The capacity of humans to understand this concept is well-illustrated in the World Wide Web. Depending on your perspective, the information on the web might be one, huge, complex, distributed, highly dynamic document, or it is millions of documents, each with an interesting, but non-explicit, set of criteria for determining each document's boundaries.

6.2 Data and metadata

Another evolutionary idea is really just an extension of what has been done in the work of computer science relative to data for many years: there's the data and then there's the data about the data, or metadata. In a database, this might mean that we know that a value is 10 and the metadata tells us that it is a date, or a string, or an amount in a given currency.

In SGML, there has been a tendency to use SGML attributes to capture metadata. So, an element may have attributes to show that it was reviewed by 'John Doe', or that it has a security classification of 'confidential'. However, there are many levels of metadata. One level that has always been a judgement call by implementers is when the 'metadata' is also part of the data. For example, the entire document may be issued on a certain date, or be written by a particular author. These are often elements within the document, but philosophically, they are also information about the document.

In the XML world of the web, metadata takes on primary significance as the *raison d'être* for a number of XML applications. There are XML applications that have little or no 'content', but rather are a series of values describing other objects. These include:

- *Desktop Management Task Force (DMTF) CIM (Common Information Model) data* – The proposed model is intended to let mainframes, Windows-based systems, and other disparate systems access and exchange management data via the Web.

- *HTTP Distribution & Replication Protocol* – proposal to improve efficiency & reliability of data distribution over HTTP (will use RDF).

- *Java Speech Markup Language (JSML)* – XML application to annotate text with additional information to improve quality/naturalness of synthesized speech.

- *Open Software Description Format (OSD)* – OSD, an application of the XML, is a vocabulary used for describing software packages and their dependencies for heterogeneous clients.

- *Platform for Privacy Preferences (P3P) Syntax Specification* – P3P applications will enable sites to automatically declare their privacy practices in a way that is understandable to users' browsers.

- *UML (Unified Modeling Language)* – emerging standard modeling language for the description of software systems.

- *Web Interface Definition Language (WIDL)* – specification of an XML application that allows interactions with Web servers to be defined as functional interfaces that can be accessed by remote systems over standard Web protocols and provides structure necessary for generating client code.

- *Translation Memory eXchange (TMX)* – developed under *Localisation Industry Standards Association (LISA)*; allows easier exchange of translation memory data between tools and/or translation vendors.

- *Web Collections using XML* – metadata syntax, an application of XML that is used to describe the properties of some object, such as a WebPage to provide information to an application using the object.

- *The Resource Description Framework (RDF)* – specification governing the interoperability of applications in terms of metadata property sets. It is being developed under the authority of the W3C. The draft specifications from W3C confirm that 'RDF will use XML as the transfer syntax in order to leverage other tools and code bases being built around XML …'

Whilst SGML focused primarily on documents, many XML proponents unfamiliar with SGML, think of XML primarily for metadata, with little or no concern for its use within the text of a document.

Certainly, users who exploit both the text-encoding and meta-data-encoding properties of SGML and XML stand to gain the most. It will mean that the processors of the contents of documents can use the same parsing engines as the processors that manipulate the network, the file system, the protocols, and the files themselves.

7   Using XML

7.1 Is there trouble in paradise? – design flaws

If XML is 'simpler' than SGML, is there a benefit of that simplicity to be reaped when creating an XML system rather than an SGML system? Some benefit will be reflected in less expensive products over time. Further, integration costs will come down eventually as product interoperability is improved. However, many of the costs incurred when creating an SGML system, such as the analysis of business requirements, the document analysis tasks, or the functional specification tasks, will still be incurred with XML.

less expensive products over time

XML is not a panacea. Design choices, made for very sound reasons during the development of XML, may have consequences during system development. Thus, there will be problems with implementations just as there are with any standard.

XML is not a panacea

An area that might cause some problems in the near term is the use of *Unicode*. The citing of the Unicode standard is an important foundation of XML and, in the long run, will make sure that there is strong, global, character set support. However, in the near term, there is less than comprehensive support for Unicode. Add to that, the few thousand code points that are unassigned, and there may be a few growing pains with the use of Unicode.

problems with Unicode?

Conversely, could the simplicity of XML mean that companies will have to compromise or give up benefits of SGML when using XML? Companies that want to use XML outside the Web may find that the use of a single concrete syntax, the lack of support for *Formal Public Identifiers*, and the requirement for the explicit specification of *System Identifiers* proves limiting compared with SGML.

7.2 XML: SGML for consenting parties

A concept that will probably cause some confusion for XML users is the optional use of DTDs, or perhaps even more confusing, the use of partial DTDs. (I must confess, the wonderful title of this section was suggested by Jeanne El Andaloussi and François Chahuneau of AIS (*Advanced Information Systems S.A.*).

Until XML came on the scene, SGML could point to the DTD as the primary construct that set it apart from all other generic tagging schemes or macro languages. Because of the DTD, the document was a self-describing text base. Like a database, you could define what could occur in a document class and then check to make sure it did occur in a particular instance by parsing the entire document, including its DTD. For many 'industrial-strength' users, this was the part of SGML that made it all worthwhile. For example, if you are building a fighter jet and have a few hundred authors working on creating the operating and maintenance documentation, the DTD could be used to make sure that they were all using the same structures in the same order and frequency. An information owner could determine the degree of control used in authoring that information by deciding to use either a stricter or more benevolent DTD.

Due to the requirement to have a DTD, SGML created a 'quiet revolution'. (This term was coined by the late Yuri Rubinsky, founder and President of *SoftQuad, Inc*). To use SGML, it was necessary for an organization to think about its documents in ways that it had never done before. The exercise of developing a DTD contributed to a change in the way organizations thought about their documentary information. Prior to SGML, there was documentation planning, but there was little rigor and no way to enforce what little there was. SGML and its use of the DTD changed all that.

When XML was formally announced in Boston at SGML '96 in November of that year, the XML Working Group explained the reasoning behind their decision to make the DTD optional. It was clear to the audience, that perhaps even the members of that Working Group did not totally agree with one another. For example, some members felt that a DTD would, 'of course', still be needed for authoring, but that for delivery, where it is assumed that the instance is already known to be valid, it would not be required. Others felt that being able to author a well-formed document, without a DTD, would be a legitimate requirement and a reasonable way of working.

What is clear, is that the minute the XML Working Group made the DTD optional, they made it necessary for XML users to have to bear an additional responsibility. Users must decide if a DTD will be used in an application, how much of a DTD will be used, and at which points in the production life cycle it will be used. For the individual user or the traditional Web user, the need for this decision may not be obvious. They may decide not to use a DTD, full-stop. However, corporate and commercial publishers will need to analyze their requirements and make informed decisions. In some ways, it's a lot like deregulating an industry. With regulation, life may not be easy, but at least you know where you stand. The rules are clear, and the decisions left to be made are few. With the advent of deregulation, there may be more chaos and more accidents initially, the responsibility is more in the hands of the user, and given time, the users grow into their new role.

Oddly enough, the vehicle that brought about the optionality of the DTD may also wind up being the catalyst for the development of a more robust replacement for it, as well. The current SGML DTD is a bit of an anomaly:

1. It plays two roles. It models the structures that can occur in a document instance and it defines the syntax of the markup in the instance, e.g., if there is minimization, etc.

2. It is in a different syntax than an SGML instance.

3. It is fairly limited in scope. For many years now, there have been calls from the user community to extend the modeling capabilities of a DTD, e.g., lexical recognition in attributes values, etc.

The XML community has put forward a number of alternate suggestions: XML-Data, XSchema (XSD), etc. These proposed DTD replacements tend to focus on the creation of a schema language that uses the syntax for XML instance markup and extends the role of the DTD to provide for inheritance and data typing (see Chahuneau 1998). As a user of SGML, I have noted that SGML moved from 'Standard Generalized *Markup* Language' to 'Standard Generalized *Modelling* Language' to 'Standard Generalized *Management* Language' in the way it was used within industry. However, it fell short of really fulfilling these roles, perhaps due to the inherent weaknesses described by Chahuneau. If XML or SGML were to have a schema language that could be used to model documentary information within the greater milieu of a corporation's overall data model, the transition to the 'document of tomorrow' might more easily be accomplished.

So, what does the 'document of tomorrow' mean? Over the past two decades, and particularly in the past five years, the corporate and commercial publishing industry has seen a shift in the definition of the document. This definition in some cases may have been pioneered in software using proprietary markup schemes. However, it is only through the use of well-structured documents, using generic markup languages, that it will be possible to realize a world-wide use of these new documents.

8 Documents as dynamic knowledge bases

knowledge = value-added information

Following on from the earlier discussion of component-based publishing, documents will continue to evolve as 'dynamic knowledge bases'. The term knowledge here refers to 'value added' information. Building on the earlier example, 10 is a datum. If we know that 10 is the value in a given currency, we have information. If we can link that value to the value last year, the value in another currency, and an indication of the market's perception of that value, we have added value to that information and now have knowledge about it. We understand it in a greater context. We can base judgements on it, we can make informed decisions.

document model simulating how we think

Today, we still struggle to find out all we need to know to interpret information. The use of structured documents; generic, content-based markup; extensive and implied hyperlinks; accessible schemas; and highly networked or interconnected systems will increase our ability to acquire knowledge. The concept of the 'all-in-one', linear document will loose its grip on our loyalty; we will move perhaps naturally toward this definition of a document over time. Why naturally, because this model more closely simulates how we think.

In his groundbreaking article, *As We May Think*, Vannevar Bush (Bush 1945) described his idea for a way to access information consistent with how our minds naturally work. He writes:

> The human mind does not work that way. It operates by association. With one item in its grasp, it snaps instantly to the next that is suggested by the association of thoughts, in accordance with some intricate web of trails carried by the cells of the brain.

He continues:

> Consider a future device for individual use, which is a sort of mechanized private file and library. It needs a name, and to coin one at random, *memex* will do. A memex is a device in which an individual stores all his books, records, and communications, and which is mechanized so that it may be consulted with exceeding speed and flexibility. It is an enlarged intimate supplement to his memory.

> Wholly new forms of encyclopædias will appear, ready-made with a mesh of
> associative trails running through them, ready to be dropped into the memex
> and there amplified.

His conclusion, therefore:

> Thus science may implement the ways in which man produces, stores, and
> consults the record of the race.

He even speculates on how this will affect the human race:

> Presumably man's spirit should be elevated if he can better review his shady
> past and analyze more completely and objectively his present problems. He
> has built a civilization so complex that he needs to mechanize his record
> more fully if he is to push his experiment to its logical conclusion and not
> merely become bogged down part way there by overtaxing his limited mem-
> ory. His excursion may be more enjoyable if he can reacquire the privilege of
> forgetting the manifold things he does not need to have immediately at hand,
> with some assurance that he can find them again if they prove important.

Now, 50 years later, we are at a stage of technological evolution where it is possible to create a 'memex', in large part because of the use of structured documents and generic markup languages.

close to create Vannevar Bush's Memex

8.1 Information (knowledge) engineers

Creating webs of information that provide 'knowledge' to the user of those webs will mean that the field of authoring must undergo a metamorphosis. Authors will be more accurately identified as information engineers. Whilst the original development of text will still be an important activity, the ability to create, enhance and maintain appropriate links to associated information will be critical to the realization of dynamic knowledge bases. We will see 'authoring' tools change dramatically as they provide for this second function of the author.

authors as information engineers

Behind the scenes, SGML and XML will be making much of this information engineering possible. They will provide the consistent information encoding standards. Their associated standards, such as HyTime, DSSSL, XLink, XSL, schema, and metadata standards, will make it possible to define global links and to present information in comprehensible formats.

9 Conclusions

For those who have been pushing for SGML to become widely accepted for the past decade, XML's popularity should be good news. XML promotes the same basic principles of SGML (limited dependence on proprietary systems, investment in a business' data assets, application of structure to text objects, etc.). It's perceived 'ease of use' should attract more users. As a company's understanding of how a generic markup language can help them to meet their business goals grows, their demands on that language may escalate. The users' increasing sophistication will lead one of two places: a move to the use of the full SGML standard or a demand for an enhancement of the XML standard.

My personal prediction is that for the majority of industrial users, keeping track of the differences between the two languages will be too bothersome. People will use the term XML to mean a standard, generic markup language with all the characteristics that such a phrase implies. For some, they will use an XML layer on an SGML product and will at times use something that is only strictly available in SGML. Will they know that? No. Will they care? No. The point will be that the use of a generic markup language is helping them to structure their documentary information and thus returning business benefit.

Those companies that currently have an SGML capability will enjoy the greatest flexibility in the future: to retain information in SGML, to transition source data to XML, to only use XML as an output format, to transform to HTML, to deliver using proprietary products. All of these are legitimate options. The investment in SGML has been a sound strategic choice and it continues to be because of this very flexibility. Companies just starting to use structured documents now have a choice of either SGML or XML, or both, depending on their business requirements.

The use of delivery platforms such as the Web can return significant business benefits not because they mimic a paper manual, but because they can be exploited to turn a set of information into a knowledge base. This is the 'added value' gained from providing the user with the ability to quickly navigate across disparate classes of information, to find important relationships and additional detail. For the corporate publisher delivering operational and maintenance information, increased use and dependence on the deployed knowledge base leads to greater consistency of actions across a shifting and perhaps unevenly skilled set of personnel, resulting in fewer safety incidents and less down time. For the commercial publisher, the ability to provide a more dynamic and rich information set means greater loyalty amongst buyers and subscribers.

Content markup, coupled with the use of small modules of information and well-defined metadata identifiers comprise a powerful arsenal for the creation, management, manipulation, and deployment of corporate knowledge. Taken together, these form the basic foundation for companies to:

- plan and execute the creation of a complete aggregate of corporate information,

- manage that information over its entire life including updates and shifts in its internal relationships, and

- deliver that knowledge base in a variety of ways that ensure use by and feedback from users.

The ultimate promise of the widespread use a generic markup language is a business environment where:

The ultimate promise

- information travels as freely and easily as desired,

- content, structure, and movement of that information can be as controlled as desired, and

- information in a file, the information about the file itself, the processes performed on that information, the results of the processes, and the environment in which it all takes place is a seamless continuum.

Prior to the advent of the World Wide Web, we did not think in these terms. SGML could not have kept this promise in its original state, primarily due to its idiosyncrasies in computer science terms. XML could not have been created as quickly nor as well, without the experience gained worldwide by the use of SGML. XML, or whatever it evolves into, will see the realization of this promise.

References

(Bush 1945)

Bush, Vannevar: As We May Think. In: The Atlantic Monthly (July 1945)

(CALS)

Originally, in 1985, CALS stood for Computer Aided Logistic Support, an initiative created by the US Department of Defense. Shortly after the term was coined, the meaning was changed to Computer-aided Acquisition and Logistic Support. In the early 90's, the meaning was again modified to Continuous Acquisition and Lifecycle Support and later to Commerce At Lightening Speed. The goal of the CALS initiative was to have all documentation in support of a weapon system available in electronic format. This implied the use of electronic data standards. By 1990, other NATO members were beginning to examine the use of CALS concepts and these ideas were also being ç pushed out to the private sector.

(Chahuneau 1998)
Chahuneau, François: SGML schemas: From SGML DTDs to XML-DATA. In: Conference Proceedings SGML/XML Europe '98, 1998

(SGML Users' Group 1989)
SGML Users' Group (Ed.): A Brief History of the Development of SGML., June 1989

Evolution and use of generic markup languages

SGML – Praxis des langen Weges

Manfred Krüger

Der Ort: Amsterdam – Konferenz-Annex eines Luxushotels in einer säkularisierten Kirche. Das Jahr: 1982. Das Thema: International Markup. Die Apostel: Charles Goldfarb, Sperling Martin (USA). Die Verheißung: SGML wird die allgemeine Basis für die Dokumentverarbeitung auf Computern. Die Gemeinde: Verlagsleute, Setzer/ Drucker und andere aus den Niederlanden, Großbritannien, Deutschland, Frankreich und den USA, unter ihnen allerdings kaum oder keine „EDV"-Spezialisten!

Das Ergebnis: Über einige kam der Geist „SGML", die meisten anderen schliefen den erholsamen Kirchenschlaf. Die Überzeugten kehrten zurück und verbreiteten die frohe Kunde in ihrem Volk, das nicht wie sie glauben wollte.

Erste Internationale Markup-Konferenz

1 Die Vorfahren und Väter

Es ist richtig, dass lebendige Menschen die Idee „SGML" hatten und sie zu einem Konzept und einer Sprache weiterentwickelten. Es wäre aber sicher falsch, dies einem Einzigen zuzuschreiben. Es ist richtig, dass es in der IBM ein Produkt gab, das zu einem sehr frühen Zeitpunkt Teile des späteren SGML-Konzepts enthielt (*Generalized Markup Language, GML*). IBM stand allerdings nicht allein; man erinnere sich an das Dokumenten-Verarbeitungssystem Scribe. Daher sollte man den Ursprung von SGML keinesfalls einer einzigen Herstellerfirma zuschreiben. Es waren nicht die Spezialisten der elektronischen Datenverarbeitung, die sich dieses Themas annahmen, sie waren noch vollauf mit den Computer-Hardware-Herausforderungen und der Zahlenverarbeitung beschäftigt. Auch die Wissenschaft ignorierte die dilettantischen Versuche der Leute, die eine formale

Ursprünge von SGML

Sprache für die Verarbeitung von Texten nicht nur entwickeln, sondern weltweit normieren wollten.

SGML wurde von ihren „Vätern" nicht eigentlich erfunden, sondern diese sichteten vielmehr die beginnende Praxis der Textverarbeitung – gute wie schlechte – und entwickelten SGML so in der intensiven Diskussion miteinander und mit den späteren Nutznießern. Ihre Leistung bestand vor allem darin, sich nicht mit den oft kurzatmigen und an den Beschränkungen der damaligen Text-Prozessoren orientierten Systemen zufriedenzugeben, sondern eine strategische Sicht einzunehmen und von gegebenen Produkten, Konzepten und Anforderungen zu abstrahieren. Als Ideengeber, Moderatoren und Integratoren sind mir damals Bill Tunnicliffe (*Graphic Communications Association, GCA*), Charles Goldfarb (damals *IBM*) und Sperling Martin aufgefallen. Charles Goldfarb wurde dann zur treibenden Kraft für die Entwicklung von SGML. Joan Smith (United Kingdom, alle anderen Genannten USA) übernahm es, SGML, besonders in Europa, bekannt zu machen. So könnte man – mit ein wenig Ironie und etwas respektlos – sagen, Charles Goldfarb ist der „Gottvater" von SGML, Joan Smith war sein „Erzengel".

Sie waren es, die eine noch kleine Schar von Anhängern gewannen, in den USA natürlich, aber insbesondere auch in Europa (Großbritannien, Niederlande, Frankreich und Deutschland) und mit diesen Überzeugten eine feste Glaubensgemeinschaft formten.

2 Vorzeitliche Ereignisse und Anwendungsprojekte

SGML wurde als Internationale Norm (ISO 8879:1986) im Oktober 1986 publiziert. Diesem Ereignis gingen viele Jahre Entwicklungsaufwand innerhalb der ISO-Arbeitsgruppe und heftige internationale Abstimmungskontroversen voraus. Dennoch ist dieses Datum – für die Anwendung von SGML in Europa – von geringerer Bedeutung als gerade die eingangs skizzierte erste *International Markup Conference* der GCA in Amsterdam. Von dieser Konferenz, die seitdem einmal jährlich stattfindet und jetzt als *SGML/XML Europe* firmiert, und von weiteren Aktivitäten der GCA gingen die ersten Impulse für den praktischen Einsatz von SGML aus.

Gelegentlich hört man, dass SGML innerhalb der *CALS-Initiative* des *US Department of Defense* zum elektronischen Publizieren entstanden sei. Die ersten SGML-Anwendungen sind aber etliche Jahre früher konzipiert worden, vor allem für den Einsatz in kommerziellen Verlagen. Hierzu gehört in den USA das heute legendäre *Electronic Manuscript Project*, das 1983 von der *Association of American Publishers (AAP)* initiiert und in Auftrag gegeben worden war. In Europa wurden meines Wissens etwa zeitgleich und unabhängig voneinander die SGML-Projekte *Elektronisches Publizieren von technisch-wissenschaftlichen Dokumenten* und das *DAPHNE-Projekt (Hahn-Meitner-Institut,* s. Abschnitt 5) im Jahre 1984 gestartet. Das Projekt Elektronisches Publizieren wurde von einem Konsortium geplant und durchgeführt, zu dem die Verlage *Poeschel* und *Springer,* das *Fachinformationszentrum Karlsruhe,* das *Deutsche Institut für Normung DIN* und die *Gesellschaft für Information und Dokumentation (GID)* gehörten. Gefördert wurde es von der *Europäischen Gemeinschaft* innerhalb des *DocDel-II-Programms.*

Wenig später wurde im Amt für offizielle Publikationen der *Europäischen Gemeinschaft,* ein Konzept für die SGML-Strukturierung dieser Publikationen entwickelt und unter dem Akronym *FORMEX* allen Produzenten von EG-Publikationen vorgegeben.

Die Zielsetzungen der genannten Projekte waren unterschiedlich, aber keines diente ausdrücklich der Erprobung von SGML, einer formalen Sprache, die sich derzeit noch in der Diskussion und der Entwicklung befand. Das Gemeinsame bestand eher darin, dass sich die Ziele dieser Projekte ohne das SGML-Konzept – deklarativ zu sein, unabhängig von Systemen und Verarbeitungen, frei in der Strukturierung der Dokumente und durch automatisch arbeitende Parser prüffähig – auch nicht annähernd verwirklichen ließen. Diese Projekte scheiterten letztlich in ihrer Realisierung. Allerdings lag dies nicht an einem unzulänglichen Konzept, sondern daran, dass die Werkzeuge (Parser, strukturgeführter Editor, Formatierer) nicht verfügbar oder für reale Anwendungen noch nicht reif waren. Hinzu kam, dass mit dem enormen Handlungsspielraum für unterschiedliche Dokumentstrukturierungen Herausforderungen entstanden, die den größten Anteil der Projekt-Ressourcen in Anspruch nahmen.

Der Erfolg der Projekte blieb vor allem auch deshalb aus, weil ihre Mitarbeiter nicht für sich selbst arbeiteten, sondern für Andere, die als Autoren, Verleger, Setzer den Nutzen aus den Projekten ziehen sollten. Letztere waren aber in dieser Zeit so sehr mit den technischen Einzelheiten der computerisierten Textverarbeitung befasst, dass sie sich mit solchen abstrakten Konstruktionen wie einer SGML-Dokumenttypdefinition nicht noch zusätzlich belasten wollten. Immerhin lieferten ihre neuen Systeme formatierte und gedruckte Seiten, was die SGML-Leute, wenn überhaupt, erst nach viel längerer Zeit und wesentlich weniger ansprechend schafften.

das verbindende Konzept

schwierige Praxis

Manfred Krüger ■ 53

Konzeptionell aber, denke ich, waren diese Projekte beispielgebend. Viele Fehlentwicklungen, besonders solche, die SGML mit bestimmten Produkten für die Dokumentenverarbeitung zu verbinden suchten, hätten vermieden werden können, wenn man die Erfahrungen der „vorzeitlichen" Projekte sorgfältig ausgewertet hätte.

3 Glaubenskriege

Die Berichte der ersten SGML-Implementierungsprojekte aus den Jahren 1984-1987 (s. Abschnitt 2) lösten bei potentiellen Nutzern keineswegs nur Begeisterung aus. Im Gegenteil, es kam zu verbissenen Diskussionen zwischen den wenigen „SGMListen" und den vielen, die für ihre Aufgaben weiterhin an Textverarbeitung und Schriftsatz festhielten. Bei denjenigen, die täglich mit den proprietären und häufig noch die Schreibmaschine oder den Fotosatz simulierenden Systemen arbeiteten, stieß das abstrakte, systemunabhängige und selbst nichts prozessierende SGML weithin auf völliges Unverständnis. Häufig wurde das SGML-Markup-Konzept als technisch überholt bezeichnet. Diese Ansicht wurde – in den Augen ihrer Verfechter –durch die folgenden parallelen Entwicklungen gestützt:

- Die Textverarbeitungsprogramme zeigten, zunehmend perfekt, auf dem Bildschirm lediglich den formatierten Text. Das Markup, mit dem dieser Text durchsetzt war, um die Formatierung zu bewirken, blieb im Hintergrund. Die Anwender zogen daraus den Fehlschluss, ihr System käme ohne Markup aus.

- Im Hochleistungsbereich (Dokumenten-Verarbeitungssysteme für technisch-wissenschaftliche Inhalte, hoch-qualitative Satzsysteme) erzielte man Ergebnisse, die in mancherlei Hinsicht den früheren, nicht-computerisierten Systemen überlegen waren. Allerdings hatten diese Systeme sämtlich eine höchst proprietäre Architektur, die den Schluss nahelegte, dies sei mit SGML-basierten Systemen nicht oder nur unter erheblich höherem Aufwand möglich, wobei letzteres auch heute noch nicht ganz falsch ist!

- Die Desktop-Publishing-Systeme kamen und demonstrierten ihre „Überlegenheit" dadurch, dass man mit ihnen in weniger als einer Stunde komplex und ansprechend gestaltete Seiten erzeugen konnte, während man mit Hilfe von SGML Wochen und Monate über die geeignete Dokumenttypdefinition nachdachte und erste, einfach formatierte Seiten erst nach dieser Phase vorweisen konnte.

Die Manager der zentralen EDV-Abteilungen misstrauten einem Standard, der von einer so bekannt schwerfälligen internationalen Organisation wie der ISO kam.

Bestenfalls gestand man SGML eine Nischenrolle im Bereich der technischen Dokumentation zu; dies aber nur mit dem Argument, die Anwender in diesem Bereich, d.h. beispielsweise die Hersteller von Flugzeugen oder Waffensystemen, könnten sich die durch SGML verursachten Mehrkosten der Dokumentation eben leisten.

SGML:
Nischenrolle
in der
Dokumentation

4 Gesellschaftsbildung

Die oben angesprochenen Verhältnisse führten zu einer gewissen Isolierung der SGML-Verfechter, die diese durch intensive Kontakte untereinander – über Landes- und Sprachgrenzen hinaus – kompensierten. Zur wichtigsten Veranstaltung, auf der man diese Kontakte pflegen und intensivieren konnte, entwickelte sich die jährliche *International Markup Conference*, die nach zwei Ausflügen in die USA und nach Kanada ausschließlich in Europa abgehalten wurde/wird und zu der sich die SGML-Experten mit jährlicher Regelmäßigkeit trafen.

Diese Konferenzen wirkten auf die gelegentlich dort erscheinenden Außenseiter als reine Insider-Treffen und wurden auch deshalb von vielen nur einmal und nie wieder besucht. Bekannte sich allerdings ein Neuling zu SGML und war bereit, in das Lager der SGML-Verfechter zu wechseln, wurde er (sie) mit großer Herzlichkeit in die Gemeinschaft aufgenommen. So wuchs die Teilnehmerzahl von etwa 50 Personen Mitte der achtziger Jahre auf etwa 200 Personen Anfang der neunziger Jahre. Die Kontakte entwickelten sich vielfach zu stabilen freundschaftlichen Beziehungen. Entsprechend stark war die Erschütterung innerhalb der SGML-Gemeinschaft als einer ihrer Väter, Yuri Rubinsky, 1996 plötzlich starb.

jährliche
Markup-
Konferenzen

Zwischen den SGML-Verfechtern und denen, die andere Konzepte bevorzugten, entwickelten sich ausgesprochene Feindschaften, die eine sachliche Diskussion der Konzepte außerordentlich erschwerten. Mir scheint heute, als wäre die Aggressivität von den SGML-Gegnern ausgegangen. Sie wurde aber durch die erkennbare gesellschaftliche Geschlossenheit der SGML-Verfechter offensichtlich auch provoziert.

5 Pionierprojekte

Nach diesem Ausflug in die „menschelnden" Aspekte der SGML-Geschichte zurück zum Technischen.

die ersten SGML-Projekte in Deutschland

Ich möchte einige frühen Projekte skizzieren, die typisch für die Entwicklung der SGML-Anwendung in Deutschland sind und die in Vergessenheit zu geraten drohen. Bei den nicht-öffentlichen Anwendungen beschränke ich mich auf diejenigen, die mir durch eigene Mitarbeit vertraut sind:

- *DAPHNE (Document Application Processing in a Heterogeneous Environment*, innerhalb des *Deutschen Forschungsnetzes, DFN*; 1984-1986)

- *Elektronisches Publizieren von technisch-wissenschaftlichen Dokumenten* (im Rahmen des EG-Programms *DocDel II, Projekt 14*; 1984-1986)

- Pharmazeutische Fachinformationen (19-5-1986)

- Strukturierung von Texten (*strukTEXT*; 1985-1986)

- Strukturierung eines zweisprachigen Wörterbuchs (*Bibliographisches Institut & F. A. Brockhaus*; 1987-1988)

- SGML-Anwendung für juristische Loseblatt-Werke des *Carl Link Verlages* (1989-1991)

- Aufbau eines SGML-basierten Redaktionssystems für Wörterbücher und Lexika (Bibliographisches Institut & F. A. Brockhaus; ab 1990).

Vor 1990 wurden außerdem erste Anwendungsprojekte in der Flugzeug-/Luftfahrt-Industrie, der Raumfahrt-Industrie und in der pharmazeutischen Industrie gestartet. In der nicht-kommerziellen Forschung befasste sich das GMD-IPSI (*Institut für Integrierte Publikations- und Informationssysteme* der *GMD – Forschungszentrum Informationstechnik mbH*) in Darmstadt mit der Nutzung von SGML für individualisierte Hypermedia-Anwendungen.

DAPHNE-Projekt

Das DAPHNE-Projekt setzte sich zum Ziel, technisch-wissenschaftliche Dokumente über Netze auszutauschen und sie beim Empfänger zu formatieren und auszugeben. Hierfür entwickelte man eine SGML-DTD, die in ihrer Strukturierung auf die Formatier-Makros von LaTeX zielte. Damit war die Gestaltungsspezifikation im Formatierer „fest verdrahtet" mit den Variationsmöglichkeiten, die LaTeX dem Anwender durch sein immanentes Styles-Konzept belässt. Die Zusammenführung von Dokumentteilen aus unterschiedlichen Quellen über das Netz (*compound documents*) spielte hier bereits eine wichtige Rolle. Es wurde meines Wissens innerhalb dieses Projekts auch der erste SGML-Parser (in Europa) geschrieben, und zwar von Craig Smith.

Vergleichsweise konservativ war die Zielsetzung für das Projekt 14 des DocDel-II-Programms: Hier ging es zunächst vorwiegend darum, die Ausgaben unterschiedlicher Textverarbeitungssysteme (damals *word processors*) auf ein einheitliches Format, nämlich SGML, zu bringen, um aus diesem Format unterschiedliche Verarbeitungssysteme – damals ausschließlich seiten- und papierorientierte Ausgaben für Verlagsprodukte – mit einem Minimum an Konvertierungen zu nutzen. Bei m Eingangsformaten und n Verarbeitungssystemen sollten also anstelle von m-mal-n lediglich m-plus-n Verknüpfungen notwendig sein. Selbstverständlich wurde auch in diesem Projekt bereits mit der Entwicklung einer eigenen DTD begonnen. Mit dem Parser aus dem DAPHNE-Projekt wurden erste Versuche mit dem Parsen von DTD und Dokumentinstanzen gemacht.

Bereits in diesem Projekt wurde die Erkenntnis gewonnen, dass die Erstellung fehlerfrei strukturierter SGML-Dokumente ohne eine besondere Unterstützung durch ein Autorensystem, das z.B. interaktives Parsen und Strukturführung bieten konnte, nicht realistisch war. In der Amsterdamer Markup-Konferenz hatten Charles Goldfarb und Sperling Martin noch behauptet, SGML würde mit jedem Texteditor erzeugt werden können und dadurch gerade frei machen von den spezifischen Funktionen bestimmter Textverarbeitungssysteme. Im Projekt 14 zog man die Konsequenz aus dieser anderen Erfahrung, spezifizierte einen SGML-Editor (mit Strukturführung) und entwickelte sogar eine erste prototypische Fassung. Dies wurde später aber nicht weiter verfolgt.

Es ist zu betonen, dass die finanziellen Mittel, die für dieses Projekt zur Verfügung standen, insbesondere auch für die Diskussion mit parallelen Projekten genutzt werden konnten. So wurden Verbindungen zu dem *Electronic Manuscript Project* und den ersten SGML-Ansätzen innerhalb des *Government Printing Office* in den USA geschaffen und Beiträge zur Entstehung der beschriebenen SGML-Gemeinschaft geleistet.

Die Konsortialpartner in diesem Projekt verdienen erwähnt zu werden. Es waren: der *Springer-Verlag* in Heidelberg (federführend in der Ausarbeitung des Projektvorschlags), der *Verlag für Technische Regelwerke* (ein Bereich innerhalb des *DIN*), das *Fachinformationszentrum Karlsruhe*, der *C.E. Poeschel Verlag* (Stuttgart) und die *Gesellschaft für Information und Dokumentation (GID)* in Heidelberg (vorwiegend im Projektmanagement tätig).

SGML in der Pharmaindustrie

Während der Laufzeit des DocDel-Projektes schlug Wolfgang Hilbig vom *Satzrechenzentrum Berlin* vor, die zwischen dem *Bundesgesundheitsamt (BGA)* und der Pharmaindustrie vereinbarte On-Demand-Publikation der pharmazeutischen Fachinformationen als SGML-Anwendung zu gestalten. Meine Firma, damals als *ConText GmbH* firmierend, bekam vom Satzrechenzentrum Berlin den Auftrag, die sehr strenge und inhaltsorientierte Strukturierungsvorgabe des BGA in einer SGML-DTD zu modellieren und sie, implementiert in den weltweit ersten SGML-Editor (WriterStation von *Datalogics*), den Pharmafirmen anzubieten, damit sie mit diesem Werkzeug fehlerfrei und standardisiert strukturierte Fachinformationsinstanzen erzeugen konnten. Innerhalb des Satzrechenzentrums wurde durch eine intern entwickelte Konvertierung die Verbindung vom Autorensystem zum Satzsystem geschaffen. Weiterreichende Pläne, die Formatierung und den Ausdruck aus einer Datenbank nach Anforderung zu produzieren, wurden nicht verfolgt. Gedruckt wurde zwar auf Anforderung, aber mit den Daten, die bereits formatiert und für den Hochleistungsdrucker aufbereitet waren.

Das Besondere an diesem Projekt – und für spätere SGML-Anwendungen nicht untypisch – war die Tatsache, dass lediglich die beiden oben genannten Firmen diese Anwendung SGML-bewusst betrieben. Die liefernden Pharmafirmen – nur etwa fünf beteiligten sich an der SGML-Erfassung mit WriterStation, die Mehrzahl lieferte konventionelle Papier-Manuskripte, die im Satzrechenzentrum im proprietären Format des Satzsystems erfasst wurden, – das BGA, der Verband der pharmazeutischen Industrie und selbstverständlich die Nutzer dieses Dienstes erfuhren von dem SGML-Konzept nichts.

strukTEXT-Projekt

Das strukText-Projekt war ein Gemeinschaftsprojekt des *Bundesverbands Druck* und des *Börsenvereins des Deutschen Buchhandels.* Es knüpfte an das *Electronic Manuscript Project* der *American Association of Publishers (AAP)* und dem Projekt 14 des DocDel-II-Programms an. Es ging ausschließlich darum, eine standardisierte, systemunabhängige Schnittstelle zu den Satzsystemen in den Setzereien und Druckereien zu formulieren. Initiator und treibende Kraft des Projekts war der Bundesverband Druck. Der Börsenverein, als Organisation der Verlage, beteiligte sich eher passiv. Das war insofern verwunderlich, weil doch die Verlage durch eine direkte Übernahme der Manuskriptdaten in die unterschiedlichen Satzsysteme profitieren würden, durch schnellere Produktion, Kosteneinsparungen, flexiblere Auftragsvergabe.

strukTEXT wurde als Entwurf im Oktober 1986 – zeitgleich mit dem Erscheinen der SGML-Norm! – publiziert. Es richtete sich, dem Produktionsfluss beim Publizieren entsprechend, an Autoren, Verlage und Druckereien.

Neben allgemeinen Regeln zur Erstellung und Weitergabe „elektronischer" Manuskripte – die zum Großteil noch heute gültig sind, sich dennoch nach mehr als zwölf Jahren nicht allgemein herumgesprochen haben – enthielt strukText die SGML-anwendungsbezogenen Strukturierungsrichtlinien. Um die Anwender nicht mehr als unbedingt notwendig zu belasten, war die Struktur sehr einfach gehalten und auf den Text-Korpus beschränkt, hatte also beispielsweise keine Titelei-Elemente. Das im Projekt formulierte Idealziel von maximal 30 Strukturelementen wurde allerdings nicht eingehalten. Immerhin umfasste strukTEXT nicht mehr als 80 Elemente, einschließlich einfacher mathematischer Formeln, einfacher Tabellen und Elemente für Links.

Die Aufnahme von strukTEXT bewegte sich bei den genannten Zielgruppen „von vornehmer Zurückhaltung bis zu schroffer Ablehnung", so drückte es der Chef eines großen Satz- und Druckhauses aus. Die Kritik bezog sich ausschließlich auf das Konzept im Ganzen, nie auf Details, von denen besonders bestimmte Strukturelemente aus heutiger Sicht durchaus kritikwürdig waren. Damit war eine durch Glaubensfragen bestimmte Diskussion eröffnet, die SGML zwar so gut wie keine Anwendung brachte, aber es bei Verlegern und Setzern immerhin weitgehend bekannt machte.

Der *Bundesverband Druck* bemühte sich in den Jahren 1987 bis 1989, strukTEXT als DIN-Norm zu etablieren. Nach umfangreichen Änderungen in der Darstellung der Richtlinien, nicht im Inhalt, wurde das Normierungsprojekt dann aber eingestellt.

strukTEXT war ein Projekt, das eine allgemeine SGML-Struktur für den breiten Gebrauch standardisieren sollte. Viele, die sich für SGML interessierten, empfanden es als Mangel, dass SGML zwar eine formale Meta-Sprache, aber kein standardisiertes Auszeichnungsschema bieten konnte. Allerdings scheiterten bis zur „Erfindung" von HTML alle derartigen Entwicklungen in der Praxis an mangelndem Interesse.

Erfolgreich wurde SGML dort eingesetzt, wo es darum ging, anwendungsspezifische Strukturen zu modellieren und diese den Anwendungen als strikt einzuhaltende Strukturierungsvorschrift vorzugeben. Dafür waren SGML-basierte Editoren mit Strukturführung eine unbedingte Voraussetzung.

So konnte der Verlag Bibliographisches Institut & F.A. Brockhaus im Jahre 1987 leicht zur Anwendung von SGML für die verteilte Redaktion eines zweisprachigen Wörterbuchs gewonnen werden. *Apples* Macintosh mit seiner für jedermann leicht zu bedienenden Oberfläche war auf dem Markt, *SoftQuad* verteilte erste Beta-Versionen seines SGML-Editors (SoftQuad Author/Editor). Im Verlag war eine umfangreiche Autoren-Richtlinie, u.a. für die Struk-

turierung der Wörterbuch-Einträge, erarbeitet worden, die innerhalb
von wenigen Stunden als SGML-DTD in den Editor implementiert
wurde. Diese Arbeit, die im direkten Gespräch mit der Herausgebe-
rin des Wörterbuchs geleistet wurde, löste spontane Begeisterung
aus: Eine solche Flexibilität und Genauigkeit für die Strukturvorgabe
hätte man vorher nicht für möglich gehalten; ohne jede Programmierung – lediglich durch Kompilation der DTD – funktionierte die
Strukturführung im Editor mit der in der DTD formulierten Rigidi-
tät; die Textansicht auf der Mac-Oberfläche mit richtigen Fonts
machte die Darstellung der Wörterbuch-Daten zu einem Vergnügen;
die Einarbeitung in die Handhabung des Computers und des Editors
erwies sich als überraschend einfach. Ein über 70 Jahre alter Professor, ein Sprachwissenschaftler, bekam für seine Arbeit erstmals einen
Computer und die SGML-Software. Nach einer eintägigen Einführung und einigen weiteren Telefonaten konnte der alte Herr seine
Arbeit ohne weitere technische Hilfe tun. Die verlagseigene Setzerei,
die mit der Übernahme von Manuskript-Daten externer Autoren
grauenvolle Erfahrungen gemacht hatte, konnte diese Daten nun
endlich fehlerlos und ohne Nachbearbeitung in das Satzsystem importieren. Das Aufsetzen der Importprozedur war allerdings nicht
ohne Aufwand und Probleme.

Die externen SGML-Experten waren für die Weiterentwicklung
der Anwendung schnell entbehrlich. Als sie nach etwa zwei Jahren
die Anwendung wieder zu Gesicht bekamen, hatte die DTD die Ver-
sionsnummer 13. Die letzten zehn Versionen hatten die Redaktions-
kräfte des Verlages völlig selbständig bearbeitet und implementiert.
Für mich war dies die erste SGML-Anwendung, die ein Redaktions-
und Produktionsproblem tatsächlich löste, und zwar sehr viel
schneller und billiger als Nicht-SGML-Konzepte oder -Produkte.

Diese Erfahrung im *Bibliographischen Institut* führte Anfang 1990
zu der Entscheidung, in Zukunft die für den Verlag zentralen Publikationen (Wörterbücher, Enzyklopädien) mit einem SGML-basierten Redaktionssystem zu erstellen und zu pflegen. Diese Entscheidung beruhte zudem auf einem Projekt, das der Verlag 1989 gemeinsam mit dem *IBM-Forschungszentrum* in Heidelberg durchgeführt hatte und in dem die Satzdaten des *Duden Deutsches Univer-
salwörterbuch* mit IBM-eigener Software analysiert und in eine
SGML-Syntax konvertiert worden war. Hier wurde die DTD also aus
der Strukturierung der Daten abgeleitet, und man kannte jetzt die in
den Satzdaten enthaltenen Strukturausprägungen und -varianten.
Diese empirisch gewonnene DTD bildete nun wiederum die Grundlage für die Entscheidung, wie diese Struktur in Zukunft gestrafft
und neuen Anforderungen der Datennutzung angepasst werden
könnte.

Die Ausschreibung für das Redaktionssystem, die der Verlag 1990 an die großen Computer- und Software-Hersteller schickte, brachte diese mit der Anforderung nach SGML-Unterstützung in große Verlegenheit. Nur das gemeinschaftlich entwickelte Konzept und Angebot zweier (kleiner) SGML-Anbieter traf die Anforderungen und wurde schließlich akzeptiert.

Aus den oben angesprochenen ersten Erfahrungen hatte man gelernt und inzwischen auch die Anforderungen an das technische System beträchtlich entwickelt. Die DTDs wurden komplexer und umfangreicher, weil auch die Nutzung der Daten ausgeweitet werden sollte und nicht mehr nur die Publikation in der Produktform Buch umfassen sollte, sondern auch die Mehrfachnutzung in unterschiedlichen Druck-Publikationen und Computer-Anwendungen. Nicht mehr der Editor stand im Mittelpunkt der Lösung, sondern der Redaktionsbetrieb mit der Koordination eines vielköpfigen Redaktionsteams zur Produktion neuer und komplexerer Publikationen. Es war nicht mehr ausreichend, dass das System funktionierte, sondern es musste durch formal gestaltete und möglichst automatisierte Prozessschritte zur besseren Wirtschaftlichkeit und der Verkürzung von Produktionszeiten beitragen.

Die Schlüsselrolle einer DTD für die Leistungsfähigkeit einer Publikationsanwendung wurde erst den Redaktionsleitern, aber schnell auch den Redakteuren selbst bewusst. Entsprechend viel Aufwand wurde der Entwicklung und Diskussion der DTDs zugestanden. Insbesondere hinsichtlich der DTDs für Enzyklopädien lernte man, dass man die inhaltsorientierte Strukturierung auch übertreiben und sich in dieser Situation einen Bärendienst erweisen konnte: Anstelle einer klaren, vom späteren Leser auch nachvollziehbaren Strukturierung im fertigen Produkt, ließen sich mit SGML völlig überzogene, in der Erstellung, Bearbeitung und Verarbeitung kostenintensive, unübersichtliche und vergleichsweise nutzenarme Anwendungen schaffen. Das Werkzeug der formalen Sprache SGML hatte das Wissen um die Strukturierung von textlichen Inhalten auf ein vor wenigen Jahren noch nicht vorstellbares Niveau gehoben (vgl. mit dem Projekt strukTEXT).

Im Zusammenhang mit der Diskussion und Entwicklung der DTDs für das Bibliographische Institut & F. A. Brockhaus wurde deutlich, dass man es hier mit Dokumenten zu tun hatte, die gerade nicht öffentlich zugänglich waren, um den Wettbewerbern keine kostenfreien Vorlagen für die eigenen Anwendungen zu bieten. In den wenigen öffentlichen Präsentationen der SGML-Anwendungen des Bibliographischen Instituts wurden bekam man daher lediglich kleine interessante Ausschnitte der Dokument-Instanzen zu sehen.

*SGML für
juristische
Loseblatt-Werke*

Drei Jahre vergingen nach der Publikation des strukTEXT-Entwurfes. Dann meldete sich ein Verleger aus Kronach in Oberfranken und verlangte, strukTEXT für die Produktion seiner juristischen Loseblatt-Werke einzusetzen. Folker O. Link-Wiesend ging es um zweierlei:

1. die aufwendige technische Produktion von Loseblatt-Werken und ihrer Austauschlieferungen durch Automatisierung der Satz- und Umbruch-Arbeit zu rationalisieren,

2. die dafür erstellten und gepflegten Datenbestände für neue, „elektronische" Lieferformen (CD-ROM) nutzen zu können, wenn es für derartige Produkte einen Markt gäbe.

*strukTEXT in der
Anwendung*

In der Analyse der Verlagsanforderungen stellte sich schnell heraus, dass die strukTEXT-Anwendung zwar eine brauchbare Ausgangsbasis bildete, aber keine Strukturelemente für die inhaltsorientierte Strukturierung der juristischen Inhalte wie Gesetze, Gesetzes-Paragraphen, Urteilsleitsätze, amtliche Erläuterungen usw. enthielt. Daher wurde die strukTEXT-DTD verändert und erweitert, so dass letzten Endes etwa zwei Drittel der Strukturelemente anwendungsspezifisch waren. Das hauptsächliche Interesse galt den Produktionsmitteln, mit denen die SGML-strukturierten Daten erstellt, korrigiert und verarbeitet werden sollten. Da Verlag und Setzerei/Druckerei im selben Haus unter der Leitung von Link-Wiesend arbeiteten, war der Verlag lediglich für die Strukturierungsentscheidungen und die Gestaltung der Loseblatt-Werke eingeschaltet, für den nicht technischen Teil also. Die Setzerei jedoch hatte die gesamte technische Produktion von der Erfassung der Manuskripte bis zur Belichtung der fertigen Seiten/Bögen zu bewältigen, ein Beispiel für die klassische Arbeitsteilung zwischen Verlag und technischen Betrieben.

Die Setzerei benötigte für diese Anwendung zwei Software-Arbeitsmittel:

1. einen Editor für die Erfassung und Strukturierung der Texte sowie die Bearbeitung und Korrektur bestehender Texte,

2. einen Formatierer für Satz und Seitenumbruch.

Das Rationalisierungsinteresse des Verlegers machte für die damals aufkommenden Alternativen unempfindlich, in denen Textbearbeitung und Formatierung in einem System mit direkten Eingriffsmöglichkeiten in die einzelnen Seiten und einer WYSIWYG-Oberfläche möglich – und zwingend – war.

*geringe Auswahl
an Werkzeugen*

Die Auswahl an Editoren war klein. Für die DOS-Plattform (mit zeichenorientiertem Bildschirm), die von der Setzerei aus Kostengründen bevorzugt wurde, gab es lediglich ein Produkt, nämlich WriterStation von *Datalogics*. WriterStation hatte – und hat bis

heute – das sonst in SGML-Editoren weitgehend verschmähte
Merkmal der Unterstützung für minimiertes Markup. Das kam den
Setzern insbesondere für die Nachstrukturierung von „roh" erfassten
Manuskripten gelegen. Die ausschließliche Bedienung des Editors
mit der Tastatur (keine Maus) machte die Handhabung durch die
Fachkräfte schnell, die höhere Produktivität erfreute die Leitung des
Druckhauses und des Verlags.

Für die Formatierung (Satz, Seitenumbruch, Seitenkontrolle mit
Generierung von a- und b-Seiten, Auswahl der geänderten Doppel-
seiten für die Belichtung, Generierung von Inhaltsverzeichnissen und
Sachregistern, usw.) wurde das Produkt DL-Pager, ebenfalls von
Datalogics, im wesentlichen aus drei Gründen gewählt:

1. SGML-Datenschnittstelle, kombinierbar mit Pager-Satz-Codes,

2. mächtige, interne Informationsverarbeitung für die oben genannten Verarbeitungen,

3. vollständige Automatisierung.

Im praktischen Betrieb zeigte es sich allerdings, dass gerade das hohe
Maß an Automatisierung in der Verarbeitung für Verlag und Setzerei typische Probleme aufwarf: Der Verlag wünschte zwar vorder-
gründig eine durchgängig konsistente Strukturierung der Werke mit
der Konsequenz einer einheitlichen Gestaltung der Ausgaben, aber
dies nur, solange einzelne Autoren keine Abweichungen verlangten.
Die Autoren allerdings hatten keine Ahnung von dem Konzept einer
DTD-kontrollierten Produktion.

Die Setzer, die auf die Entwicklung und Modifikation der Pager-
Instruktionen – in Form kompilierter Stylesheets – keinen direkten
Einfluss hatten, entwickelten einen großen Eifer, den Sonderwün-
schen einzelner Verlagslektoren oder Autoren durch Tricks in der
Nutzung der vorgegebenen DTD und durch Einstreuung von Pager-
Satz-Codes zu entsprechen. Da zudem Pager auch nicht fehlerfrei
parsende Daten, so gut es eben geht, formatiert, stellte man erst nach
Jahren fest, als die Daten tatsächlich für „elektronische" Produkte
genutzt werden sollten, dass dies wiederum umfangreiche Nachbe-
arbeitungen notwendig macht. Diese Umwege zu einer individuali-
sierten Gestaltung innerhalb des Satzsystems schadeten der Akzeptanz durch die Setzer keineswegs. Im Gegenteil, ein Setzer äusserte
sich so: „Pager ist kein gutes Satzsystem, es ist ein sehr gutes!"

Das Ziel der parallelen Datennutzung war trotz der SGML-
Konzeptualisierung und aller sorgfältiger Vorarbeit durch den Verle-
ger nicht befriedigend erfüllt. Der Rationalisierungsaspekt mit der
Konsequenz der kostengünstigen Produktion wurde erst gewürdigt,
als ein neuer Setzereileiter die Kombination von WriterStation und
Pager durch ein „modernes" SGML-basiertes WYSIWYG-System

automatisierte
Verarbeitung
schafft
Probleme

parallele
Datennutzung
unbefriedigend

mit integriertem Editor ersetzte. Die Reaktion der SGML-erprobten Setzer: „Wo ist da der Fortschritt?", der Hinweis der Betriebsleitung an den Verlag: „So billig wie mit dem alten System werden wir in Zukunft wohl nicht mehr produzieren können!".

Diese Pionierprojekte machen u.a. verständlich, warum man SGML in der öffentlichen Diskussion die hässlichen Etiketten der Nicht-Praktikabilität und Erfolglosigkeit anheftete: Die öffentlich diskutierten Projekte konnten nicht in die Praxis umgesetzt werden, und die proprietären Projekte wurden nicht öffentlich diskutiert.

Häufiger wird in der Praxis die Ansicht geäußert, dass SGML im wissenschaftlichen Bereich entwickelt und erstmals eingesetzt wurde. Damit verbunden ist meist die Kritik, dass SGML unpraktisch und akademisch sei. Richtig ist, dass SGML erst mit Beginn der neunziger Jahre ein Thema der breiteren wissenschaftlicher Diskussion in Deutschland wurde. Ausnahmen hierzu sind das DAPHNE-Projekt und einige Projekte des GMD-IPSI, die ab 1988 unter der konzeptionellen Leitung von Roberto Minio standen.

Roberto Minio kommt hinsichtlich des Einsatzes von SGML in Deutschland eine wichtige, allgemein unterschätzte Bedeutung zu. Als wissenschaftlicher Lektor im Springer-Verlag (Heidelberg) beschäftigt und in den Jahren von 1984 bis 1987 an der *Carnegie Mellon University* (Pittsburgh, USA) arbeitend, begleitete er mit entscheidenden Beiträgen das oben beschriebene Projekt 14 des DocDel-II-Programms und beriet mich beispielsweise in allen meinen SGML-Projekten. Ich kenne niemanden, der mehr SGML-Projekte angestoßen, konzeptualisiert und befruchtet hat als er. Dies betrifft insbesondere Projekte in Deutschland und innerhalb der Europäischen Gemeinschaften.

Es wird Leser geben, die in der Liste der Pionierprojekte die Anwendung des DIN, publiziert unter dem Titel *Rechnergestützte Dokumentbearbeitung von Normen* im DIN-Fachbericht 27 (1990), vermissen. Hinsichtlich der SGML-Anwendung beruhte dieses Projekt einmal auf den Ergebnissen des Projekts 14 des DocDel-II-Programms und zum anderen ganz entscheidend auf der Entwicklung von Anders Berglund für die Internationalen Normen (vgl. ISO/TR 9573; 1988). Ich erkenne deshalb diesem Projekt keine eigenständigen Pionier-Merkmale zu.

6 Pionierwerkzeuge

Obwohl es sich einfach nachvollziehen lässt, wann wer ein SGML-unterstützendes oder SGML-basiertes Produkt zum ersten Mal öffentlich angeboten hat, gibt es eine Reihe von Firmen, die für sich beanspruchen, die ersten gewesen zu sein. Insbesondere gilt dies für Editor-Produkte, die eine Seiten-Formatierung in WYSIWYG-Form einschlossen, sog. Dokumenten-Verarbeitungssysteme.

Relativ schwierig ist es dagegen, die Produkte, die die SGML-Unterstützung normgerecht – vor allem mit der Implementierbarkeit beliebiger, syntaktisch korrekter DTDs – integriert hatten, von denen zu unterscheiden, die lediglich eine oder wenige Strukturen mehr oder weniger „fest verdrahtet" enthielten und somit für die praktischen Projektanforderungen, eigene DTDs einzusetzen, nicht so gut geeignet waren

Noch Anfang der neunziger Jahre konnte man häufig das Argument hören, SGML sei ja als Konzept beeindruckend, leider aber wegen fehlender Werkzeuge zur praktischen Nutzung nicht tauglich.

Der WriterStation-Editor von *Datalogics* kam im Herbst 1986 auf den Markt. Meines Wissens war er tatsächlich der erste SGML-Editor, mit dem man beliebige, wenn auch in ihrem Umfang nicht unbeschränkte DTDs implementieren konnte und der Formatier-Definitionen verwendete, in denen man kontextabhängig und unter Nutzung der hierarchischen Vererbung von Formatinstruktionen Formatvorlagen erstellen konnte, die zur Laufzeit auf die SGML-Daten angewendet wurden.

WriterStation (WS) unterstützte das Parsen und Formatieren auch für Markup-minimierte Dokumente, ja sogar für *Shortrefs* und *Datatags*. Es konnte komplexe Texte und Nummerierungen als Formatierungsmerkmale *on the fly* generieren. Sämtliche Funktionen waren in einem dem Anwendungsentwickler zugänglichen Writer-Station-Basic geschrieben und wegen des reichen Bestandes an WS-Basic-Primitives konnten komplexe, spezifische Anwendungsanforderungen durch Programmierung des Editors erfüllt werden.

Datalogics hatte WriterStation nicht in erster Linie als selbständigen SGML-Editor geplant, sondern insbesondere als Frontend für das hauseigene Satzsystem Pager, das damals das Kernprodukt für Datalogics darstellte und ebenfalls schon 1986 mit einer SGML-Datenschnittstelle glänzen konnte.

Anders als bei anderen Satzsystemen und Dokumenten-Verarbeitungssystemen mit SGML-Schnittstelle konnte man mit Pager auf die SGML-Konstrukte für bedingte Verarbeitungen, Textgenerierungen und Gestaltungen in den Format-Spezifikationen zugreifen, indem Attributwerte und Umgebungsbedingungen interpretiert wurden. Damit konnte Pager auch die in den DTDs impliziten Anforderungen zur Navigation auf den SGML-Strukturen und zu ihrer Verarbeitung, beispielsweise die Ebenen rekursiv verwendeter Elemente zu unterscheiden, erfüllen. Pager war also bereits damals mit mehr „Intelligenz" ausgestattet als viele heute in Mode befindlichen Systeme mit ihrem „Baby-SGML"-Interface.

Pager war und ist immer noch ein Satz- und Umbruch-System, das vollständig automatisiert im Batchbetrieb arbeitet. Die Verweigerung einer interaktiven Nutzung war und ist in den Augen des Herstellers, Steven Brown, dem Gründer und langjährigen Inhaber von *Datalogics*, keine Schwäche des Produkts, sondern entspricht der Überzeugung, dass SGML-strukturierte Dokumente ausschließlich völlig automatisiert verarbeitet werden sollten. Typisch für die Mehrzahl von Pager-Installationen und -Anwendungen ist, dass das völlig im Hintergrund arbeitende Produkt selbst bei vielen Anwendern nahezu unbekannt bleibt.

Pager nutzte eine derzeit als Standard bezeichnete Computer-Plattform, VAX-Rechner von *Digital Equipment*. Mit dem Siegeszug von UNIX und DOS-Windows für die Dokumentenverarbeitung geriet das Produkt allerdings aus dem Blickfeld. Erst mit der Verfügbarkeit auf UNIX-Systemen und auf Windows/NT erlebt Pager eine Renaissance, und dies nahezu ohne funktionale Erweiterung oder Veränderung gegenüber dem Ende der achtziger Jahre.

Mit der Publikation der SGML-Norm machten sich auch andere Software-Hersteller Gedanken über eine SGML-Unterstützung. Im Jahr 1987 – auf der Markup-Konferenz in Torremolinos, wegen der geringen Teilnehmerzahl unbestrittener Tiefpunkt der SGML-Konferenzen – präsentierte Yuri Rubinsky den SGML-Editor von *SoftQuad*, den Author/Editor, auf einem Macintosh. Die etwa 50 Teilnehmer der Konferenz waren begeistert von Yuri Rubinsky und seiner Kunst, ein solches Produkt zu präsentieren, aber auch von der ansprechenden Oberfläche und leichten Handhabbarkeit des Editors selbst. Die Teilnehmer konnten vergleichen, denn innerhalb der Konferenz hatten sie einen ersten SGML-Hands-on-Workshop absolviert, der mit WriterStation durchgeführt wurde.

Author/Editor glänzte durch die einfache und schnelle Implementierbarkeit einer DTD, die ebenfalls einfache Möglichkeit, Styles aus der graphischen Oberfläche heraus mit WYSIWYG-Kontrolle zu erstellen, die Maus-Handhabung und die tadellose Integration in die Macintosh-Oberfläche. Author/Editor wurde als Autoren-Werkzeug für Autoren ohne professionellen Hintergrund in der Satztechnik oder Programmierung akzeptiert.

Die völlig anderen Schwerpunkte, wie WriterStation sie gesetzt hatte, gerieten in den Hintergrund, ebenso die unterschiedlichen Einsatzgebiete. Leider hatte das anfängliche Urteil, Author/Editor würde das SGML-Werkzeug für Jedermann, keinen Bestand. Trotz bester Voraussetzungen – einfache und intuitive Handhabung verbunden mit leistungsfähiger Strukturführung – kam Author/Editor nur selten bei den echten Autoren (im Unterschied zu Erfassern fremder Texte) zum Einsatz.

Im Sommer 1988 wurde Author/Editor dann regulär ausgeliefert. Zeitgleich mit der englischsprachigen Version wurde in Deutschland eine vollständig eingedeutschte Version einschließlich eines Handbuches angeboten. Das Handbuch wurde übrigens mit dem Arbor-Text-Publisher, dem ersten SGML-basierten Dokumenten-Verarbeitungssystem mit hoch-qualitativer Satzverarbeitung erstellt und gesetzt. *Launching customer* für diese deutsche Version des SoftQuad-Produkts war das Bibliographische Institut & F. A. Brockhaus (s. Abschnitt 5) mit 20 Lizenzen auf einen Schlag.

ArborText begann 1986 mit der Entwicklung eines SGML-basierten Dokumenten-Verarbeitungssystems. Dabei ging man von dem Seiten-Formatierer TeX der *American Mathematical Society* aus, für den man eine Editor-Unterstützung entwickeln wollte. Gleichzeitig wollte man neben der TeX-Domäne (wissenschaftliche, insbesondere mathematische Dokumente) auch reguläre Büro-Anwendungen (Briefe, Memos, Berichte und Präsentationen) unterstützen, in denen die Stärken von TeX zur Geltung kommen: tadellose Mikro-Typografie und automatisierter Spalten- und Seitenumbruch, Einbeziehung von vielen Sonderzeichen und Symbolen, Tabellen- und Formelunterstützung, Grafik-Integration, automatisierte Generierung von Verzeichnissen und Registern.

Die Erstfassung des ArborText-Publishers erschien 1987 und ließ sich von den potentiellen Nutzern nur schwer einordnen: Das TeX hatte eine attraktive Editor-Oberfläche bekommen, aber dafür wurden die Anwender in die Dokumenttypen von Brief, Buch und Memo gezwungen. Die bisher schon erstellten TeX-Dokumente ließen sich in dieser Editor-Oberfläche nicht fortführen. Sie war zwar typografisch anspruchsvoll, entsprach aber nicht der aufkommenden WYSIWYG-Mode. Die Formatierung im Editor war bildschirmorientiert; und nur in einem separaten Fenster konnte man die TeX-Ausgabe „previewen". Der ArborText-Publisher unterstützte SGML, allerdings waren die Dokumenttypen vorgegeben und nur sehr eingeschränkt adaptierbar. Dazu kam, dass sie nicht in regulären SGML-DTDs modelliert und dokumentiert waren und einige Syntax-Regeln von SGML recht willkürlich eingesetzt wurden.

ArborText-Publisher

TeX mit attraktiver Oberfläche?

Aber: Vom Standpunkt der Architektur war bereits dieses Arbor-Text-Produkt vorbildlich – und ist es bis heute geblieben. Einige Argumente: Trennung von Bearbeitungsoberfläche und Seiten-Darstellung; die Strukturführung im Editor macht die fehlerfreie Verarbeitung sicher; das Dokumenten-Verarbeitungssystem ist nicht an den implementierten Formatierer gebunden; hinter der system-neutralen SGML-Schnittstelle können relativ einfach unterschiedliche Verarbeitungssysteme integriert werden; der strukturgeführte Editor mit seiner übersichtlichen und bildschirmgerechten Gestaltung macht die Erstellung/Bearbeitung von Dokumenten einfach und schnell; die hervorragenden, aber sonst schwierig zu handhabenden Merkmale des TeX-Formatierers lassen sich wie selbstverständlich und ohne Kenntnisse des Formatierers (und ohne die Hilfe der TeX-Hacker) nutzen.

Mit dem zweiten großen Schritt zum ADEPT-Editor und zum ADEPT-Publisher wurden die SGML-Beschränkungen beseitigt. Heute ist der ADEPT-Editor unbestritten das führende SGML-Editor-Produkt, ohne daß sich die Architektur über die mehr als zehn Jahre wesentlich hätte zu verändern brauchen.

Fast ausnahmslos wurden die genannten Produkte im Zusammenhang mit den bereits beschriebenen Pionierprojekten eingesetzt. Anders war dies mit dem ArborText-Publisher. An vielen Universitäten und Forschungseinrichtungen waren mindestens einige Lizenzen verfügbar. Typischerweise ignorierten die Anwender allerdings das diesem Produkt zugrundeliegende SGML-Konzept. Für sie war der ArborText-Publisher einfach ein bequem zu bedienendes TeX-System.

Auch im Zusammenhang der Pionierprodukte muss zu den diesbezüglichen Behauptungen im bereits zitierten DIN-Fachbericht 27 etwas richtiggestellt werden: Der auf dem Technical Publishing System (TPS) von *Interleaf* beruhende und von dem *Zentrum für Graphische Datenverarbeitung (ZGDV)* in Darmstadt entwickelte „SGML-Editor INES" (vgl. Abschnitt 3 des Fachberichts) war weder das erste kommerzielle SGML-System, noch erfüllte es „alle Anforderungen aus dem Normenwesen". Die Behauptung, „die SGML-unterstützenden Editoren konnten nur feste DTDs verarbeiten" ist nicht korrekt, traf aber absurderweise im wesentlichen auf das INES-Produkt selbst zu. Die INES-Entwicklung hat die SGML-Anwendung für Normen und andere Industrie-Projekte in Deutschland eher verzögert als gefördert.

Die oben diskutierten wenigen Pionierprodukte bezogen sich im wesentlichen auf die Editor- und die Formatierfunktion für die Druckausgabe. Selbstverständlich gibt es weitere Pionierprodukte für die computergestützte Dokumenthandhabung und -verwendung.

Zu ihnen gehören HyperText-Produkte wie beispielsweise DynaText von *Electronic Book Technologies*. Solche kamen dann aber erst nach 1990 und haben nach meinem Dafürhalten die Anwendung von SGML nicht mehr wesentlich beeinflusst oder gefördert. Vielmehr kam die Schubkraft für die Ausweitung der Anwendungen aus anderen Quellen, über die jetzt zu sprechen sein wird.

7 Die Neuzeit

War die Pionierzeit durch viele ideologische Debatten und vorsichtige Versuche geprägt, in denen man sich vorrangig mit den Möglichkeiten der formalen Sprache hinsichtlich der Modellierung der Strukturen in DTDs und der Implementierung in die meist noch sehr wenig perfekten Werkzeuge beschäftigte, traten in den Projekten ab Beginn der neunziger Jahre mehr und mehr organisatorische und management-orientierte Aspekte in den Vordergrund.

SGML wurde zu einem Mittel, mit dem man die Erstellung, Pflege und Produktion großer Dokumentbestände innerhalb großer Organisationen und über Organisationsgrenzen hinweg zu verwalten begann. Besonders wichtig waren dabei auf das Dokumentmanagement bezogene Aspekte wie die Fragmentierung großer Dokumente, die Mehrfachverwendung einzelner Dokumentteile, die Behandlung unterschiedlicher Dokumentfassungen.

SGML für das Dokumenten-Management

Dieser Fokus auf den organisatorischen Ablauf hat allerdings in den meisten Anwendungen eher zu Problemen als zu schnellen Lösungen geführt: Mit der zunehmenden Kontrolle von Dokumentstrukturen durch SGML-Parser und der zunehmend fehlerfreien automatisierten Weiterverarbeitung geparster Dokumente hatte die Organisation der Dokumentenbearbeitung in den Redaktionen der Verlage und in der Produktion der technischen Betriebe nicht Schritt gehalten. Um diese gewonnenen Möglichkeiten zu nutzen, musste erst einmal das Umfeld neu organisiert werden. Diese notwendige Reorganisation provozierte heftige innerorganisatorische Auseinandersetzungen und langwierige Neuorientierungen und Umstellungen. Nach aussen drangen weiterhin überwiegend schlechte Nachrichten von SGML-Anwendungsprojekten.

Neuordnung des Ablaufs

Andererseits begann man aber jetzt auch, die schon länger diskutierte Idee der multimedialen Nutzung von SGML-strukturierten Dokumenten in die Praxis umzusetzen. Erste Produkte entstanden, in denen SGML-strukturierte Dokumente *on the fly* für die formatierte Bildschirmdarstellung verarbeitet wurden und als Hypertext

SGML für Hypertexte: DynaText

genutzt werden konnten. Hierzu gehört DynaText, das ab 1990 kommerziell verfügbar war.

Auch diese Möglichkeiten der „elektronischen" Nutzung lösten zunächst keine Begeisterung aus, weil man nämlich feststellte, dass die vorliegenden SGML-strukturierten Dokumente zwar technisch für diese Nutzung vorbereitet, aber in ihrer Strukturierung völlig ungeeignet waren. Von vielen inhaltlichen Fehlern in den Dokumenten, auf die man beim Recherchieren und Browsen, im Unterschied zum mehr linearen Lesen in der Druckausgabe, schnell stieß, einmal abgesehen, stellte man fest, dass sich die auf die Druckausgabe bezogenen Strukturen nur schlecht für diese innovative Nutzung eigneten, da sie sehr stark format- und seitenorientiert waren und keine oder nur wenig leistungsfähige Verweise zur Generierung von Hyperlinks enthielten.

Die Umstellung und Anreicherung der Strukturen in den Dokumenten sowie die Beseitigung inhaltlicher Fehler hat viele Projekte nicht unwesentlich aufgehalten. Ausserdem hat man vielfach die daraus resultierenden Aufwendungen zur Dokumentenbearbeitung dem SGML-Konzept angelastet („SGML ist kompliziert, zeitaufwendig und teuer"), nicht, wie es richtig wäre, den veränderten und erweiterten Nutzungen zugeordnet.

8 Das Zeitalter der Expansion

Etwa mit Beginn der neunziger Jahre begann die Zahl der Anwendungen und ihre Bedeutung für die sie betreibenden Institutionen stetig mit hohen Zuwachsraten zuzunehmen. Die – im Vergleich zu gängigen Desktop-Publishing-Anwendungen (DTP) – relativ lange Planungs- und Implementierungszeit von SGML-Projekten erweckte dennoch in der Öffentlichkeit den Eindruck, dass sich „in Sachen SGML nur wenig bewege".

Hinter den Kulissen aber wurde fleißig gearbeitet. Als deutliches Zeichen dieser Aktivitäten mag die schnell wachsende Zahl von Experten gelten, die ihre Dienste zum Aufbau und zur Unterstützung von SGML-basierten Dokumenten-Anwendungen anboten. Hierzu gehörten die Datenverarbeitungsspezialisten von Satzfirmen, Berater für technische Dokumentation und auch um Drittmittel aus der Industrie bemühte wissenschaftliche Institutionen.

Kennzeichen dieser neuen SGML-Unterstützer war, dass sie zwar die technischen und formalsprachlichen Aspekte von SGML-Anwendungen schnell virtuos beherrschten, aber die Organisation des Umfelds der Anwendung sowie die Verwertungsaspekte, d.h. die

Produkt-Gestaltung, vernachlässigten. Dies führte meiner Beobachtung nach häufig zu erheblichen Problemen und Enttäuschungen mit den neuen SGML-Systemen und -Anwendungen, und insofern haben SGML-Experten selbst dazu beigetragen, die Durchsetzung von SGML in der Praxis zu bremsen.

Die Anwendungen im Einzelnen zu beschreiben, die diese Expansionsphase in Deutschland prägten, würde den Umfang dieses Beitrags sprengen. Allerdings lässt sich ein typisches Muster für die Expansion von SGML-Anwendungen erkennen: SGML breitet sich in solchen Industrien flächendeckend aus, wo der „Leidensdruck" mit bestehenden Dokumentations- und Publikationskonzepten besonders groß ist. Anwendungen in einem der Industriezweige hatten über lange Zeit kaum stimulierende Wirkung über seine Grenzen hinaus. Erst wenn die Diskussion über den Einsatz und den Nutzen von SGML innerhalb eines Industriezweiges begonnen hatte und erste industrie-interne Anwendungen bekannt geworden waren, breitete sich die Anwendung schnell innerhalb dieses Industriezweiges aus. So erscheint SGML wie ein Virus mit geringer Neigung zu einer selbständigen Infizierung fremder Wirte, der sich allerdings, nachdem er einmal eingeimpft worden ist, schnell und nicht wieder eindämmbar im Wirt verbreitet.

Nach meiner Beobachtung ist dieses Expansionsverhalten eng mit der Intensität der Verflechtung innerhalb einer Industrie und dem Ausbau der internen Kommunikationseinrichtungen verknüpft.

So ist es kein Wunder, dass sich SGML-Anwendungen zuerst im Bereich der Flugzeughersteller und ihrer Kunden, den Luftfahrtgesellschaften, verbreiteten, mit einiger Verzögerung innerhalb der Automobil-, Fahrzeug- und Zuliefer-Industrie, parallel dazu in der Telekommunikationsindustrie, der Computer- und Software-Industrie und in bestimmten, ausgewählten Bereichen der Verlagsindustrie (Rechtsinformationen, Wörterbücher, Enzyklopädien).

Zur Zeit (1998) scheint SGML seinen Siegeszug in der Dokumentenverarbeitung von Versicherungen und Banken fortzusetzen, also solchen Unternehmen, die ein besonderes Interesse an einer hoch-automatisierten Dokumentenverarbeitung mit äußerst hohen Anforderungen an die Verarbeitungssicherheit, -geschwindigkeit und Wirtschaftlichkeit haben.

9 Unvermutet und revolutionär(?): das Web

Nun hatte man sich daran gewöhnt, gerade auch in Deutschland, dass der Entwicklungshauptstrom der Dokumentenverarbeitung an SGML vorbeifließt, als plötzlich dieses „Spitzklammer-Format" unter der euphemistischen und verwirrenden Bezeichnung *Hypertext Markp Language* (*HTML*) das bestehende Internet eroberte und schnell die bis dahin bestehenden Internet-Dienste in den Schatten stellte. Das so schwerfällig gelöste Problem des Dokumentenaustauschs über Netze (s. DFN-Projekt DAPHNE, Abschnitt 5) wurde mit einem Mal zu einem Kinderspiel: Ohne jedes Zutun des Empfängers erschienen die Dokumente in ansprechender Gestaltung, Bilder und Grafiken waren in die Texte eingebettet, die Hyperlinks in den Web-Seiten brachten mit einem bloßen Klick Dokumente auf den Bildschirm, die irgendwo in dieser Welt gespeichert waren. Die spezifischen Hürden zwischen Computern und Betriebssystemen unterschiedlicher Hersteller schienen mit einem Mal wie „weggeblasen".

Dies bedeutete, dass all die wunderbaren Zielsetzungen, die mit der Anwendung von SGML propagiert worden waren, jetzt mit HTML Wirklichkeit geworden waren. War HTML verglichen mit SGML die mächtigere Sprache? Und das Schönste: Niemand meckerte, alle wollten teilhaben.

Verdutzt rieben sich die SGML-Experten die Augen und fragten sich, was sie wohl falsch gemacht hatten. Denn HTML war – nach einer konzeptionellen Nachbesserung durch Yuri Rubinsky (s. Beitrag von Pamela Gennusa, Abschnitt 3) – schlicht eine SGML-DTD, wenn auch eine, in der die Prinzipien generischer Markupsprachen wie SGML, d.h. die Medien- und Gestaltungsneutralität, mit Füßen getreten wurden. Ein Dokument gegen die HTML-DTD parsen, bevor man es „ins Web stellt"? Warum, wenn man gerade durch Verletzungen der Strukturvorgabe die schönsten Effekte im Browser des Empfängers hervorrufen konnte: mehrere Body-Starttags hintereinander mit unterschiedlichen Farb-Attributen für den Hintergrund geben ein dynamisches Farbspiel im Browser.

Die Medien fragten, wer hat uns diese neue Welt des Webs eröffnet, wer ist der Erfinder dieses Webs? Die Antwort war schnell gefunden und passte so gut zu der Vorstellung, wie neue Technologien in nimmermüder Forscher-Arbeit – diesmal an der *Europäischen Organisation für Kernforschung, CERN*, wo eigentlich die Hauptzielsetzung in der Beschleunigung kleinster Materie-Teilchen, nicht in der von Bits und Bytes liegt – erfunden werden: Tim Berners-Lee wird nun in den Medien, insbesondere in Deutschland, als der einsame Erfinder des Webs gefeiert (vgl. *Die Zeit* vom 15. 8. 1997). Für Viele, die das Web mit dem Internet gleichsetzen, wird er damit sogar zum Erfinder des Internets.

Durch die weitere Entwicklung des Webs mit seinen HTML-Anwendungen merkten die „SGMLer" aber schnell, dass diese Entwicklung ihr Anliegen, d.h. die Förderung von SGML-Anwendungen, so beschleunigte wie keine der von ihnen ausgehenden Aktivitäten, diejenigen der *International SGML Users' Group* oder die von *SGML-Open*, jetzt *OASIS*, eingeschlossen. Die Zahl der Organisationen und Personen, die jetzt eine SGML-Anwendung (HTML) nutzten, verdoppelte sich jeweils in wenigen Monaten.

SoftQuad als Hersteller des SGML-Editors Author/Editor entwickelte auf dieser Technologie-Basis den HTML-Editor HoTMetaL und lieferte nach mir vorliegenden, von SoftQuad nicht bestätigten Informationen statt in etwa zehn Jahren 10.000 Author/Editor-Lizenzen nun in etwa drei Jahren mehr als 500.000 HoTMetaL-Lizenzen aus.

Zu den immer häufigeren Web- und Internet-Konferenzen kamen Tausende, die vorher niemals etwas von SGML gehört hatten oder die HTML tatsächlich für eine originäre, völlig innovative Technologie hielten. Die kleine Zahl von SGML-Anwendern und Konferenzteilnehmern, meist auch höheren Lebensalters, konnte nur staunen. Immerhin, nicht nur bei dieser Gelegenheit kamen diese sich vorher völlig Fremden miteinander ins Gespräch und fanden schnell gemeinsame Diskussionsthemen. Ich erinnere mich z.B. an eine heftige, inhaltlich interessante Diskussion über das Stylesheet-Konzept von DynaText, die Vertreter der beiden unterschiedlichen Lager am Rande der Web-Konferenz in Darmstadt 1995 führten.

Die SGML-Dienstleister spürten mit einem Mal, dass der Wind nicht mehr ins Gesicht blies, sondern in den Rücken und die Entwicklung vorantrieb: Kommerzielle Institutionen wollten die Web-Technologie für ihre regulären Dokument-Anwendungen (meist technische Dokumentation) großflächig einsetzen, stellten aber fest, dass die HTML-DTD für ihre Strukturierungserfordernisse nicht ausreichend war. Sie wollten selbstverständlich auch organisierte und zentral steuerbare Anwendungen haben und nicht lediglich die nur schwer organisierbaren DTP-Anwendungen mit anderen Mitteln fortsetzen. Sie waren in der Regel schnell davon zu überzeugen, dass HTML, als SGML-Anwendung richtig verstanden und eingesetzt, viele Probleme lösen würde, an denen man seit mehreren Jahren vergeblich gearbeitet hatte. Diesen Anwendern, die bisher statt auf „Standard-Konzepte" auf von den Herstellern so genannte „Standard-Produkte" gesetzt hatten, standen jene gegenüber, die sich

Konzepte ohne
erschwingliche
Software stehen
auf verlorenem
Posten

teilweise seit mehreren Jahren bemüht hatten, ihre SGML-Anwendungen in den Firmen durchzusetzen. Letztere liefen mit einem Mal offene Türen ein: „Aha, HTML ist ja im Kern SGML. Nur habt Ihr SGMLer uns ja nicht klarmachen können, was uns dieses Konzept nützt. Jetzt sehen wir es. Toll!"

Heute, nach einiger Zeit der Erfahrung mit HTML-Anwendungen, gerade auch in der Industrie und Wirtschaft, muss konstatiert werden: Ein technologisches Konzept, das nicht ausreichend durch erschwingliche Werkzeuge, hier Software, unterstützt wird, steht auf verlorenem Posten angesichts weltweiter Marketing-Bemühungen von Herstellern, die erschwingliche – wenn auch auf proprietären Konzepten beruhende – Produkte anbieten. Umgekehrt kann sich auch der größte Hersteller einschlägiger Produkte, also *Microsoft*, nicht einer offenen und standardisierten Technologie verschließen, die von der Masse der Anwender als Standard begriffen wird.

das Web – nicht
nur revolutionär

Vielfach wird das Web als revolutionär bezeichnet. Dies schiene gerechtfertigt, wenn das Web entscheidende, abrupte Veränderungen verursacht hätte. Abgesehen von ihrem plötzlichen Eindringen in die Praxis der Dokumentenverarbeitung und des Dokumentenaustauschs über Netze, und abgesehen von ihrem enormen Wachstum, sehe ich allerdings eher die adaptiven Aspekte der Web-Anwendung. Die Web-Technologie nahm nicht nur die schon vorher verfolgten Zielsetzungen auf, beispielsweise die des DAPHNE-Projekts (s. Abschnitt 5), sondern stützte sich auch auf Technologien, die bereits vorher entwickelt worden waren und eingesetzt wurden, beispielsweise SGML.

In der Praxis der Entwicklung von Web-Dokumenten zeigten sich die gleichen Merkmale, Schwächen und Stärken, wie in gleichgerichteten Projekten vorher: Eine quasi standardisierte DTD provoziert schnell viele und teilweise konträre Anforderungen an ihre Änderung und Erweiterung. Wo die Anwender die fest an eine Gestaltung gebundene DTD oder die Gestaltung nicht ändern können, wird die DTD trickreich für individuelle Gestaltungen ausgeschlachtet und umgebogen. Die Struktur der Web-Dokumente zählt kaum, entscheidend ist der gestalterische Effekt. Die Güte einer SGML-Anwendung entscheidet sich nicht an der formalen Sprache SGML, sondern der gestalterischen Qualität der DTD und der darauf aufbauenden Verarbeitungen.

Insofern war es logisch, dass nach nur wenigen Jahren der Praxis der Wunsch artikuliert wurde, dieser in vielen Details und in vielen Anwendungssituationen durchaus problematischen und beschränkten SGML-Anwendung mit der Bezeichnung HTML die Mächtigkeit von SGML „einzuhauchen", ohne selbstverständlich die generelle Praktikabilität von HTML einzubüßen und ohne auf die technisch glanzvollen und wohlfeilen Web-Technologien wie Server, Web-Browser, Navigation im Netz verzichten zu müssen. „SGML minus unnötiger Komplexität plus Netzwerk-Effizienz plus neuer Name ist gleich XML", so formulierte Tim Bray in dem Technologie-Workshop von *Daimler Benz* zum Thema XML im November 1997.

Da XML in diesem Band von Pamela Gennusa besprochen wird, gehe ich nicht weiter darauf ein. Aus lokaler Sicht ist dem auch nichts hinzuzufügen, weil die deutsche Beteiligung an dem Entwicklungs- und Standardisierungsprojekt XML gering war. Immerhin vermied man die Peinlichkeiten früherer deutscher Beteiligungen an den SGML-Normierungsprojekten der ISO, bei denen man sich gelegentlich in eine feindselige Obstruktion der Projekte hineinsteigert hatte.

Bereitwillig wird jetzt auch in Deutschland das Akronym SGML durch XML ersetzt, in der Hoffnung, damit auf *die* Publishing-Technologie der Zukunft zu setzen.

XML =
HTML plus und
SGML minus

10 SGML/XML die Publishing-Technologie der Zukunft?

Arnoud de Kemp, der weithin anerkannte Experte für die Entwicklung von Zukunftsmärkten für Publikationen im Springer-Verlag, äußerte bei einem seiner zahlreichen Vorträge, dass SGML wohl die wichtigste Publishing-Technologie der Zukunft, d.h. des kommenden Jahrhunderts, sei. Eine solche öffentliche Äußerung tut gerade denjenigen gut, die sich seit nun schon mehr als zwölf Jahren bemühen, diese Botschaft in Deutschland, Europa und der Welt zu verbreiten. Diese Äußerung fördert nicht unbeträchtlich die allgemeine Akzeptanz und öffnet die Märkte für diese Technologie.

Nur, diese Akzeptanz der formalen Sprache schafft lediglich und bestenfalls eine technische Basis für die Industrialisierung der Dokumentenverarbeitung und -nutzung. Wie diese Sprache eingesetzt wird, ob für eine wirtschaftliche Dokumenten- und Publikationen-Produktion, für die Zwecke technischer Dokumentation und Fachinformation, oder zur Strukturierung des immer umfangreicheren und komplexeren Wissens, bleibt offen. Deshalb vermute ich, dass SGML/XML in ihrer Anwendung mit wachsender Erfahrung der Dokumenten-Produzenten sehr schnell selbstverständlich und damit unwichtig wird.

SGML/XML –
die Botschaft ist
angekommen

Nicht die eilig dem W3-Konsortium vorgelegten XML-Addenda werden die Diskussion bestimmen und die Entwicklung vorantreiben, sondern die oft mühseligen Arbeiten an den Konzepten für

- eine zweckgerechte Strukturierung der informationshaltigen Inhalte,

- eine zweckgerechte und wirtschaftliche Produktion, hier vor allem die Abstimmung des Einsatzes menschlicher Intelligenz und manueller Arbeit mit automatisierten Prüfungen, Kompilierungen und Verarbeitungen, und

- die Vernetzung von Dokumenten und Publikationen, um den Lesern (was für ein altmodischer Begriff!) die Orientierung und Navigation in dem durch die Dokumente verfügbaren Wissen zu erleichtern.

Leider hat gerade die Entwicklung der SGML/XML/HTML-Anwendungen (zu schweigen von den Nicht-xxML-Anwendungen) unter diesen letztgenannten Aspekten mit den formalsprachlichen Möglichkeiten von xxML nicht Schritt gehalten.

Weiterhin ignorieren die meisten Autoren von technischen Dokumentationen und Publikationen ihre Verantwortung für die leserfreundliche Strukturierung ihrer Informationen und sonstigen Inhalte. Weiterhin vernachlässigen die meisten kommerziellen Verlage (*commercial publishers*) und institutionellen Distributoren (*corporate publishers*) ihre Verantwortung für die Koordination der Autoren, die leserfreundliche und mediengerechte Gestaltung der Dokumente und die Vernetzung der Inhalte über die Grenzen der einzelnen Dokumente und Publikationen hinaus.

Dabei ist es recht einfach, diesen Aspekten mehr Beachtung zu schenken: Die formale Sprache SGML in den Dokumenten und im Kopf der Autoren, Redakteure, Publizisten, Organisatoren erlaubt – am besten unter Einsatz eines SGML-Parsers und einer SGML-Suchmaschine – eine schnelle und sichere Prüfung der Dokumentinhalte und ihrer Strukturierung, von „SGMListen" gelegentlich als semantische Validierung bezeichnet. Außerdem erlaubt sie durch den Einsatz von Automatismen die Korrektur und Erweiterung der Strukturierung und die formale und anwendungssichere Verknüpfung von Inhalten (Hyperlinks).

SGML wird ein allgemein eingesetztes, aber selbstverständliches Werkzeug in der Dokumentenverarbeitung sein, ohne das vieles nicht (wirtschaftlich) geht, mit dem allein aber auch weiterhin die Qualität beliebig niedrig, die Produktionskosten hoch und die Wirtschaftlichkeit gering sein können.

Praxis – heute

Innovation für Nachrichtenagenturen

Klaus Sprick

1 Agenturen und Nachrichten

1.1 Nachrichtenagenturen – Aufgabe und Funktion

Nachrichtenagenturen sind die Großhändler der Nachricht. Ihr Geschäftszweck ist es, Nachrichten aller Art aktuell zu sammeln, zu verarbeiten und an eine Vielzahl von Kunden, vorwiegend in den Medien, zu verbreiten. Nachrichten in diesem Sinne schließen alle möglichen technischen Mediaformen wie Text, Bild, Ton, Grafik und Video mit ein, wobei die frühen „klassischen" Formen Text und Bild sind und erst in den letzten Jahrzehnten Grafik, Audio und das Fernsehmedium hinzukamen.

Nachrichtenagenturen müssen dicht am Geschehen sein, deshalb unterhalten sie üblicherweise ein Netz von Büros und Korrespondenten zur aktuellen Berichterstattung über Ereignisse in ihrem Tätigkeitsbereich. Je nach Auftrag der Agentur ist dies ein inhaltlich bestimmter Sektor (z.B. Sport) oder, bei Abdeckung aller Themen, ein Land (nationale Agentur) oder die ganze Welt (Weltagentur).

Agenturjournalisten nutzen die gesamte Vielfalt der verfügbaren technischen Übermittlungswege zum Transport der von ihnen geschöpften Nachricht an ihre Redaktionen. Diese prüfen, ergänzen, recherchieren weiter, stellen alle einlaufenden Nachrichten zu kompletten Diensten zusammen und liefern sie an ihre Kunden nach deren Anforderungsprofil. Es ist das Wesen der Agenturen, daß sie einer Vielzahl von Kunden die gleichen Dienste liefern und dafür spezialisierte Verteilnetze benutzen (Abbildung 1).

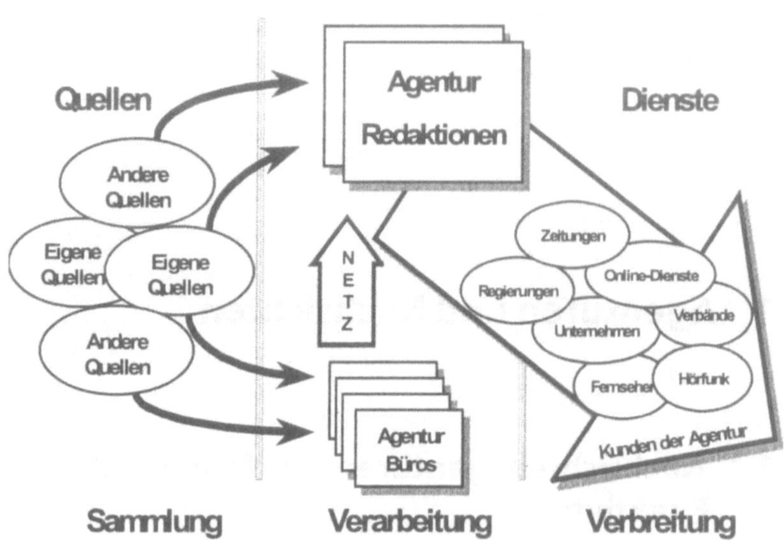

1.2 Nachrichtenagenturen – Technologie

Informations-
technik bestimmt
den Fortschritt

Seit Erfindung des Telegrafen im 19. Jahrhundert, dem wichtigsten Impuls zur Gründung der Agenturen heutigen Zuschnitts, ist die Technologie bis heute der Motor für ihre weitere Entwicklung und für neue Märkte. Seit Beginn der elektronischen Übermittlung Mitte des letzten Jahrhunderts ist der Transport der Nachricht ständig schneller, preiswerter und zuverlässiger geworden. Seit den siebziger Jahren des heutigen Jahrhunderts werden Computer für die Verteilung und Bearbeitung der Nachrichten eingesetzt. Informationstechnik bestimmt seitdem den Fortschritt der Agenturen.

An die Seite der herkömmlichen Medienformen wie Zeitungen, Zeitschriften und Rundfunk sind innovative Arten des Publizierens (Online-Dienste, multimediale Formen) getreten, die nicht nur neuen Technikeinsatz erfordern, sondern auch veränderte Geschäftsprozesse der Agenturen notwendig machen. Daß eine Geschäftsprozeßoptimierung ihrerseits neueste Technologie einsetzen muß, ist nur logisch.

Der Grund hierfür liegt in dem großen und ständig steigenden Volumen an Nachrichten, die unter hohem Kostendruck zu schöpfen, zu selektieren, zu verifizieren und zu publizieren sind. Nur fortschrittliche Verfahren der Informatik vermögen hier den unter hohem Zeitzwang stehenden intellektuellen Prozeß des Journalisten effizient zu unterstützen

1.3 Nachricht als Dokument

Nachrichten sind Dokumente, die sehr aktuelle Ereignisse enthalten und vorwiegend für den sofortigen Gebrauch bestimmt sind. Zur Einordnung und Bewertung dieser Ereignisse, zur Bereitstellung des historischen Hintergrunds und zur korrekten Wiedergabe von Fakten benötigen Agenturen Archive und Dokumentationen, die ebenfalls sehr eng am Zeitgeschehen geführt werden müssen

Ursprünglich hatte bei den Nachrichten nur ihr – ausschließlich intellektuell interpretierbarer – Inhalt Bedeutung; die Form (das Format) wurde nur beeinflußt durch die Wirtschaftlichkeit der Übertragung, nicht durch die Verarbeitung oder Nutzung. Kosten der Übertragung berechneten sich beispielsweise bei Telegrammen nach Wörtern und führten mitunter zu kuriosen neuen Wortschöpfungen, sogar zu einer eigenen Nachrichtensprache.

Die Interpretation des Inhalts von Nachrichten war ursprünglich allein dem Menschen vorbehalten; technische Werkzeuge, wie wir sie heute kennen (z.B. Volltextsuche, Kontextanalyse), gab es nicht. Präsentationsformen orientierten sich daher überwiegend an der Ausgabe auf Druckern und der Interpretation durch den Menschen. Diese Form der Präsentation hat sich bis heute erhalten und bestimmt noch weitgehend die Textdienste der Agenturen.

1.4 Format der Nachricht

In den siebziger und achtziger Jahren wurden die ersten Textformate von Agenturmeldungen international genormt, ein wichtiger und dringend erforderlicher Fortschritt. Diese Formate wurden sowohl für die Ausgabe auf Druckern (Fernschreibgeräten) entworfen, als auch für die elektronische Speicherung. Nachrichten können seitdem bei den Agenturen in Rechnersystemen verarbeitet und automatisch zu ihren Kunden gesendet werden. Diese können einige wenige strukturelle Meldungselemente ebenfalls durch Computer erkennen und so die Nachricht dem Bearbeiter zuleiten. Weltweit sind im wesentlichen zwei Formate für Meldungstexte verbreitet:

1. ANPA 89-3 des amerikanischen Verlegerverbandes *NAA* (*Newspaper Association of America*),

2. IPTC 7901 des *IPTC*, des internationalen Verbandes der Agenturen und Verleger für Telekommunikation (*International Press Telecommunications Council*).

Ein nächster wichtiger Schritt in der Normierung von Nachrichtenformaten war 1991 die Einführung des *Information Interchange Model* (*IIM*), das *NAA* und *IPTC* vor allem im Hinblick auf die digitale Bildtechnik entwickelt haben. Das IIM benutzt eindeutig definierte (*tagged*) Felder für eine Fülle von Daten und Metadaten von Nachrichten. Es ist ein Format, das für Multimedia-Anwendungen ständig weiterentwickelt wurde und seit Oktober 1997 in der Version 4 besteht (IPTC-NAA 1997). Es ist bei Agenturen vorwiegend für Bild, Grafik und Audio im Einsatz, für Textdienste eher vereinzelt.

Inhalte werden in beiden Formattypen durch *Stichworte* beschrieben, die aber nur Bedeutung für die aktuelle Vermittlung und redaktionelle Verarbeitung haben, nicht für die Beschreibung von Fakten im Meldungstext über den aktuellen Zeitbezug hinweg. Eine Einteilung in Ressorts (*categories*) gibt ein sehr grobes Raster inhaltlicher Zuordnung zu Themenkomplexen. Diese *categories* sind überholt, Agenturen ersetzen sie neuerdings durch einen systematischen, inhaltsbezogenen Thesaurus, der 1998 von *IPTC* und *NAA* gemeinsam als *Subject Reference* – einer strukturierten Definition der im Dokument behandelten Themen – normiert wurde (IPTC-NAA 1998b).

Hier zeichnet sich eine neue Dimension der aktuellen Nachrichtenverarbeitung ab: Erschließung der Nachricht durch inhaltsbezogene (semantische) Strukturelemente, die durch technische Werkzeuge erkannt werden können. Ihre logische Fortsetzung findet sich in einem SGML-basierten Format, das im nächsten Abschnitt beschrieben wird.

2 Nachrichtenformate für Multimedia

2.1 Problemstellung

2.1.1 ANPA 89-3 und IPTC 7901

Telegrafen, Fernschreiber und Drucker sind obsolet, aber die für sie *Textformate*
geschaffenen Formate bestimmen noch heute den Nachrichtenfluß.
Die aus den neuen Anforderungen resultierenden Probleme mit
diesen alten Formaten sind:

- Es gibt keine klare Trennung zwischen Metadaten (Informationen, welche die Nachricht selbst beschreiben oder managen) und dem eigentlichen Nachrichteninhalt.

- Die Nutzung der Nachrichten auf allen Stufen verursacht hohe Kosten, weil sie nur gut durch Menschen interpretiert, schlecht aber durch Maschinen selektiert und verarbeitet werden können.

- Sie bieten keinen Ansatz für automatische Verknüpfungen mit anderen Informationen, wie sie z.B. im Internet oder Online-Diensten benötigt werden und dort üblich sind.

- Eine inhaltliche Erschließung für Datenbankanwendungen ist sehr schwierig.

2.1.2 IPTC/NAA Information Interchange Model (IIM)

Das IIM ist ein für den Austausch von Nachrichten auf der OSI- *Multimedia-*
Anwendungsschicht sieben konstruiertes Format und ist seinerseits *formate*
in mehrere Ebenen (*records*) unterteilt. Es trennt Inhalt von beschreibenden Informationen, ist unabhängig von Übermittlungsarten (dafür gibt es einen *envelope record*) und erlaubt Verknüpfungen.
Dieses modernere Format bietet bereits alle für Multimedia und
Nachrichtenmanagement nötigen Eigenschaften und Funktionen. Es
eignet sich gut für Datenbankstrukturen und ist deshalb auch in der
Branche weit verbreitet.

Das IIM definiert Nachrichten als Objekte und stellt für den *Nachricht als*
Nachrichteninhalt einen eigenen *record* bereit (*ObjectData*), der in *Objekt*
einer Vielzahl verschiedener Dateiformate dargestellt werden kann.
Der vielleicht einzige Nachteil:

- Das IIM ist proprietär, nur in der Branche üblich und keine „Mainstream-Technologie".

Die aus dem Internet und dem World Wide Web stammende dynamische Entwicklung setzt auf SGML, HTML, XML und verwandte Technologien und stellt nur dafür preiswerte Werkzeuge bereit.

2.2 Die Anforderungen an eine neue Norm

Nachrichtenvolumen steigen

Die im vorhergehenden Abschnitt beschriebene grundsätzliche Problematik der heutigen Informationsstruktur der Agentur-Berichterstattung wird dadurch verschärft, daß das Volumen der verbreiteten Nachrichten stetig stark expandiert. Weltweiter Trend ist, daß die Kosten der intellektuellen/manuellen Arbeit steigen und die der Technik sinken.

neue Standardformate nötig

Den in den Gremien von *NAA* und *IPTC* tätigen Fachleuten war schon Anfang der neunziger Jahre klar, daß nur ein neuartiges Nachrichtenformat auf der Basis akzeptierter und verbreiteter internationaler Standards die Anforderungen und Herausforderungen neuer Technologien erfüllen kann.

Anforderungen

Diese sind folgendermaßen definiert:

- Unabhängigkeit von technischen Plattformen

- Verwendbar in allen Sprachen

- Nutzbar für alle Formen des Publizierens

- Multimedial mit Verknüpfungen

- Basierend auf internationalen Standards

- Verfügbarkeit von Werkzeugen zur Bearbeitung

- Einbindung der vorhandenen Formate

- Computergerechte Formatierung

- Nachrichtenspezifische Strukturierung für

  - Formatelemente und

  - Inhalt

- Flexibilität gegenüber künftigen Entwicklungen

2.3 Der Weg zu einem neuen Standard

Der Weg war lang und begann schon 1991, als man auf SGML, die
ISO 8879, als mögliche Norm für das Vorhaben stieß. Die Gremien
von *IPTC* und *NAA* begannen mit der Sammlung aller Anforderungen, insbesondere der nachrichtenspezifischen Elemente. Diese lagen
durch das IIM bereits im wesentlichen vor. Die neue Technologie
stellte aber erweiterte Möglichkeiten bereit, die auch genutzt werden
sollten. Sie betrafen insbesondere die inhaltliche Markierung von
Texten.

Welches sind die Elemente einer Nachricht?

Es wurde klar, daß die in einer *Document Type Definition (DTD)*
enthaltene Festlegung für Nachrichten zusammen mit einer klaren
Definition der Bedeutung von Elementen und einer darauf aufset-
zenden Anwendung ein Geschäftsmodell darstellen, welches weltweit
nicht einheitlich vorhanden ist. Für eine internationale Norm, die
unterschiedliche Sprachen, Gebräuche oder gar Kulturen umfassen
soll, keine leichte Aufgabe. Außerdem gab es auch Schwierigkeiten,
die Technologie selbst zu verstehen; auch das braucht Zeit.

DTD ist Geschäftsmodell

1993 wurde der Entwurf eines *Universal Text Format (UTF)* vorgestellt, welches die erste SGML-konforme Dokumenttypdefinition
von *IPTC* und *NAA* war.

erster Entwurf nach SGML-Norm UTF

Das UTF war eine (seinerzeit) sehr revolutionäre und für viele
unverständliche Art, ein Format zu definieren. Die häufigsten Einwände lauteten:

- Ein Journalist kann niemals die Markierungen schreiben.

- Markierungen dauern zu lange.

- Der Ballast (Overhead) ist zu groß und kostet Zeit und Geld in
  der Übertragung.

- Es gibt keine Software, die das Redigieren markierter Nachrichten durch Journalisten unterstützt.

2.4 Der Einfluß des World Wide Web

Das Aufkommen des World Wide Web (WWW) führte zu der
Überlegung, HTML für das neue Format zu verwenden. Dies wurde
jedoch bald wieder verworfen, da HTML (seinerzeit) mit SGML
unzureichend kompatibel und zu begrenzt einsetzbar war. Erst die
neueren Versionen ab HTML 3.0, die HTML zu einer DTD gemäß
SGML machten, ließen die Architekten umdenken.

WWW verändert die Sicht

Die DTD wurde 1996 so umkonstruiert, daß eine Reihe von Elementen mit denen von HTML 3.0 übereinstimmen und somit von frei verfügbaren Browsern erkannt werden können. Alle anderen Elemente gehen nicht verloren, sondern sind mit eigenen Anwendungen oder entsprechenden Werkzeugen erkennbar.

Besondere Probleme bereitete die Definition der Tabellen, da hier ganz spezielle Anforderungen gestellt wurden. Die DTD muß es erlauben, daß man Tabellen in Dokumenten bei den Zeitungen direkt in den Satz geben kann, gleichzeitig aber auch deren Nutzung in Online-Systemen sichert. Die letztlich getroffene Festlegung wird weiter unten beschrieben.

DTDs können sehr komplizierte Gebilde sein, die nur von wenigen Fachleuten völlig verstanden werden. Ein Fehler bei der frühen Entwicklung der UTF-DTD lag in der Rekursion von Elementen. In den ersten Fassungen war es z.B. möglich, eine Tabelle in einer Tabelle in einer Tabelle usw. zu haben, was in der Praxis nicht vorkommt und zu letztlich unbeherrschbaren Strukturen führen würde.

Die erste Version des neuen Standards, der nun endgültig *IPTC-NAA News Industry Text Format (NITF)* heißt, wurde schließlich 1996 vorgestellt und befindet sich nunmehr in Version 2.0b1 (August 1998; IPTC-NAA 1998a). Aus der relativ langen Zeitspanne von 1991 bis 1997 ist erkennbar, wie schwierig und langwierig Normung auf internationaler Ebene sein kann, wenn sich ehrenamtlich tätige Fachleute mit Normungsfragen in neuen Technologien beschäftigen müssen. Dazu gibt es aber kaum eine sinnfällige Alternative.

3 News Industry Text Format (NITF) – eine Norm für aktuelle Nachrichten

3.1 Einführung in das NITF

Das NITF ist als ein SGML-basiertes Format unabhängig von Plattformen und ausgelegt für die Markierung von Texten und Tabellen für Nachrichten und deren Verknüpfungen. Es eignet sich für alle Arten verlegerischer Betätigung, elektronisch wie konventionell. Die Markierung umfaßt zwei Arten:

- Formatstrukturen des Textes
- inhaltsbezogene Elemente

Der Grundgedanke beim NITF ist, daß zu einem möglichst frühen Zeitpunkt, d.h. schon bei der ersten Entstehung des Dokuments, Markierungen angebracht und im Laufe der weiteren Verarbeitung und Verwendung (im Rahmen der DTD) ergänzt und verändert werden können. Bei Nachrichten spielt die Zeit bis zum Kunden eine sehr große Rolle; in den meisten Fällen wird die Eilbedürftigkeit höher als eine ausführliche Erschließung zu bewerten sein.

Markierungen jederzeit erweiterbar

Das NITF kann Verknüpfungen mit eigenen Elementen wie auch mit externen Dokumenten wie weiteren Texten, Bildern, Grafiken, Audiostücken und Videoclips herstellen. Dazu bedient es sich der Methoden von *HyTime* (ISO 10744) CLINK und ILINK. Es bildet damit die Basis für multimediale Dienste von Nachrichtenagenturen.

Verknüpfungen auch für Multimedia

Das NITF ist stark an HTML angelehnt und wie HTML eine Anwendung, die mit dem ISO-Standard 8879 konform ist. Dieser Grundsatz stellt sicher, daß für diesen Standard eine maximale Anzahl von Werkzeugen und Systemen verfügbar ist; Web-Browser können große Teile von NITF direkt darstellen.

mit ISO 8879 konform

NITF ist sowohl eine selbständige Norm als auch kompatibel zu dem IPTC-IIM. Bei der Definition wurde darauf geachtet, daß die im IIM vorhandenen Elemente übernommen wurden. Zur Übermittlung kann NITF als registriertes Dateiformat in das IIM eingebettet werden und dessen Beschreibungsdaten nutzen.

kompatibel mit dem IPTC-NAA IIM

Das NITF soll letztlich die veralteten Formate ANPA 1312 (98-3) und IPTC 7901 ablösen.

löst alte Formate ab

3.2 Überblick über die NITF-Struktur

Das NITF kann in zwei Hauptabschnitte unterteilt werden (s. Abbildungen 2 und 3):

- HEAD – der Nachrichtenkopf mit Metadaten
- BODY – die eigentliche Nachricht

Der Zeichensatz ist standardmäßig ISO 8859-1, kann aber auf alle anderen Alphabete – auch *Multibyte Coded Character Sets* – erweitert werden.

Zeichensatz ISO 8859-1

Im Nachrichtenkopf HEAD (Abbildung 2) sind die Informationen über das NITF-Objekt (TITLE, BANNER, BASE, META) enthalten, wie auch Informationen über die Nachricht selbst definiert (TOBJECT, IIM und diverse Elemente in DOCDATA).

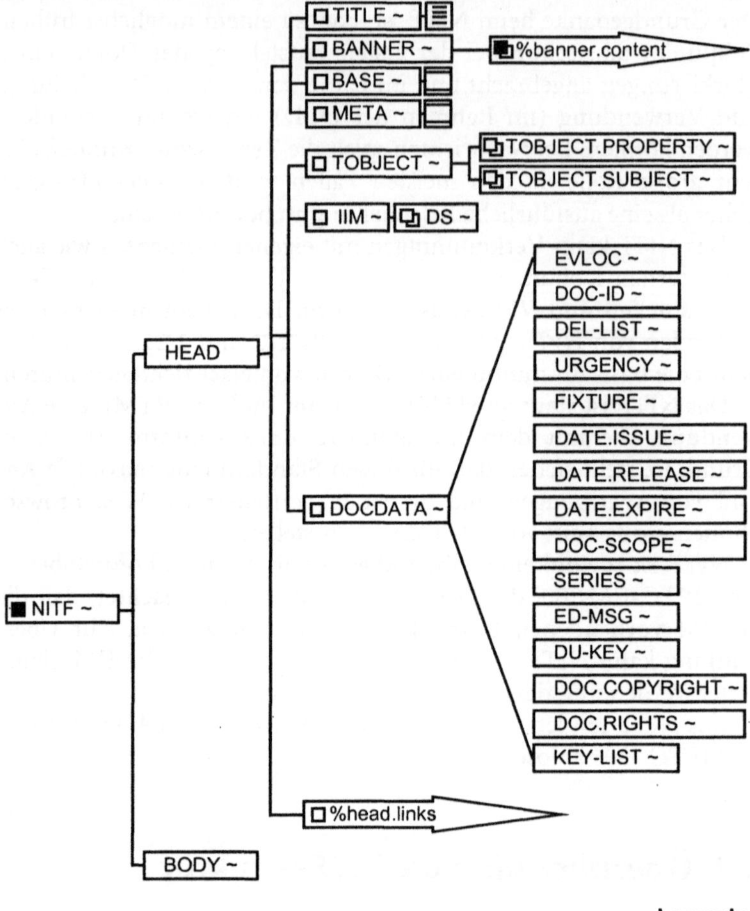

Legende

Symbol	Bedeutung	Symbol	Bedeutung
NITF ~	NITF mit Content	□	Eins
HEAD	Head Element	■	Keins oder eins
BANNER ~	1 Banner Element		Eins oder mehr
%banner.content	Banner Inhalt		Null oder mehr
	PCDATA	%	Parameter Entität
	Leeres Element	~	Mehr Inhalt folgt

Eine Besonderheit ist die aus HTML 3.0 entlehnte Funktion eines BANNER. In einem Browser bleibt der Banner fix oben im Fenster stehen, währen der Inhalt scrollt. Damit sollen z.B. Firmenlogos, Copyright-Hinweise oder Navigationshilfen dargestellt werden.

Der eigentliche Nachrichtenkörper BODY enthält die für eine Nachricht notwendigen Strukturelemente und Inhaltsmarkierungen.

Fast alle Elemente können mehrfach auftreten; dies ist ein Indikator
für die grundsätzlich sehr freie Form im Nachrichtenaufbau.

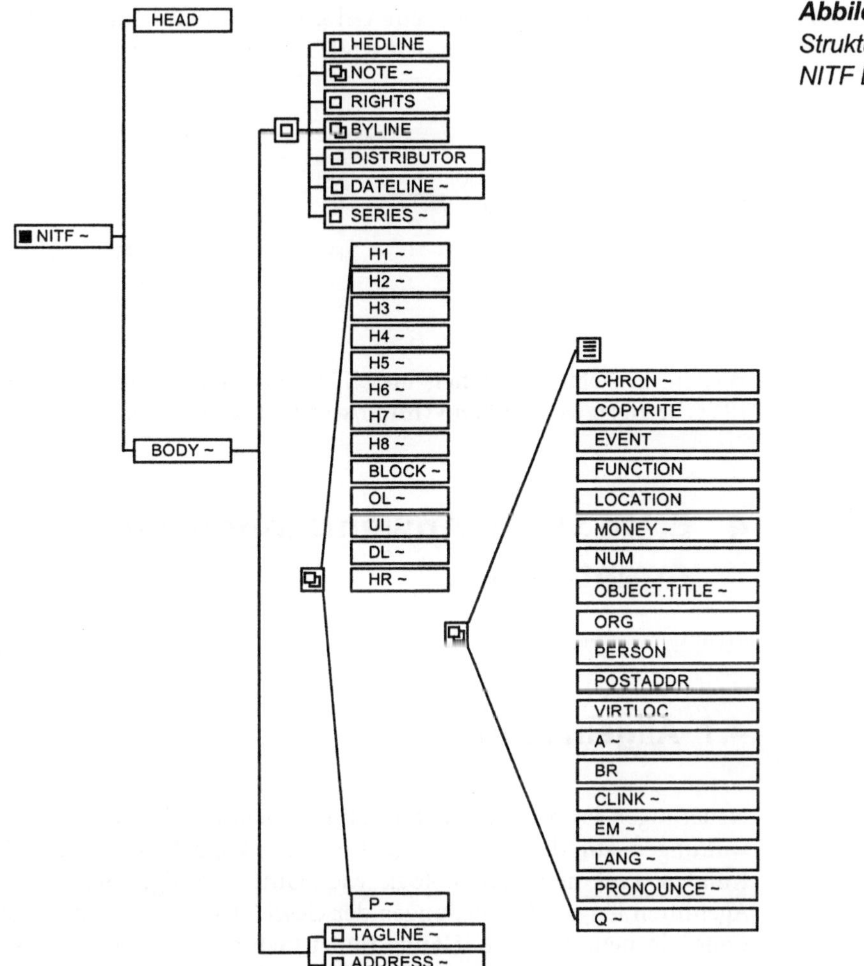

Abbildung 3
*Struktur des
NITF BODY*

Bei den Tabellen hat man auf die sehr mächtige Definition nach
CALS (ursprünglich: Computer Aided Logistics Support, s. Beitrag
von Pamela Gennusa, References) verzichtet; diese erschien zu komplex. Die in NITF gewählte Form für Tabellen entspricht der DTD
von HTML 4.

Tabellen

3.3 Die SGML-Deklaration des NITF

große Kapazität nötig

Eine Abweichung von üblichen SGML-Deklarationen ist aus der Notwendigkeit entstanden, sehr viel größere Dokumente als üblich zuzulassen. Daher erscheint in der *NITF Declaration*:

```
CAPACITY
SGMLREF TOTALCAP 1000000
ENTITYCAP    300000
ELEMCAP      300000
GRPCAP     300000
EXGRPCAP   300000
EXNMCAP    300000
```

Weitere Einzelheiten stehen im NITF Dokument selbst, das beim IPTC bezogen werden kann (http://www.iptc.org/iptc/).

4 Erste SGML-Anwendungen bei Agenturen

4.1 Allgemeines

Neuerungen brauchen Zeit

Neuerungen im Nachrichtenformat der Agentur haben direkte Auswirkungen auf die an das Agenturnetz gekoppelten Systeme der Kunden. Eine neue Technologie wie SGML benötigt auch bei den Agenturen längere Umstellungen der Geschäftsprozesse und Investitionen in neue Systeme. Häufig findet man ältere Redaktionssysteme, die sich an Änderungen schlecht anpassen lassen und durch neue Hardware und Software z.T. beträchtliche Investitionen erfordern. Dies und anderes mag erklären, daß auch bei eindeutigen Verbesserungen die neuen Technologien sich nur langsam durchsetzen.

Diese konservative Haltung gilt dann nicht, wenn

- neue Dienste geschaffen werden, die von Anfang an die neue Technik benutzen, oder

- für Fälle, in denen die Verhältnisse einer Änderung überschaubar und die Auswirkungen berechenbar sind.

Aus diesem Grund fallen die nachfolgenden Beispiele für die ersten Anwendungen in eine der beiden Kategorien.

4.2 dpa Deutsche Presse-Agentur GmbH

dpa ist eine große internationale Nachrichtenagentur mit Sitz in Hamburg und rund 1000 Beschäftigten in aller Welt. In der *dpa*-Gruppe werden Dienste in Text, Bild, Grafik und Ton herausgegeben, die Textdienste in deutsch, englisch, spanisch und arabisch. Mit dem Schwerpunkt der Medienversorgung unterhält *dpa* in Deutschland und der Welt ein eigenes dichtes Netz an Büros und Korrespondenten.

Kurzprofil

4.2.1 Fernsehprogrammdienst

Schon 1990 startete *dpa* die erste SGML-Anwendung bei Agenturen: Den *dpa-Fernsehprogrammdienst*, welcher den Zeitungen komplette Fernsehprogramme satzfertig liefert. Nur wenige Zeitungssysteme konnten bei Aufnahme des Dienstes SGML-Dokumente direkt annehmen.

erste Vorläufer-Anwendung

Zur Zeit der Einführung des Dienstes hat *dpa* hierfür noch keine DTD definiert, sondern eine vom Bundesverband Druck geschaffene Struktur *StrukText* benutzt. Die für Fernsehprogramme relevanten Texte und Daten werden in einer Datenbank gehalten, aus der die SGML-markierten Elemente laufend oder zu bestimmten Zeiten innerhalb des Formats IPTC 7901 an bis zu 30 Abnehmer in gleicher Form via Satellit geliefert werden. Im PC der Kunden wird die SGML-Markierung dann zur Konvertierung auf die Sprache des jeweiligen Satzsystems benutzt.

4.2.2 dpa-Online

Mit dem Aufkommen der Online-Dienste stellte sich der *dpa* – in ihrer Rolle als „Großhändler" – die Aufgabe, den neuen Online-Verlegern (Web-Publishers) ein für die neue Technologie verwendbares Nachrichtenprodukt zu liefern. Der Dienst *dpa-Online* soll einen Detaillierungsgrad besitzen, der es Kunden ermöglicht,

SGML und HTML

- ganze Seiten direkt und ohne Aufwand, d.h. per Software, in beliebigen Strukturen in die eigenen Websites zu übernehmen, sowie

automatisierte Verwendung

- einzelne Elemente des gesamten Angebots zu erkennen und in die eigenen Produkte in beliebiger Art und Weise einbinden zu können.

Die Antwort auf diese Herausforderung heißt NITF in einer für diesen Dienst typischen Ausprägung. Im Frühjahr 1997 wurde der Testbetrieb aufgenommen, Ende 1998 sind rund 40 Kunden bereits Bezieher von *dpa-Online* (Abbildung 4), 50 Prozent davon mit der NITF-Variante, die sich steigenden Zuspruchs erfreut.

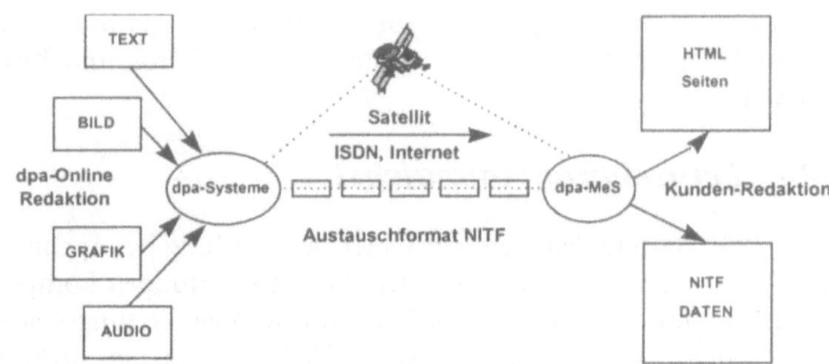

Abbildung 4
Schema des dpa-Online Dienstes

Der Erfolg von *dpa-Online* ist nicht zuletzt auf die große Flexibilität zurückzuführen, welche die Kunden durch die feine „Granularität" der NITF-Daten erhalten und ist in diesem Punkt Wettbewerbsangeboten überlegen.

4.2.3 Weiteres Vorgehen

Technologien im Modell erprobt

dpa hat in einem Technologieprojekt *CLIP-ING* neue Technologien wie SGML in der realen Umgebung einer Agentur studiert und im Modell erprobt. Die Ergebnisse führen zu weiteren konkreten Projekten, in deren Mittelpunkt die Schaffung eines neuartigen Editors „M-PET" und eines Multimedia-Servers stehen. Es ist beabsichtigt, die allgemeinen Nachrichtendienste künftig auch im NITF-Format anzubieten.

4.3 Schwedische Agentur TT

Die schwedische nationale Agentur *Tidningarnas Telegrambyå (TT)* hat ca. 150 Kunden im Medienbereich. *TT* gibt allgemeine Nachrichtendienste wie auch einen Internet-Dienst heraus und liefert fertig gesetzte Seiten für Zeitungen. *TT* hat 150 Beschäftigte in Stockholm, Malmö, Göteborg und Sundsvall. *Kurzprofil*

TT hatte schon in den siebziger Jahren mit „Fernsatz" begonnen, in dem sie den Kunden satzfertig ausgeschlossene Texte (für normierte Spaltenbreiten) lieferte. Die Kunden forderten jetzt eine aktuellere Belieferung und ein flexibleres Format ohne Satzkommandos, das auch für das elektronische Publizieren geeignet war. *Erfahrung mit Fernsatz*

TT ist ein Mitglied des IPTC und gewann in der Mitarbeit am NITF die Überzeugung, daß dies auch das geeignete Format zur Erfüllung der neuen Anforderungen ist. Zum Zeitpunkt, an dem die ersten NITF-Versionen herauskamen (1995), wurde die Entwicklung begonnen. Von Anfang an hat *TT* dabei eng mit den Herstellern von Redaktionssystemen für Zeitungen zusammengearbeitet. So kommt es, daß kurz nach Aufnahme des NITF-Dienstes schon 38 der 150 Kunden den Dienst nutzen können. *NITF übernommen*

In der Agentur selbst mußte das alte System durch eine moderne Client/Server-Umgebung ersetzt werden. Besonderes Gewicht legte das TT Management auf die Ausbildung des Personals, das von zeichenorientierten Terminals auf die grafische Oberfläche von Windows 95 wechseln mußte. *TT* verfolgte dabei das Ziel, daß die Reporter und Redakteure selbst die notwendige Markierung in die Texte einfügen sollten. Da für die zeitkritische Arbeit in Agenturen kein geeignetes Werkzeug am Markt verfügbar war, hat TT-Software einen eigenen an die NITF-DTD gekoppelten Editor entwickelt, der einer der Hauptgründe für den großen Erfolg des Projekts ist. Unter anderem hat *TT* eine Rechtschreibprüfung mit 1,3 Mio. Wörtern aus dem Altsystem in den NITF-Editor integriert. *neues Redaktionssystem mit NITF-Editor*

Im September 1997 begann *TT* mit der Aussendung des Textmaterials mit markierter Struktur; 1998 wurden die Tabellen hinzugefügt. Danach will *TT* mit der inhaltlichen Erschließung der Nachrichten durch Content-Markup beginnen. Im Laufe des Projekts waren nur kleinere Änderungen der DTD notwendig. *Inhaltsmarkierung geplant*

4.4 Die amerikanische Agentur Associated Press (AP)

AP ist eine der weltweit operierenden Weltagenturen mit Sitz in New York, die Dienste in allen Medien herausgibt. *AP* ist in vielen Ländern der Welt mit Diensten in deren Sprachen vertreten, so auch in Deutschland mit Sitz in Frankfurt.

AP hat Parser-Software erstellt, welche die existierenden Dienste in das NITF-Format umsetzt. Mit diesem Angebot will die *AP* mögliche künftige Nachfrage befriedigen.

5   Perspektiven weiterer Entwicklung

5.1 Der NITF-Standard

Unter den Fachleuten des *IPTC* und *NAA* bleibt die weitere Entwicklung der Standards IIM und NITF auch in Zukunft auf der Tagesordnung. So hatten die beiden Gremien 1997/1998 die Entwicklung eines themen-orientierten Thesaurus von sog. subjects zur feineren inhaltlichen Kategorisierung von Nachrichten abgeschlossen, der in diese beiden Normen integriert wurde.

Der NITF-Standard in der Version 2.0b wird - von seiner inhaltlichen Definition her - als vorläufig abgeschlossen betrachtet; er befindet sich in einem „reifen" Stadium. Es werden jedoch die bei Nutzung normalen Ergänzungs- und Änderungswünsche erwartet, die in eine laufende Pflege einmünden sollen.

Eine andere Frage ist, ob durch neue Technologien Änderungen notwendig werden.

5.2 SGML und XML

Durch die Rasanz der Entwicklung des Internet und besonders des World Wide Web gibt es laufend neue Impulse für die Entwicklung neuer Verfahren, Sprachen und Werkzeuge. Besondere Aufmerksamkeit ist der Sprache *Extensible Markup Language* (*XML*) zu widmen, die mächtiger und reicher als HTML ist, aber nicht die Komplexität von SGML aufweist (Abbildung 5).

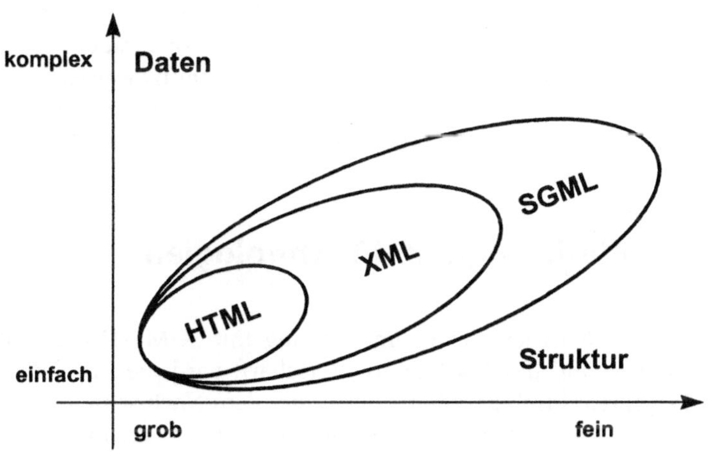

Abbildung 5
Sichtweise des
IPTC auf die
Standards

Namhafte Hersteller haben angekündigt, XML künftig in ihren Produkten zu unterstützen, bzw. zum eigenen Speicherformat zu machen. Dies dürfte der Durchbruch für eine weite Anwendung werden, weil dann keine besonderen und teuren Werkzeuge zur Erstellung und zur Anzeige von NITF-Dokumenten mehr nötig sind. Die Vorstellung, ohne Verteilung von Client-Software komplexe Anwendungen mühelos zum Endnutzer transportieren zu können, beflügelt die weitere Entwicklung der SGML-Technologie.

XML-Support

IPTC und *NAA* haben aus diesem Grunde das NITF überarbeitet und Ende 1998 vollständig mit XML kompatibel gestaltet. Der Aufwand hierfür erwies sich als nicht allzu groß. Wegen der grundsätzlich einfacheren Strukturen wurden komplexere Konstrukte in SGML auf die simplere Basis von XML reduziert. Änderungsbedarf gab es z.B. in den folgenden Festlegungen:

Änderungsbedarf gering

- Tag-Minimierung ist nicht erlaubt.

- Keine Kommentare in Markup Deklarationen;

- Keine Namensgruppen in Element- und Attributdeklarationen;

- Attributwerte sind auf Zeichenketten reduziert.

- *Mixed Content* ist zu vereinfachen.

- XML unterscheidet Groß- und Kleinschreibung.

- Syntaxregeln sind strikter.

*Funktionsverlust
vernachlässigbar*

Der Verlust an Funktionalität bei der Konvertierung zu XML wird als sehr gering angesehen. Dagegen wird bei der erwarteten großen Akzeptanz von XML der Gewinn an Effizienz und Kostengünstigkeit sehr hoch bewertet. Dies trifft insbesondere dann zu, wenn man ein *well-formed document* ohne Notwendigkeit einer DTD schafft, wobei angemerkt werden sollte, daß die volle Funktionalität des NITF auch bei XML nur unter Verwendung der DTD genutzt werden kann.

Die neue DTD mit XML-Kompatibilität `nitf` (Kleinbuchstaben), ist auf der IPTC Homepage www.iptc.org/iptc abrufbar.

5.3 Werkzeuge und Technologien

*Markierung unter
Zeitdruck*

Eine der Schwierigkeiten im Umgang mit SGML-Dokumenten ist der Aufwand des Markierens. Verschärft wird die Problematik bei Agenturen durch den Zeitdruck, unter dem Nachrichten erstellt und redigiert werden müssen. Bisher am Markt verfügbare SGML-Editoren erwiesen sich in Tests als für Agenturen ungeeignet (Erfahrungen von *dpa* und *TT*). Die Lösung ist, einen für das NITF geeigneten eigenen Editor zu bauen, der die Besonderheiten der DTD beachtet und die in Agenturen nötigen Funktionen bietet (*TT*: NITF-Editor; *dpa*: M-PET).

*Struktur leichtes
Problem*

Die strukturelle Markierung ist dabei jedoch der leichtere Teil des Problems, die Inhaltsmarkierung der schwerere. Die Aufgabe, im freien Text in wenigen Minuten strukturiert und verständlich Nachrichten zu formulieren, deren Inhalt dann nach den Vorgaben des NITF markiert sein soll, ist nur mit massiver Unterstützung durch IT-Systeme zu erreichen. Journalisten arbeiten allerdings auch heute nach *Stylebooks* und Formatvorgaben; die mögliche geforderte Tiefe eines NITF-Dokuments stellt jedoch sehr viel höhere Ansprüche.

*semantische
Markierung*

Die dabei zu beachtenden Umstände haben David Allen und Wiebke Möhr in einem *Beitrag Considerations for the Semantic Markup with NITF* beschrieben (Allen/Möhr 1998; s.a. Beitrag von Gerhard Knorz und Wiebke Möhr).

Dabei ging es um die folgenden semantischen Elemente:

`PERSON`	Personennamen
`FUNCTION`	Funktion oder Rolle einer Person
`ORG`	Name einer Organisation
`LOCATION`	Name eines Ortes
`EVENT`	Ereignis in der Nachricht
`OBJECT.TITLE`	Name des Nachrichtenobjekts
`CHRON`	Beschreibung einer Zeit

MONEY	Geld oder Währung
NUM	Zahlenausdruck
Q, BQ	Zitat oder zitierte Information

Daß Inhaltsmarkierungen im Agenturjournalismus möglich sind, hat ein von *dpa* geführtes und von *DeTeBerkom* gefördertes Projekt CLIP-ING ergeben, in dem die *GMD – Forschungszentrum Informationstechnik mbH* wissenschaftliche Untersuchungen zu diesem Thema betrieben hat. Eines der Ziele war es, aus den Nachrichtentexten die Fakten zu extrahieren und umgekehrt, in Kenntnis der Fakten, Nachrichten in einem „Markup-Server" zu markieren.

Faktenextraktion im CLIP-ING Projekt

Das Ergebnis war, bezogen auf die begrenzte Menge des Modellversuchs, ein Regelwerk für NITF-Elemente für das automatische Markieren. Weitere Einzelheiten sind dem Artikel von Lothar Rostek und Melina Alexa: *Marking up in TATOE and exporting to SGML* (Rostek/Alexa 1998) zu entnehmen.

Markup-Server

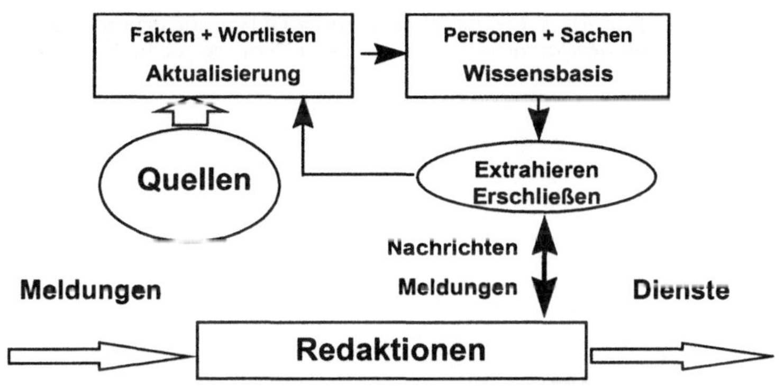

Abbildung 6
Informatorischer Kreisprozeß

Aus den Ergebnissen hat *dpa* ein mögliches theoretisches Modell künftiger neuer Geschäftsprozesse einer Redaktion erarbeitet. Dies sieht einen „Markup-Server" als Baustein eines Kreisprozesses vor, der mit Rückgriff auf eine Wissensbasis die neuen in den Nachrichten enthaltenen Fakten extrahiert, sodann mit dem gespeicherten Wissen vergleicht und markiert, aber auch auf Abweichungen aufmerksam macht. Auf diese Weise könnte in einem „informatorischen Kreisprozeß" nicht nur die semantische Markierung erzeugt werden, sondern gleichzeitig die Wissensbank aktualisiert werden (Abbildung 6).

Wieweit der oben geschilderte Prozeß in die Realität umgesetzt wird, ist eine Frage des wirtschaftlichen Nutzens gegenüber den hohen Kosten der Realisierung.

Welcher Nutzen?

Literatur

(Allen/Möhr 1998)

Allen, David; Möhr, Wiebke: Considerations for the Semantic Markup with the NITF: IPTC-NAA NITF Supporting Documentation. o.O. 1998. Erhältlich im Internet: www.iptc.org/iptc

(IPTC-NAA 1997)

IPTC-NAA (Hrsg.): IPTC-NAA Information Interchange Model (IIM). Version 4, Oktober 1997. o.O., 1997. Erhältlich im Internet: http//www.iptc.org/iptc

(IPTC-NAA 1998a)

IPTC-NAA (Hrsg): IPTC-NAA News Industry Text Format (NITF). Version 2.0b1, August 1998. o.O., 1998. Erhältlich im Internet: http://www.iptc.org/iptc

(IPTC-NAA 1998b)

IPTC-NAA (Hrsg.): IPTC-NAA Information Interchange Model: Draft Guideline 3 (Subject Codes), 1998. o.O., 1998. Erhältlich im Internet: http://www.iptc.org/iptc

(Rostek/Alexa 1998)

Rostek, Lothar; Alexa, Melina: Marking up in TATOE and exporting to SGML – Rule development for identifying NITF categories. In: Computers and the Humanities, 31 (1998), S. 311-326

Der Einsatz von XML bei der Süddeutschen Zeitung

Lucky Kuffer

1   Die Anfänge ... mit Pam

Kaum zu glauben, aber Pam Anderson gilt als die „Glücksfee" der *SZonNet* – zumindest sehen wir vom SZonNet-Entwicklungsteam das so. *SZonNet* ist die Online-Ausgabe der *Süddeutschen Zeitung*, die seit dem 6. Oktober 1995 anläßlich des 50jährigen Jubiläums der *SZ* im Internet (http://www.sueddeutschte.de) zu finden ist. Die kalifornische Strandnixe aus der amerikanischen Serie *Baywatch* ist das Schmuckstück unseres ersten SZonNet-Prototypen gewesen – erstellt Ende '94 auf einem NeXT-Rechner am *Institut für Computerlinguistik der Ludwig Maximilian Universität* in München. Zwischen *Streiflicht, Aufmacher, Seite Drei* und der *Meinungsseite* räkelte sich die schöne Blonde immer dann im Wasser, wenn man auf den Namen des Präsidenten der Bundesanstalt für Arbeit, Bernhard Jagoda, klickte: Der Hyperlink war wohl „zufällig etwas daneben geraten", vielleicht mit ein Grund, warum diese ersten SZonNet-Seiten oft für heiter entspannte Mienen sorgten und die treibenden Kräfte innerhalb der *Süddeutschen* positiv für die Idee *SZonNet* stimmten.

Die Anfänge mit Pam zeigen aber auch, wie vergleichsweise spielerisch man mit dem Thema Internet, HTML oder SGML umgegangen ist. Und auch jetzt sehen wir XML mit ihren Layout- und Verlinkungssprachkonstrukten als Toolbox, um Möglichkeiten für ein besseres Online-Publishing auszutesten.

die Glücksfee der SZonNet

2 HTML versus HTxML

Ganz ehrlich, die ersten Prototypseiten waren nicht unbedingt für einen möglichen Webauftritt gedacht, sondern sollten einigermaßen passabel die mit SGML beschriebenen SZ-Artikel darstellen. Dazu mußte die SZ-Struktur mit HTML-Elementen ergänzt werden. Ohne HTML und einen WWW-Browser wäre es schwer gewesen, dem Laien den Nutzen von Zeitungsartikeln in spitzen Klammern nahezubringen. HTML war Mittel zum Zweck – mißbraucht als „Layout-Krücke". Und so „verpacken" auch wir unsere Artikel in HTML-Tabellen und justieren die Absätze pixelgenau mit transparenten Platzhalterbildern.

Mitten hinein in diese HTML-Informationsgrauzone ist der Zeitungsartikel plaziert: klar gekennzeichnet mit Artikel-Tags. Mittlerweile nennt man diese Strukturierungsvariante gern HTxML. Wir haben das HTML <META>Tag mit Nichtbeachtung bestraft in der Hoffnung auf eine „SGMLight-Lösung".

Wir haben auch mit C.M. Sperberg-McQueen und Robert F. Goldstein argumentiert, die in ihrem Plädoyer *HTML to the Max: A Manifesto for Adding SGML Intelligence to the World Wide Web* bereits im September 1994 die Möglichkeiten erörtert hatten, mit einer abgespeckten SGML-Variante im Internet zu publizieren. Mit der steigenden internationalen Akzeptanz von XML sehen wir uns bestärkt, auf XML zu setzen und unsere Datenstrukturen dahingehend anzupassen.

3 Warum SGML/XML?

Unser primäres Ziel ist es, die Archivierung der SZ-Inhalte und den Datenexport in einem möglichst neutralen Format zu gewährleisten, unabhängig von spezifischen Software- oder Systemanforderungen. Das Kernthema ist offensichtlich: Ein Verlag erzeugt täglich ein Meer an Information, kann aber nicht zu jeder Zeit frei über diese verfügen, weil die Daten vom Satz her nicht in einheitlicher Form vorliegen. Die Information klebt am Papier, ein Zustand, den sich ein

Der Einsatz von XML bei der Süddeutschen Zeitung

moderner Zeitungsverlag nicht leisten kann. Eine einheitliche digitale Form der Inhalte dagegen schafft Freiräume und ist daher eine wesentliche Voraussetzung für die weitere Vermarktung über CD-ROM, externe Datenbanken oder das Internet. Hier gilt die Datenstrukturierung in SGML seit langem als erfolgversprechender Lösungsansatz. Auch Nachrichtenagenturen wie die *dpa* oder andere Zeitungsverlage wie z.B. die *Frankfurter Allgemeine*, die *Neue Zürcher Zeitung* und auch der *Axel Springer Verlag* können hier auf Erfahrungen mit SGML zurückgreifen, – ein Vorteil, wenn es darum geht, untereinander regelmäßig Daten auszutauschen. So wäre es durchaus wünschenswert, wenn jede Agentur oder jeder Verlag seine Datenstruktur über eine *Document Type Definition (DTD)* offen kommuniziert, so daß es in absehbarer Zeit vielleicht zu einem allgemein gültigen Zeitungsstandardformat kommen könnte. Das SGML-Engagement der *dpa* für ein einheitliches Nachrichtendatenformat auf der Basis eines IPTC-Vorschlags (s. Beitrag von Klaus Sprick) ist hier vorbildlich: auf Initiative des *International Press Telecommunications Council (IPTC)* und der *Newspaper Association of America (NAA)*, der führenden Interessenvertreter der gesamten Nachrichtenbranche in Amerika, ist im Laufe der letzten Jahre ein SGML-basiertes Datenbeschreibungsmodell für Nachrichten entstanden. Die *dpa* vertritt hier die deutschen Interessen und leistet – z.B. mit ihrem News-Box-Angebot – ihren Beitrag dazu, daß dieses Format Akzeptanz in Deutschland findet. Auch die *Süddeutsche Zeitung* ist Geschäftspartner der *dpa* und erhält permanent aktuelle Daten aus der *dpa-News-Box* – z.B. für die *SZonNet*.

4 Die Struktur der Süddeutschen – Artikel und Mappen

Die *Süddeutsche Zeitung* wird im HERMES/Unysis-Produktionssystem erstellt und kurz darauf ins Archivsystem REGIS eingelesen (s. Abbildung 1). Hier läuft der erste SGML-Filter: neben Datum, Seitenangabe, der Titelei und anderen Informationen zum Artikel werden auch die Positionsangaben der Absätze und weitere technische Informationen ausgezeichnet. Sie werden beim Datenexport nicht berücksichtigt und ausgefiltert.

    Die zentrale Produktionseinheit HERMES ist das Herzstück der Zeitung, unser „Heiligtum" – also *untouchable*. Durch seine Mächtigkeit überläßt es dem Benutzer eine Vielzahl von Möglichkeiten und Freiheiten bei der Texterstellung. Kein Journalist der *Süddeut-*

Produktions–
system
HERMES

schen wird z.B. von einem SGML-Editor gemaßregelt, wie er seine Texte zu verfassen und zu strukturieren hat – manchmal zum Leidwesen derer, die für die Qualität der elektronischen Daten zuständig sind.

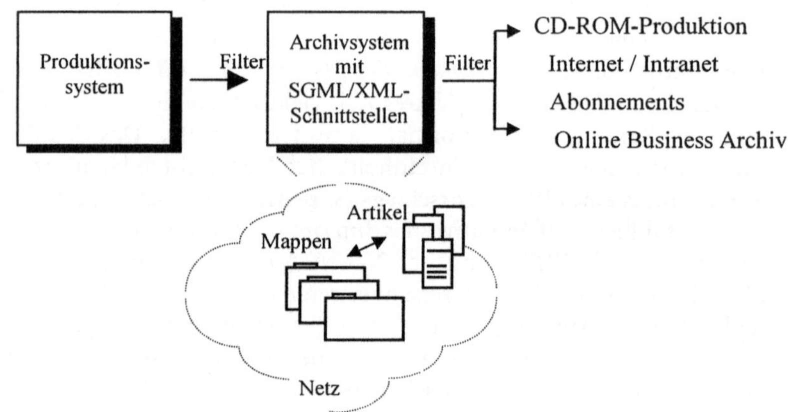

Abbildung 1
*Architektur des
SZ-Systems*

Nicht immer kann die strenge Logik des Filters schritthalten mit der Kreativität des einzelnen Journalisten am Redaktionsarbeitsplatz. Das Ergebnis ist immer wieder eine Herausforderung an denjenigen, der für den Input-Filter des Archivsystems zuständig ist.

*Archivsystem
REGIS*

Das REGIS-Archivsystem ist ein ADABAS-basiertes Datenbank-Managementsystem mit Erweiterungen, die über den relationalen Ansatz hinausgehen. Die archivierten Artikel sollen jederzeit in einem standardisierten Datenformat aus dem Archiv gelesen werden können, inklusive der Information über Verknüpfungen zu weiteren Artikeln oder zu den Tausenden von Informationsmappen: Als Äquivalent zu den Papiermappen in einem klassischen Archiv gibt es im elektronischen Archiv des *Süddeutschen Verlages* elektronische Mappen, in denen Dossiers zu einem bestimmten Thema aufbereitet und bereitgestellt werden. Diese Informationsobjekte sind über bestimmte Eigenschaften klassifiziert und stehen in Beziehung zu anderen Dossiers und Artikeln. Ein Artikel bezieht sich im Normalfall auf einen anderen, und/oder auf ein Thema, das bereits in einer elektro-

   ■
■
■   *Der Einsatz von XML bei der Süddeutschen Zeitung*

nischen Mappe behandelt ist. So gibt es z.B. eine Mappe über Bill Clinton (Person), über die Regierung Clinton (Institution), die Innenpolitik Clintons (Vorgang) oder die Sexaffäre Clintons (Ereignis). Die Clinton-Dossiers sind miteinander vernetzt, ebenso wie die Dokumente in diesen Mappen – untereinander oder mit sonstigen relevanten Berichten. Zur Unterscheidung und als Zugangshilfen dienen neben dem Dossiertitel verschiedene Suchnamen, hierarchische Klassifikationen, Signaturen und ein Geographiethesaurus. Neben Artikeln und Artikelverweisen können Bilder, Graphiken, Ganzseitendokumente in PDF und theoretisch weitere Medien archiviert sein.

Mit *SZML*, der Markup Language für die *SZ*, werden alle Artikel und Mappen neutral in ASCII abgebildet – mit den Metainformationen und Verknüpfungen. Ein Beispiel für die Auszeichnung des *Streiflichts* ist in Abbildung 2 zu sehen. Metainformationen zum Artikel wie z.B. Artikel-ID, Ressort, Rubrik, Datum und weitere Klassifizierungen werden im Artikel-Tag als Attribute gekennzeichnet; der Ausdruck `PUBLIC='yes'` zeigt an, daß der Artikel bereits online veröffentlicht wurde.

Markupsprache für die SZ

Die unterschiedlichen Angaben zur Ausgabe (`<ISSUE>`) machen Sinn, wenn man bedenkt, daß ein Artikel auf verschiedenen Seiten in der jeweiligen Ausgabe (Fernausgabe, Bayern- oder Münchenausgabe) gedruckt sein kann. Technische Informationen sind in einem Element `<TECH>` als Attributwerte abgelegt. Der Artikeltext wird eigens als solcher gekennzeichnet, damit er sich zusätzlich von den Referenzangaben zu anderen Artikeln (`<REF-ART>`), zu Autoren (`<REF-AUTHOR>`) oder elektronischen Dossiers (`<REF-FOLD>`) abhebt. Über Schlüsselelemente (*Unique Identifiers* bzw. IDs) werden die Artikel und Mappen miteinander verknüpft.

Markup der Metainformation

Im Moment sind die Links als einfache Anker in HTML abgebildet – nachdem die *Architectural Forms* aus HyTime nach einigen Tests wieder in der Schublade verschwunden sind. Hier könnten die XML-Verknüpfungssprachen *XLink* und *XPointer* einen echten Fortschritt für komplexere und kreativere Links (z.B. bi- oder multidirectional) bedeuten, sobald eine für alle verfügbare Standardsoftware diese auch verarbeiten kann.

Links

Abbildung 2
SZML-Auszeichnung eines Streiflichts

```
<?xml version='1.0'?>
<!DOCTYPE SZML SYSTEM "szml_v4.dtd" >
<SZML>
<ARTICLE ID='A6859171' SECTION='Nachrichten' CO-
LUMN='Streiflicht' DATE='19980613' CLASS='SZ' SUB-
CLASS='SZ' PUBLIC='yes'>
<ISSUE REGION='M&uuml;nchen' PAGE='1'/>
<ISSUE REGION='Deutschland' PAGE='1'/>
<ISSUE REGION='Bayern' PAGE='1'/>
<TECH SOURCE='HERMES' PAGELEV='12.2.1'
OBJLEV='12.2.1' ORIGFILE='0612S1F2'
ARTID='12.2.1.streifli.1306.10'/>
<TEXT>
<P><SZ.T><H1>
Das Streiflicht
</H1></SZ.T></P>
<P>
(SZ) Halt ein, o Christenmensch, geh in dich und denk nach,
wie das zusammenpa&szlig;t: Einerseits behauptet der bra-
silianische St&uuml;rmerstar Ronaldo, das 2:1 gegen
Schottland sei &#132;mit Gottes Hilfe&#147; erarbeitet wor-
den; andererseits r&auml;t der Essener Weihbischof Franz
Grave ab von Gebeten um den Titelgewinn, weil Gott sich
nicht auf diese Weise f&uuml;r unsere W&uuml;nsche
&#132;einspannen&#147; lasse. ...
</P>
<P>...</P>
</TEXT>
<REF-AUTHOR>
<UL>
<LI><A HREF='I0000066'>Unterst&ouml;ger, Her-
mann</A></LI>
</UL>
</REF-AUTHOR>
<REF-FOLD>
<UL>
<LI><A HREF='I0086815'>Fu&szlig;ball-
Weltmeisterschaft 1998 / Sport</A></LI>
<LI><A HREF='I0013323'>Theologie in Deutschland /
Religion Religion</A></LI>
<LI><A HREF='I0085045'>Bibel / Literatur</A></LI>
</UL>
</REF-FOLD>
</ARTICLE>
</SZML>
```

Ein Beispiel für Verknüpfungen zwischen Artikel und Mappen, so wie sie aktuell vorkommen, gibt Abbildung 3:

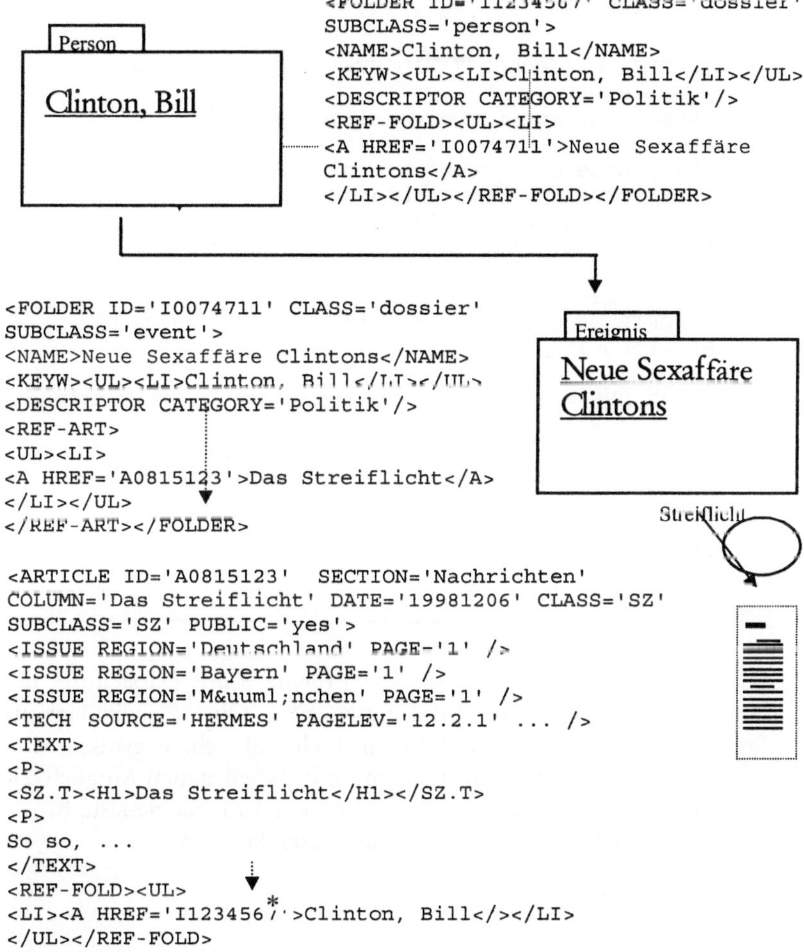


```
<FOLDER ID='I1234567' CLASS='dossier'
SUBCLASS='person'>
<NAME>Clinton, Bill</NAME>
<KEYW><UL><LI>Clinton, Bill</LI></UL>
<DESCRIPTOR CATEGORY='Politik'/>
<REF-FOLD><UL><LI>
<A HREF='I0074711'>Neue Sexaffäre
Clintons</A>
</LI></UL></REF-FOLD></FOLDER>
```

```
<FOLDER ID='I0074711' CLASS='dossier'
SUBCLASS='event'>
<NAME>Neue Sexaffäre Clintons</NAME>
<KEYW><UL><LI>Clinton, Bill</LI></UL>
<DESCRIPTOR CATEGORY='Politik'/>
<REF-ART>
<UL><LI>
<A HREF='A0815123'>Das Streiflicht</A>
</LI></UL>
</REF-ART></FOLDER>
```

```
<ARTICLE ID='A0815123'  SECTION='Nachrichten'
COLUMN='Das Streiflicht' DATE='19981206' CLASS='SZ'
SUBCLASS='SZ' PUBLIC='yes'>
<ISSUE REGION='Deutschland' PAGE='1' />
<ISSUE REGION='Bayern' PAGE='1' />
<ISSUE REGION='M&uuml;nchen' PAGE='1' />
<TECH SOURCE='HERMES' PAGELEV='12.2.1' ... />
<TEXT>
<P>
<SZ.T><H1>Das Streiflicht</H1></SZ.T>
<P>
So so, ...
</TEXT>
<REF-FOLD><UL>
<LI><A HREF='I1234567'>Clinton, Bill</></LI>
</UL></REF-FOLD>
</ARTICLE>
```

Abbildung 3
Verknüpfung zwischen Artikel und Mappen

Auch ein Mappe besitzt eine eindeutige ID und die Angaben für Klasse und Unterklasse. Neben der Mappenbezeichnung sind ein oder mehrere Schlüsselwörter aufgeführt, denen Angaben der Kategorie folgen. Als Verknüpfung sind Referenzen zu den Autoren

<REF-AUTHOR>, anderen Dossiers <REF-FOLD> und Artikeln
<REF-ART> zugelassen.

Ein einfaches Beispiel für die Struktur einer elektronischen Mappe
zeigt Abbildung 4:


```
<?xml version='1.0'?>
<!DOCTYPE SZML SYSTEM "szml_v4.dtd" >
<SZML>
<FOLDER ID='I0009137' IDREF='' CLASS='dossier' SUB-
CLASS='event'>
<NAME>Kinoszene in Deutschland</NAME>
<KEYW><UL>
<LI>Kinoszene in Deutschland</LI>
<LI>Filmtheater: Deutschland</LI>
<LI>Kino: Zuschauer</LI>
<LI>Zuschauer: Kino</LI>
<LI>Multiplex-Kinos</LI>
</UL></KEYW>
<DESCRIPTOR CATEGORY='Film'/>
<REF-FOLD TYPE='Parent'>
<UL>
<LI><A HREF='I0010287'>Filmindustrie in Deutschland
/ Film</A></LI>
<LI><A HREF='K0009535'>Filmtheater</A></LI>
<LI><A HREF='G0001651'>Deutschland</A></LI>
</UL>
</REF-FOLD>
</FOLDER>
</SZML>
```


Die HTML-Listenelemente stehen für eine klare Darstellung der
Schlüsselwörter und Verknüpfungsbegriffe. Obwohl wir Layout-
Sprachen wie CSS1 bzw. CSS2 oder auch XSL sehr begrüßen, sind
wir noch sehr vorsichtig im Umgang mit diesen neuen Möglichkeiten, da wir bei unseren Lesern die Bereitschaft für die neueste Brow-
sersoftware nicht ohne weiteres voraussetzen können.

5 Online Business Archiv mit Hyperwave

Im Moment steht der Aufbau eines Online Business Archivs an, das unter Mithilfe der Lüneburger Firma *Werum GmbH* mit dem Hyperwave Information Server realisiert wird. *Hyperwave* verfolgt eine ausgereifte Verknüpfungsstrategie auf der Basis eines objektorientierten Datenbank-Managementsystems. Für das elektronische Archiv ist dies ein Test, inwieweit die historisch gewachsene Archivstruktur in Form von eigenständigen Informationsprodukten vermarktet werden kann.

Seit April dieses Jahres wird dieses Archiv von dem neu gegründeten *Dokumentations- und Informationszentrum München* vermarktet. Die *DIZ GmbH* ist ein gemeinsames Tochterunternehmen des *Süddeutschen Verlages* und des *Bayerischen Rundfunks*, das die langjährigen Dokumentations- und Archiverfahrungen beider Häuser gemeinsam in Form von verschiedenen Dienstleistungen weitergibt. Auch hier dient die SZML-Struktur als Austauschformat zwischen REGIS, Hyperwave und weiteren Systemumgebungen.

6 Zusammenfassung

Seit ungefähr vier Jahren ist SGML bei der *Süddeutschen Zeitung* ein Thema

- als Austauschformat zwischen den verschiedenen Systemen im Haus,
- als Austauschformat zwischen den verschiedenen Geschäftspartnern im Bereich Verlage und Archive,
- als Mittel zum Qualitätsmanagement und
- als Format für die Publikation im Internet und auf CD-ROM.

XML wird oft fälschlicherweise als „Hype" gesehen, der durch die Internet-Euphorie entstanden sei. Doch genau das Gegenteil ist der Fall: XML macht unabhängig von allen „Hypes" dieser hochtechnischen Welt aus Betriebssystemen, Softwareprodukten, Anwendungen und DV-Methoden. SGML/XML hilft, das „eigene Schiff" in ruhigerem Fahrwasser zu halten und gelassen abzuwarten, was an technischen Neuerungen auf einen einprasseln könnte.

MARTIF – ein SGML-basiertes Austauschformat für terminologische Daten

Klaus-Dirk Schmitz

1 Motivation

Eine zielgerichtete und effizient ablaufende fachsprachliche Kommunikation ist ohne korrekte Terminologie nicht denkbar. Deshalb benötigen Fachleute, technische Redakteure, Dokumentare und Informationsvermittler einen Zugriff auf vorwiegend einsprachige Fachwörter mit ihren entsprechenden Definitionen und Erläuterungen. Erfolgt die fachsprachliche Kommunikation über Sprachgrenzen hinweg, müssen Übersetzer und Dolmetscher die Informationen adressatenspezifisch in die Zielsprache übertragen; Recherchen in mehrsprachigen Terminologiebeständen sind eine Voraussetzung für qualitativ hochwertige Übersetzungen. Sprachplaner, Normungsfachleute, Fachlexikographen und Terminologen unterstützen die genannten Terminologienutzer durch die Erarbeitung und Dokumentation ein- und mehrsprachiger Fachwortbestände.

fachsprachliche Kommunikation braucht korrekte Terminologie

Traditionelle Medien für die Erarbeitung, Weitergabe und Nutzung von Terminologie – wie (Fach-)Wörterbücher, Glossare oder Karteikarten-Sammlungen – wurden durch Entwicklungen im Bereich der elektronischen Datenverarbeitung immer stärker verdrängt. Die Ergänzung bzw. Ersetzung dieser traditionellen Medien, die Mitte der sechziger Jahre mit dem Aufbau von Terminologiedatenbanken auf Großrechneranlagen begann, hat dazu geführt, daß heute eine Vielzahl von meist PC-basierten Programmen zur Terminologieverwaltung von den oben erwähnten Nutzergruppen eingesetzt werden.

elektronische Mittel statt traditioneller Medien

Da eine qualitativ hochwertiger Terminologie nur durch einen sehr zeit- und damit kostenintensiven Prozeß erarbeitet werden kann, ist die Gemeinschaft der Terminologienutzer daran interessiert, terminologische Datenbestände auszutauschen. Die jeweiligen Terminologiebestände sind allerdings unterschiedlich strukturiert, da die Anforderungen an die benötigten Sprachen und Informationskategorien von der Nutzergruppe und ihrem organisatorischem Umfeld abhängen. Ein Austausch von Terminologiebeständen zwischen verschiedenen Anwendern und/oder Systemen wird hierdurch enorm erschwert und konnte bisher nur durch individuelle Konvertierungsprogramme bewerkstelligt werden.

2 Entwicklung eines Austauschformats

Die nationalen Normungsinstitutionen sowie die *ISO (International Organization for Standardization)* haben dieses Problem erkannt und bereits Anfang der achtziger Jahre einen Standard für den Austausch terminologischer Daten definiert (ISO 6156: *Magnetic tape exchange format for terminological/lexicographical records (MATER)*; auch DIN 2341-1). Diese Norm war wegen der unzeitgemäßen Ausrichtung auf das Magnetband als Datenträger für den Austausch zwischen modernen Terminologieverwaltungssystemen wenig geeignet. MATER als Austauschstandard wurde deswegen bis auf wenige Ausnahmefälle, z.B. für den Datenaustausch zwischen TEAM, der Terminologiedatenbank der *Siemens AG*, und EURODICAUTOM, der Terminologiedatenbank der *EU-Kommission*, in der Praxis nicht eingesetzt.

Bereits Ende der achtziger Jahre wurde in den USA mit den Arbeiten an der Definition eines „moderneren" Austauschformats für terminologische/lexikographische Daten begonnen (Melby 1991). Diese unter dem Namen *MicroMATER* bekannten Ansätze orientierten sich an den Konzeptionen der neu aufkommenden PC-basierten Terminologieverwaltungsprogramme.

Mit der Publikation des SGML-Standards (ISO 8879:1986) wurde ein genormter Formalismus zur Beschreibung von Textstrukturen zur Verfügung gestellt. Nachdem dann ein Jahr später die *Text Encoding Initiative (TEI)* u.a. mit dem Ziel gegründet worden war, anwendungsorientierte Beschreibungsstrukturen für unterschiedliche Dokumenttypen zu entwickeln, kam die MicroMATER-Gruppe zu dem Entschluß, das neue Austauschformat auf der Basis von SGML und in Kooperation mit der TEI zu entwickeln. Mit der Gründung der Terminological Data Work Group (AI7) innerhalb der TEI im Jahr 1991 wurden die Arbeiten an einem Austausch für terminologische Daten unter dem Namen *TEI-TERM* weitergeführt. Später löste man sich von der TEI und führte die Entwicklung des Austauschformats – ohne die SGML-Basis zu verlassen – im Rahmen des technischen Komitees ISO/TC37/SC3 unter den Arbeitstiteln *TIF* bzw. *E-TIF (Electronic Terminology Interchange Format)* und schließlich unter der Bezeichnung *MARTIF (Machine-readable Terminology Interchange Format)* weiter.

3 MARTIF

Auf der Basis dieser Vorarbeiten wurde 1997 das Terminologie-Austauschformat MARTIF als ISO-Norm verabschiedet (*ISO FDIS 12200-1: Terminology – Computer applications – Machine-readable Terminology Interchange Format (MARTIF)*).

Der Hauptteil des MARTIF-Standards legt im wesentlichen den Formalismus fest, in dem terminologische Einträge eines auszutauschenden Terminologiebestandes beschrieben werden, d.h. er spezifiziert die *Document Type Definition (DTD)* des SGML-Dokuments mit den entsprechenden Tags (Markierungen) für die Strukturierung der Daten. Der normative Anhang A des Standards definiert die einzelnen terminologischen Datenkategorien und deren Repräsentation in MARTIF. Er basiert auf der parallel zur MARTIF-Norm entwickelten *ISO FDIS 12620 (Terminology – Computer applications – Data categories)*.

Ein MARTIF-Dokument, d.h. eine entsprechend der MARTIF-Norm kodierte Datei mit terminologischen Daten, besteht aus dem `<martifHeader>` mit Angaben zum gesamten Datenbestand und dem `<text>` mit den einzelnen Datensätzen. Der `<text>` wiederum enthält im `<body>` die eigentlichen terminologischen Einträge, die in `<termEntry>`-Tags eingeschlossen sind, und im `<back>` zusätzliche Angaben (z.B. bibliographische Daten), auf die von den Einträgen des `<body>` aus verwiesen wird. Abbildung 1 veranschaulicht diese Grundstruktur.

Abbildung 1
Grundstruktur eines MARTIF-Dokuments

```
<martif>
<martifHeader>
... (The header goes here.)
</martifHeader>
<text>
     <body>
          <termEntry ID='XXX1'>
          ...(The first terminological entry goes here.)
          </termEntry>
          ...(More terminological entries go here.)
     </body>
     <back>
          <refObjectList type='bibl'>
          ...(The bibliographical <xref>s go here.)
          </refObjectList>
          ...(Any other external references also go here.)
     </back>
</text>
</martif>
```

Term-Eintrag: Informationen zu einem Begriff

Wie erwähnt, wird der terminologische Eintrag, der alle Informationen zu einem Begriff einschließlich der sprachspezifischen Daten in den jeweiligen Sprachen enthält, entsprechend der MARTIF-Konvention in eine `<termEntry>`-Struktur eingebettet. Innerhalb dieser Struktur folgen nach den begriffsorientierten und für die Verwaltung des Eintrags notwendigen Informationen (`<AuxInfo>`) die in `<LangSet>` eingeschlossenen Sprachblöcke. Dabei sind wiederum alle benennungsorientierten Datenelemente, die zu genau einer Benennung gehören, in einer `<ntig>`-Struktur eingeschlossen. Der Aufbau eines `<termEntry>` wird in Abbildung 2 deutlich gemacht.

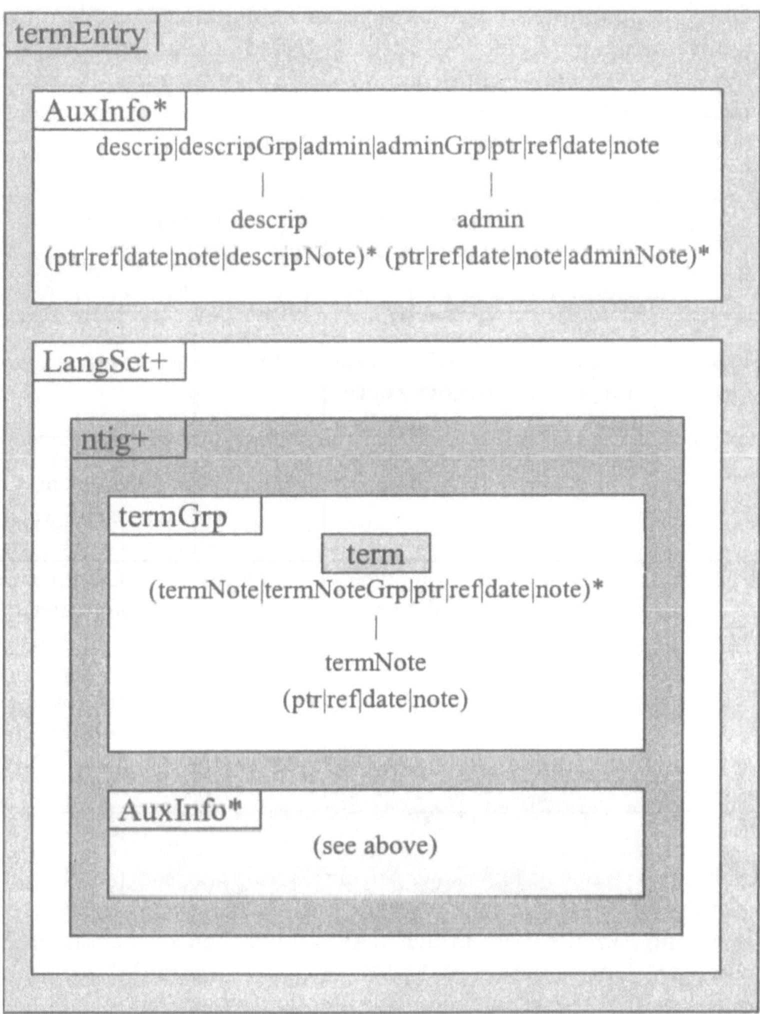

Bei der Entwicklung der MARTIF-DTD verfolgte man die Philosophie, relativ wenige, und damit relativ allgemeine, terminologische Datenkategorien zu definieren, um sicherzustellen, daß die Norm auf möglichst alle in der Praxis vorkommenden Strukturen von Terminologiebeständen anwendbar ist. Deshalb hat man vorwiegend strukturelle Elemente wie `<termEntry>`, `<LangSet>`, `<ntig>` oder `<termGrp>` und Obergruppen terminologischer Datenkategorien wie `<descrip>`, `<admin>` oder `<termNote>` festgelegt. Die einzelnen terminologischen Datenkategorien werden meist nicht als eigenständige Elemente, sondern durch Attributierung der

Obergruppen mittels `type` beschrieben. Abbildung 3 aus dem normativen Anhang A der ISO 12200 (MARTIF) zeigt, daß beispielsweise die MARTIF-Repräsentation der Datenkategorie *Wortklasse* nicht als Element `<partOfSpeech>` sondern als `<termNote>` mit entsprechendem `type`-Attribut realisiert ist.

Table A.3 MARTIF data category representation Group 1: Terms and term-related data categories Subgroup 2: Term-related information, cont. 6				
Pos. no.	Data category name	MARTIF data category representation	Value	Examples
A.2.2	grammar	<termNote type= 'grammar'>	Perm. instance	Used only where there is no finer degree of granularity.
A.2.2.1	part of speech	<termNote type= 'partOfSpeech'>	Perm. instance	Common permissible instances include: *n, v, adj.* <termNote type= 'partOfSpeech'>v </termNote>

Abbildung 4 zeigt ein Beispiel für ein Terminologieaustauschdokument in MARTIF, wobei aus Gründen der besseren Lesbarkeit Umlaute und Akzente nicht in der MARTIF-üblichen zeichensatzunabhängigen Repräsentation als SGML-Entities („Tür" für „Tür" oder „contrôle" für „contrôle") dargestellt werden.


```
<!DOCTYPE martif PUBLIC "MARTIF (framework) //EN" [
<!ENTITY % mtf-body.PUBLIC "MARTIF (base) //EN" >
<!ENTITY % mtf-ents PUBLIC "ENTITIES for MARTIF //EN" >
    ] >
```

```
<martif>
  <martifHeader>
   <fileDesc>
     <titleStmt><title>Example 1</title></titleStmt>
     <publicationStmt><p>not published</publicationStmt>
     <sourceDesc><p>modified from ISO 12200</sourceDesc>
   </fileDesc>
   <revisionDesc>
     <change><p>1996.Jan.10: modified by KDS</change>
   </revisionDesc>
  </martifHeader>

  <text>
   <body>
     <termEntry>
       <descripGrp>
         <descrip type='subjectFieldLevel1'>appearance of
         materials</descrip>
         <note>this domain is for the sake of appearance</note>
       </descripGrp>
       <note>this note applies to the entire termEntry </note>

       <ntig lang=en>
         <termGrp>
           <term>opacity</term>
           <termNote type='partOfSpeech'>n</termNote>
           <termNote type='termType'>preferred term
           </termNote>
         </termGrp>
       </ntig>

       <ntig lang=de>
         <termGrp>
           <term>Opazität</term>
           <termNote type='partOfSpeech'>n</termNote>
           <termNote type='grammaticalGender'>f</termNote>
         </termGrp>
         <descripGrp>
           <descrip type='definition'>Maß für Lichtundurchläs-
           sigkeit</descrip>
           <ref type='sourceIdentifier' target=DIN-
           6730:1992-08'>p.5</ref>
         </descripGrp>
       </ntig>

       <ntig lang=fr>
         <termGrp>
           <term>opacité</term>
           <termNote type='partOfSpeech'>n</termNote>
           <termNote type='grammaticalGender'>f</termNote>
         </termGrp>
       </ntig>
     </termEntry>
```

Abbildung 4
MARTIF-
Dokument:
Instanz
(Fortsetzung)

```
    <termEntry>
    . . . . . . .
    </termEntry>
  </body>
  <back>
   <refObjectList type='bibl'5>
    <refObject>
      <item id='DIN-6730:1992-08'>
      ** Place bibliographic reference here</item>
    </refobject>
   </refObjectList>
  </back>
 </text>
</martif>
```

Mit dem MARTIF-Standard steht ein offenes und flexibles Format für den Austausch terminologischer Daten zwischen verschiedenen Terminologieverwaltungssystemen zur Verfügung. MARTIF kann aber nicht nur benutzt werden, um terminologische Daten an andere Nutzer weiterzugeben. Es kann auch eingesetzt werden, wenn in einem Unternehmen Daten bei einer Umstellung auf eine andere Software von einem Datenbankformat in ein anderes überführt werden müssen. Weiterhin kommt als Vorteil hinzu, daß die terminologischen Daten durch die SGML-Konformität des MARTIF-Formalismus wie andere SGML-Dokumente weiterverarbeitet werden können, z.B. für eine Publikation als gedrucktes Wörterbuch.

4 Weiterentwicklung von MARTIF

Auch wenn durch die beiden Normen ISO 12200 (MARTIF) und ISO 12620 (Data categories) der Austausch von terminologischen Daten im wesentlichen exakt definiert wird, so ist doch zu vermuten, daß zusätzliche Informationen über den Inhalt von Datenkategorien der beiden am Austausch beteiligten Terminologieverwaltungssysteme angegeben werden müssen, damit der Austausch ohne Informationsverlust und Informationsverfälschung korrekt ablaufen kann. Ein sogenannter *blind interchange* ohne zusätzliche Absprachen scheint auch mit dem MARTIF-Standard nicht zwischen allen Systemen möglich zu sein.

Deshalb haben an verschiedenen Stellen Forschungsvorhaben begonnen, die den Austausch von MARTIF-konformen Daten zwischen Terminologieverwaltungssystemen mit unterschiedlicher Eintragsstruktur und unterschiedlichen Datenkategorien anhand konkreter Terminologiebestände empirisch untersuchen. Sie wollen Aufschluß darüber gewinnen, ob ein *blind interchange* ohne zusätzliche Wandlungs- und Konvertierungsroutinen möglich ist und ob über den MARTIF-Standard hinaus weitere Festlegungen für einen Terminologieaustausch erfolgen müssen (Hardman 1996, Melby/Schmitz et al. 1996, Reinke/Schmitz 1998, Wright 1996).

Zur Zeit liegt ein erster Entwurf für den *blind interchange* mit MARTIF vor (Alder/Corradini et al. 1998). Dieser Vorschlag, der als Grundlage für die Definition eines 2. Teils der ISO 12200 (hier: MARTIF Teil 2) dienen soll, versucht im wesentlichen, die im folgenden diskutierten Eigenschaften des jetzt als Teil 1 bezeichneten MARTIF-Standards (MARTIF Teil 1) zu verändern.

4.1 Zeichensatzproblematik

MARTIF Teil 1 benutzt zur Darstellung der Zeichen den in ISO 646 definierten 7-Bit Zeichensatz; Umlaute, akzentuierte Zeichen sowie sonstige Sonderzeichen werden entsprechend des Annex D der SGML-Norm ISO 8879 durch Ersatzdarstellungen repräsentiert (s. hierzu das Beispiel der SGML-Entities vor Abbildung 4). Diese Zeichensatzlösung ist jedoch für Sprachen mit nicht-lateinischem Alphabet vollkommen unzureichend.

MARTIF Teil 2 benutzt zur Kodierung der Daten *XML (Extensible Markup Language)*, eine unter Federführung des *World Wide Web Consortiums* definierte Untermenge von SGML (World Wide Web Consortium 1997, Microsoft Corporation 1998). Hierdurch trägt MARTIF Teil 2 nicht nur der augenblicklichen Entwicklung im Bereich der Markup-Sprachen Rechnung, auch die Zeichensatzproblematik beim Austausch terminologischer Daten wird vernünftig gelöst, da XML auf dem 16-Bit Unicode-Zeichensatz (Unicode Consortium 1996) basiert. Der Unicode-Zeichensatz enthält in seinen 38.885 definierten Zeichen nahezu alle Zeichen, die in unterschiedlichsten Sprachen der Welt benutzt werden, so auch für Arabisch, Chinesisch, Japanisch oder Thai.

4.2 Mehrdeutigkeiten in der Modellierung

In der ISO 12620 (Data categories) und entsprechend im normativen Anhang der ISO 12200 (MARTIF) sind eine Vielzahl von terminologischen und verwaltungstechnischen Datenkategorien aufgeführt.

Bestimmte Informationen gleicher Art können jedoch je nach Konzeption der eigenen Terminologieverwaltung in unterschiedlichen Datenkategorien untergebracht werden, ohne gegen diese beiden Normen zu verstoßen. Als Beispiel können die in Abbildung 3 aufgeführten Kategorien „grammar" und „part of speech" dienen; in beiden kann die Wortklasse einer Benennung kodiert sein.

Bei einem *blind interchange* können derartige Spielräume zur Dateninkonsistenz führen, da ohne Absprache nicht eindeutig klar ist, wie eine bestimmte Art von Information im Austauschformat abgebildet wird. Deshalb wurden in MARTIF Teil 2 diese Mehrdeutigkeiten durch die Definition einer eindeutigen Untermenge der ISO 12610 aufgelöst.

Wie in Abschnitt 3 erwähnt, werden in der MARTIF-DTD nur die strukturellen Elemente definiert und die eigentlichen Datenkategorien durch die Type-Attribute spezifiziert; diese Attribute werden in MARTIF Teil 1 nicht durch die DTD überprüft. In MARTIF Teil 2 sind jedoch die Datenkategorien der eindeutigen Untermenge der ISO 12620 explizit als Attribute in der DTD definiert, so daß ein Parser Verletzungen der MARTIF-Norm Teil 2 erkennen kann.

4.3 Inhalte von Datenkategorien

In der ISO 12620 werden terminologische Datenkategorien definiert, im Anhang der ISO 12000 die entsprechenden MARTIF-Repräsentationen der Datenkategorien. Die Inhalte von Datenkategorien sind jedoch in beiden Normen nicht festgelegt. Es werden höchstens bei den Beispielen Empfehlungen gegeben, wie die Werte von Datenkategorien aussehen können (Abbildung 3). Deshalb kann beim Austausch terminologischer Daten eine nominale Wortklasse durch *noun, n., sub, sub.* oder *Substantiv* kodiert sein, ohne die MARTIF-Norm zu verletzen.

Für einen *blind interchange* müssen jedoch die Inhalte von Datenkategorien eindeutig definiert sein. MARTIF Teil 2 legt die Inhalte aller Datenkategorien fest, bei denen dies möglich ist. Während bei textlichen Datenkategorien wie *Benennung, Definition, Kontext* oder *Anmerkung* eine Überprüfung des Inhalts nicht sinnvoll ist, müssen bei Datenkategorien mit einer festgelegten Menge von Werten wie *Wortklasse, Genus* oder *Benennungstyp* die Inhalte kontrolliert werden. Problematisch ist eine Festlegung von Inhalten bei Kategorien wie *Fachgebiet,* da es hierbei zwar um eine festlegbare Wertemenge handelt, die aber je nach Anwender und Anwendungsgebiet stark differiert. Für diesen Fall sollen bestimmte, in den entsprechenden

Fachgebieten akzeptierte Klassifikationen bei einer zentralen Stelle registriert werden. MARTIF-Austauschdokumente geben dann an, welche Klassifikation benutzt wird, und dies kann dann validiert werden.

Bei der Entwicklung von MARTIF Teil 2 wird die Strategie verfolgt, die Inhalte von Datenkategorien nicht mittels einer entsprechenden DTD zu definieren und durch einen Parser zu testen. Vielmehr wird ein eigenständiges Validierungswerkzeug entwickelt, das speziell auf die Überprüfung von Datenkategorie-Inhalten ausgerichtet ist. Ob ein Dokument mit terminologischen Daten der MARTIF-Norm Teil 2 entspricht, wird dementsprechend durch einen XML-Parser und ein Validierungswerkzeug festgestellt.

5 Schlußbemerkung und Ausblick

Mit MARTIF Teil 1 liegt eine internationale Norm für den Austausch terminologischer Daten vor, die es erlaubt, die einzelnen Datensätze und Datenkategorien sowie die Abhängigkeiten der einzelnen Informationen untereinander eindeutig zu identifizieren. Wegen der hohen Flexibilität kann MARTIF alle Formen und Strukturen von Terminologiebeständen adäquat abbilden. Diese Flexibilität hat aber auch ihren Preis: Ein verlustfreier und korrekter Austausch von Daten zwischen stark unterschiedlich kodierten Terminologiebeständen ist nur durch zusätzliche Absprache möglich. Durch die SGML-Basiertheit von MARTIF wird die Weiterverwendung der Terminologiebestände in anderen Umgebungen und der Austausch mit anderen nicht-terminologischen Daten erleichtert.

Das in MARTIF Teil 2 definierte striktere Terminologieaustauschformat erlaubt einen *blind interchange* ohne zusätzliche Absprachen. Durch die Benutzung von XML als zugrundeliegendem Formalismus wird der derzeitigen Entwicklung bei den Markup-Sprachen Rechnung getragen, was auch einer leichteren Überführung der MARTIF-Daten in HTML zur Präsentation im World Wide Web dient. Unicode als Basis für die Zeichendarstellung ermöglicht auch die Kodierung von Terminologiebeständen in Sprachen mit nicht-lateinischem Zeichensatz.

Zur Zeit sind Bemühungen im Gange, eine gewisse Kompatibilität zwischen MARTIF Teil 2 und anderen Austauschformaten wie *OLIF (Open Lexicon Interchange Format)* oder *TBX (TermBase eXchange)* zu erreichen. OLIF wurde in dem von der EU-Kommission geförderten Otelo-Projekt definiert, um einen Austausch zwischen lexikalischen Datenbeständen zu ermöglichen, die als Wörterbücher für verschiedene maschinelle Übersetzungssysteme dienen (s. Thurmair/Ritzke et al. 1998). Innerhalb der *LISA (Localization Industry Standards Association)* wurde eine spezielle Arbeitsgruppe mit Namen *OSCAR (Open Standards for Container/Content Allowing Re-use)* gegründet, die das Austauschformat *TMX (Translation Memory eXchange)* für Datenbestände aus Übersetzungsspeichern und das Format *TBX (TermBase eXchange)* für Bestände aus Terminologiedatenbanken definieren wird. Es existiert eine enge Kooperation zwischen den an den jeweiligen Formaten arbeitenden Entwicklern (s. Melby 1998).

Literatur

(Alder et al. 1998)
Alder, Aaron D.; Corradini, Ryan A.; Melby, Alan K.; Schmitz, Klaus-Dirk; Wright, Sue Ellen: Future Development in ISO 12200. In: TermNet (Hrsg.): TAMA'98. Wien: TermNet, 1998 (Proceedings of the 4th International Symposium on Terminology in Advanced Microcomputer Applications). Erhältlich im Internet: http://www.ttt.org/clsframe

(DIN 2341 Teil 1 Entwurf 1986)
DIN 2341 Teil 1 Entwurf 1986. Format für den maschinellen Austausch terminologischer / lexikographischer Daten (MATER) - Kategorienkatalog

(GTW 1994)
Gesellschaft für Terminologie und Wissenstransfer: Empfehlungen für Planung und Aufbau von Terminologiedatenbanken. Saarbrücken: GTW, 1994 (GTW-Report)

(Hardman1996)
Hardman, Daniel: A Practical Proposal for the Blind Interchange of Terminological Data. Provo (Utah), Brigham Young University, unpublished Master's Thesis, 1996

(ISO 6156 1987)
ISO 6156 1987. Magnetic tape exchange format for terminological / lexicographical records (MATER)

(ISO 8879 1986)
ISO 8879 1986. Information processing - Text and office systems - Standard generalized markup language (SGML)

(ISO FDIS 12200 Part 1 1998)
ISO FDIS 12200 Part 1 1998. Computer Applications in Terminology - Machine-readable Terminology Interchange Format (MARTIF) - Part 1: Negotiated Interchange

(ISO FDIS 12620 1998)
ISO FDIS 12620 1998. Computer Applications in Terminology - Data Categories

(ISO/IEC 646 1991)
ISO/IEC 646 1991. Information technology - ISO 7-bit coded character set for information interchange

MARTIF – ein SGML-basiertes Austauschformat für terminologische Daten

(Melby 1991)

Melby, Alan K.: MicroMATER: A proposed standard format for exchanging lexical/terminological data files. In: Meta 36(1991), Nr. 1, S. 135-160

(Melby 1998)

Melby, Alan K.: Data Exchange Standards from the OSCAR and MARTIF Projects. Paper presented at the Int. Conference on Language Resources and Evaluation, May 28-30, 1998, Granada

(Melby et al. 1996)

Melby, Alan K.; Schmitz, Klaus-Dirk; Wright, Sue Ellen: The Machine Readable Terminology Interchange Format (MARTIF): Putting Complexity in Perspective. In: TermNet News, (1996), Nr. 54/55, S. 11-21

(Melby/Hardman1996)

Melby, Alan K.; Hardman, Daniel: Importing Terminology from Multiple Sources in Three Phases: Inspection, Adjustment and Adoption. In: Galinski, Christian; Schmitz, Klaus-Dirk (Hrsg.): Proceedings of TKE '96: Terminology and Knowledge Engineering. Frankfurt (Main): Indeks Verlag, 1996, S. 197-204

(Microsoft 1998)

Microsoft: XML: A Technical Perspective. Erhältlich im Internet: http://www.microsoft.com/xml/xmlwhite.htm

(Reinke/Schmitz 1998)

Reinke, Uwe; Schmitz, Klaus-Dirk: Testing the Machine Readable Terminology Interchange Format (MARTIF). Saarbrücken: Universität des Saarlandes, 1998

(Schmitz 1996a)

Schmitz, Klaus-Dirk: MARTIF: Ein neuer ISO-Standard für den Austausch terminologischer Daten. In: Technische Dokumentation (1996), Nr. 3, S. 8-9

(Schmitz 1996b)

Schmitz, Klaus-Dirk: Martif: A New ISO-Standard for the Interchange of Terminological Data. In: TermNet News (1995), Nr. 50/51, S. 6-8

(Thurmair et al. 1998)

Thurmair, Gregor; Ritzke, Johannes; McCormick, Susan: The Open Lexicon Interchange Format OLIF. In: TermNet (Hrsg.): TAMA'98. Vienna: TermNet, 1998 (Proceedings of the 4th International Symposium on Terminology in Advanced Microcomputer Applications)

(Unicode Consortium 1996)

Unicode Consortium: The Unicode Standard, Version 2.0. Reading, MA: Addison-Wesley, 1996

(World Wide Web Consortium 1997)

World Wide Web Consortium: Extensible Markup Language (XML). Erhältlich im Internet: http://www.w3.org/XML

(Wright 1996)

Wright, Sue Ellen: Blind Interchange of Terminological Data: Problems and Possibilities. In: Multilingualism in Specialist Communication. In: Vienna: TermNet, 1996 (Proceedings of the 10th LSP-Symposium), S. 1123-1130

(Wright 1997)

Wright, Sue Ellen: Mapping Local Data Categories to Categories Defined in ISO 12620. In: IITF Journal. Im Druck.

(Wright/Budin 1994)

Wright, Sue Ellen; Budin, Gerhard: Data Elements in Terminological Entries: An Empirical Approach. In: Terminology 1(1994), Nr. 1, S. 41-60

Eine SGML-basierte bibliographische Datenbank für Nachschlagewerke

Sascha Höning

1 Kleine Typologie von Literaturangaben in Nachschlagewerken

Literaturangaben sind ein wichtiger Bestandteil von Nachschlagewerken und Lexika. Dem Leser begegnen sie in drei Varianten:

Varianten von Literaturangaben

1. *Angaben zur Primärliteratur im Text eines Lexikonartikels*
   Das Erwähnen bedeutender Werke eines Schriftstellers oder Wissenschaftlers im laufenden Text ist insbesondere in biographischen Artikeln unverzichtbar (Kafka, Newton, Virchow). Aber auch in Sachartikeln (Literatur, Kunst, Philosophie) gibt es zahlreiche Gelegenheiten, Primärliteratur anzuführen. Weil diese Literaturangaben in den Textfluss eingebunden sind, werden sie vom Leser kaum als das wahrgenommen, was sie im Grunde sind: „harte" bibliographische Daten.

2. *Angaben zur Primärliteratur im Anhang eines Lexikonartikels*
   Die zweite Variante bietet separate Abschnitte, meist in kleinerer Schrift oder anderer Schrifttype, um sie vom eigentlichen Artikel abzuheben. Diese Anhänge enthalten Hinweise zur Primärliteratur, die man erwähnen möchte, die aber nicht im Text des Artikels untergebracht werden können oder sollen.
   Ein solcher Annex kann sich wiederum in zwei Unterabschnitte gliedern: den Werkkatalog und den Ausgabenkatalog. Bölls Brot der frühen Jahre ist im Werkkatalog aufgeführt, die von B. Balzer herausgegebenen zehnbändigen Werke Heinrich Bölls stehen unter den Ausgaben.

3. *Angaben zu weiterführender Literatur*
Die dritte Form enthält, ebenfalls in einem separaten Abschnitt, Hinweise zur Sekundärliteratur: Klaus Schröters rororo-Monographie über Böll findet man hier zitiert.

Jede der drei Kategorien *Werke*, *Ausgaben*, *Sekundärliteratur* kann auch unabhängig von den anderen vorkommen: also nur Werke, nur Ausgaben, nur Sekundärliteratur. Auch unterschiedliche Kombinationen gibt es, z.B. Werke und Sekundärliteratur, aber keine Ausgaben – oder Werke und Ausgaben, aber keine weiterführende Literatur. Unabhängig von den Kombinationsmöglichkeiten, die sich daraus ergeben, ist die Reihenfolge festgelegt: zuerst Werke, danach Ausgaben, Sekundärliteratur zuletzt.

*Miniatur-
bibliographien
für Leser*

Innerhalb jedes dieser Abschnitte sind die Literaturzitate „Stück für Stück" – in meist chronologischer Abfolge – aneinandergereiht. Bei Bedarf werden Untergruppen gebildet, im Werkkatalog eines Literaten z.B. *Romane*, *Lyrik*, *Dramen*. Die Anzahl der Zitate richtet sich nach dem Lexikonartikel und ist von Stichwort zu Stichwort unterschiedlich groß. Oft dienen diese „versteckten Miniatur-Bibliographien" Lesern als Anregung und Ausgangspunkt, um auf eigene Faust weitergehende Literaturrecherchen nach dem Schneeballsystem anzustellen.

2 Bibliothekarische Bibliographie vs. lexikographische Bibliographie

*Hauptaufgaben
für die
redaktionelle
Bearbeitung*

Für eine effektive redaktionelle Bearbeitung von Literaturangaben in Nachschlagewerken und Lexika gilt es, drei Hauptaufgaben anzugehen:

1. Die Daten sollen nur einmal erfasst werden, einfach und schnell aktualisierbar und beliebig oft verwendbar sein.

2. Es bedarf einer angemessenen Strukturierung der Textsorte Bibliographie.

3. Die Bearbeitung der Daten soll in die redaktionelle Arbeitsumgebung integriert sein.

*die bibliographi-
sche Datenbank*

Darüber hinaus muss die Einbindung der Daten in redaktionelle Texte möglich sein. Das Mittel hierfür ist eine eigenständige bibliographische Datenbank.

Zunächst liegt es nahe, sich auf dem Markt umzusehen und herauszufinden, ob eine solche bibliographische Datenbank nicht schon existiert. Schließlich gab es derartige Systeme schon lange vor den

Zeiten des Internet. Doch die am Markt verfügbaren bibliothekarischen Datenbanken eignen sich nicht für die Einbindung in ein Redaktionssystem. Zu diesem Zweck wurden sie ja schließlich auch nicht gemacht. Sie erfüllen im Wesentlichen die Funktion von Katalogen und Verzeichnissen (Eversberg 1998).

Wollte man sich ihrer dennoch bedienen, müsste man mit Blick auf das angestrebte Ziel vor einigen ihrer Eigenschaften kapitulieren: Die bibliothekarischen Systeme sind, teilweise absurd anmutend, hoch gezüchtet, ihre atomistische Struktur erweckt den Anschein größerer Wichtigkeit als der, die dem Inhalt beigemessen wird, und es gibt keine Möglichkeit, die Inhalte textlich und zugleich strukturiert weiterzuverarbeiten. Der Lexikograph braucht in diesem Zusammenhang aber nicht nur die Möglichkeit, Literaturangaben in eigens strukturierten Abschnitten anzulegen. Er möchte auch im laufenden Text seines Artikels bibliographische Angaben einbinden. Aber: Einer Strukturierung bibliographischer Angaben im Fließtext wird er nur dann zugeneigt sein, wenn dadurch seine Formulierungsfreiheit nicht eingeschränkt wird. Das bedeutet im Endeffekt: Struktur ja, aber bitte flexibel. Das ist im Markt jedoch nicht zu haben.

Auf der einen Seite also: ein – von Bibliothekaren meist selbst mitgebautes, teils geliebtes, teils erlittenes – Schlaraffenland mit unterschiedlichsten Programmen, Schemata und abfragbaren Datenbanken ..., denn schließlich sind bibliographische Daten ganz hervorragend dazu geeignet, nach Herzenslust durch und durch (sozusagen well done) strukturiert zu werden. Die Frage dabei ist: wo hört man am besten auf? (Beim Steak jedenfalls ist die Sache klar.)

Auf der anderen Seite: die Gegebenheiten und Zwänge, denen ein Erfassungs- und Bearbeitungssystem ausgesetzt ist und mit dem in einem Verlag so verschiedenartige Dokumente wie Texte, Tabellen, Formeln usw. gehandhabt werden. Ein Redaktionssystem ist – wie alle anderen Anwendungen auch – immer aufs Neue mit den bekannten Problemen konfrontiert: Kurzlebigkeit von Programmen und Betriebssystemen sowie Fortschritte in der Hardwaretechnik, die es eigentlich nach jeder CeBIT notwendig machen, sich neu auszustatten. Diese unabänderliche Tatsache bedroht das wichtigste Wirtschaftsgut, das Verlage besitzen: die elektronisch gespeicherten Textsubstanzen. Es ist wichtig, die relative Unabhängigkeit dieser Substanzen von verschiedenen Hard- und Softwareumgebungen sicherzustellen.

So reicht es nicht aus, verlegerische Textmaterialien nur zum Zweck der Druckaufbereitung mit Satz- bzw. Desktop-Publishing-Programmen zu gestalten. Dieses Stadium liegt jenseits redaktioneller Bearbeitung und Pflege. Die Texte müssen schon vor der Übergabe an den Satzrechner nach inhaltlichen Kriterien gegliedert und durch Redakteure bearbeitet werden können. Außerdem ist von Bedeutung, die Daten möglichst dauerhaft verfügbar zu halten.

3 SGML: das Format der Wahl

Die Schlussfolgerung ist klar: Längst ist SGML als Format für die Daten ins Spiel gekommen. Fachleuten zufolge stellt SGML derzeit die einzig bekannte Datenstruktur zur Verfügung, bei der auch nur mit annähernder Sicherheit davon ausgegangen werden kann, dass sie auch über die kommenden zehn Jahre noch Verwendung finden wird (Leuser/Tscheke 1996). Dass dies hoffentlich mehr als nur ein EDV-frommer Wunsch ist, mag dadurch belegt werden, dass SGML immerhin seit 1986 eine internationale Norm (ISO 8879) ist.

Die Wahl eines neutralen Datenformates gilt natürlich auch für bibliographische Daten. Auch diese Textsorte sollte im Lexikonverlag über Jahre, z.T. auch Jahrzehnte, verfügbar sein. Einerseits ist erleichternd, dass mit Sicht auf bibliographische Daten nur ein Bruchteil an puristisch-bibliothekarischer Strukturierungsphantasie benötigt wird, um für ein Lexikon zum Ziel zu gelangen. Andererseits steht dem aber nun einmal das vielfache Vorhandensein komplizierter Strukturen und Systeme am Markt gegenüber (Eversberg 1998).

Der Lexikonredakteur ist für das Bearbeiten der lexikalischen Texte zuständig und muss dabei auch Literaturangaben verarbeiten. Allerdings soll er sich mit bibliothekarischen Spezialitäten nicht auseinandersetzen müssen. Das ist Aufgabe des Bibliographieredakteurs, der sich auf der Grundlage „seiner" Datenbank, der bibliographischen Datenbank, um die Literaturversorgung kümmert und sich mit passendem Handwerkszeug und entsprechenden Methoden im Kanon der fachmännisch-bibliothekarischen Profession bewegt.

4 Der Weg: ein SGML-basiertes Redaktionssystem

Für die mit einem solchem Szenario verbundenen Anforderungen scheiden vorgefertigte Datenbanken und Systeme als Handwerkszeug gänzlich aus. Bei *B. I. & Brockhaus* war das Ergebnis die Entwicklung einer eigenen bibliographischen Datenbank, die in das bestehende SGML-basierte Redaktionssystem integriert werden konnte.

Nach Ablauf einer mehrjährigen Vorbereitungs- und Pilotphase, in der die gesamte Arbeitsumgebung hard- und softwareseitig aufgebaut worden war, erarbeiten *B. I. & Brockhaus* seit nunmehr ca. fünf Jahren im Routinebetrieb Lexika und Wörterbücher mit dem hauseigenen elektronischen Redaktionssystem. Am Mannheimer Verlagsstandort besteht es derzeit aus rund 100 UNIX-Workstations, mehreren Servern sowie umfangreicher (ebenso üblicher wie notwendiger) Peripherie, also Druckern, Bandlaufwerken, *Storage Arrays* usw. Eine weniger umfangreiche, aber qualitativ gleichwertige Anlage ist auch im Leipziger Verlagshaus installiert; die beiden Redaktionssysteme stehen miteinander über ein Intranet in Verbindung.

Die Hardware stammt von SUN, als Datenbankprogramm wird Sybase eingesetzt, und für die Textbearbeitung wird der ADEPT-Publisher verwendet. Die Satzaufbereitung erfolgt mit PageOne. Den Aufbau des Gesamtsystems bewerkstelligte die *STEP GmbH* in enger Zusammenarbeit mit dem Verlag.

Mit der Einrichtung von Fachzirkeln und deren Besetzung mit engagierten und interessierten Mitarbeitern aus dem Kreis von Redaktion und Technik konnten *B. I. & Brockhaus* im Laufe der Zeit eine bemerkenswerte Eigenkompetenz aufbauen. Eine motivierte Crew im eigenen Haus ist übrigens für ein solches System lebenswichtig und sollte sich der wohlwollenden Aufmerksamkeit der Geschäftsleitung sicher sein dürfen. Da das Investitionsvolumen erheblich ist, muss den Verantwortlichen an der steten Pflege des Systems durch Entwicklungsteams gelegen sein, die man für diese Aufgabe mit gewissen Freiräumen vom Tagesgeschäft ausstattet. Ein solch komplexes System kann nie wirklich fertig werden.

5 Die Bibliographische Datenbank innerhalb des Redaktionssystems

Im Redaktionssystem liegt für jedes Lexikon eine eigene sog. *Werkapplikation* auf. Mit Werkapplikation ist eine Datenbank gemeint, mit der die Redakteure interaktiv arbeiten und aus deren Inhalt am Ende ein Buch produziert wird. So gibt es spezielle Produktionsdatenbanken für die *Brockhaus-Enzyklopädie*, den *Brockhaus* in einem Band, drei und fünf Bänden, für Meyers Taschenlexika, für die DUDEN-Wörterbücher und zahlreiche weitere Nachschlagewerke.

Innerhalb dieses Datenbankspektrums bildet die Bibliographische Datenbank (kurz: BibDB) keine eigentliche Produktionsdatenbank: Es wird kein Buch, das nur Bibliographie enthält, geben. Sie ist eine Referenzdatenbank, deren Aufgabe darin besteht, für alle in Frage kommenden Werke als bibliographische Informationsquelle zu dienen. Im Vergleich zu den reinen Werkapplikationen, den Lexikondatenbanken also, schlägt die BibDB daher etwas aus der Art.

*Konzept einer
Referenz-
datenbank*

Das Konzept einer Referenzdatenbank, die viele andere Applikationen in immer gleicher Weise versorgt, bietet sich nicht nur unter sachlichem Aspekt an. Es ist aus ökonomischen Gründen naheliegend, dass bibliographische Informationen unabhängig von einem bestimmten Lexikontyp immer in der gleichen Struktur vorliegen sollten, was nicht notwendigerweise bedeutet, daß sie gleich ausführlich sein müssen. Beispielsweise will man in dem einen Lexikon generell auf die Erwähnung von Untertiteln verzichten, in einem anderen Lexikon hingegen nicht. Literaturzitate in *Meyers Taschenlexikon* können auch in der *Brockhaus-Enzyklopädie* verwendet werden – warum also für jedes Werk von Neuem mit einer eigenen Literaturdokumentation beginnen?

*Literatur-
information wird
zentral
vorgehalten*

In der Papierwelt war das bisher nicht zu verhindern, hinzu kamen meist noch Besonderheiten von Lexikon zu Lexikon. Im Rahmen des Redaktionssystems konnte nun erreicht werden, dass es genügt, die einmal ermittelte Literaturinformation in der Bibliographischen Datenbank vorzuhalten, die Aktualität der Literaturzitate im Bedarfsfalle sicherzustellen und die gewünschte Ausführlichkeit eines Literaturzitates in der Zielapplikation anzuwenden. Voraussetzung ist, dass die Dokumenttypdefinition (DTD) der Zielapplikation die entsprechenden Bausteine kennt, wie sie in der DTD der Bibliographischen Datenbank vorgegeben sind.

6 Aufbau von Lexikonartikeln

*Struktur eines
Allgemein-
lexikons*

Bevor die BibDB nun detaillierter dargestellt wird, sollen zuvor am Beispiel eines Allgemeinlexikons dessen grundlegende Bausteine und Strukturen aufgezeigt werden, um später den Zusammenhang der – im Prinzip einfachen – Wechselwirkung zwischen Werkapplikation und BibDB herzustellen.

In einem Allgemeinlexikon findet man in der Hauptsache

- Sachartikel
- biographische Artikel
- geographische Artikel (z.B. Städte, Staaten)

- Werkartikel (z.B. musische, architektonische, bildnerische, schriftstellerische Werke von Persönlichkeiten)
- Übersichtsartikel
- Sonderartikel
- Literaturangaben
- Bilder
- Bildunterschriften
- Tabellen
- Legenden
- Verweise
- Übersichten

Auf einer CD-ROM-Version eines Lexikons findet der Leser zudem

- multimediale Elemente wie Ton, Animation, Video und
- ein im Vergleich zur Printausgabe meist umfangreicheres Verweissystem (Hyperlinks).

Diese nicht vollständige Aufzählung mag zeigen, dass recht viele Artikeltypen sowie weitere Bausteine in einer Lexikonapplikation zum Tragen kommen können. Die DTD repräsentiert alle diese Bestandteile und gestattet es beispielsweise, einen Lexikonartikel zu erstellen, der aus folgenden Teilen besteht:

- dem Lemma, also dem (Such-)Stichwort,
- dem Kopfteil, der bestimmte Informationspartikel enthält, der aber abhängig von Lexikon- und/oder Artikeltyp in Umfang und Aufbau anders definiert sein kann (z.B. Lebensdaten einer Person im einem biographischen Artikel; statistische Angaben zu Beginn eines Staatenartikels);
- dem Artikeltext (Korpus),
- den Werk- und Literaturhinweisen sowie
- gegebenenfalls Verankerungen von Tabellen und Multimediainformationen.

Es soll darauf verzichtet werden, näher auf den Aufbau dieser Bestandteile einzugehen. Im Zusammenhang mit der Bibliographischen Datenbank sind nur die Literaturhinweise von Interesse.

7 Aufbau von BibDB-Dokumenten

7.1 Struktur bei Bedarf

Material aus der BibDB

Wie eingangs dargestellt wurde, gibt es in einem Lexikonartikel zwei Stellen, an denen Literaturzitate vorkommen können: im laufenden Artikeltext sowie in eigenen Literaturabschnitten. Auf die Literaturangaben im Fließtext soll später eingegangen werden. Zunächst zur Darstellung der separaten Literaturabschnitte. Sie sind es, die originär durch die BibDB mit Material versorgt werden.

Um alle Publikationstypen abzudecken, die für ein Lexikon relevant sind, benötigt die bibliographische Applikation nur vier verschiedene Artikeltypen (mithin Literaturzitattypen):

1. das selbständige nichtperiodische Werk (SWDOK, Abbildung 1)

2. das periodische Werk (ZSDOK, Abbildung 2)

3. das unselbständige Werk aus einem selbständigen nichtperiodischen Werk (UWDOK, Abbildung 6)

4. das unselbständige Werk aus einem periodischen Werk (UZDOK, Abbildung 4)

Anders als die unterschiedlichen Dokumentstrukturen einer Lexikonapplikation unterscheiden sich diese vier Artikeltypen nur in Details. Sie folgen dem gleichen Bauplan. Dieser sagt: Innerhalb eines BibDB-Artikels, (auch Titelaufnahme und im Weiteren einfach Dokument genannt) gibt es zwei Teile. Der erste Teil unterliegt strenger SGML-Strukturführung. Im zweiten Teil, dem sog. Containerteil, ist Struktur möglich, aber nicht erzwungen.

Struktur- und Containerbereich

Mit der Definition dieser Zweiteilung in Struktur- und Containerbereich schafft man sich die Möglichkeit, unstrukturierte oder anders als SGML-strukturierte Daten in Form von *plain text* in einem SGML-Dokument abzulegen. Struktur- wie auch Containerteil sind in Umfang und Größe natürlich variabel.

Vorteile der Zweiteilung

Dieses Verfahren der qualitativen Zweiteilung in ein und demselben Dokument hat Vorteile.

- Der Strukturteil stellt sicher, dass erstens die Einheitlichkeit der Form aller Literaturangaben gewahrt wird. Und da die Literaturangabenstruktur in allen betreffenden Applikationen identisch ist, wird zweitens die Kompatibilität zwischen der BibDB und den Zielapplikationen garantiert.

- Das Anwendungsspektrum der Datenbank kann mit Hilfe der Container über den eigentlichen Zweck hinaus erweitert werden, wie später noch ausgeführt wird.

bibdb:dstat=0> zsdok:art-id=402264> zeitschr> titlit:form=periotit>
Zeitschrift für Bibliothekswesen u. Bibliographie, <titlit
periozhl> Jg. (&spvgev) 1 (&spvgev) ff. <periozhl erschang> erschort>
(Frankfurt am Main <erschort erschjhr> 1954 (&spvgev) ff.);
<erschjhr <erschang <zeitschr <zsdok
c1>
¶ titlit:form=periotit> ZfBB <titlit ⁋
¶ verlag> (Klostermann) <verlag ⁋
¶ Begr. u. hg. v. autor:typ=hrsg> Hanns W. Eppelsheimer,
<autor autor:typ=hrsg> Gustav Hofmann, <autor autor:typ=hrsg>
Hermann Tiemann. <autor ⁋
¶ 1. 1954; 8. 1962; 11. 1964; 21. 1974; 31. 1984; 41. 1994; 44.
1997 ⁋
<c1
c2>
¶ Zur Vereinigung mit dem titlit:form=periotit> Zentralblatt für
Bibliothekswesen (ZfB) <titlit ab 1991 vgl. die editor. Notiz von
autor> Klaus–Dieter Lehmann <autor in: ZfBB 38 (1991), 1. S.
1–2. ⁋
¶ bibref> Autopsie. <bibref ⁋
¶ letzte 2 Jahrgänge stosig> im Haus vorhanden; <stosig
ehemals vorhanden ab Jg. 8.1962; als Geschenk abgegeben an die
stosig> Bibliothek des Landesmuseums für Technik in
Mannheim; <stosig bei Bedarf dort abrufbar. ⁋
¶ wll> BEATE / Bibliothek <wll ⁋
<c2
<bibdb

Abbildung 1 *Dokumentstruktur für ein selbständiges Werk*

- Die Speicherung unstrukturierter Informationen in den Containern hat zur Folge, dass diese Informationen ebenfalls Teilnehmer am Datenbestand sind und mittels Volltextrecherche abfragbar zur Verfügung stehen. Der mit Volltextanfragen einhergehende Mangel an *Precision* auf der Ergebnisseite ist, wie die Praxis zeigt, vernachlässigbar.

- Strukturierung ist nicht a priori für alle Dokumente als Voraussetzung zwingend, sie kann bei Bedarf nachgeführt werden.

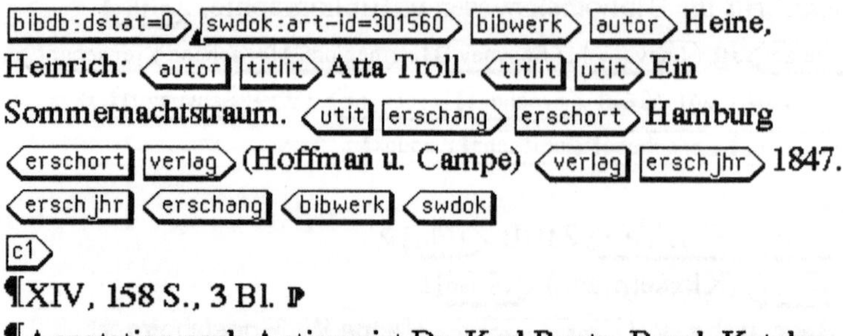

Dieses Vorgehen hat weitere positive Konsequenzen:

- Die bibliographische Information ist bereits in der Datenbank verfügbar. Sie muss im Bedarfsfalle nicht erneut recherchiert werden: Auf diese Weise werden unnötige Kosten vermieden.

- Die Kosten, die durch bibliographie-redaktionellen Bearbeitungsaufwand für diese Titel entstehen, können dem Lexikon zugerechnet werden, das sie verursacht, in unserem Beispielfall dem Lexikon B.

Damit ist eine vor allem ökonomisch und konzeptionell begründete Maxime verwirklicht: Strukturieren bringt Aufwand mit sich; diesen leistet man für den Einzelfall produktbezogen und erst bei Bedarf.

Eine weitere Facette dieser Maxime zeigt sich in der Zielsetzung, in der Bibliographischen Datenbank im Strukturteil möglichst alle relevanten Daten zu einem Literaturzitat vorzuhalten (Autor, Titel, Erscheinungsort, Auflage, Erscheinungsjahr). Kürzen bzw. Anpassen eines Zitats hat dort zu geschehen, wo es verlangt wird: in der Zielapplikation. Entscheidet die Redaktion, dass grundsätzlich keine Erscheinungsorte in Lexikon A angegeben werden sollen, in Lexikon B aber durchaus, so erfolgt das Eliminieren der Erscheinungsortangaben für Lexikon A in dessen Applikation, nicht in der BibDB. Die Bibliographische Datenbank soll keine lexikonspezifischen Eigenheiten der Literaturdarbietung vorwegnehmen (müssen).

Im Gegensatz zum Containerteil bietet der Strukturteil SGML sozusagen in Reinform. Er bildet im Wesentlichen die an der *ISBD* (*International Standard Bibliographic Description*) orientierte bibliographische Beschreibung nach. Die Ausformung der Struktur kann bei Bedarf ausführlicher ausfallen als in den Abbildungen dargestellt. Da, wie schon erwähnt, die Literaturangabenstruktur in allen betreffenden Applikationen identisch ist, wird es möglich, aus der BibDB jede Produktionsdatenbank durch einen einfachen Kopiervorgang mit Literaturangaben zu füttern (Abbildung 3).

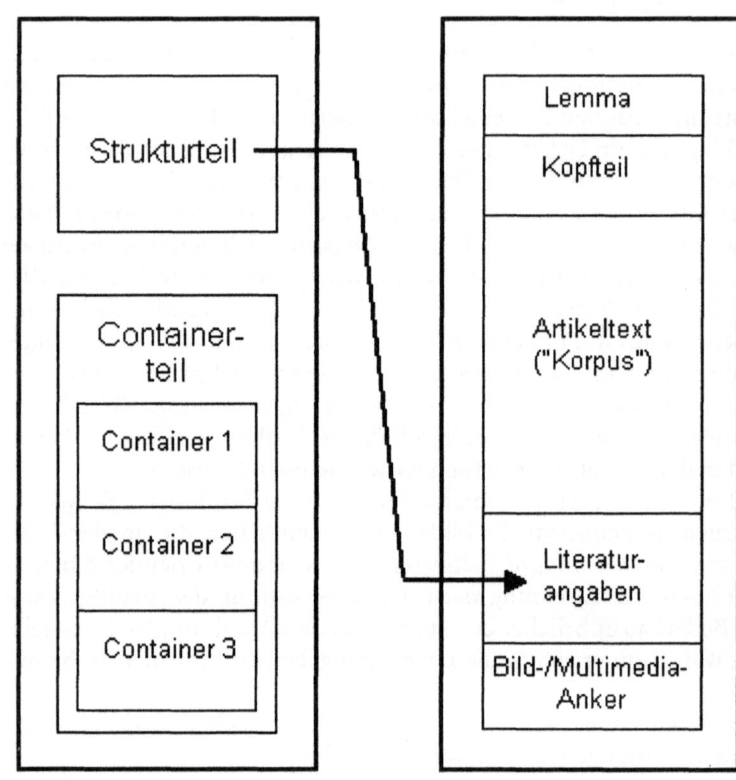

Abbildung 3
Versorgung eines Lexikonartikels mit Literaturangaben aus der BibDB durch Kopieren einzelner Zitate

7.2 Exkurs

Um den Kopiervorgang zu ermöglichen, sind für Literaturzitate die Strukturen in den Zielapplikationen identisch mit der Struktur in der BibDB. Die Einzelzitate werden zu einem Katalog zusammengefügt und in chronologischer Abfolge aneinandergereiht.

Dieses Verfahren könnte man sich noch eleganter vorstellen. Der Bearbeiter kopiert das Dokument nicht aus der BibDB in die Zielapplikation A, B, C, ... (kopieren heißt auch: duplizieren, Redundanz erzeugen), sondern er setzt in der Zielapplikation lediglich einen Verweis auf die BibDB-Artikel-Identnummer des Titels. Im weiteren Verlauf der Verarbeitung werden dann bei der Zielapplikation jeweils die entsprechenden Strukturteile aus der BibDB zugespielt; in der Lexikonsubstanz selbst gibt es gar keine Literarungaben.

weitere Lösungsmöglichkeiten

Ein Vorteil dieses Verfahrens wäre, dass Aktualisierungen und Korrekturen immer für alle Applikationen zum gleichen Zeitpunkt automatisch wirksam wären. Ein aktives Nachführen einer Aktualisierung durch den Bibliographiebearbeiter, Zielapplikation für Zielapplikation, könnte entfallen.

Das klingt freilich gut, allerdings kann man sich auch Gründe vorstellen, diesen Vorteil nicht nutzen zu wollen. Zum einen macht ein solches Vorgehen sicher die technische Bewältigung der Umfangskontrolle in den Zielapplikationen komplizierter. Zum anderen ist nachvollziehbar, dass der Bearbeiter eines Lexikonartikels diesen gerne komplett vor sich haben möchte, inklusive der Literaturangaben. Ein solches Verfahren setzt außerdem voraus, dass Literaturangaben in jedem der verschiedenen Lexika in immer der gleichen Art und Weise zitiert werden; das ist aber redaktionell wie auch marketingtechnisch nicht gewünscht. Weiterhin kann diese Methode nur für die Literaturanhänge, nicht für die Zitate im laufenden Text eines Artikels eingesetzt werden. Auf Literaturangaben im Fließtext muss der Lexikonbearbeiter ja direkt schreibend zugreifen können, sonst kann er seinen Text in der Weise, wie er es möchte, nicht verfassen.

Diese Schwierigkeiten wären technisch sicher alle in den Griff zu bekommen – fragt sich nur, zu welchen ökonomischen Bedingungen. Gleiches gälte auch für Veränderungen im Workflow und die Auswirkungen auf die Tätigkeit der Lexikonredakteure einerseits und der Bibliographiebearbeiter auf der anderen Seite. All diese Einwände bedeuten aber nicht, dass die oben angerissene Vision nicht zumindest konzeptionell erörtert werden sollte. Die denkbare Anwendbarkeit liegt vielleicht irgendwo in der Mitte.

wichtiger Faktor: ökonomische Bedingungen

8 Zusatzinformationen in den Containern

Alle Zusatzinformationen, die man sich, übrigens nicht nur als Bibliograph, zu einer Literaturangabe denken und wünschen kann, die im Lexikon aber nichts verloren haben, werden im Containerteil abgelegt.

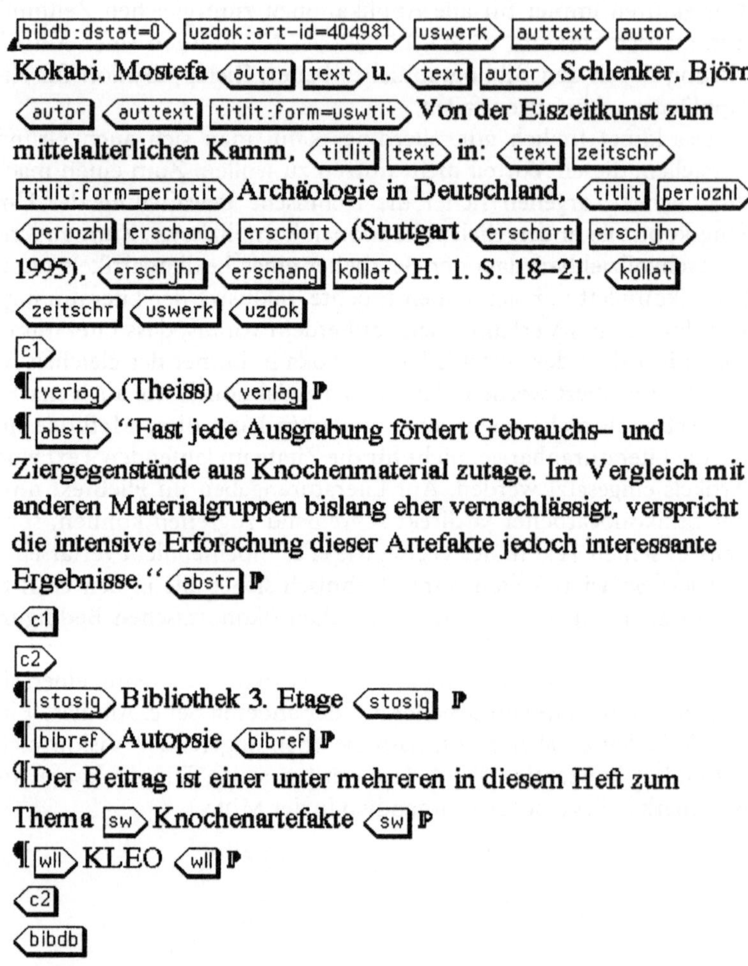

Abbildung 4
Dokumentstruktur für ein unselbständiges Werk aus einem periodischen Werk

Aufbau des Containerteils

Klammerelemente mit den Namen c1, c2 und c3 (vgl. Abbildung 4) stehen für die drei implementierten Container. Sie können wiederum Unterelemente beinhalten, müssen es aber nicht. Sie bieten zudem die Möglichkeit, beliebig *plain text* einzugeben. Welche Art der Information in welchem Container abgelegt wird, kann bei der definitionsgemäßen Gleichartigkeit dieser drei Elemente nicht in der Struktur selbst festgelegt sein. Dies ist auch nicht nötig. Es ist viel weniger geheimnisvoll: Die Mitarbeiter der für die BibDB zuständigen Arbeitsgruppe haben vereinbart, welche Art von Informationen in welchen Container eingetragen wird.

In Container 1 (`c1`) werden zusätzliche bibliographische Informationen abgelegt. Sie helfen dem Bearbeiter, ein Zitat näher zu beurteilen. Oft enthält `c1` auch hilfreiche weiterführende Hinweise, auch Klartextkommentare.

Container 2 (`c2`) beinhaltet im Wesentlichen allgemeine Erschließungsinformationen. Dazu gehören etwa für literarische Werke die Zuordnung zu einer Gattung wie Lyrik, Drama, Hörspiel, die Angabe einer bibliographischen Referenz, mit deren Hilfe ein Zitat verifiziert wurde, Schlagwörter usw.

Container 3 (`c3`) ist für die Aufnahme (noch) nicht verifizierter oder fraglicher Daten vorgesehen. Sobald die unsicheren Daten geklärt sind, wandern sie in Container 1 oder 2. Der Container 3 hat dann keine Funktion mehr und wird gelöscht.

Die Elemente sind weitgehend mit sprechenden Kürzeln versehen. Als Beispiele seien genannt `autor` für Autor, `titlit` für *Titel* einer *Literatur*angabe, `erschort` für *Ersch*einungs*ort*, `sw` für *S*chlag*w*ort, `stosig` für *Sto*ndort/*Sig*natur.

8.1 Erweiterung der Aussagefähigkeit von Elementen mit Hilfe von Attributen

Durch Attribute kann man einem Element unterschiedliche Eigenschaften bzw. Bedeutungsnuancen zuweisen. Das `<autor>`-Tag soll als Beispiel dafür dienen, dass in namhaftem Umfang Attribute eingesetzt werden, um die Strukturierung der Daten zu verfeinern. Die Verwendung jeweils eigener Elemente für alle denkbaren Formen einer Autorenschaft, wie z.B. echter Verfasser, Mitverfasser, Herausgeber, Bearbeiter, Beitragender, Übersetzer, Illustrator führt die Anzahl der Elemente rasch ins Uferlose. Eleganter ist es, alle diese Formen der Urheberschaft schlicht als Autorenschaft zu sehen, und die einzelnen Typen durch Attribute zu charakterisieren. Auch pseudonym gebrauchte Namen können auf diese Weise gekennzeichnet werden. Wenn es sich um einen körperschaftlichen Urheber handelt, kann auch dies ausgedrückt werden.

Differenzierung durch Attribute

Attribute können außerdem bei der Recherche nutzbar gemacht werden, indem man mit ihnen das gesuchte Element näher spezifiziert, also nicht nur das Element selbst, sondern auch das jeweilige Attribut sucht (z. B.: Autor vom Typ Herausgeber).

Schließlich können Attribute auch genutzt werden, um den Formatierern (Editor, Satzprogramm) mitzuteilen, wie der Inhalt eines Elements typographisch ausgegeben werden soll.

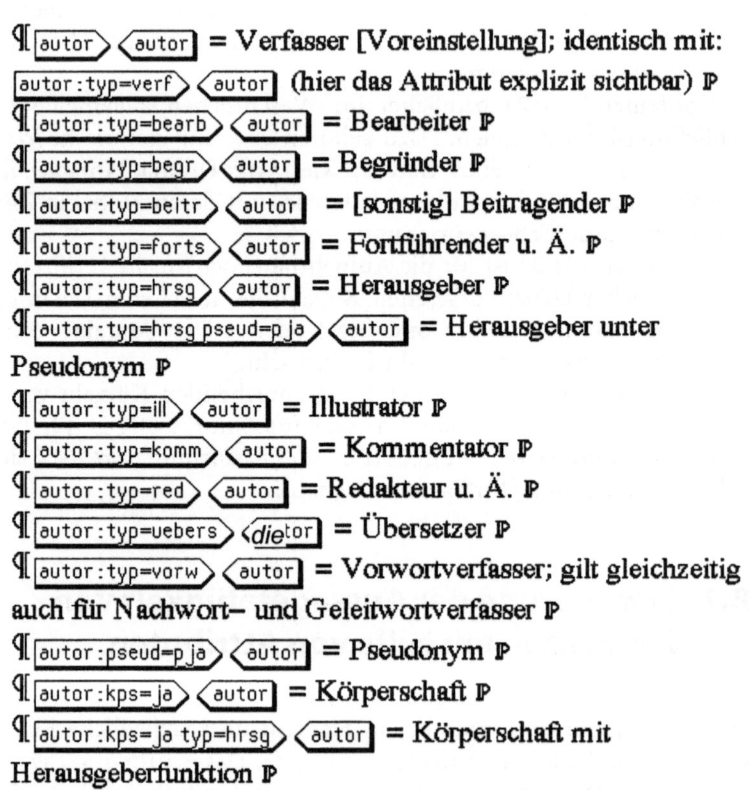

Abbildung 5
Beispiele für Eigenschaften, die das Element autor mit Hilfe von Attributen annehmen kann

8.2 Preview-Funktion

Der Editor bietet dem Bearbeiter eine Vorschaufunktion, ein sog. *Preview*, mit dessen Hilfe der Überblick über den Inhalt eines Dokuments besser gelingt. Um dies zu erreichen, werden zum einen die Tags ausgeblendet (vgl. Abbildungen 6 und 7), zum anderen diejenigen Attribute in den Elementen ausgewertet, die typographische Auswirkungen nach sich ziehen. Einem Autor des Typs Herausgeber kann man auf diese Weise für die Schriftformatierung die Groteske, einer Körperschaft die Grundschrift zuweisen. In anderen Fällen ist die *Kursive* oder die **Halbfette** gewählt.

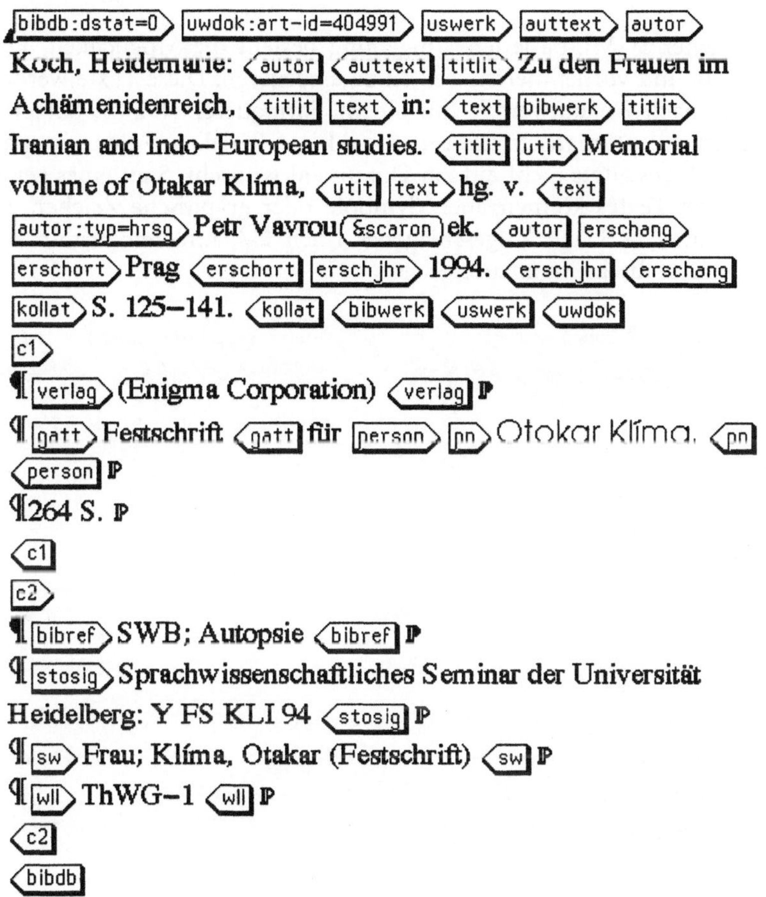

Abbildung 6
Dokumentstruktur für ein unselbständiges Werk aus einem selbständigen Werk

Für die spätere Verarbeitung im Satzprogramm sind die Umsetzungen des Editor-Previews jedoch ohne Bedeutung. Sie wirken nur auf die Bildschirm- bzw. Hardcopy-Ausgabe. Die für den Druck maßgeblichen typographischen Festlegungen werden erst durch das Satzprogramm vorgegeben. Das Ergebnis des Previews ist daher nicht identisch mit dem Endergebnis, welches sich aus der exakt gerech-

Preview als Simulation des Endergebnisses

neten Satzaufbereitung ergibt. Für die Aufgaben des Redakteurs reichen aber die Funktionen des Editor-Previews.

8.3 Generierte Texte

In einer SGML-basierten Umgebung besteht die Möglichkeit, Elemente mit vordefinierten Texten zu assoziieren. Diese Texte werden – je nach Defaultwert – von einem Formatierer (Editor, Satzprogramm) automatisch erzeugt, sobald der Redakteur eine typographisch gestaltete Sicht auf ein Dokument wünscht. Statt eines generierten Textes können auch Symbole oder graphische Zeichen erscheinen (z.B. ein aufgeschlagenes Buch 📖, um den Beginn des Literaturabschnitts anzuzeigen).

Die Verwendung derart automatisch erzeugter Dokumentteile ist sinnvoll, wenn man innerhalb einer Applikation immer die selben Textbausteine in immer der gleichen Art und Weise darstellen, aber nicht jedesmal neu schreiben möchte. So verhindert man auch, dass sie Bestandteil der eigentlichen Datensubstanz werden. Denn in einer anderen Applikation will man zwar durchaus die selben Daten, aber man will mit den Elementen andere generierte Texte verbinden.

Abbildung 7 zeigt den Inhalt von Abbildung 6 typographisch gestaltet. *Standort/Signatur:* und *Schlagwörter:* sind generierte Texte.

9 Nutzbare Zusatzeffekte der Strukturierung

Die aus den Abbildungen ersichtlichen Beispielinhalte zeigen, dass die BibDB nicht nur für ihre Hauptaufgabe, nämlich die Bereitstellung von Literaturangaben für die Zielapplikationen verwendet werden kann. Zusatznutzen lässt sich aus ihr in mehrfacher Art ziehen:

Zusatznutzen der BibDB

- Sie ist für jeden Redakteur in Bezug auf die Lexikonsubstanzen, aber auch allgemein die erste maßgebliche und direkt an seinem Arbeitsplatz(rechner) erreichbare bibliographische Quelle.

- Sie dient als hausinterner Bibliothekskatalog (mit Hilfe des Elements `stosig`, Standort/Signatur).

- In gleicher Weise informiert sie als eine Art „Verbundkatalog en miniature" mit Hinweisen, aus welchen Bibliotheken Literatur rasch besorgt werden kann, wenn sich das Gesuchte nicht im Hausbestand findet und beim ersten Ausleihvorgang die entsprechenden Daten festgehalten wurden.

- Sie ist abfragbar als Schlagwortkatalog.

- Sie kann mit Hilfe ihrer Container als Volltextspeicher dienen und beispielsweise. Buchrezensionen, Klappentexte und andere Zusatzinformationen beliebiger Art speichern. Diese Informationen können, wenn es als sinnvoll erachtet wird, ebenfalls einer mehr oder weniger tief gehenden Strukturierung unterzogen werden.

- Die Container, deren Inhalte nicht in die Lexikonsubstanzen exportiert werden, erlauben es, Bearbeitungshinweise und sogar Mitteilungen an Kollegen abzulegen; auf diese Weise kann im Dokument selbst eine Korrespondenz über das Dokument innerhalb der Arbeitsgruppe bzw. Redaktion geführt werden.

In der Praxis können aus Kosten- und Kapazitätsgründen natürlich nicht alle diese Möglichkeiten in einheitlicher Weise von vornherein mit Leben erfüllt werden. Wichtig ist aber, dass die Optionen dazu bestehen; denn dann können sie im konkreten Bedarfsfalle aktiviert und genutzt werden.

wichtig: Optionen offenhalten

10 Literaturangaben im Fließtext

Noch offen geblieben ist bis jetzt die Bearbeitung von Literaturangaben im Fließtext. Der Redakteur soll seinen Text formulieren können, ohne durch Literaturzitierregeln eingeengt zu werden. Eine Eins-zu-eins-Umsetzung der festgelegten Strukturen aus der BibDB kann deshalb nicht vorgegeben werden.

Um dennoch die Literaturangaben in der Lexikonsubstanz in strukturierter Weise zur Verfügung zu haben, gibt es auf der Seite der Zielapplikationen ein Klammerelement, das seinerseits Elemente der BibDB aufnehmen kann. Innerhalb dieser Klammer ist die Anordnung der bibliographischen Tags nicht wie in den Literaturabschnitten und der BibDB festgelegt, sondern frei wählbar. Um die Elemente herum kann der Redakteur seinen Text schreiben. Zwei Ziele werden somit erreicht:

- Der Lexikonredakteur kommt zu seinem Recht, den Text nach seinen Vorstellungen formulieren zu können, ohne auf die „Grammatik" der bibliographischen Strukturen Rücksicht nehmen zu müssen.

- Der Bibliographieredakteur erreicht den Zweck, dass auch im Fließtext vorkommende Literaturangaben bibliographisch strukturiert sind – und nicht als *plain text* von den Tausenden Textzeilen aufgesogen werden.

11 Metadaten

Alle Daten im Redaktionssystem müssen auch verwaltet werden. Die Dokumente einer Lexikonapplikation sind nicht Selbstzweck in Form alleinigen Datenbankdaseins; mit ihnen soll etwas geschehen. Wenn der Zeitpunkt gekommen ist, sollen die Inhalte der Datenbanken an ein Satzsystem weitergereicht werden. Daneben gibt es zahlreiche Anlässe und Fragestellungen statistischer Art, denen die Substanzen unterworfen werden sollen.

Zu diesem Zweck gibt es die Möglichkeit, Metainformationen mit Hilfe des sog. Planungsteils verfügbar zu machen. Ein solcher Planungsteil existiert zu jedem einzelnen Dokument einer Applikation. Er ist nicht Bestandteil des Dokumentinhalts, sondern er bildet einen Dokumentbestandteil bzw. -annex auf der Metaebene. Hier werden alle Verwaltungsinformationen *über* die Dokumente der Datenbank festgehalten. Die Verwaltung dieser Metadaten geschieht dynamisch, d.h., sie sind auf den Einzelfall bezogen immer aktuell.

Beispiele für einfache Planungsteilfelder sind: Anzahl der Zeichen, die ein Dokument enthält, Datum der Erstellung, Datum der letzten Änderung. Felder dieser Art können vom System automatisch mit Inhalt gefüllt werden.

Eine andere Art von Feldern enthält Codes. Auf diese Weise können z.B. alle Dokumente, die einen bestimmten Code tragen, von einem Bearbeiter zu einem beliebigen Zeitpunkt gezielt auf der Metaebene recherchiert werden, ohne dass er etwas über den konkreten Inhalt der einzelnen Dokumente wissen muss. Beispiel hierfür ist ein Aktualisierungscode, mit dessen Hilfe alle Dokumente aufgefunden werden können, die nach Ablauf einer bestimmten Zeitspanne einer Nachbearbeitung unterzogen werden sollen. *Retrievalhilfe*

Der Aktualisierungscode wird von den Redakteuren in den Planungsteil der betreffenden Artikel eingetragen; anders als Datum und Zeichenumfang, die vom System hinzugefügt werden, muss eine solche Information aktiv eingebracht werden. Ebenso verhält es sich mit dem Code namens *Bibliographiestatus*, den die Bibliographieredakteure im Planungsmanager setzen, um kenntlich zu machen, dass sie mit ihrer Arbeit fertig sind, also der Hinzufügung der Literaturabschnitte und der Strukturierung der Literaturangaben im Fließtext.

Von großer Wichtigkeit ist der Planungsteil für die Produktions-, also die Lexikondatenbanken. Je nach Zielsetzung verfügt jede Lexikonapplikation über einen eigenen Planungsmanager, der Datenfelder in unterschiedlicher Art und Anzahl bereitstellt. Allen Planungsmanagern gemeinsam sind jedoch Felder, mit denen der Bearbeitungsstatus eines jeden Dokuments festgehalten und aktualisiert wird. Der Projektleiter eines Lexikons wird dadurch in die Lage versetzt, an einem Stichtag alle Dokumente der Datenbank, die z.B. in der Stichwortstrecke *Orthopraxie* bis *Ostkirchen* liegen, für die redaktionelle Bearbeitung zu sperren, indem er sie mit einem anderen Status versieht. Die Textstrecke, kenntlich am veränderten Status, steht schließlich für die Übergabe an ein Satzprogramm bereit. *Information für die Produktionsdatenbanken*

Es ist schon gefallen: Die Bibliographische Datenbank schlägt als Referenzdatenbank etwas aus der Art. So auch für die Metadaten. Solange nicht daran gedacht wird, ein eigenes Produkt aus den Dokumenten der BibDB herzustellen, genügt es, den Einsatzbereich des Planungsteils auf statistische Felder und einige wenige Codes zu beschränken.

für viele Fälle
gerüstet

Wenn man allerdings daran denkt, nicht nur indirekt, sondern auch direkt aus der BibDB ein Produkt abzuleiten – sei es eine CD-ROM oder eine Online-Anwendung – so wird man auch hier den Planungsteil entsprechend gestalten müssen. Die berühmten Schubladen jedenfalls, in denen man seine Ideen für die passende Gelegenheit aufbewahrt, sind mit Blick auf eine solche Entwicklung der Dinge nicht leer.

Literatur

(Eversberg 1998)
> Eversberg, B.: Was sind und was sollen Bibliothekarische Datenformate. o. O., 1998. Erhältlich im Internet:
> http://www.biblio-tu-bs.de/allegro/formate/index.htm

(Leuser/Tscheke 1996)
> Leuser, M.; Tscheke, T.: Daten unabhängig und langfristig erhalten. In: Börsenblatt für den Deutschen Buchhandel (1996), Nr. 35, S. 156-158

Realisierung eines SGML-basierten Publikationsprozesses im Verlag: kritische Anmerkungen

Marion Spengler

1 Einführung

Viele Verlage haben inzwischen erkannt, daß die Anwendung von SGML sinnvoll ist und einige bestehende Probleme in Publikationsprozessen lösen kann. Als eine große Stärke der Nutzung von SGML gilt dabei, daß mit einem kontrollierten Datenbestand möglichst automatisch eine Vielzahl unterschiedlicher Produkte erstellt werden kann.

Für den Einsatz von SGML im Verlagsbereich werden noch viele andere Gründe genannt, die häufig anhand eines einfachen Publikationsmodells (Abbildung 1) illustriert werden, so beispielsweise bei Maler/El Andaloussi (1996) oder Ensign (1997).

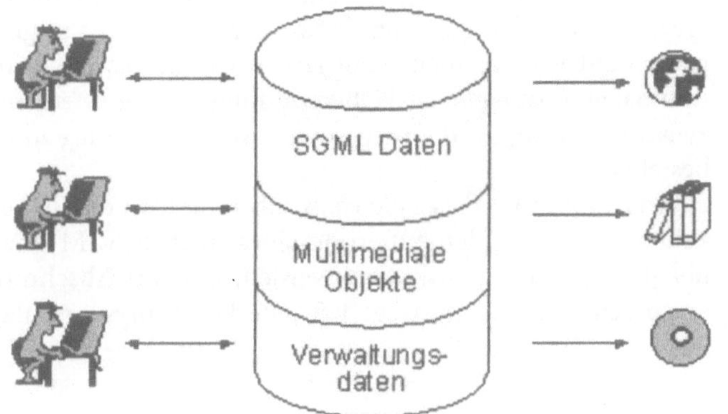

Abbildung 1
Vereinfachtes Modell für einen SGML-basierten Publikations-prozeß

SGML-basierte
Produktion:
Vorteile

Es wird argumentiert, daß die Vorteile eines solchen Produktionsprozesses in den folgenden Punkten liegen:

- *flexible Mehrfachnutzung*, d.h. die Wiederverwendung eines zentralen Datenbestandes für vielfältige Produkte

- *die Möglichkeit, elektronische Publikationen und gedruckte Produkte parallel herzustellen*
  Dies bedeutet, daß das Elektronische Publizieren kein nachgelagerter und verzögerter Prozeß mehr sein muß, was insbesondere für Online-Produkte interessant wird.

- *die Verringerung der Produktionskosten und -zeiten für alle Produkttypen durch höhere Automation*
  Der Aufwand der inhaltlichen Aufbereitung wird im Prozeß nach vorne verlagert und ist damit Basis für eine automatisierte Produkterstellung.

- *die Verbesserung der Qualität und Konsistenz der Daten in allen Produkttypen*
  Die Struktur der Publikationen wird von Beginn an durch DTDs kontrolliert. Durch die automatisierte Zuordnung der Strukturelemente zu ihren Layoutdefinitionen wird die Darstellung gesteuert und einheitlich.

- *die Kostenersparnis für die Konvertierung proprietärer Datenformate bei jeder Umstellung des Produktionssystems*
  Durch die Verwendung von SGML wird Systemunabhängigkeit erreicht.

- *die Verbesserung des internen Zugriffs, der Verwaltung und Kontrolle aller Daten*

keine optimalen
Lösungen

Die meisten der bereits bestehenden SGML-Anwendungen sind jedoch nicht optimal für den gesamten Produktionsprozeß implementiert, d.h. sie nutzen die Vorteile von SGML nicht vollständig aus. Die Mehrfachnutzung eines SGML-Datenbestandes für die Herstellung vielfältiger Publikationstypen ist selbst in großen Verlagen so gut wie gar nicht realisiert. Auch gibt es noch immer keine optimalen Lösungen zur Überwindung einiger Medienbrüche, die zwischen Autor und Verlag sowie zwischen Verlag und Druckerei bestehen.

Im Abschnitt 2 dieses Beitrags sollen deshalb mögliche Schwierigkeiten bei der Implementierung eines solchen SGML-basierten Publikationsprozesses diskutiert werden, und im Abschnitt 3 werden entsprechende Lösungswege bzw. Verbesserungsvorschläge angeboten.

2 Implementierungsschwierigkeiten von SGML im Verlag

Die in diesem Abschnitt beschriebenen Schwierigkeiten konzentrieren sich im wesentlichen auf die Bereiche der eigentlichen Produktherstellung innerhalb eines Verlages. Auf die zahlreichen Probleme, die mit dem Thema der Datenübernahme von externen Autoren und mit der Konvertierung nach SGML beim Dateninput verbunden sind, wird nur hingewiesen.

2.1 Seitenumbruch bei der redaktionellen Arbeit

Neben der redaktionellen Arbeit mit den Inhalten besteht insbesondere bei Zeitungs- und Zeitschriftenverlagen eine wichtige Aufgabe der Redakteure darin, Dokumente so zu bearbeiten, daß sie in ein vorgegebenes Layout passen. Dies ist für elektronische Produkte i.d.R. nicht relevant, aber bei Druckerzeugnissen mit vorgegebenen Text- und Anzeigenbereichen wichtig.

Für den Produktionsprozeß bedeutet dies, daß Redakteure keineswegs nur in der logischen Struktur und damit unabhängig vom Layout arbeiten können, sondern daß sie permanent auf Layout- und andere Begrenzungen wie beispielsweise Seitenumbrüche achten und reagieren müssen. Dazu benötigen sie Werkzeuge, die das endgültig gewünschte Layout schon im Bearbeitungsstadium erzeugen können. Die derzeit am Markt erhältlichen SGML-Editoren haben jedoch nur unzureichende Layout-Funktionalitäten, die lediglich dazu dienen sollen, die Bildschirmansicht übersichtlicher zu gestalten, aber nicht in der Lage sind, den endgültigen Umbruch zu erzeugen oder zu simulieren.

2.2 Produktherstellung ist keine Einbahnstraße

In den grafischen Darstellungen des modellhaften Produktionsprozesses wird der Weg von der zentralen Datenbasis zum jeweiligen Produkt meist nur in eine Richtung dargestellt (s. Abbildung 1). Für die Realität ist ein solches Modell aber nicht immer zutreffend.

Elektronische Produkte sind nicht immer autark, d.h. vollständig unabhängig von den gedruckten Äquivalenten. Häufig müssen noch Erscheinungsdaten bzw. Quellenangaben der entsprechenden gedruckten Publikation sowie z.B. bei Loseblatt-Werken und juristischen Zeitschriften auch Seitenumbruchinformationen in Online-Datenbanken oder CD-ROM-Anwendungen mit verzeichnet sein. Dies bedeutet, daß solche Informationen auch in den SGML-Datenbestand nach der Imprimatur bzw. Drucklegung zurückgeschrieben werden müssen, damit sie für die Herstellung elektronischer Produkte zur Verfügung stehen. Ein Produktionsprozeß, der vorsieht, daß aus einem Datenbestand alle Produkte parallel hergestellt werden, ist in solchen Fällen nicht realisierbar.

2.3 Nachträgliche Korrekturen im fertigen Produkt

Häufig kommt es vor, daß in einem fertig formatierten Produkt oder auch bei den Testversionen eines elektronischen Produktes „in letzter Sekunde" noch inhaltliche Fehler bzw. Rechtschreibfehler auffallen und entsprechende Korrekturen vorgenommen werden müssen. Damit alle anderen Produkte auch davon profitieren können, müssen diese Korrekturen in den zentralen SGML-Datenbestand einfließen. Dies ist jedoch häufig nicht so einfach, wie man vielleicht denken mag.

- Die Erzeugung von Produkten aus dem SGML-Bestand ist nicht immer voll automatisiert, sondern insbesondere bei hohen Layoutanforderungen mit manuellen Eingriffen im jeweiligen Produktionssystem verbunden. Das heißt, daß man die Korrekturen nicht im zentralen Datenbestand vornehmen und auf Knopfdruck das Produkt neu erzeugen kann. Vielmehr ist es meist so, daß die SGML-Daten zwar in das proprietäre Format des jeweiligen Produktionssystems überführt werden, daß dort aber noch sowohl Layout- als auch inhaltliche Korrekturen vorgenommen werden. Teilweise werden sogar die Postscript-Daten noch geändert.

- Die meisten Satzsysteme und auch Anwendungsprogramme für elektronische Produkte sind nicht in der Lage, die Daten auch wieder im SGML-Format zu exportieren, so daß Korrekturen, die in diesen Systemen durchgeführt wurden, nicht automatisch wieder in den zentralen Datenbestand zurückgeschrieben werden können.

- Die aufgrund dieser Korrekturen häufig notwendige manuelle Nachbesserung der Korrekturen im zentralen Datenbestand bedeutet doppelten Aufwand und ist natürlich auch sehr fehleranfällig.

Dies hieße konsequenter Weise, daß – sobald die SGML-Daten einmal in das proprietäre Format des Produktionssystems umgesetzt wurden – eigentlich keine inhaltlichen Änderungen mehr vorgenommen werden dürfen oder daß das System in der Lage sein muß, später korrektes SGML auch wieder zurückzuschreiben.

2.4 Umsetzung von SGML-Daten in gestaltete Produkte

Im Vergleich zur technischen Dokumentation wird insbesondere bei gedruckten Verlagserzeugnissen viel mehr Wert auf das Layout einer Publikation gelegt, da sich u.a. über das Layout Konkurrenzpublikationen voneinander absetzen. Bei der Umstellung des Publikationsprozesses muß deshalb bedacht werden, daß auch ein SGML-basiertes Produktionssystem den bestehenden und zukünftigen Layoutanforderungen gerecht werden muß.

Layout für den Wettbewerb

Will man SGML-strukturierte Daten mehrfach verwenden, so sollte die DTD nicht nach dem Layout eines Produktes definiert sein. Je generischer jedoch die Repräsentation eines Dokumenttyps durch die DTD definiert ist, desto komplexer müssen die Programme sein, die logisch strukturierte SGML-Dokumente automatisch in aufwendig gestaltete Produkte umsetzen können. Ein Großteil der am Markt befindlichen Systeme sind beispielsweise nicht in der Lage, Fußnoten beliebig zu plazieren und zu verwalten. Von der automatischen Formatierung von Tabellen, Formeln, Text-Bild-Integration, Ausrichtung von Text usw. ganz zu schweigen. Auch die Textdarstellung in elektronischen Produkten läßt vielfach zu wünschen übrig, da beispielsweise nur selten Algorithmen verwendet werden, die ästhetische Zeilenumbrüche und Zeichenabstände darstellen können (*H&J: hyphenation and justification*).

hohe Anforderungen an Produktionssysteme

Auch die für einen SGML-basierten Publikationsprozeß propagierte Systemunabhängigkeit sei hier in Frage gestellt, weil die jeweiligen Methoden der Umsetzungen von SGML-Daten in Produkte nicht standardisiert sind und somit langfristig auch schwierig zu pflegen sind. In der Realität hat jedes auf dem Markt befindliche Produktionssystem seine eigene Sprache für die Definition von Stylesheets. Diese Sprache muß zunächst erlernt werden, und bei

fehlende Standardisierung

neuen Versionen eines Systems müssen die Stylesheets häufig angepaßt werden. Komfortablere Anwendungen stellen einen Stylesheet-
Editor mit grafischer Benutzeroberfläche zur Verfügung. Dies ändert
allerdings nichts an der Tatsache, daß ein Wechsel des Produktionssystems trotz Nutzung von SGML häufig aufwendig bleibt.

2.5 Zentrale Verwaltung der Daten

echnisches und inhaltliches Know-how

Die Einführung eines zentralen Datenbanksystems oder eines zentralen Dateiverwaltungssystems kann schwierig sein, schon weil zunächst geklärt werden muß, welcher Verlagsbereich (Redaktion,
Lektorat, Herstellung, Satz oder EDV-Abteilung) ein solches System
auswählen, integrieren und betreuen soll. Bei diesen Tätigkeiten ist
eine enge Verbindung von technischem und inhaltlichem Know-
how sehr wichtig, aber oft schwer zu realisieren.

Anforderungen an die Technik

Neben der Frage der Zuständigkeiten sind natürlich vor allem die
Fragen bezüglich der Funktionalität des benötigten Systems zu beantworten. Wenn sich der Verlag nicht frühzeitig darüber im klaren
ist, welche Anforderungen beim Umgang mit den Daten bestehen,
kann sich die Entscheidung über die richtige Strategie und das richtige System lange hinziehen. Dies fängt bei der Entscheidung an, ob
das Dateisystem zur Verwaltung der Daten ausreicht. Wenn man
sich für ein Datenbanksystem entscheidet, geht es weiter bei der
Betrachtung der unterschiedlichen Philosophien der Datenbank-
technologie und Datenstrukturierung: relational oder objektorientiert oder eine Mischung aus beidem. Performanz, Einfachheit der
Abfrage- und Auswertungssprache sowie Pflegbarkeit der Datenbank
und die speziellen Anforderungen im Zusammenhang mit der Nutzung von SGML (Sicherstellung der DTD-Konformität, Entity-
Management usw.) sind weitere Punkte, die geklärt werden müssen.

Anforderungen an die Nutzung

Bei diesen Entscheidungsprozessen müssen neben den technischen Anforderungen auch die Belange der späteren Anwender berücksichtigt werden. Das Umdenken, das den Mitarbeitern beim
Wechsel vom gedruckten Manuskript zur Datei abgefordert wird, ist
weniger einschneidend als der Sprung von einer Datei zur Datenbank. Bei unzureichendem Einblick in die Funktionsweise einer
Technologie kann leicht der Eindruck entstehen, daß man weniger
Kontrolle über die Dokumente hat statt mehr. Bei zunehmender
Speicherung von Zugriffsdaten, Bearbeitungsdaten wie z.B. Korrek-
turvolumina, kann der Eindruck entstehen, daß eine stärkere Kontrolle über die Mitarbeiter ausgeübt wird. Hier kann es zu Problemen kommen, wenn nicht frühzeitig über spezifisch vorgegebene

Zugriffsrechte nachgedacht und möglicherweise auch Datenschutz-
berater und Betriebsrat eingeschaltet werden.

2.6 Verwaltung der DTDs und Stylesheets

In einem integrierten Publikationsprozeß zur parallelen Herstellung
verschiedener Produkte aus einem Datenbestand ist nicht nur die
Verwaltung der Daten wichtig, sondern auch die Verwaltung der
damit verbundenen DTDs und den dazugehörigen Stylesheets. Diese
Verwaltung wird erschwert, wenn jeweils verschiedene Versionen
dieser Regelwerke vorhanden sind.

Einsatz von DTD-Varianten

- Für einen SGML-basierten Publikationsprozeß im Verlag werden meist mehrere Dokumenttypen definiert, da Zeitschriften
  oder Bücher ganz unterschiedliche Arten von Beiträgen enthalten. Es ist nicht immer ratsam, komplexe und umfangreiche
  Werke mit nur einer DTD zu beschreiben, weil sonst auch die
  Dokumentinstanzen zu groß werden. *Beispiel*: Buch.DTD, Arti-
  kel.DTD

- In der Regel haben verschiedene Produkte unterschiedliche
  Strukturen und Inhalte, z.B. können bei elektronischen Pro-
  dukten verschiedene multimediale Bestandteile vorkommen.
  Beispiel: Internet.DTD, CDROM.DTD

- Tiefe und Umfang der Strukturierung und Auszeichnung kann
  im laufenden Prozeß von Bearbeitungsschritt zu Bearbeitungsschritt variieren. Viele Dokumente werden von ihrer Entstehung
  bis zur Veröffentlichung an verschiedenen Stellen unterschiedlich angereichert. *Beispiel*: Erfassungs.DTD, Produktions.DTD

Für diese Fälle wird häufig eine Sammlung von DTD- und entsprechenden Stylesheet-Modulen aufgebaut, die jeweils nur bestimmte
Elemente oder Elementgruppen definieren. Diese Module werden
dann für verschiedene Stadien und Produkttypen individuell zu-
sammengebunden. Dabei empfiehlt es sich, jeweils ein Modul für
jeden Typ zu bilden und Elemente, die in verschiedenen Modulen
vorkommen, in einem gemeinsamen Modul zu sammeln, das von
den anderen referenziert wird (Abbildung 2).

DTD- und Stylesheet-Module

   Zur Verwaltung verschiedener Varianten eines Elementes in verschiedenen Produkttypen oder Bearbeitungsstadien werden oft *Marked Sections* benutzt, um Deklarationen in DTDs beliebig „ein- und
auszuschalten" (Maler/El Andaloussi 1996).

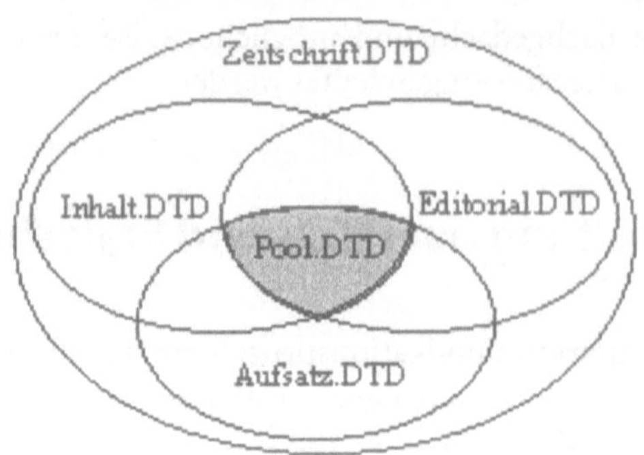

Abbildung 2
DTD-Module für
eine Zeitschrift

Neben verschiedenen Produktvarianten und Produktionsstadien, kann es auch langfristig gesehen zu verschiedenen DTD- und Stylesheet-Versionen kommen:

- Produktanforderungen und Quellen verändern sich im Laufe der Zeit, so daß sich auch DTDs und Stylesheets ändern müssen. Dies kann zur Folge haben, daß ältere Dokument-Instanzen mit den aktuell geänderten DTDs nicht mehr konform sind. Grundsätzlich sollte man darauf achten, daß Änderungen rückwärts kompatibel sind, aber das läßt sich bei gravierenden Veränderungen der Produktstruktur nicht immer sicherstellen. *Beispiel*: Version1.DTD, Version2.DTD

- Größere Alt-Datenbestände, die nach SGML konvertiert wurden, sind zum Teil durch die mit der Konvertierung verbundenen Schwierigkeiten nicht so stark strukturiert wie die aktuell erzeugten SGML-Daten. *Beispiel*: AltDaten.DTD, Aktuell.DTD

Systeme für die DTD-Verwaltung sind nötig

In beiden Fällen kann es Schwierigkeiten bereiten, Überblick über die einzelnen DTDs und Stylesheets bzw. deren Module zu behalten. Es ist insbesondere bei komplexen DTDs notwendig, einen effizienten Mechanismus zur Verwaltung der Module zu haben, so daß die Abhängigkeiten zwischen den Modulen immer deutlich sind und kontrolliert werden können. Sonst können beispielsweise Änderungen oder Löschungen von Elementen in einem Modul zu unerwünschten Effekten in einem anderen Modul führen. Ein ausgeklügeltes System zur Dokumentation der DTDs und der Änderungen ist notwendig, insbesondere wenn die Verantwortung für die DTDs bei mehreren Personen liegt oder wechselt. Dedizierte Systeme für diese Verwaltungsaufgaben haben sich allerdings bisher auf dem Markt nicht durchgesetzt.

2.7 Kosten-Nutzen-Kalkulation

Es ist für Verlage häufig sehr schwierig einzuschätzen, ob sich die
Umstellung auf einen SGML-basierten Publikationsprozeß finanziell
auch rechnet. Da es noch wenige Erfahrungen auf diesem Gebiet gibt
und diese in der Regel auch nicht publik werden, ist es nur schwer zu
beurteilen, wie hoch die Kosten einer solchen Umstellung sein können und wo die Einsparungen genau liegen. Systemkosten oder
Konvertierungskosten lassen sich noch relativ leicht ermitteln, aber
Kosten und Einsparungen, die mit den Veränderungen im Arbeits-
aufwand und -ablauf von Autoren oder Redakteuren zu tun haben,
sind schwerer zu kalkulieren. Auch läßt sich nur schwer vorhersagen,
wie stark tatsächlich der Umsatz steigt, weil grundsätzlich die Möglichkeit besteht, neuartige Produkte flexibler zu erstellen. Aus diesem
Grund werden in der Regel zunächst nur die Prozesse umgestellt, die
in der kürzesten Zeit den größtmöglichen *return on investment* erwarten lassen, und das ist betrifft vielfach die eigentliche Herstellung
bestimmter Produkte. Der redaktionelle Prozeß bleibt im wesentlichen unberührt.

3   Es gibt noch viel zu tun ...

Die oben aufgeführten Punkte sollen nicht den Eindruck erwecken,
daß der Realisierung eines SGML-basierten Publikationsprozesses in
einem Verlag nur Barrieren im Weg stehen. Sie sollen jedoch auf
mögliche Hindernisse hinweisen, denn nur wenn diese im Vorfeld
erkannt werden, können verlagsspezifische effiziente Strategien zur
Einführung von SGML entwickelt werden.

Es gibt natürlich eine Reihe von Lösungsansätzen und verschiedene positive Beispiele von SGML-Einführungen bei Verlagen. Im
Zusammenhang mit den im vorherigen Abschnitt beschriebenen
Schwierigkeiten fällt jedoch auf, daß insbesondere die derzeit verfügbaren Redaktions- und Produktionssysteme noch erweitert und
verbessert werden müssen, um eine SGML-basierte Produktion
effizienter zu ermöglichen.

SGML-basierte *Redaktionssysteme* zur Bearbeitung und Verwaltung der Dokumente sollten

- verschiedene Standard-Systeme für die Erstellung, Bearbeitung
  und Produktion mit einem zentralen Datenverwaltungssystem
  so integrieren, daß Redakteure sowohl mit „einfachen" SGML-
  Editoren als auch in fertig umbrochenen Seiten bzw. elektroni-

schen Prototypen noch Korrekturen vornehmen und jederzeit
Überblick über den Dokumentenstatus behalten können (Walter 1997). Diese Integration sollte mit flexiblen und standardisierten Methoden erfolgen, die es den Anwendern erlauben, eigenständig Systeme einzubinden oder zu entfernen.

- neben den Daten auch eine integrierte Verwaltung der DTDs, der Stylesheets und der Transformationsprogramme anbieten. Sie sollten Systeme beinhalten, die Versionsverwaltung und Dokumentation dieser Regelwerke unterstützen, anzeigen wie Module miteinander verknüpft sind und wo welche Elemente verwendet werden. Dies sollte integriert mit den eigentlichen Daten erfolgen, so daß man beispielsweise den Überblick darüber behält, welche Elemente bei bestimmten DTD-Versionen nicht mehr valide sind.

Produktions-
systeme

SGML-basierte *Produktionssysteme* zur Herstellung verschiedener Produktvarianten sollten

- entweder direkt auf SGML aufsetzen, anstatt proprietäre Formate zu nutzen, oder zumindest nach der Bearbeitung korrekte SGML-Daten exportieren können.

- viel mehr Funktionalität und Flexibilität für die automatisierte Formatierung anbieten. Dieser Bereich ist im Zuge der Desktop-Publishing-Welle, die seit Jahren vorherrscht, leider stark vernachlässigt worden. Systeme wie einst TeX könnten da wieder Vorbild sein.

- standardisierte und flexiblere Methoden zur Generierung von Produkten aus SGML-Daten anbieten. Sicher würde SGML weiter verbreitet sein, wenn der Standard DSSSL (Document Style Semantics and Specification Language – ISO/IEC 10179: 1996) früher existiert hätte und implementiert worden wäre. Erst wenn auch die Verbindung von strukturierten Daten zum fertigen Produkt standardisiert ist, werden wir vollständige Systemunabhängigkeit erreicht haben.

Zudem bestehen zusätzlich zu den Anforderungen an die derzeit verfügbaren Systeme natürlich auch Verbesserungsvorschläge zu der Art und Weise, wie SGML in den Verlagen implementiert wird.

- Die Möglichkeiten zur effektiven Umsetzung von SGML-Daten für Produkte ist oft stark davon abhängig, wie die Daten strukturiert sind bzw. wie sie in der DTD abgebildet wurden. Bei der Entwicklung von DTDs sollte man frühzeitig sowohl die Druck- als auch die elektronischen Produkte berücksichtigen. Es sollte vermieden werden, bei der Dokumentanalyse und Konzeption nur einen Produkttyp in Betracht zu ziehen.

- Eine detailliertere SGML-Auszeichnung von Dokumenten erlaubt eine höhere Automatisierung bei der Produktion, bedeutet
  aber auch höheren Aufwand bei der Erstellung der Dokumente.
  Um hier den geeigneten Mittelweg zu finden, sollte die Definition der Produktanforderungen, Dokument-Analyse und DTD-
  Entwicklungsarbeit intensiv betrieben werden. Zusätzliche Arbeit, die an dieser Stelle investiert wird, zahlt sich immer aus.

- Grundlegende Veränderung der Publikationsprozesse, wie sie
  hier dargestellt wurden, setzen natürlich meist auch Veränderungen in den Arbeitsabläufen und Verantwortungsbereichen
  verschiedener Mitarbeiter voraus. Dies ist ein wichtiger Punkt,
  der sorgfältig geplant und behandelt werden muß und deshalb
  nicht unerwähnt bleiben soll. Es ist aber eigentlich ein Manage-
  ment-Thema und die weitere Behandlung würde den Rahmen
  dieses Beitrags sprengen.

3.1 Heilsbringer XML!?

Die Schwierigkeiten, die hier beschrieben wurden, liegen zum
Großteil darin, daß die SGML-Gemeinschaft der praxisgerechten,
aber auch standardisierten Umsetzung der SGML-Daten in Produkte
und Anwendungen bisher zuwenig Beachtung geschenkt hat. Echte
Systemunabhängigkeit und flexible Mehrfachverwendung der Daten
sind erst erreicht, wenn nicht nur die Dokument-Formate standardisiert sind, sondern auch die Methoden, mit denen die Daten in den
Anwendungssystemen verarbeitet werden.

standardisierte Umsetzungsmethoden

Die Lösung vieler Probleme in diesem Zusammenhang kommt
möglicherweise mit der *Extensible Markup Language XML* (Bray et
al. 1997). Im Zuge der Entwicklung von XML sind nämlich auch
eine Reihe komplementärer Standards in Arbeit, die sich mit der
Umsetzung von strukturierten Daten in Online-Produkte beschäftigen. Hier seien exemplarisch folgende genannt:

- *XSL (Extensible Style Language)* basiert auf DSSSL und wird zur
  Definition von Stylesheets entwickelt. Mit einem XSL-Stylesheet
  wird definiert, wie XML-Elemente im World Wide Web darzu-
  stellen sind. Auch Definitionen aus bisher im Internet teilweise
  verwendeten sog. *Cascading Style Sheets (CSS)* können in XSL
  integriert werden.

- *XLL (Extensible Linking Language)* bietet mit XLink und XPointer Mechanismen an, mit denen sich XML-Dokumente beliebig
  miteinander zu verknüpfen lassen. XLL geht dabei weit über

HTML hinaus und unterscheidet zwischen einfachen und erweiterten Links. Erweiterte Links können z.B. mehrere Ziele haben oder wahlweise das Zieldokument direkt in das aktuelle Dokument integrieren oder in einem neuen Fenster anzeigen.

- *DOM (Document Object Model)* soll eine neutrale und systemunabhängige Programmierschnittstelle für den Zugriff auf XML- (und HTML-)Daten werden. Standardisiert werden soll die Art und Weise, wie beispielsweise JavaScripts auf den Inhalt, die Struktur und das Layout von XML-Daten zugreifen, Inhalte verändern und je nach Nutzer-Aktion Dokumente dynamisch darstellen (Wood 1998).

Für die Massen-Anwendung World Wide Web sind solche Standards unabdingbar, weil die Programme, die XML-Daten darstellen und verarbeiten, systemunabhängig auf allen Plattformen weltweit nutzbar sein müssen. Es gibt auch bereits einige Systeme, die zumindest bei Online-Produkten relativ flexibel mit Stylesheets umgehen und zusätzlich die Druck-Ausgabe integrieren können. Hieran zeigt sich ein Trend, der zunehmend den Schwerpunkt auf die standardisierte Zuweisung von Formaten und Funktionalitäten zu den Strukturelementen legt.

Nutzung von SGML-Daten mit XML-Systemen

Es bleibt dabei zu hoffen, daß die heutigen und zukünftigen Nutzer von SGML von dieser Bewegung durch die Entwicklung besserer Systeme profitieren können und daß die mit einigem Aufwand aufgebauten SGML-Datenbestände auch mit den neuen XML-Systemen ohne großen Zusatz-Aufwand umgesetzt werden können.

Literatur

(Bray et al. 1997)
Bray, Tim; Paoli, Jean; Sperberg-McQueen, C. M.: Extensible Markup Language (XML). In: XML: Principles, Tools and Techniques. o.O.: O'Reilly & Associates 1997 (World Wide Web Journal, 1997, Bd. 2, Nr. 4)

(Ensign 1997)
Ensign, Chet: $GML: The Billion Dollar Secret. Upper Saddle River (N.J.): Prentice Hall, 1997

(Maler/El Andaloussi 1996)
Maler, Eve; El Andaloussi, Jeanne: Developing SGML DTDs: From Text to Model to Mark. Upper Saddle River (N.J.): Prentice Hall, 1996

(Walter 1997)
Walter, Mark: Online Journals: Print Publishers Move from Pilot to Full Rollout. o. O., Februar 1997 (The Seybold Report on Internet Publishing)

(Wood 1998)
Wood, Lauren: The Web Document API. In: Conference Proceedings SGML/XML Europe '98. o.O., 1998

Eines für alle: auf der Suche nach dem universellen Redaktionssystem für Verlage

Angelika Binding

1 Einführung

Ein SGML-basiertes Redaktionssystem zu implementieren, bedeutet einen großen zeitlichen und finanziellen Aufwand. Um vor allem den Buch-Verlagen den Weg zur Nutzung dieser Technologie zu ebnen, stellt in der *Verlagsgruppe Georg von Holtzbrinck* eine Betrei berfirma ein Redaktionssystem zur Online-Nutzung zur Verfügung.

Redaktions-system zur Online-Nutzung

Die Verlagsgruppe Georg von Holtzbrinck umfaßt eine Reihe renommierter und bekannter Verlage wie *Rowohlt, S. Fischer* (beide Belletristik und Sachbuch), *Gustav Fischer* (Medizin), *Verlagsgruppe Handelsblatt, Macmillan* und *Die Zeit*. Die Firmen operieren mit größtmöglicher Unabhängigkeit voneinander und erhalten von der Holding keine Vorgaben für operative Entscheidungen.

In Zeiten großer technischer Innovationen, wie wir sie in der Verlagsbranche gegenwärtig erleben, bringt dieses Firmenkonzept zwei wesentliche Nachteile mit sich: Einerseits können kleinere Firmen eventuell nicht die Ressourcen für die Einführung neuer Produktionsmethoden und Produkte aufbringen, andererseits besteht die Gefahr, daß ähnliche oder gleiche Systeme mehrfach entwickelt werden.

Zur Förderung und Koordinierung der Einführung neuer Publikationstechnologien und elektronischer Produkte hat die Verlagsgruppe *Holtzbrinck* daher 1996 eine *Stabsstelle Elektronische Medien* eingerichtet. Drei sog. *Competency Centres* für die Bereiche *Online*, *Multimedia* und *Content Management* wurden zur Durchführung

Koordination neuer Technologien

der konkreten Projektarbeit gegründet. Sie sind zur Wahrung der nötigen Praxisnähe jeweils in einem Verlag der Gruppe angesiedelt (Ziffzer/Moss 1996).

Das *Competency Centre for Content Management* (*CCCM*) betreut die Gebiete medienneutrale Datenhaltung und -archivierung sowie Datenstrukturierung, insbesondere SGML.

Die Mitarbeiter des CCCM befaßten sich zunächst mit dem Bereich Bücher und buchähnliche Werke. Hierzu sollen auch die Loseblattwerke zählen, obwohl sich die Fachwelt nicht einig ist, ob sie den Büchern oder eher den Zeitschriften zuzuordnen sind oder sogar eine eigene Gattung bilden. Die Gebiete Zeitungen und Zeitschriften stellen im Hinblick auf Produktionsgeschwindigkeit, Strukturierungstiefe und Wiederverwendbarkeit jeweils ihre eigenen Anforderungen an die Datenarchivierung und -erzeugung und werden daher separat bearbeitet.

2   Situation in den Holtzbrinck-Verlagen

In einer konzernweiten Erhebung wurden die Produktpaletten der Buchverlage in produktionstechnischer Hinsicht untersucht und die bereits eingesetzten Techniken im Bereich *Elektronisches Publizieren und Produzieren* abgefragt.

Es zeigte sich, daß alle befragten Buchverlage u.a. Lexika, Wörterbücher, Loseblattwerke, Gesetzeskommentare, kritische literarische Gesamtausgaben oder regelmäßig überarbeitete Sachbücher in ihrem Programm haben. Allen diesen Produkte ist gemeinsam, daß sie eine oder mehrere der folgenden Eigenschaften aufweisen:

- *Die Inhalte eignen sich für Spin-off-Produkte.* Dies sind neue Bücher, die Extrakte oder Querextrakte aus mehreren bereits erschienenen Werken enthalten. Spin-off-Produkte generieren zusätzlichen Umsatz bei häufig geringen Kosten, da die Inhalte aus dem bestehenden Fundus geschöpft werden.

- *Die Inhalte eignen für die Umsetzung in elektronische Produkte.* Dies gilt für Offline- und Onlineprodukte. CD-ROMs und Online-Publikationen sind heute zwar unter Ertragsgesichtspunkten noch nicht mit Büchern vergleichbar, die Marktsituation legt ein Engagement auf diesen Gebieten jedoch nahe.

- *Die Werke erfordern eine regelmäßige inhaltliche Überarbeitung.*

- *Die Werke haben eine sehr komplexe Struktur.* Beispiele hierfür sind Lexika, Wörterbücher, aber auch kritische Gesamtausgaben mit Sekundärliteratur.

2.1 Anforderungen an die redaktionellen und herstellerischen Abläufe

Die hier angesprochenen Publikationstypen werden über mehrere Jahre hinweg vorbereitet und stellen eine enorme Investition für den Verlag dar. Um am Markt bestehen zu können, sowie zur Reduktion ihrer Produktionszeiten und -kosten müssen erhöhte Anforderungen an die redaktionellen und herstellerischen Abläufe gestellt werden. Hierzu gehören:

große Investition der Verlage

- *Bequeme Extraktion und Rekombination.* Die Kosten für Spin-offs werden gering gehalten, wenn Textauswahl und Textbearbeitung bequem erledigt werden können und die Ausgangsinhalte leicht zugänglich sind.

- *Konsistente Datenstruktur.* Wenn die Ausgangsdaten für elektronische Produkte gut strukturiert sind und in anwendungsneutralen Datenformaten vorliegen, müssen sie keiner umfangreichen Vorbereitung unterzogen werden. Die Produktionskosten verringern sich damit.

- *Kurze Produktionszeiten.* Mit dem Einsatz geeigneter Werkzeuge kann die Produktion von Werken, die regelmäßig überarbeitet werden, schneller und kostengünstiger gestaltet werden und die Produkte können schneller am Markt sein.

- *Teilautomatisierung von ermüdenden Arbeitsgängen, die gleichwohl Konzentration erfordern.* Lexika haben ein ausgedehntes System von Verweisen, deren Gültigkeit geprüft werden muß. Enzyklopädien und Gesamtausgaben umfassen eine Reihe von Registern, deren Einträge aus den Texten extrahiert werden müssen. Oft müssen die Bestandteile eines Werkes nach speziellen Regeln sortiert werden. All dies zieht Arbeitsvorgänge in den Redaktionen nach sich, die zwar langwierig und langweilig sind, aber dennoch intellektuellen Einsatz erfordern und deshalb nicht an weniger qualifizierte Mitarbeiter delegiert werden können. Diese Arbeiten werden durch den Einsatz geeigneter elektronischer Werkzeuge wesentlich erleichtert.

- *Unterstützung bei der Verwaltung der Inhalte und der Arbeitsgänge.* Die Werke bestehen vielfach aus einer großen Menge von

Einzelkomponenten, die von einer großen Zahl an Autoren, Herausgebern und Dienstleistern erstellt werden. Ein gut konfiguriertes Werkzeug zur Kontrolle des Workflows reduziert den hierdurch induzierten Verwaltungsaufwand.

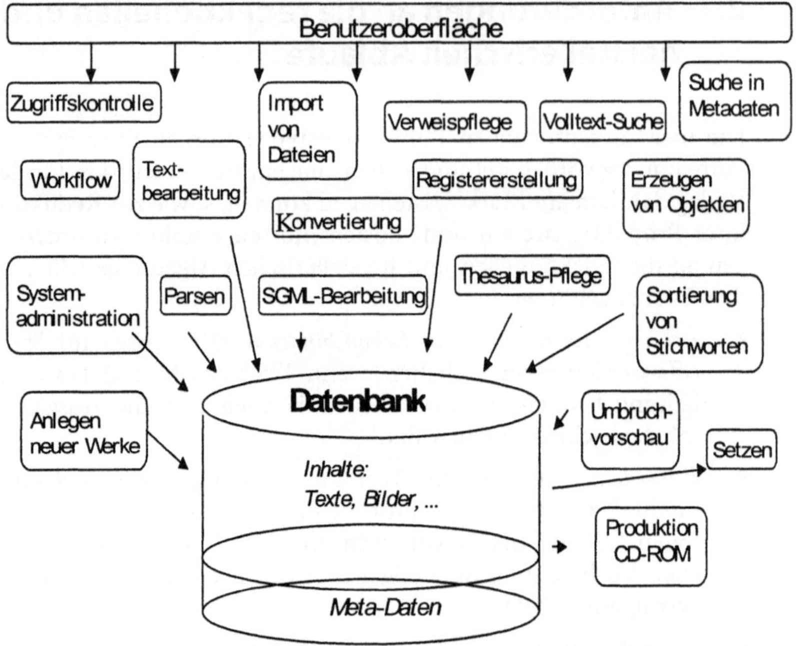

Abbildung 1
Produktion von Referenzwerken (Arbeitsschritte)

2.2 Strategische Überlegungen

Neben den produktionstechnischen Belangen sind Markterfordernisse zu berücksichtigen.

- *Time to market und Aktualität.* Für eine Reihe von Werken sind Aktualität und frühe Verfügbarkeit am Markt kritische Erfolgsfaktoren. Beispiele hierfür sind Jahrbücher, Gesetzes- und Steuerkommentare, Wörterbücher und Bücher zu speziellen Ereignissen, z.B. Kongreßbände, Bildbände zu großen Sportereignissen.

- *Added value.* Bei Gesamtausgaben, deren Urheberrecht in naher Zukunft auslaufen wird, ist es wichtig, dem Leser einen Mehrwert, z.B. in Form zusätzlicher Register, zu bieten, um die Marktstellung halten zu können. Dies gilt auch für Gesetzessammlungen oder bestimmte Arten von Sachbüchern.

- *Spin-off-Produkte.* Die Inhalte, auch als *assets* oder Verlagssubstanzen angesprochen, sind das Kapital eines Verlages. Nur durch Mehrfachveröffentlichung kann dieses Kapital auch mehrfache Erträge bringen. Bieten diese Spin-offs zusätzliche Vorteile im Hinblick auf Aktualität, so erzeugt dies weitere Wettbewerbsvorteile.

2.3 Fehlende EDV-Hilfsmittel für die redaktionelle Arbeit

Die Untersuchungen haben gezeigt, daß in den Redaktionen noch sehr wenig auf elektronische Werkzeuge, von einfacher Textverarbeitung abgesehen, zurückgegriffen wird. Zu den Aufgaben, die besser unterstützt werden könnten, gehören:

elektronische Unterstützung benötigt

- *Kollationieren verschiedener Textfassungen.* Dies geschieht durch Korrekturlesen der Ausdrucke, Vergleichsprogramme werden nicht eingesetzt.

- *Seitenumfangsbedingte Textkürzungen* erfolgen durch zeitraubende Arbeitszyklen zwischen Redaktion, Herstellung und Setzerei.

- *Vereinheitlichung der Schreibweise von Namen und Fachausdrücken* werden beim Korrekturlesen anhand von Papierlisten durchgeführt.

- *Sortierung* von Registerbegriffen oder Einträgen in Lexika geschieht über Karteikartensysteme.

- *Pflege der Verwaltungsdaten* von Aufträgen für Abbildungen oder Textteile wird mit Papierlisten durchgeführt.

- *Übernahme von Autorendaten* ist oft nicht sehr kostengünstig, da diese in verschiedenen Formaten mit oft unerwünschten Formatierungen angeliefert werden. Nicht immer werden den Autoren Hilfsmittel wie Word-Makros zur Verfügung gestellt.

- *Archivierung der Inhalte* erfolgt bisher lediglich im proprietären Satzformat und ggf. in Postscript bei der Setzerei. Der Verlag hat vielfach keine Kopie dieser Daten.

3 Medienneutrale Datenpflege mittels SGML-basierter Redaktionssysteme

Die Aufgaben, die bei den oben angesprochenen Werktypen besonders auftreten, sind leichter zu erledigen, wenn die Substanzen in einer möglichst anwendungsneutralen Form vorgehalten werden. Für Texte hat sich hier seit einigen Jahren SGML durchgesetzt. Die Eigenschaften und Vorzüge von SGML sind vielfach in der Fachliteratur diskutiert worden, so daß hier auf eine Wiederholung verzichtet wird. Für andere Inhalte wie Abbildungen, Tonsequenzen und Video gibt es derzeit keine anwendungsunabhängigen Formate, jedoch bewährte Standards, auf die zurückgegriffen werden kann.

Entschließt sich ein Verlag, seine Inhalte in standardisierter Form zu archivieren und weiterzuverarbeiten, so ist hierfür der Aufbau einer entsprechenden integrierten Produktionsumgebung sinnvoll. Eine solche Umgebung sprechen wir als *Redaktionssystem* an.

3.1 Definition eines Redaktionssystems

Man versteht unter einem Redaktionssystem ein System zur

- Speicherung und Archivierung,
- Bearbeitung,
- Suche und Auswahl sowie
- Verwaltung von Verlagsinhalten.

Komponenten Typischerweise besteht ein solches Redaktionssystem aus einer Datenbank, in der sowohl die Inhalte als auch die sog. *Metadaten*, d.h. die für die Verwaltung und Auswahl notwendigen Daten, gespeichert werden.

Auf diese Datenbank wird dann mit verschiedenen Programmen wie einem Editor, einem Suchprogramm und einem Anzeigeprogramm (*Viewer*) zugegriffen. Werkzeuge zur Anlage und Prüfung von Verweisen, zur Erstellung von Registern und zur Konvertierung unterstützen Autor, Redakteur und Hersteller bei ihrer Arbeit.

Die Texte werden zweckmäßigerweise in SGML kodiert, da für die Wiederverwertung von Verlagsinhalten eine medienneutrale, aber strukturierte Archivierung wichtig ist.

Ziel ist die Anlage eines gut gepflegten Datenbestandes, aus dem dann für ein – gedrucktes oder elektronisches – Produkt Teile exportiert und weiterverarbeitet werden können.

Immer häufiger ist ein Redaktionssystem mit einer Workflow-Komponente zur Überwachung, Steuerung und teilweise zur Automatisierung von Vorgängen mit Terminkontrolle ausgestattet.

3.2 Vorteile eines SGML-basierten Redaktionssystems

Der Einsatz eines guten SGML-basierten Redaktionssystems bietet eine Reihe von Vorteilen.

Die Erzeugung von Registern und Navigationshilfen kann unterstützt werden. und Werkzeuge können beispielsweise bei der Verweispflege helfen, wodurch die Fehlerrate reduziert wird. Beides führt zu einer Qualitätssteigerung der Produkte. *Steigerung der Qualität*

Die konsequente Trennung von Texterstellung und Textformatierung befreit den Autor von der mitunter auch nur subjektiv empfundenen Verpflichtung, sich während des Schreibens um das Layout des Textes zu kümmern. Konsistent strukturierte Texte können automatisiert gesetzt werden. Beides führt zu einer Verkürzung der Produktionszeit.

Die Automatisierung des Satzes führt überdies zu einer Kostenersparnis. Hier ist natürlich die sorgfältige Auswahl der weiterverarbeitenden Setzerei ausschlaggebend. *Kostenersparnis*

Konsistent strukturierte Daten müssen für eine Umsetzung in ein elektronisches Produkt nicht erst manuell vereinheitlicht und aufbereitet werden, ein Hauptkostenfaktor solcher Projekte wird damit eliminiert.

Häufig möchte der Verlag Spin-offs von bereits publizierten Werken produzieren, um zusätzliche Erlöse zu erzielen. Sind diese Inhalte in layout-unabhängiger Weise archiviert und leicht zugänglich und durchsuchbar, bedeutet dies Zeit- und Kostenersparnis bei der Produktion. *Sekundärverwertung*

3.3 Verlagsseitige Prämissen bei der Einführung eines SGML-basierten Redaktionssystems

Für die erfolgreiche Umstellung eines Publikationsprozesses auf eine redaktionssystem-gestützte Produktion ist eine sorgfältige Vorbereitung essentiell. Zu Beginn muß eine exakte Kosten-Nutzen-

Analyse erarbeitet werden, in die neben dem Anschaffungspreis des Systems alle neu hinzugekommenen Kosten und alle durch das System zu erreichenden Einsparungen und Erträge Eingang finden.

Ist im Verlag nicht genug technisches Know-how, etwa im Management von Softwareprojekten, vorhanden, muß man auf entsprechende Beratung von außen zurückgreifen.

Es ist in jedem Fall zu klären, wer später das System im Verlag betreuen wird. Die hierbei anfallenden Aufgaben sind vielfältig und meist nicht von einer einzelnen Person zu leisten. Man benötigt vielmehr mehrere Spezialisten, wobei vor allem bei einem kleinen Verlag lediglich ein „Viertel-" oder „Achtelexperte" ausgelastet ist.

Der Verlag wird sein Programm einer detaillierten Prüfung unterziehen, um festzustellen, welche Werke sich für die Bearbeitung mit einem Redaktionssystem eignen und ob genug solcher Werke zur Auslastung des Systems vorliegen.

3.4 Redaktionssystem und externe Autoren

Die Umstellung auf SGML und ein SGML-basiertes Redaktionssystem muß natürlich auch die Zusammenarbeit mit den Autoren einbeziehen. Diese stehen den neuen Konzepten nicht immer positiv gegenüber. Grund hierfür ist, daß SGML allen Beteiligten gewisse Regeln im Aufbau der Texte auferlegt, die der Verlag zwar schon früher gewünscht hat, in der Vergangenheit jedoch schwer durchsetzen konnte. Durch die Formalisierung der Textstruktur in SGML ist der Autor an ihre strikte Einhaltung gebunden.

Auf dem Markt erhältliche SGML-basierte Redaktionssysteme sind vielfach von den Anforderungen der Dokumentationsabteilungen großer technischer Betriebe geprägt. Diese unterscheiden sich jedoch in fundamentaler Weise von der Autorentätigkeit für einen Verlag.

In der technischen Dokumentation eines Industriebetriebes arbeiten in der Regel fest angestellte Redakteure, deren Tätigkeit überwiegend bis ausschließlich im Verfassen von Texten für diese bestimmte Firma besteht. Es handelt sich um eine definierte Personengruppe, die die zu verwendende Software von ihrem Arbeitgeber gestellt bekommt und der genau vorgeschrieben werden kann, wie die Texte zu erfassen, zu formulieren und zu strukturieren sind.

Für einen Fachverlag hingegen schreiben vielfach Autoren, die dies neben ihrer eigentlichen Arbeit, nur zeitweise und mitunter für verschiedene Verlage tun. Die Autoren eines Verlages fluktuieren. Es ist wirtschaftlich in der Regel nicht tragbar, sie mit teurer Spezialsoftware auszurüsten, und der Verlag ist ihnen gegenüber nicht weisungsbefugt.

Darüber hinaus gehören die Autoren im allgemeinen zu den Besten ihres Faches und sind so in einer starken Position gegenüber dem Verlag: entweder dieser akzeptiert die Form, in der der Autor sein Manuskript liefert, oder der Autor wechselt den Verlag. Die Autoren sind vielfach nicht bereit – und machmal auch nicht in der Lage – viel Arbeit in die Strukturierung ihres Textes zu investieren, sich überhaupt einem engen Korsett beim Aufbau ihrer Texte zu unterwerfen, geschweige denn eine andere Software als die ihnen vertraute zu verwenden.

Autoren in starker Position

Ein Konzept, das in der Verlagsbranche Erfolg haben will, muß dieser Tatsache Rechnung tragen und preisgünstige Lösungen für die Kooperation mit wechselnden externen Autoren bieten.

3.5 Grundsatz: Organisation vor Technik

Verlage wünschen sich oft ein System, das sich vollständig an die bisherige Produktionsweise anpaßt. Ein Redaktionssystem, das eine wirkliche Verbesserung der Produktion bietet, wird jedoch auch Änderungen an den Arbeitsabläufen notwendig machen. (Auch mit der Einführung des Autos mußte auf Peitsche und Hafer verzichtet werden.)

Änderung der Arbeitsabläufe

Zur Vermeidung unnötiger Ausgaben sind jedoch zuerst die Produktivitätsverbesserung durch organisatorische Maßnahmen und erst dann die Einführung neuer technischer Hilfsmittel zu prüfen.

Die Einführung eines Redaktionssystems bedeutet eine Reorganisation des Produktionsablaufes im Verlag und kann nicht „so nebenbei" erledigt werden.

3.6 Weiterverarbeitung der Daten

Eine Datenbank ist kein Selbstzweck: Aus den SGML-Dokumenten sollen Bücher, CD-ROMs und Web-Seiten werden.

Konsistent kodierte Dateien sind ein Segen für die weiterverarbeitenden Betriebe, aber nicht jede Setzerei und nicht jeder CD-ROM-Programmierer kann diesen Vorteil voll ausschöpfen. Bei der Lieferantenauswahl ist daher auf das Vorhandensein von Programmierkräften im Haus und den Einsatz eines geeigneten Satzsystems zu achten.

Vorteile ausschöpfen

letzte
Korrekturen

Letzteres wird besonders wichtig, wenn während der Satzphase inhaltliche Korrekturen notwendig werden und der Verlag nach Abschluß der Arbeiten SGML-Dateien zum Reimport in seine Datenbank zurückerhalten möchte. Anzustreben ist zwar, diese Phase so kurz wie möglich zu halten, so daß mit aktuellen Daten gearbeitet wird, aber ganz werden sich letzte Korrekturen nicht vermeiden lassen. Mitunter ist jedoch ein separates Nachführen der Korrekturen in den SGML-Daten effektiver als ein Reimport.

3.7 Beschaffung eines gemeinsamen Systems

Die Hürde der Implementierung eines Redaktionssystems kann gesenkt werden, indem eine Reihe von Verlagen oder – wie in unserem Falle – die Verlagsgruppe ein gemeinsames System für alle in Frage kommenden Buchprojekte ihrer Verlage beschafft.

gemeinsames statt individuelles Vorgehen

Ein unabhängiges Vorgehen hat zwar auf den ersten Blick eine Reihe von Vorteilen: Jeder Verlag kann das für sich optimale System beschaffen. Es enthält eventuell weniger, aber genau die Komponenten, die der betreffende Verlag benötigt. Auch ist zu erwarten, daß ein individuell konzipiertes System billiger ist als ein System, das die Anforderungen vieler Verlage erfüllt. Weiterhin sind keine langwierigen Abstimmungsprozesse mit anderen Verlagen erforderlich, ein solches individuelles System ist daher eventuell in kürzerer Zeit zu realisieren als ein umfassendes für die Verlagsgruppe.

Aus der Perspektive der Verlagsgruppe ergibt sich jedoch ein anderes Bild: Viele der kleineren Verlage werden eventuell den Schwellenaufwand, der für eine tragfähige Konzeption unerläßlich ist, nicht erbringen können. Unnötige Doppelentwicklungen würden zusätzliche Kosten für die Verlagsgruppe verursachen und inkompatible Systeme eine Kooperation auf Produktionsebene verhindern.

Betrieb durch einen Dienstleister

Durch gemeinsamen Einkauf hingegen kann ein System beschafft werden, das bessere Funktionalität bietet und dessen Kostenanteil gleichzeitig für den Einzelverlag vergleichbar ist mit dem eines eigenen kleinen Systems. Nicht zuletzt kann die Pflege und der Betrieb des Systems an einen Dienstleister vergeben werden, so daß die Einzelverlage von dieser Aufgabe befreit werden.

Da die Vorteile einer gemeinsamen Beschaffung die eventuellen Nachteile überwiegen, wurde im Sommer 1997 ein Projekt zur Beschaffung eines *Holtzbrinck-Redaktionssystems* gegründet.

4 Projektierung des Holtzbrinck-Redaktionssystems

In der ersten Ausbaustufe sollten folgende Werke mit dem System bearbeitet werden können:

- Fischer Weltalmanach
- Loseblattwerke
- Gesetzeskommentare
- Lexika z.B. in den Bereichen Medizin und Kultur

Weiterhin wurden sowohl gedruckte als auch elektronische Publikationsformen betrachtet.

Auf gute Anpaßbarkeit des Systems an die verschiedenen Projekte durch geschulte Mitarbeiter der Verlage wurde daher großen Wert gelegt.

4.1 Anforderungsprofil des Holtzbrinck-Redaktionssystems

Eine Projektgruppe mit Mitgliedern aus verschiedenen Holtzbrinck-Verlagen sammelte zunächst Anforderungslisten, die bereits früher für verlagsinterne, werkbezogene Projekte erstellt worden waren und vereinigte diese in mehreren Sitzungen zu einem Gesamtkatalog. Dabei legten die Diskussionen häufig unterschiedliche Vorstellungen über die verschiedenen Funktionen und ihre Wichtigkeit offen. Diese wurden dann Stück für Stück zur Deckung gebracht.

Gesamtkatalog der Anforderungen

Das Ergebnispapier beschreibt eine Redaktionsumgebung, die neben dem eigentlichen Redaktionssystem weitere Programme umfaßt, die nicht in das Redaktionssystem integriert sein müssen.

Die Einzelanforderungen wurden hinsichtlich ihrer Dringlichkeit für die einzelnen Projekte klassifiziert. Dies geschah auch, um festzustellen, ob ein gemeinsames System wirklich sinnvoll ist, oder ob die Projekte in verschiedene Gruppen mit völlig unterschiedlichen Anforderungsprofilen zerfallen. Dies war jedoch nicht der Fall. Zur Abrundung des Bildes wurden die Anforderungen einiger Projekte hinzugefügt, in deren Rahmen bereits ein anderes System einsetzt wird oder die erst mittelfristig auf eine SGML-basierte Produktion umgestellt werden sollen.

Dringlichkeit

Folgende Komponenten wurden als wesentlich für ein SGML-basiertes Redaktionssystem identifiziert:

- *integrierte Speicherung* von SGML-Texten und anderen Komponenten wie Word-Texte, Abbildungen und Tabellen in einer Datenbank;

- *flexibler Zugriff* auf Informationseinheiten beliebiger Größe;

- *spezifisch definierbare Zugriffsrechte* auf die Datenbank, Einrichtung von Benutzern und Rollen;

- Bearbeitung der redaktionellen Inhalte mit einem leistungsfähigen *SGML-Editor*;

- *Bearbeitung nicht SGML-strukturierter Texte* z.B. mit Word, auch in Verbindung von Formatvorlagen zur Erfassung von teilstrukturierten Texten durch externe Autoren;

- *bequemer Import von Fremdtexten*, die die Autoren in mehr oder weniger strukturierter Form geliefert haben, verbunden mit einer Möglichkeit zu komfortablen Nachstrukturierung;

- *Export von Daten* zur maschinellen Weiterverabeitung etwa durch ein Satzsystem;

- *SGML-gestützte Suche* auf den Inhalten, kombinierbar mit einer Suche in den Metadaten;

- *Unterstützung bei der Verweispflege* und der *Generierung von Registern*;

- *Verwaltung verschiedener Versionen*, d.h. zeitlich aufeinander folgender Fassungen eines Textes, und von *Varianten*, d.h. von verschiedenen Fassungen eines Textes, die für verschiedene Verwendungszwecke geschrieben wurden;

- *Sortierung von Texten* nach unterschiedlichen Sortierregeln, z.B. ö wahlweise wie oe oder wie o, Sortierregeln für Sonderzeichen.

Wie sich im weiteren Verlauf des Projektes zeigte, mußte der Wunsch nach einer genauen Umbruchvorschau zurückgestellt werden, da dies die Integration der vollständigen Funktionalität desjenigen Satzsystems bedeutet hätte, das von der weiterverarbeitenden Setzerei verwendet wird.

4.2 Systemauswahl

Es war der Projektgruppe von Anfang an klar, daß es auf dem Markt kein System gibt, das bereits alle gewünschten Eigenschaften aufweist. Es galt daher das System zu identifizieren, dessen Funktionenprofil den erarbeiteten Anforderungen am nächsten kommt, bzw. sich am besten in diese Richtung weiterentwickeln läßt. Hierzu wurde ergänzend zum Anforderungskatalog ein Fragebogen erarbeitet, mit dem die technischen Konzeptionen der Systeme, die zu erwartenden Kosten und die anbietenden Firmen verglichen werden konnten.

Von den acht Systemen, die die Gruppe im Verlauf ihrer Arbeit untersuchte, wurden schließlich zwei ausgewählt, die genauer getestet werden sollten.

zwei Systeme in der engeren Wahl

Damit endete die Aufgabe der Projektgruppe, denn der weitere Verlauf des Testens, Auswählens und Implementierens wurde von einem neuen Team übernommen.

5 Betrieb des Redaktionssystems durch einen Dienstleister

Schon vor einiger Zeit wurde in der Verlagsgruppe Holtzbrinck die Frage diskutiert, ob die Verlage das Redaktionssystem auf hauseigenen Servern nutzen sollen oder ob der Betrieb eines solchen Systems besser an eine Firma vergeben wird.

Diese Firma würde das System auf einem Rechner installieren und ihren Kunden gegen monatliche Gebühr zur Verfügung stellen. Die Verlage speichern ihre Daten auf dem zentralen Server und greifen über ISDN-Leitung oder über das Internet auf das System zu.

Gegen das Modell eines Redaktionssystem-Rechenzentrums wurden anfangs einige Bedenken vorgebracht. Zunächst einmal verfügt noch nicht jedes Haus der Verlagsgruppe Holtzbrinck über ein leistungsfähiges lokales Netz (LAN) oder über einen Internet-Zugang. Auch externe Partner wie Autoren, Herausgeber, Redaktionen und Dienstleister sind vielfach noch nicht Online. Hier kämen also zusätzliche Investitionen auf die Verlage zu. Allerdings müßten die Verlage für eine Inhouse-Lösung ebenfalls über ein LAN verfügen und zur Anbindung externer Autoren und Redaktionen Internet-Anschlüsse bereitstellen.

Modell: Rechenzentrum

Man war darüber besorgt, daß ein solches System möglicherweise nicht gegen Hacker abgeschottet werden kann. Einige Redakteure scheuten sich davor, ihre Inhalte überhaupt in fremde Hände zu geben, weil sie eine Vermischung der Daten mit denen anderer Häuser oder neue Abhängigkeiten von einem befürchteten. Dem ist entgegenzuhalten, daß das Einwählen in das System auf bestimmte

Besorgnisse

anrufende Telefon-Nummern beschränkt werden kann. Die Inhalte der einzelnen Projekte werden in getrennten Datenbanken abgelegt, sind daher nicht von unbefugten Nutzern einsehbar. SGML-Daten können jederzeit aus dem System exportiert und in ein anderes Redaktionssystem geladen werden.

Viele erkannten jedoch, daß die Vorteile des Modells im Vergleich zu den Einwänden bei weitem überwiegen:

Die Investitionen sind für den einzelnen Verlag niedriger. Eine bessere Ausnutzung der Geräte (Plattenplatz, Rechenzeit) spart Betriebskosten ein. Auch können Spitzenbelastungen einzelner Verlage durch Zugriff auf gemeinsame Gerätekapazität abgefangen werden.

Eine zentrale Programmpflege, Datensicherung und Lagerung erhöhen die Betriebssicherheit.

Die Verlage können sich auf ihre Kernkompetenzen konzentrieren, da ein Help-Desk mit EDV-Fachleuten ihnen zur Beratung zur Verfügung steht und die Möglichkeit existiert, Routineaufgaben wie Konvertierungsläufe im Batchverfahren, die keine inhaltlichen Kenntnisse, wohl aber EDV-technische Fertigkeiten erfordern, an entsprechende Fachkräfte zu delegieren.

Ein solches Rechenzentrum kann darüber hinaus eine Reihe interessanter Zusatzdienste anbieten, beispielsweise:

- Datensicherung, -auslagerung und -archivierung

- Index-Läufe und Konvertierung

- Erfassung und Rohstrukturierung

- Weiterverarbeitung der Daten im Satz, für CD-ROMs oder Online-Dienste

- Beratung und Einrichten des Systems für neue Projekte

Es wurde daher beschlossen, den Verlagen das System im Rahmen einer eigens gegründeten Tochterfirma anzubieten, die ihre Dienste gegen entsprechende Vergütung erbringt. Diese Firma wird für die Wahl des Systems verantwortlich sein, da ihr wirtschaftlicher Erfolg im wesentlichen davon abhängt.

Die Entscheidung, das System bei dieser neuen Betreiberfirma zu nutzen, lieber eine eigene Lösung zu beschaffen/entwickeln oder weiterhin konventionell zu arbeiten, liegt hingegen bei den jeweiligen Häusern.

6 Nachtrag

Das System wurde inzwischen ausgewählt und die Firma *Activ Publishing* mit Sitz in Mannheim gegründet.

Wir entschieden uns für den *Information Manager* der Firma *Texcel*, da dieser auf einer objekt-relationalen Datenbank beruht, die es ohne großen Implementierungsaufwand erlaubt, auf beliebige Elemente eines SGML-Dokumentes lesend und schreibend zuzugreifen. Weiterhin bietet das System interessante Funktionen bei der Suche in den Texten, bei der Nutzung von Textbausteinen in verschiedenen Dokumenten, bei der Versionenverwaltung und dem Vergleich von Versionen.

Mit der Implementierung der ersten Projekte wurde begonnen.

Literatur

(Ziffzer/Moss 1996)
  Ziffzer, Stefan; Moss, Sebastian: Neue Medien: Know How, Aufbau und Wissenstransfer in einer dezentralisierten Verlagsgruppe. In: Zeitschrift für Führung und Organisation (1996), Nr. 6, S. 343-346

SGML für dynamische Publikationen – das Beispiel Fischer Weltalmanach

Thomas Kamps, Christoph Obermeier
Klaus Reichenberger und Ingrid Schmidt

1   Schöne neue Welt

Die Magie elektronischen Publizierens hat seit einigen Jahren die Verlagsbranche ergriffen. Die Buchmessen legen beredtes Zeugnis davon ab: Das Zauberwort heißt Multimedia, und fast jeder Verlag hat eine CD-ROM im Sortiment. Die anfängliche Faszination dieser neuen Welt weicht jedoch – immer noch viel zu häufig – rasch der Ernüchterung, spatestens dann, wenn der begeisterte Käufer die CD-ROM zu Hause benutzt. Ohne vielleicht genau sagen zu können, was er sich im Unterschied zum Buch davon erhofft hat, macht sich ein dumpfes Gefühl der Enttäuschung breit. Multimedia allein macht eben noch kein gutes Produkt. Und eine CD-ROM ist nicht dann besonders gut, wenn sie dem Layout des zugrundegelegten Printprodukts nahe kommt.

Wir wollen hier nicht Qualitätskriterien für elektronische Produkte unter die Lupe nehmen, sondern vielmehr anhand der CD-ROM-Produktion des Fischer Weltalmanach '99 zeigen, wie SGML in Verbindung mit wissensbasiertem Publizieren zu einer neuen Generation elektronischer Produkte führen kann; wie deren Funktionalität den Möglichkeiten des Mediums gerecht wird, sie gewinnbringend nutzt und neuartige Zugangsstrukturen zu den Informationen schafft.

*Zauberwort
Multimedia*

2 Publikationskonzepte

2.1 SGML und die Zukunft kann kommen?

Black-box-
Publishing

Die Gegenreaktion auf Multimedia heißt manchmal SGML. Dabei gilt SGML-basiertes Publizieren als Synonym für Qualität, der nach SGML ausgezeichnete Datenbestand als Garantie für uneingeschränkte Publikationsmöglichkeiten. Diese Vorstellung wird vor allem von dem Schlagwort „neutrales Format" genährt. Aber in welcher Hinsicht neutral? Die ursprünglich gemeinte Plattformunabhängigkeit wird jetzt Medienunabhängigkeit genannt, ohne daß sich die dahinter liegende Bedeutung ändert. Dies bewirkt keine Veränderung in der Anwendung von SGML, es erhöht lediglich die Erwartungen. Die Dokumente werden, immer noch im Hinblick auf ihr Printlayout, nun mit SGML statt mit Satzcodes markiert. Allein dieses Spitzklammerformat, eingespeist in einen Datenpool, soll auf Knopfdruck die Generierung der verschiedensten Medienprodukte ermöglichen: der Datenpool als *black box* (s.a. Beitrag von Marion Spengler). Anforderungen an die Struktur des Datenpools; wie das Generieren vor dem Knopfdruck eigentlich vonstatten gehen soll; ob der Dienstleister für das elektronische Produkt überhaupt mit SGML umgehen kann, all diese wichtigen Fragen werden in der Regel nicht berücksichtigt. Das Ergebnis dieser Vorstellung sind häufig lange Gesichter, da die Praxis meist gravierend von der Theorie abweicht. Mit der Zeit kristallisiert sich immer mehr die Erkenntnis heraus, daß es nicht ausreicht, SGML einzusetzen, ohne ein Konzept für das „Wie" zu haben. Nach dem „Wie" zu fragen heißt, darüber nachzudenken, welche Ziele dieses Auszeichnungskonzept verfolgt und welche Inhalte überhaupt ausgezeichnet werden sollen.

Cross-Media-
Publishing

Genau da setzt das weitergehende Modell des *Cross-Media-Publishing* an. Es steht für die elektronische Aufbereitung der Inhalte einer Publikation ohne vorherige Festlegung auf ein bestimmtes Publikationsmedium. Damit wird das Dokumentenparadigma durch der Idee der Informationseinheit ersetzt. Die Strukturierung hangelt sich nicht mehr am Printprodukt entlang, sondern greift den Informationsgehalt. Dieser Paradigmenwechsel wirkt sich auch auf den Umgang mit den Inhalten selbst aus. Auf diese weitreichenden Veränderungen werden wir jedoch in diesem Zusammenhang nicht eingehen. Sie sind einen eigenen Beitrag wert.

Beim Cross-Media-Publishing müssen die inhaltsorientierten Auszeichnungen hauptsächlich zwei Anforderungen genügen:

1. Sie müssen alle für die verschiedenen Produkte notwendigen Informationen enthalten (*Medienunabhängigkeit*), und

2. ihr Format muß systemunabhängig sein (*Plattformunabhängigkeit*).

Beiden Punkten kann durch die Anwendung von SGML Rechnung getragen werden. Der Standard an sich steht schon für die system-neutrale Speicherung. Die Medienneutralität wird über die Art und Weise der DTD-Modellierung erreicht, die darauf ausgerichtet ist, die Inhalte zu markieren und nicht die Layoutstruktur. So eingesetzt wird der Nutzen von SGML, der bei der Black-box-Idee noch Wunschdenken war, – langsam – Realität:

- Verwertung der Ressourcen eines Titels für mehrere Medien wie Print oder CD-ROM sowie für Zweitverwertungen,

- damit verbunden eine Kostenreduktion und

- die Produktionsbeschleunigung bei den einzelnen Verwertungs-formen.

Es wäre jedoch falsch, die Vorteile, die mit Cross-Media-Publishing verbunden sind, nur im Bereich der Produktion und unter Rationalisierungsgesichtspunkten zu sehen. Die Möglichkeiten, die sich dadurch für die Verlage eröffnen, gehen weit darüber hinaus. SGML-strukturierte Inhalte lassen sich je nach Güte und Tiefe ihrer Strukturierung sehr gut in einer Form repräsentieren, die von einem elektronischen Produkt ebenso genutzt werden kann wie für das Retrieval zur Herstellung von Zweitverwertungen.

2.2 Wozu Wissen, wenn es Dokumente gibt?

Damit SGML effizient eingesetzt werden kann, muß das Dokument als Ressource für eine *Wissensbasis* begriffen werden (s. Beitrag von Pamela Gennusa). Ohne in diesem Zusammenhang den Begriff der Wissensbasis diskutieren zu wollen, verstehen wir sie als die Summe der miteinander vernetzten Objekte und Fakten, die aus Dokumenten extrahiert werden können. In einem solchen Netz kann jedes Objekt und jede Verknüpfung zwischen den Objekten (Relation) Informationen über sich aus den verschiedenen Dokumenten sammeln. Je stärker die Objekte und Fakten miteinander verknüpft sind, desto dichter wird das Netz. Eine solche Wissensbasis kann zusätzlich um anderes, externes Wissen, wie Thesauri zu bestimmten Themen, erweitert werden.

Ein Publikationsmodell, das auf einer solchen Wissensbasis aufsetzt, ist eine notwendige Voraussetzung für effektives Cross-Media-Publishing, und es muß ein konkretes Konzept des geplanten Cross-Media-Publishing vorliegen, damit der Aufbau einer Wissensbasis wirklich unterstützt wird. Eine am Informationsgehalt des Verlagstitels orientierte SGML-Auszeichnung wird möglichst viele Fakten semantisch auszeichnen, so daß sich der Aufbau der Wissensbasis eng an die SGML-Modellierung anlehnen kann, indem Elemente in Objekte übersetzt werden und Relationen teilweise aus den Attributwerten abgeleitet werden können. Eine für diesen Zusammenhang nicht unwesentliche Schwäche von SGML ist, daß es kein SGML-Feature gibt, um explizit Relationen zu modellieren.

```
<!ELEMENT    sprachen      - -   (#PCDATA | sprache)+ >
<!ATTLIST    sprachen      id    CDATA                 #REQUIRED
                           jahr  NUMBER                #IMPLIED >


<!ELEMENT    sprache       - -   (#PCDATA) >
<!ATTLIST    sprache       typ   (national|amt|regional|handel|
                                 handel-bildung|verkehr|
                                 verwaltung|bildung-verkehr)
                                                       #IMPLIED
                           ca-attr  (ca|gr-als|kl-als)
                                                       #IMPLIED
                           prozent  NUTOKEN            #IMPLIED >
```

Nur auf dem Hintergrund solcher Wissensbasen, die in Teilen aus einer abstrahierten Darstellung der Dokumente gespeist werden, können neuartige, dynamische elektronische Publikationen entstehen, die eine völlig neue Qualität in der Interaktion aufweisen.

3 Das elektronische Produkt Fischer Weltalmanach

3.1 Das Projekt

Der Fischer Weltalmanach ist eines der Schlüsselprodukte des *Fischer Taschenbuch Verlages* in Frankfurt am Main. Er erscheint seit 1959 jährlich und ist seit der ersten Ausgabe Marktführer im Bereich der deutschsprachigen aktuellen Nachschlagewerke. Er umfaßt derzeit 672 Seiten und enthält über 250.000 ständig aktualisierte Daten zu sämtlichen Staaten der Welt. Das Produkt ist einem sachlich knappen, präzisen Stil und einem hohen Qualitätsanspruch verpflichtet. Jährlich werden aus einer Fülle von statistischen und anderen Quellen die essentiellen Daten und Fakten des vergangenen Jahres herausgefiltert. So versammelt der Weltalmanach statistische Basisdaten zu allen Staaten der Welt, teilweise ergänzt durch eine Chronik wichtiger Ereignisse, enthält Biographien führender nationaler und internationaler Politiker sowie ausführliche Kapitel über Internationale Organisationen, Wirtschaft, Umwelt und Kultur. Zum Text treten eine Vielzahl von Karten, Grafiken und Tabellen.

Zeitlich leicht versetzt bringt der *Systhema Verlag* in München seit 1997 eine elektronische Version als CD-ROM heraus, die das Buch durch weitere Informationen ergänzt.

Beide Verlage, der Fischer Taschenbuch Verlag und der Systhema Verlag, gehören zur *Verlagsgruppe Georg von Holtzbrinck*. Die Verlagsgruppe kam zu der Einsicht, daß sich eine SGML-basierte Datenhaltung positiv auf den Produktionsprozeß auswirken würde und darüber hinaus die Qualität der Produkte steigern kann. Aus diesem Grund fällte sie eine strategische Entscheidung für den Einsatz von SGML und wählte den Fischer Weltalmanach zum geeigneten Pilotprojekt.

Hierfür war die komplexe inhaltliche Struktur des Weltalmanachs entscheidend, die sich für einen Versuch, SGML für eine tiefe semantisch-orientierte Strukturierung einzusetzen, besonders anbot. Für eine SGML-Strukturierung des Weltalmanachs sprechen

- die vielen, meist kleine Informationseinheiten,
- die Inhalte, die häufig überarbeitet werden und
- die komplexe Struktur der Texte.

Darüber hinaus war auch der Fischer Taschenbuchverlag mit seinen Überlegungen zum elektronischen Publizieren – im Vergleich zu anderen Verlagen der Gruppe – relativ weit fortgeschritten.

Die nun beginnende SGML-Modellierung der Almanach-Inhalte war dem Konzept des Cross-Media-Publishing verpflichtet. Es wurde ein modulares DTD-Konzept entwickelt, das auf einer Element-Attribut-Bibliothek aufbaut. Dadurch wird es möglich, die anfänglich relativ flach ausgebaute Inhaltsstruktur nach und nach durch das gleichzeitig entwickelte komplexe Inhaltsmodell auszutauschen. Ein solches Vorgehen war notwendig, da bei aller Neuerung stets eine reibungslose Produktion des Buches gewährleistet sein mußte. Die neuartige Strukturierung der Informationen zog auch eine Umstellung in der Arbeit bei allen Beteiligten nach sich und sollte daher

Pilotprojekt für
SGML

SGML-Migration

stufenweise geschehen: In der Redaktion galt es, zunächst mit einem einfachen SGML-Editor Informationseinheiten zu bearbeiten statt der bisherigen Dokumente, die Herstellung mußte neue Kommunikationsformen mit der Setzerei finden, die Setzerei mußte sich auf ihre neue Aufgabe einstellen, diese SGML-strukturierten Informationseinheiten in ein Print zu überführen, und alle damit verbundenen neuen Arbeitsabläufe mußten sich einspielen.

erste CD-ROMs

Die Produktion der ersten beiden Weltalmanach-CD-ROMs brachte einige Schwierigkeiten mit sich: Einerseits mußte ein wahrer „Zoo" von Datenformaten gebändigt werden – für den Staatenteil gab es SGML-strukturierte Dokumente, die anderen Teile bestanden aus einer Vielzahl von Datenformaten und Medien –, andererseits wurde die bereits vorliegende SGML-Struktur nicht ausgenutzt. Trotz dieser anfänglich schlechten Kosten-Nutzen-Rechnung beschloß der Fischer Taschenbuchverlag ein SGML-basiertes Redaktionssystem einzuführen und die SGML-Strukturierung auf den gesamten Weltalmanach auszudehnen.

die neue CD-ROM

Daß diese Entscheidung richtig war, zeigt die CD-ROM des Fischer Weltalmanach '99, für deren Produktion die Firma *Intelligent Views*, mit Unterstützung des *Instituts für Integrierte Publikations- und Informationssysteme der GMD (GMD-IPSI)* ein wissensbasiertes Publikationsmodell realisiert hat. Der Grundstock der Wissensbasis wird dabei direkt aus den SGML-strukturierten Inhalten gewonnen.

3.2 Der wissensbasierte Publikationsprozeß

Datenbestand und Objektnetz

Der SGML-ausgezeichnete Datenbestand macht beim Fischer Weltalmanach '99 etwa die Hälfte des Gesamtbestandes aus. Die andere Hälfte besteht aus wenig strukturierten, print-optimierten Daten, die in RTF, Excel, QuarkXpress, Bitmap und anderen Datenformaten vorliegen. Durch diese unterschiedlichen Formate wird der effiziente Zugriff auf gleichartige Daten erschwert. So ist beispielsweise ein Teil der Faktendaten SGML-strukturiert und ein anderer Teil als Excel-Tabellen erfaßt. Für die Weltalmanach-CD-ROM, die als interaktives, individualisiertes, elektronisches Arbeitswerkzeug konzipiert ist, ist es von zentraler Bedeutung, daß gleichartige Daten auch miteinander verglichen werden können. Daher muß der Originaldatenbestand zunächst homogenisiert, d.h. in ein uniformes Datenformat transformiert werden. Dieses Zielformat ist eine als Objektnetz gespeicherte spezielle Datenbank, die Objekte von unterschiedlichem Typ (Regionen, Staaten, Kontinente, Personen, Texte, Grafiken, thematische Karten, etc.) durch semantische Beziehungen miteinander verknüpft.

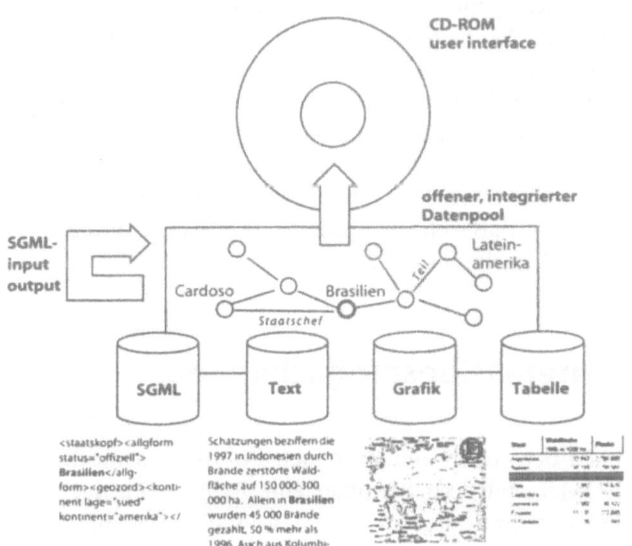

Abbildung 1
*Publikations-
architektur*

Abbildung 1 zeigt, daß Fakten wie etwa die Produktionsdaten, die als Excel-Tabellen vorlagen, und Fakten, die im Staatenteil des Fischer Weltalmanachs SGML-strukturiert waren, nunmehr für den Zugriff unifiziert und an einem Staatenobjekt gespeichert sind.

Die Modellierung der Objektstruktur orientierte sich an der SGML-DTD für den Staatenteil. Darüber hinaus spielt die DTD eine wichtige Rolle für den standardisierten Import der Daten in die Datenbank sowie für deren standardisierten Export aus der Datenbank.

Aufbau der Wissensbasis

Der SGML-strukturierte Datenbestand konnte direkt in das Wissensnetz überführt (s. Beispiel in Abschnitt 2.2) und dort mit zusätzlichen Informationen angereichert werden, wohingegen die anderen Daten weiter aufbereitet werden mußten, und – aufgrund der nicht expliziten Struktur – auch nicht so vielfältig mit anderen Objekten verknüpft werden konnten. Für diese Aufbereitung waren für jedes Datenformat verschiedene, speziell zu entwickelnde Parsingmechanismen notwendig. Dabei lag eine Schwierigkeit darin, daß die verschiedenen Datenformate unterschiedlich viele hierarchische und semantische Strukturinformationen transportieren, und daß daher der Aufwand, diese Informationen möglichst automatisiert zu gewinnen, unterschiedlich groß war. QuarkXPress-Daten etwa enthalten keine expliziten Strukturinformationen, wohingegen RTF-Dateien wenigstens eine Inhaltsstruktur in Form von Überschriften,

*Thomas Kamps, Christoph Obermeier
Klaus Reichenberger und Ingrid Schmidt*

Unterüberschriften etc. aufweisen, die für den Aufbau der Objektstruktur genutzt werden konnten.

Kosten   Die Heterogenität der Datenformate sowie die darin enthaltene
unterschiedliche Tiefe der semantischen Auszeichnungen hat weit-
reichende Konsequenzen für die Komplexität der Wissensbasis und
damit auch für ihren effizienten Aufbau. Gerade dieser Punkt wirkte
sich erheblich auf die Kostenstruktur des Projektes aus, da gerade die
individuelle Behandlung der einzelnen Formate einen hohen Ko-
stenfaktor darstellte. Die Erfahrung von Intelligent Views in diesem
Projekt zeigt, daß sich die semantische Auszeichnung in SGML hier
um ein Mehrfaches bezahlt macht.

3.3 Interaktionsmöglichkeiten

Hauptfenster   Die nach dem oben beschriebenen Publikationsmodell entstandene
CD-ROM bietet dem Benutzer eine Reihe neuartiger Interaktions-
möglichkeiten mit den Inhalten des Fischer Weltalmanachs. Er kann
sich geographische, demographische, politische, wirtschaftliche und
umweltbezogene Fakten zu allen Staaten der Erde ansehen oder sich
ausführlich über nationale wie internationale Politiker, Umwelt,
Wirtschaft, Internationale Organisationen, Kulturpreise und im
vorangegangenen Jahr verstorbene Personen informieren, indem er
im Hauptfenster (Launcher) – dem Ausgangspunkt seiner Informationsexploration – zwischen diesen einzelnen Rubriken hin- und
herschaltet.

textuelle   Dabei unterscheidet sich die Rubrik der Staaten, da sie faktenori-
Rubriken   entiert ist, grundlegend von den anderen, vornehmlich textuellen
Rubriken. Die Themen der letzteren werden im Hauptfenster zur
Auswahl angeboten. Hat sich der Benutzer durch Anklicken für ein
Thema entschieden, geht ein sogenanntes Infofenster auf, das den
zusammenhängenden Text zeigt und seine Gliederung als Zugangs-
struktur zu den Inhalten links daneben stellt (Abbildung 2). Der
Leser kann sich über dieses Inhaltsverzeichnis im Text bewegen und
es als Orientierungshilfe, etwa beim Scrollen oder Verfolgen von
Links, benutzen: Seine aktuelle Position im Text ist stets durch Her-
vorhebung der entsprechenden Abschnittsüberschrift markiert.

Sehr viel interessantere, weil vom Buch grundlegend verschiedene Möglichkeiten der Informationsexploration werden für den fakten-orientierten, semantisch ausgezeichneten Staatenteil angeboten. Einige der SGML-markierten Fakten werden im Hauptfenster als Einschränkungs- oder Sortierkriterium für die Staatenliste bereitge-stellt und unterstützen so den Leser bei seiner individuellen Staaten-auswahl. Beispielsweise kann er sich alle Staaten anzeigen lassen, deren Fläche 10.000 km^2 übersteigt, oder er kann sich die Liste aller mitteleuropäischen Staaten nach deren jährlichem CO_2-Ausstoß ordnen lassen. Abbildung 3 zeigt eine Auswahl der Staaten nach der Amtssprache.

faktenorientierter Staatenteil

Abbildung 3
Staatenauswahl-Fenster –Liste der Staaten mit Spanisch als Amtssprache

Jede Staatenliste kann die Ausgangsbasis für weitere Informationsabfragen bilden. Durch Anklicken eines Staates im Hauptfenster öffnet sich auch hier ein Infofenster und zeigt den ausgewählten Staat mit einem voreingestellten Set von Basisinformationen, wie Fläche in km^2, Bevölkerungsanzahl, Hauptstadt, Bruttosozialprodukt. Links daneben erscheint eine vollständige, gruppierte Liste aller einen Staat charakterisierenden Fakten. Die fettgedruckten Namen stehen dabei für eine ganze Gruppe von Fakten. Um die Liste übersichtlicher zu machen, kann durch Anklicken eines fettgedruckten Namens die zugehörige Gruppe zusammengezogen und wieder expandiert werden (Abbildung 4). Der Benutzer kann diese Faktenliste benutzen, um die voreingestellte Auswahl zu verändern, indem er durch einfaches Anklicken weitere ihn interessierende Fakten hinzufügt und andere entfernt. Jeder Selektionsvorgang verändert unmittelbar die Darstellung des Staates im Infofenster.

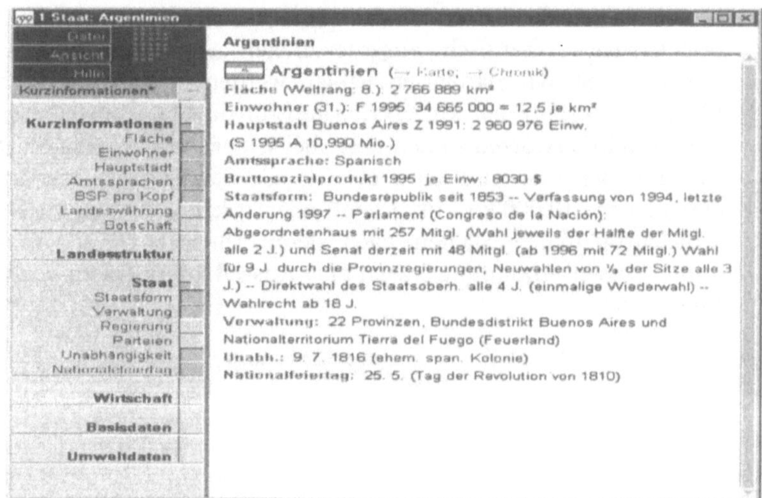

Abbildung 4
Selektionsmechanismus (Infofenster Staatenteil)

Um mehrere Staaten gleichzeitig im Infofenster zu sehen, kann man sie entweder durch doppeltes Anklicken in der Staatenliste oder über drag & drop einfügen. Ein neu hinzugenommener Staat zeigt automatisch das zuvor selektierte Faktenprofil.

individuelle Profile

Jede Faktenauswahl ist eine spezifische Sicht auf den Datenbestand des Weltalmanachs. Sichten, die der Benutzer für seine speziellen Fragen und Aufgaben häufiger benötigt, kann er sich als Profil unter einem eigenen Namen abspeichern; es steht ihm damit für spätere Explorationen wieder zur Verfügung.

Alle Infofenster sind gleich aufgeteilt: links befindet sich die Informations- und Zugriffsstruktur, rechts davon wird der Inhalt dargestellt. Dieselbe Einteilung für alle Fenster zu wählen, ist eine der Konsistenzregeln, die für eine einfache Erlernbarkeit im Umgang mit dem System sorgt. Andere solcher Regeln betreffen die direkte Manipulation von Informationsobjekten mit Hilfe von drag & drop bzw. die Funktionsauslösung durch Doppelklick. Beide Interaktionsmechanismen zusammen stellen sicher, daß die Informationseinheiten nach einem einheitlichen intuitiven Muster zwischen den verschiedenen Fenstern bewegt werden können.

Im Staatenteil sind die semantischen Einheiten in ein festes Schema eingebunden. In den textuellen Teilen des Fischer Weltamanachs gibt es ebenfalls solche Einheiten, die jedoch nicht fest in einer Struktur verankert sind, sondern nur dann ausgezeichnet werden, wenn sie vorkommen. So werden beispielsweise in allen textorientierten Teilen wie Umwelt, Wirtschaft, Internationale Organisationen die Personennamen ausgezeichnet. Aus diesen SGML-Markierungen kann später automatisch ein Register generiert werden. Gerade hier ist es allerdings unabdingbar, daß nicht nur die Textstellen markiert sind, sondern daß auch die Wissensbasis ein entsprechendes Objekt enthält, das mit diesem markierten Textteil verbunden wird. Nur so können bei der Registererstellung z.B. Schreibvarianten eines Personennamens im Text einer einzigen Person zugeordnet werden. Ohne die Einbindung in das Wissensnetz würde jede Schreibvariante getrennt im Register aufgeführt sein.

3.4 Zugriffsmedien

Zugriffsmedien dienen der Kommunikation von Informationseinheiten und sind daher abhängig von strukturellen und quantitativen Eigenschaften der zu kommunizierenden Daten. Daher werden Textdaten in geeigneten Textbrowsern, Photos bzw. thematische Karten in skalierbaren Medienbrowsern präsentiert. Anders verhält es sich bei Fakten. Diese können durch verschiedene Zugriffsmedien kommuniziert werden: Ein automatisch generierter Text, eine Visualisierung als Tabelle oder Diagramm, aber auch markiertes Kartenmaterial können geeignete Mittel sein, um die darzustellenden Fakten ausdrucksvoll grafisch umzusetzen. Da die Wahl des Mediums entscheidend vom Aufgabenkontext, von individuellen Wahrnehmungsaspekten und von den Vorlieben und Gewohnheiten des Benutzers abhängt, liegt es nahe, daß dieser auch die Entscheidung trifft, wie die Fakten präsentiert werden sollen. Wie solche Sichten

*Thomas Kamps, Christoph Obermeier
Klaus Reichenberger und Ingrid Schmidt*

mit Hilfe der verschiedenen Medientypen umgesetzt werden, wird im folgenden erläutert. Dabei werden vier verschiedene Typen von Infofenstern unterschieden, die als Text-, Tabellen-, Diagramm- und Kartenscreen bzw. -browser bezeichnet werden.

Der Benutzer wird vielfach die Fakten zu mehreren Staaten vergleichen wollen, um daraus weitere Erkenntnisse ableiten zu können. Im Fall der Textsicht liegen dafür klare quantitative Beschränkungen vor. Denn obwohl es bei der Weltalmanach-CD-ROM theoretisch möglich ist, beliebig viele Staaten in der Textsicht miteinander zu vergleichen, ist es sinnvoll, die Anzahl auf zwei oder maximal drei Staaten zu beschränken, da die Komplexität der Darstellung – eventuell verstärkt durch die Notwendigkeit, zu scrollen – die Wahrnehmung überfordert. Im Gegensatz dazu ermöglicht eine Tabellendarstellung den Vergleich beliebig vieler Staaten. Darüber hinaus können auf Tabellen Sortieroperationen ausgeführt werden. Die Diagrammsicht wiederum erlaubt, die Daten holistisch und abstrahiert zu betrachten. Kommastellengenauigkeit ist diesem Medium fremd. Im Kartenscreen ist es möglich, staatenbezogene Fakten, wie etwa die Zugehörigkeit zu Internationalen Organisationen oder die Arbeitslosigkeitsraten auf Karten einzutragen und damit geographisch zu erfassen. Da die Diagrammgenerierungskomponente in der Weltalmanach-Anwendung eine herausgehobene Rolle spielt, wird der unterliegende Mechanismus im folgenden Abschnitt detailliert dargestellt.

3.5 Diagrammgenerierung

Das Modul für Diagrammgenerierung erlaubt dem Benutzer, individuell zusammengestellte Fakten, die aus allen Teilen des Weltalmanachs kommen können, visuell vergleichbar zu machen. Da jeder Benutzer andere, spezifische Informationswünsche hat, muß der Visualisierungsprozeß automatisch erfolgen. Es können nicht für beliebige Datenverknüpfungen a priori Diagramme berechnet und gespeichert werden, die dann gegebenenfalls nur noch abgerufen werden müßten. Mit automatischer Visualierung ist die Bedingung verbunden, daß das System in der Lage sein muß, gewisse Visualisierungsentscheidungen zu treffen, etwa welche Art von Diagramm für welche Sorte von Fakten generiert werden soll.

Für ein Produkt wie die Weltalmanach-CD-ROM ist von entscheidender Bedeutung, daß diese Systementscheidungen in einem ausgewogenen Verhältnis zu den Möglichkeiten des Benutzers stehen, manuell auf die Visualisierung Einfluß zu nehmen. Der Vorteil dieses Designkonzepts besteht darin, daß sich der Benutzer auf der einen Seite nicht um die Generierung der Diagramme kümmern muß, andererseits aber die Möglichkeit hat, auf die Präsentation eines Diagramms entscheidenden Einfluß auszuüben, etwa durch Einstellung unterschiedlicher Ordnungs- und Gruppierungskriterien oder durch Änderung der Eigenschaften des Präsentations-Stylesheet, die beide das „Look and Feel" der Darstellung festlegen.

Prinzipiell startet die Visualisierung mit einer Benutzeranfrage, welche eine Menge von Eingabedaten (Fakten) an den Generierungsprozeß liefert. Diese Fakten werden vom System analysiert und hinsichtlich spezifizierter grafischer Kodierungsstrategien visuell kodiert. Mittels prozeduraler Layoutalgorithmen werden die kodierten Fakten schließlich in ein Diagramm umgesetzt. Dieser Prozeß wird im folgenden erläutert.

3.5.1 Eingabe

Um den Visualisierungsprozeß in Gang zu setzen, wählt der Benutzer im Diagrammscreen ihn interessierende Staaten und Kategorien aus, analog zur Interaktion im Textscreen des Staatenbrowsers (s. Abschnitt 3.3). Diese Benutzeranfrage startet einen Kommunikationsprozeß zwischen dem Visualisierungssystem und der Weltalmanach-Datenbank, welche eine Menge von Datentupel an den Visualierungsmodul zurückliefert. Diese Datentupel werden sortiert, abhängig davon, ob der Benutzer die Daten nach Kategorien oder nach Staaten geordnet sehen möchte, und an den Analysemechanismus weitergereicht.

3.5.2 Analysefunktionalität

Die Qualität von Datenanalyseverfahren hängt wesentlich von der Reichhaltigkeit und der Strukturiertheit der zu analysierenden Daten ab. Insofern sind die im Falle der Weltalmanach-Anwendung vorliegenden stark strukturierten SGML-Daten von großem Wert. Sie erlauben, über die strukturierte Benutzerführung in den Browsern mittels Unterkategorienbildung bzw. über die Bereitstellung strukturierter Suchergebnisse hinaus, die Abbildung eines differenzierten Einheitensystems, das für die Diagrammgenerierung von großer Bedeutung ist. Auf diesen Aspekt wird im folgenden näher eingegangen.

Konkret untersucht der Analysemechanismus, inwieweit die Kategorien der Benutzeranfrage in Gruppen geordnet werden können. Diese Gruppenbildung dient der Strukturierung des zu generierenden Diagramms. Ein Kriterium für die Gruppenbildung ist die Vergleichbarkeit der Daten, die sich aus gemeinsamen Einheiten ergibt. Beispielsweise können einwohnerbezogene Größen verglichen werden, während Einwohner und Fläche disjunkte Kategorien sind. Basierend auf dieser Gruppenbildung werden die Kategorien des weiteren nach Kategorietypen klassifiziert, die unterschiedlich visualisiert werden müssen. So erfahren prozentuale Anteile eine andere Visualisierung als absolute Werte. Darüber hinaus werden typspezifische Analysemethoden implementiert, z.B. für fehlende Prozentangaben wird das Komplement berechnet und als „sonstige" ausgewiesen.

3.5.3 Kodierungsfunktionalität

Die Kodierungsfunktionalität wird durch die Angabe der grafischen Abbildung der Fakten, durch die Formulierung von Konsistenzregeln und durch eine Reihe formal-ästhetischer Konventionen festgelegt.

Grafische Abbildung

Allgemein werden Kategorien und Staaten durch folgende grafische Elemente abgebildet:

Kategorie	→	Balken (Farbe, Position, Länge, Unterteilung)
		Quadrat (Farbe)
		Linie (Strichelung, Farbe)
		Attribut von Karteneintrag (Farbe)
Staat	→	Symbol
		Attribut von Balken (Farbe)
		Attribut von Linie (Strichelung)
		Karteneintrag

Entsprechend der obigen Zuordnung können Kategorien als Balken, Quadrate oder als Linien dargestellt werden. Die Kategoriewerte werden entsprechend der unten angeführten Zuordnung durch die in Klammern gesetzten Attribute der grafischen Elemente umgesetzt. Insbesondere werden für die unterschiedlichen Wertetypen adäquate grafische Umsetzungsmöglichkeiten spezifiziert:

absolute Zahl	→	Länge des Balkens
%-Anteile	→	Unterteilung des Balkens in Anteile
%-Zahlen	→	Länge des Balken

Qualität   →   Wahl grafischer Elemente ohne
Länge, deren Farbkodierung in
einer Legende erklärt wird

Symbol   →   x/y-Position

Staaten werden demgegenüber durch Symbole bzw. durch qualitative Attribute der die Kategorien visualisierenden grafischen Elemente umgesetzt.

Konsistenzregeln

Im Hinblick auf eine gute Lesbarkeit und Wiedererkennbarkeit ist es notwendig, die Konsistenz der Darstellungen zu gewährleisten. Diese ist besonders wichtig, da das Diagramm-Modul in einem interaktiven Prozeß zur Anwendung kommt. Ein einfaches Mittel, die Konsistenz dynamisch sicherzustellen, besteht darin, eine feste Reihenfolge der o.a. Kategorietypen festzulegen, die sich in allen generierten Diagrammen widerspiegelt. So repräsentiert im Fischer Weltalmanach die Reihenfolge „absolute Zahl, %-Anteile, %-Zahlen, Qualität" die Ordnung der visualisierten Kategorien. Konkret werden zunächst Balken absoluter Länge dargestellt, darunter folgen Prozentbalken und dann die Qualitätsdarstellungen.

Reihenfolge

Neben der Reihenfolge ist eine konsistente Farbauswahl von großer Bedeutung. Daher sollte innerhalb einer interaktiven Sitzung sichergestellt sein, daß etwa die Farbkodierung eines Staates oder einer Kategorie konstant bleibt, damit gleiche Sachverhalte einfach wiedererkannt werden können. Diese Konsistenzregeln der Darstellung gehen unmittelbar einher mit den Konsistenzregeln der anderen Module, aber auch mit den in Abschnitt 3.3 beschriebenen Konsistenzregeln auf der Interaktionsebene.

Farben

Diagrammtypen

Im letzten Abschnitt wurde der grundsätzliche Mechanismus erklärt, welcher der Visualisierungstechnik in der Weltalmanach-Anwendung zugrunde liegt. In diesem Abschnitt soll auf die generierbaren Diagrammtypen und auf die Interaktionen auf diesen Typen eingegangen werden. Die Diagrammtypen beruhen zum einen auf den o.a. Abbildungsvorschriften, auf Konsistenzregeln und ästhetischen Konventionen, aber auch auf expliziten Benutzeranforderungen, die sich etwa als Ordnungskriterien niederschlagen. Konkret können die Fakten nach Staaten, nach Kategorien, nach Zeit und nach Orten klassifiziert werden; die Ordnung nach Zeit und Orten ist derzeit noch nicht implementiert.

Klassifikation nach Staaten

Klassifikation nach Staaten bedeutet, daß eine Menge von Fakten –
nach Staaten gruppiert – visualisiert wird. Die Visualisierung erfolgt
in Form von alphabetisch nach Staaten geordneten Päckchen von
Balkendiagrammen. Darüber hinaus werden aus der Gruppenbildung, die sich aus gemeinsamen Einheiten ableitet (s. Abschnitt
3.5.2), Alinierungsregeln berechnet, die dafür sorgen, daß die grup-
pierten Balken links aliniert werden. Kategorien, die nicht vergleichbar sind, werden untereinander, nach links versetzt angeordnet (Abbildung 5). Diese Maßnahmen dienen der Strukturierung der Diagramme und damit auch der besseren Lesbarkeit.

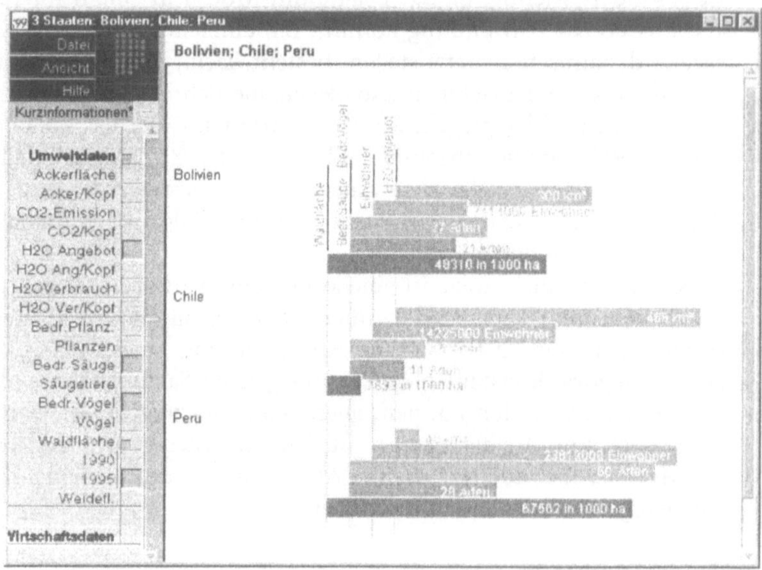

spezialisierte Sichten

Solche Diagramme können sehr komplex werden, insbesondere
wenn viele Staaten und Kategorien vom Benutzer ausgewählt wurden. Daher gibt es die Möglichkeit spezialisierter Sichten: Per Doppelklick auf ein Einheitenpäckchen werden nur die Kategorien dieser
Einheit über alle gewählten Staaten hinweg hervorgehoben; alle anderen Kategorien werden „ausgegraut" und treten damit in den
Hintergrund. Zur besseren Orientierung schaltet sich zusätzlich ein
Koordinatensystem ein, dessen Einheitenraster am längsten Balken
ausgerichtet ist. Dadurch wird die Vergleichbarkeit einzelner Katego-
rienmengen quer zur Staatenordnung möglich, und gleichzeitig geht
der Kontext aller ausgewählten Kategorien nicht verloren, da diese
sichtbar bleiben.

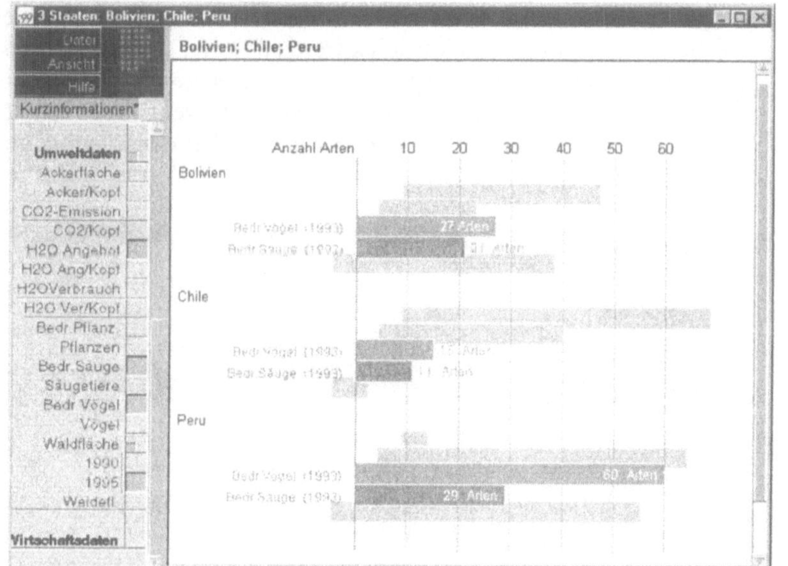

Abbildung 6
Diagrammsicht nach Staaten geordnet, mit Fokus (Infofenster Staatenteil)

Klassifikation nach Kategorien

Klassifikation nach Kategorien bedeutet, daß eine Menge von Fakten – nach Kategorien gruppiert – visualisiert wird. Jedes dieser Balkenpäckchen setzt Balken der gleichen Kategorie zueinander in Beziehung. Die Balken konnen daher automatisch links aliniert werden. Eine spezialisierte Sicht ist für diesen einfachen Diagrammtyp, der auch als Aneinanderreihung nicht vergleichbarer Diagramme betrachtet werden kann, nicht vorgesehen. Die Päckchen werden untereinander angeordnet, entsprechend der oben angegebenen Typreihenfolge (Abbildung 7).

Klassifikation nach Zeit

Viele der Kategorien des Fischer Weltalmanachs wurden über mehrere Jahre erhoben und liegen somit als Zeitreihen vor. Insofern sind zeitbezogene Sichten auf die Fakten wichtige Hilfsmittel der grafischen Datenanalyse. Solche Sichten werden durch Liniendiagramme unterstützt, in denen auf der x-Achse die Zeit (gegebenenfalls sind mehrere x-Achsen vorhanden) und auf den y-Achsen die Einheiten der ausgewählten Kategorien abgetragen werden; die Linienzüge repräsentieren die verschiedenen Kategoriewerte. In diesem Diagrammtyp werden die Verbindungselemente der Linien durch Symbole repräsentiert, so daß die Kombination von Symbol und Linientyp eine eindeutige visuelle Kodierung von Kategorie und Staat ermöglicht. Ähnlich wie bei der Klassifikation nach Staaten, kann ein solches Diagramm schnell komplex werden. Daher sind spezialisierte Sichten, etwa auf einzelne Aspekte wie „nur Kategorien mit der Einheit Tonne" oder „nur Fakten, die Schweden betreffen" als Hervorhebungen auf die gleiche Weise realisiert, wie bei der Klassifikation nach Staaten.

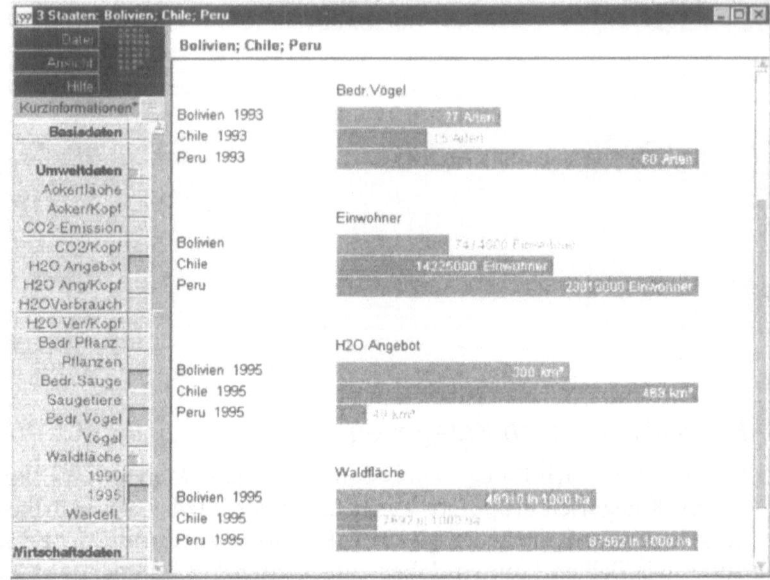

__Abbildung 7__
Diagrammsicht nach Kategorien geordnet (Infofenster Staatenteil)

Klassifikation nach Ort

Karten Fakten, Staaten betreffend, sind auf natürliche Weise in einen geographischen Kontext eingebettet. So kann eine Reihe von Staaten, etwa bezüglich der Inflationsrate oder der Zugehörigkeit zur selben Internationalen Organisation (OPEC, Nato), auf einer geographischen Karte markiert werden. Dabei wird die Verbindung von normiertem Wissen (Thesaurus) und individuellen Verknüpfungen von Fakten seitens des Benutzers beachtet. Verschiedene Zoomstufen erlauben dem Benutzer, seinen Blick auf ganz bestimmte Staaten zu richten. Von der geographischen Sicht kann auch in andere Sichten gewechselt werden.

4 Zusammenfassung und Ausblick

Anhand der Produktion der Fischer Weltalmanach '99 CD-ROM wurde gezeigt, wie ein wissensbasierter Publikationsprozeß implementiert werden kann, der es erlaubt, dynamische Publikationen effizient zu produzieren. Die Grundkomponente ist eine spezielle Datenbank, in der zum einen die Fakten und Medieninhalte (Text, Grafik) gespeichert werden und zum anderen ein Objektnetz, das Informationseinheiten – die über spezielle Parsingmechanismen aus heterogenen Datenformaten herausgefiltert werden – uniform integriert. Die SGML-Modellierung des Fischer Weltalmanachs war die Grundlage für den Aufbau der Wissensbasis und trug damit erhebliche dazu bei, ein reichhaltiges elektronisches Produkt zu schaffen und die Produktionskosten zu senken. Darüber hinaus diente SGML als standardisiertes Input- und Output-Format für die Datenbank.

Es wurde weiterhin gezeigt, wie durch die Bereitstellung einer geeigneten Zugriffsfunktionalität ein individualisierter Zugang zu den Informationen möglich werden kann. In diesem Zusammenhang sind Präsentationsmechanismen, wie Diagramm- oder Tabellengenerierungsverfahren, aber auch Kartendarstellungen von besonderer Wichtigkeit, da individualisierter Zugriff immer auch unvorhergesehene Datenkonstellationen impliziert. Dadurch entsteht ein Darstellungsproblem, das nur automatisch adäquat gelöst werden kann.

Durch die in der elektronischen Ausgabe des Fischer Weltalmanachs '99 bereitgestellten Explorationsmechanismen wurde das Feld „dynamische Publikationen" eher eröffnet als schon vollkommen ausgelotet. Den Leser bei der anspruchsvollen Aufgabe des Sammelns und Klassifizierens von Informationen, des Erkennens und der Analyse von Zusammenhängen vielfältiger zu unterstützen, wird auch die zukünftigen elektronischen Ausgaben des Weltalmanach vor neue Herausforderungen stellen. Dies gilt für die Strukturierung und redaktionelle Bearbeitung der Inhalte ebenso wie für die Visualisierung. In diesem Zusammenhang werden ein Arbeitsmappenkonzept und eine sogenannte Outlinefunktion eine große Rolle spielen. Arbeitsmappen dienen dazu, für den Leser interessante Informationen zwischenzuspeichern, um sie im Outliner mit anderen Materialien zu einem eigenen Dokument zusammenzustellen.

Für die Visualisierung heißt das, spezialisierte Diagramme zu erzeugen, die eine eingeschränkte Menge von Kategorien noch sehr viel direkter in Beziehung setzen und gleichzeitig einen allgemeingültigen Mechanismus für die Diagrammgenerierung nicht in Frage stellen. So lassen sich z.B. prozentuale Anteile klarer in einem Tortendiagramm darstellen oder zeitabhängige Daten können mittels

*Thomas Kamps, Christoph Obermeier
Klaus Reichenberger und Ingrid Schmidt*

Kurven vergleichbar gemacht werden. Neue Möglichkeiten, Werte grafisch in Beziehung zu setzen, werden durch Funktionen ergänzt, die es dem Leser erlauben, Zusammenhänge, die er erkannt hat, auch festzuhalten. So wird er existierende Kategorien zu neuen verrechnen können, etwa dadurch, daß „pro Einwohner" oder „pro Fläche" Werte gebildet werden, oder er wird sich statistischer Funktionen bedienen können.

Kundendienst-Information bei Rolls-Royce Motor Cars Ltd.

Renate Mayer und Leszek Wawrzyniak

1 Einführung

Dieser Artikel beschreibt, wie die *Rolls Royce Motor Cars Ltd.* SGML-Technologie einsetzt, um den Erstellungsprozeß von Rolls-Royce-Produktinformationen für Händler und Wartungspersonal zu unterstützen. Dabei war es das Ziel, die papierbasierte Produktinformation abzulösen, die Daten statt dessen strukturiert aufzubereiten, um sie als Teil eines elektronischen Handbuches, eines elektronischen Service-Katalogs oder anderer elektronischer Dokumenttypen anzubieten. Zu diesem Zweck hat *CSC Ploenzke* für Rolls-Royce in einem zweijährigen Projekt ein objektorientiertes integriertes System zur automatischen Übernahme von Alt-Daten, zur Erstellung von Neu-Daten und zur Verwaltung von SGML-Dokumenten implementiert. Die zugrundeliegende Architektur, die Module dieses Autorensystems sowie die wichtigsten Phasen des Realisierungsprojekts werden im folgenden beschrieben.

Ablösung papierbasierter Dokumentation

1.1 Rolls-Royce Motor Cars

Die *Rolls-Royce Motor Cars Ltd.* – zu Projektbeginn der etablierteste britische Hersteller von Luxus-Limousinen, mittlerweile Teil des *VW Konzerns* – produziert jährlich etwa 3000 PKW in mehreren Varianten, die sowohl viele Standardzubehörteile als auch exklusives Zubehör haben.

Die für das Fahrzeug notwendige technische Dokumentation wird von der Abteilung Kundeninformation, der *Customer Information Group*, für das weltweite Händlernetz von Rolls-Royce erstellt. Sie wird zuerst auf englisch geschrieben und danach in die vier Hauptsprachen Deutsch, Französisch, Italienisch und Spanisch übersetzt. Eine Unterstützung weiterer Sprachen, wie z.B. des Japanischen, ist geplant.

Diese technische Information ist äußerst wichtig und muß, um die qualitativ hochwertige Wartung und Reparatur eines Fahrzeugs sicherzustellen, während seines gesamten Lebenszyklus zur Verfügung stehen. Beispielsweise werden detaillierte Informationen über Montage, Demontage und Einstellung von komplexen Autoaggregaten sowie über Ersatzteile oder Drehmomente vorgehalten. Ferner werden Erfahrungen, die in der Praxis gemacht wurden, als abrufbare Ratschläge angeboten. Auf diese Weise sollen Techniker in die Lage versetzt werden, die Wartung und Reparatur eines Rolls-Royce fehlerfrei und effizient durchzuführen.

Eines der Hauptprobleme der Autohersteller, die kleine Auto-Serien produzieren, sind die Kosten für die unterstützende Dokumentation pro Fahrzeug, die nicht von der Stückzahl, sondern von der Vielfalt und Komplexität der Fahrzeuge herrühren. Sie entstehen bei der Erstellung der Dokumentation, bei ihrer Übersetzung in viele Sprachen, bei der Druckvorbereitung, und schließlich auch bei der Verteilung. Zu den Kosten kommen noch relativ lange Bearbeitungszeiten hinzu und, damit verbunden, das relativ schnelle Veralten der Information.

1.2 Das Projekt IETIS

Im September 1995 suchte Rolls-Royce Motor Cars Ltd. nach einer Lösung für ihre technische Dokumentation und trat, beraten durch die *UK SGML User Group* und von Mitgliedern der *Arbeitsgruppe SAE J2008*, an mehrere Unternehmen heran. Die Arbeitsgruppe SAE J2008 (SAE J2008 ist das amerikanische Standard-Austauschformat für unabhängige Auto-Händler) hat die Aufgabe, ihre Mitglieder, zu denen auch Rolls-Royce gehört, über die Verfügbarkeit neuer Technologien, über zeitgemäße Lösungen und mögliche Lösungsanbieter zu informieren. Die UK SGML User Group empfahl Rolls-Royce, sich an *CSC Ploenzke* zu wenden, nicht zuletzt wegen eines SGML-basierten Autoren- und Viewing-Systems, das CSC zu dieser Zeit bei der Firma *Ford Motor Corporation* weltweit implementiert hatte. Aufgrund dieser Erfahrungen erhielt CSC den Projektauftrag.

Das Projekt, das den Namen *IETIS, Integrated Electronic Technical Information System*, erhielt, startete im November 1995 mit einer ersten Analyse der vorliegenden Daten. Ein Prototyp folgte im Sommer 1996. Die Realisierung des Produktionssystems begann anschließend und wurde in der Grundversion im Sommer 1997 fertiggestellt. Einige Erweiterungen, wie die Implementierung eines neuen CD-Viewers, haben das Projekt bis März 1998 verlängert.

1.3 Besonderheiten der Kundendienst-Information

Als Kundendienstinformation bezeichnet man die technische Information, die notwendig ist, um eine zufriedenstellende Wartung und Reparatur eines Fahrzeuges während seines gesamten Lebenszyklus von zehn, zwanzig oder gar fünfzig Jahren zu gewährleisten.

Die Kundendienstinformation muß folgenden Kriterien genügen:

- *Sie muß gleichzeitig mit der Produktauslieferung verfügbar sein,* und zwar bei neuen wie modifizierten Produkten. Um Händler und Servicepersonal mit der richtigen Information zu versorgen, müssen Autoren und Übersetzer der Dokumentation nahezu zeitgleich mit dem Produkt fertig sein. Hierfür braucht man eine ökonomisch sinnvolle und schnelle Methode für die Verteilung der neuen Information.

- *Sie muß korrekt und spezifisch für jeden Fahrzeugtyp sein.* Ein technischer Autor, der ein wichtiges Mitglied der „Engineering-Mannschaft" darstellt, muß dafür sorgen, daß neue Konstruktionen oder Konstruktionsänderungen schnell und verständlich für den Kundendienst dokumentiert werden.

- *Sie muß während des gesamten Lebenszyklus vorgehalten werden.* Der Prozeß der Aktualisierung der Kundendienstinformationen erstreckt sich über den gesamten Lebenszyklus eines Fahrzeuges und wird durch Konstruktionsänderungen und -erweiterungen angestoßen. Die Änderungen sind meistens für eine bestimmte Serie von Fahrzeugen gültig, wobei noch jeder einzelne Wagen, der von einem Techniker gewartet wird, durch eine *VIN (Vehicle Identification Number)* gekennzeichnet ist.

- *Sie muß einfach in der Handhabung sein.* Benutzer der Kundendienstinformation sind die Automechaniker und Ersatzteilverkäufer, die die für die jeweilige Reparatur oder Wartung notwendigen Informationen selbstverständlich möglichst schnell und einfach finden möchten. Dabei sind es vor allem die unterschiedlichen Such- und Navigationsmöglichkeiten, die die meisten Nutzer überzeugen können. Die Verfügbarkeit preiswerter PCs und preiswerter CD-ROM-Technologie hat die Erstellung und Verteilung von Information revolutioniert.

2 Das Kundendienst-Informationssystem IETIS

2.1 Anforderungen an das IETIS

Die ursprünglichen Anforderungen der Rolls-Royce Motor Cars an das Kundendienst-Informationssystem IETIS (Integrated Electronic Technical Information System) waren:

- Es sollte ein Autorensystem implementiert werden, das sich allein durch die Kostenersparnis gegenüber dem herkömmlichen Prozeß finanziert. Diese Ersparnis sollte durch die Verkürzung der Redaktions- und CD-Erstellungskosten, durch eine möglichst hohe Wiederverwendbarkeit der Information und durch eine erhöhte Kontrolle und Kostenreduktion bei der Sprachübersetzung zustande kommen.

- Prozeßänderungen und Personalentwicklung sollten sich schnell und problemlos mit minimaler Schulung realisieren lassen. In der Vergangenheit hatten die Autoren lediglich einfache Texteditoren und Graphikwerkzeuge verwendet. Auch die neuen Werkzeuge sollten von diesen nicht computer-geschulten Autoren einfach zu benutzen sein.

- Es sollte weiterhin eine einheitliche und integrierte Autorenumgebung für alle im Service-Bereich notwendigen Informationstypen geben. Hierzu gehören z.B. Anleitungen für Demontage/Montage und Reparatur, Wartungspläne, illustrierte Teilekataloge, Elektro-Schaltpläne, das Kundendienst-Bulletin.

- Alle technischen Service- und Teile-Informationen sollen sich auf einer CD-ROM des ASSIST (After-Sales Service Information SysTem) befinden.

- Der Export der Informationen zu anderen Viewing-Systemen, wie z.B. Intranet und SAE J2008, sollte sichergestellt werden.

- Eine vollständige Verwaltung der Informationen war sicherzustellen, und zwar in bezug auf Links und die Zugehörigkeit zu Hierarchien, auf Versionen, Varianten (Sprachen und Formate), auf Workflow und Status (Freigabe, Check-In und Check-Out) und auf die Zugriffsrechte zu Funktionen und Informationen.

- Weiterhin war zu gewährleisten, daß die Informationen von anderen firmeninternen und externen Systemen importiert und wiederverwendet werden können.

Im Laufe des Projektes kamen weitere Anforderungen hinzu: Es sollte ein CD-Viewer entwickelt werden, der die vielen neuen Möglichkeiten, die durch die Erzeugung der Daten im IETIS entstanden, auch anzeigt. Und es sollte eine Lösung für die Online-Aktualisierung der CDs über ein Internet-Download gefunden werden.

2.2 Das IETIS-System

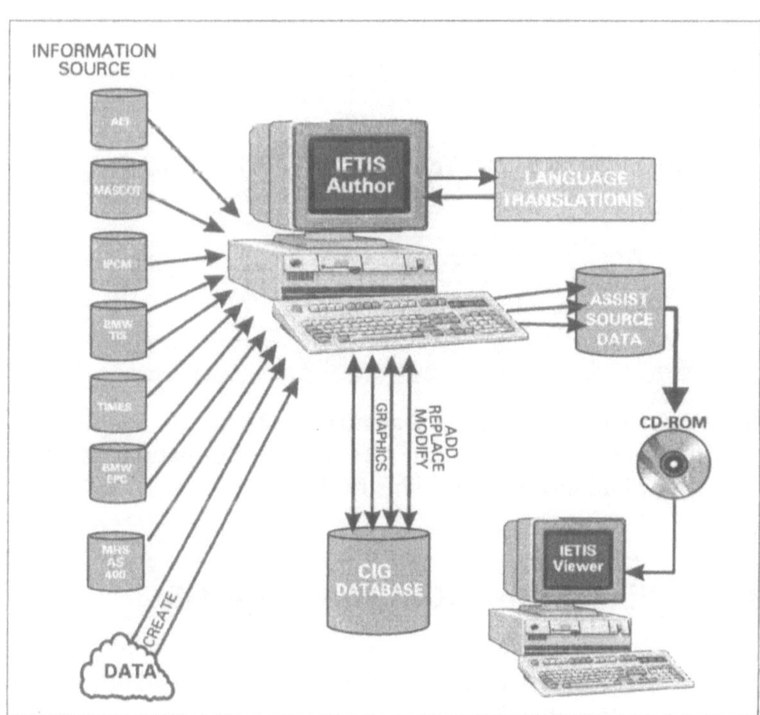

Abbildung 1
Informationsfluß-
Diagramm

Den oben aufgelisteten Anforderungen entsprechend wurde das IETIS Service-Informationssystem als ein integriertes, interaktives, Client/Server-System unter Windows NT implementiert.

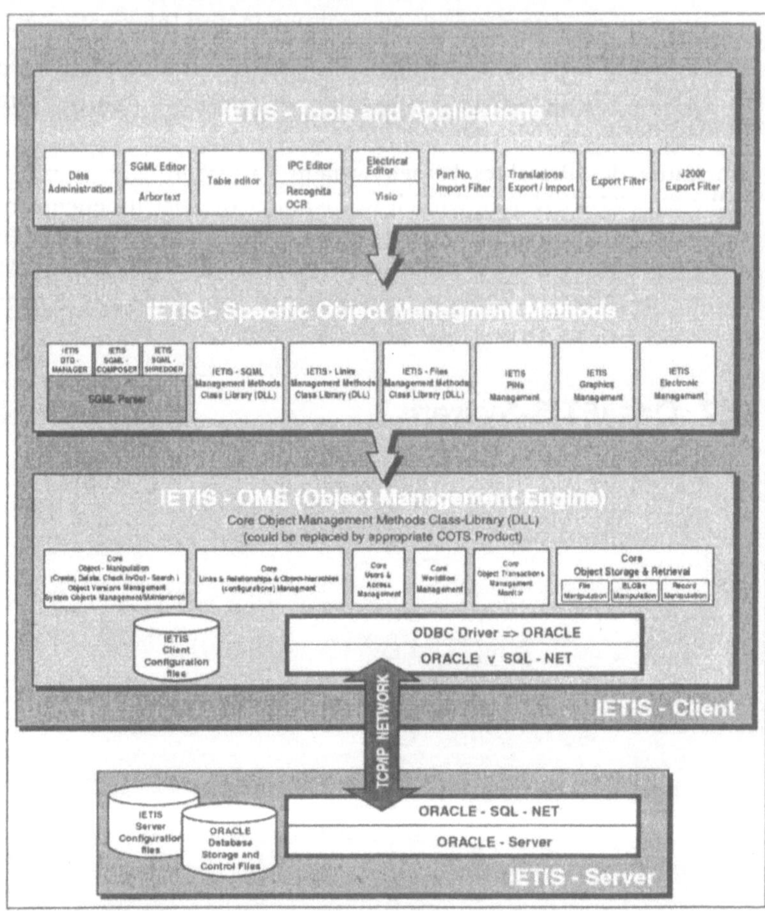

Es basiert auf einer relationalen Datenbank (ORACLE). Der Informationsfluß und die Architektur des IETIS-Informationssystems sind in den Abbildungen 1 und 2 illustriert.

2.3 Der Einsatz von SGML für das IETIS

Der größte Teil der Service-Information besteht aus strukturierten, miteinander verknüpften Texten, Tabellen und Graphiken. Um eine zukunftssichere Basis für die Implementierung zu gewährleisten, entschied man sich, einige der erprobten CALS- und J2008-Standards zu akzeptieren. Dies führte zur Anwendung von SGML für strukturierte Texte, von *HyTime* für die Hyperlinks und die Verwendung des *TIFF-Formats* (GruppeIV) für Graphiken.

SGML und die damit verbundene Technologie hatten bei den Rolls-Royce Managern in der Vergangenheit den Ruf „sehr kompliziert und kostspielig" zu sein. Durch verschiedene Präsentationen und eine Vorstudie konnten ihre Einwände diesbezüglich entkräftet werden. Insbesondere die Sorge, daß die bisherigen Autoren SGML-basierte Werkzeuge nicht beherrschen würden, konnte anhand konkreter Experimente zerstreut werden. So wurde noch im Rahmen der Vorstudie innerhalb eines Tages eine prototypische Dokumenttypdefinition (DTD) für die Service-Informationen entwickelt und von den Autoren an einigen einfachen Rolls-Royce-Dokumenten mit etwas fachlicher Unterstützung erfolgreich getestet.

Abbildung 3 illustriert diese DTD. Abbildung 4 präsentiert ein SGML-Fragment, das auf der DTD aufsetzt.

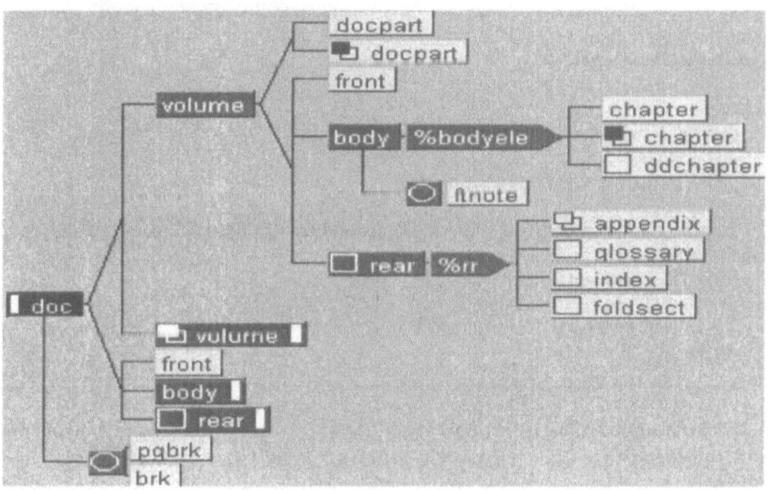

Abbildung 3
*Graphische
Darstellung der
DTD*

SGML mit seiner Technologie bietet – wenn man den ganzen Umfang ausschöpfen wollte – unzählige und sehr komplexe Möglichkeiten. Es kann aber auch pragmatisch und relativ einfach an der richtigen Stelle eingesetzt werden. Die Kunst besteht darin, die Architektur eines Systems so zu gestalten, daß die Vorteile von SGML zur Geltung kommen, ohne daß die Nachteile sichtbar werden.

Diese Mischung ist bei der IETIS-Implementierung offensichtlich gelungen, und sie führte zu einer hohen Akzeptanz durch die Benutzer. Die Kosten hielten sich in den geplanten Grenzen.

```
<!-- Fragment document type declaration subset:
ArborText, Inc., 1988-1995, v.4001
<!DOCTYPE RRTOPIC PUBLIC "Rolls-Royce Motor Company Inc.//DTD To-
pics//EN" [
<topic aid="0009">
<topic-title>Assembly oil filter (V12)<?Pub Caret> &mdash; To remove and fit
</topic-title>
<step>
<para>Drain any oil from the oil filter assy.<refer-to-pin pin="0925" oid="0"
mv="0" sv="0" vi="0"></para>
<para>Remove the two nuts securing the oil filter to the bracket.</para>
<graphic graphicname="G:\Graphics_Database\092500W0004.tif " size="" height="not
found ! "width="not found !" magnify="75" oid="12314" mv="1" sv="1" vi="1"
pins="092500W0004">
</step>
<step>
<para>Pull the oil filter assy upwards to ease the access to the pipe connections
and sensor connections.</para>
<para>Disconnect the oil cooler pipes.</para>
<installation>
<para>Replace the sealing rings</para>
</installation>
<graphic graphicname="G:\Graphics_Database\092500W0007.tif" size="0"
height="1470" width="1470" magnify="75" oid="20203" mv="1" sv="1" vi="1"
pins="092500W0007">
</step>
<step>
<para>Disconnect the oil pipes to the engine.</para>
<installation>
<para>Replace the sealing rings</para>
</installation>
<graphic graphicname="G:\Graphics_Database\092500W0003.tif" size="10146"
height="1535"
width="1535" magnify="75" oid="6256" mv="1" sv="1" vi="1"
pins="092500W0003">
</step>
</topic>
```


Ein wichtiger Erfolgsfaktor war, daß die zukünftigen Nutzer die Autorenwerkzeuge frühzeitig und stufenweise zum Austesten zur Verfügung hatten und auch ihre Änderungswünsche einbringen konnten. Damit fühlten sie sich in den Entwicklungsprozeß integriert und waren von den vielfältigen Möglichkeiten neuer Funktionen nicht überfordert.

Etwa zehn interne und bis zu zehn externe Mitarbeiter arbeiten zur Zeit interaktiv mit dem IETIS-System. Um mit den neuen Werkzeugen umgehen zu können, genügt in der Regel ein Tag Einarbeitung.

Rund 200 weltweit verteilte Händler und eine ähnliche Anzahl von Rolls-Royce-Mitarbeitern benutzen den IETIS-Viewer bei der täglichen Wartung, Reparatur oder im Ersatzteilverkauf.

2.4 Die IETIS-Architektur

Das IETIS verwaltet Objekte, deren Attribute und die Abhängigkeiten zwischen Objekten und Attributen. Die IETIS-Objekte sind meistens in Hierarchien eingebunden (s. Abbildung 5) und/oder mit anderen IETIS-Objekten verknüpft. Dies bedeutet, daß die IETIS-Objekte auf andere IETIS-Objekte verweisen oder von ihnen referenziert werden. Objekt-Hierarchien und Links dienen unter anderem dazu, die Navigationspfade, die der Endbenutzer später im Viewer verfolgen kann, innerhalb der komplexen Service-Information zu definieren.

IETIS-Objekte

Die wichtigsten IETIS-Objekte sind in folgende Klassen unterteilt:

- *Table Of Contents Objects (TOC Objects)*. Sie definieren die hierarchischen Strukturen.

- *Service Information Elements (SIEs)*. Das sind strukturierte SGML-Text-Fragmente, die der IETIS-DTD entsprechen.

- *Tabellen*, die aus praktischen Gründen nicht in SGML definiert sind;

- *Graphiken*;

- *Illustrated Parts Catalogue Frames (IPC Frames)*. Sie repräsentieren den illustrierten Teilekatalog und umfassen Subklassen für Teile-Informationen.

- *Elektrische Schaltkreise (Electrical Circuits)*, die noch Subklassen für Komponenten, Stecker und Drähte enthalten.

Die drei wichtigsten Komponenten der IETIS-Architektur sind die Object Management Engine, die IETIS-spezifischen Erweiterungen und die IETIS-Werkzeuge (s.a. Abbildung 2).

OME, die Object Management Engine, ist eine universelle objektorientierte Erweiterung einer gängigen relationalen Datenbank, sie basiert auf ODBC und ist damit RDB-unabhängig. OME setzt bei Rolls-Royce auf ORACLE auf und verwaltet die Objekte mit ihren Attributen, Hierarchien und Links, Versionen, Varianten, mit Workflow- und Statusinformationen.

*Objekt-
Management*

Die IETIS-spezifischen OME-Erweiterungen umfassen z.B. die zusätzlichen Rolls-Royce Objekt-Methoden und allgemeine Algorithmen.

Die IETIS-Werkzeuge können als eigentliche Applikationen direkt und interaktiv von den IETIS-Benutzern bedient werden. Sie bieten anwendungsspezifische Graphische Benutzerschnittstellen (GUIs) und Funktionalitäten. Zu den IETIS-Werkzeugen gehören:

- der integrierte *SGML-Editor* zur Bearbeitung von strukturierten und verlinkten Texten, die von der für IETIS entwickelten DTD kontrolliert werden;

- der integrierte *Tabellen-Editor*,

- der integrierte *Illustrated Parts Catalogue Editor (IPC Editor)* mit einem graphischen Hotspots-Editor zur interaktiven Erstellung des Teilekatalogs,

- die *integrierte OCR Engine* zur automatischen OCR-Erkennung der Hotspots auf vorgefertigten Graphiken,

- der integrierte *Electrical Circuits Editor (EC Editor)* mit eng integrierter Graphik-Engine zur interaktiven Erstellung der Elektroschaltpläne und zur Erfassung und Verwaltung der ECE-Objekte,

- die *Print-Engine* für Service-Informationen, die aus rechtlichen Gründen weiter auf Papier geliefert werden müssen, wie z.B. die Karosserie-Instandsetzung und das Kundendienst-Bulletin;

- der *Importfilter* für Daten aus Hostsystemen, z.B. Teile-Daten aus der Konstruktion und Fahrzeug-Identifikationsnummern aus der Produktion (sog. VINs);

- *Export- und Import-Tools* für die Sprachübersetzung durch externe Firmen.

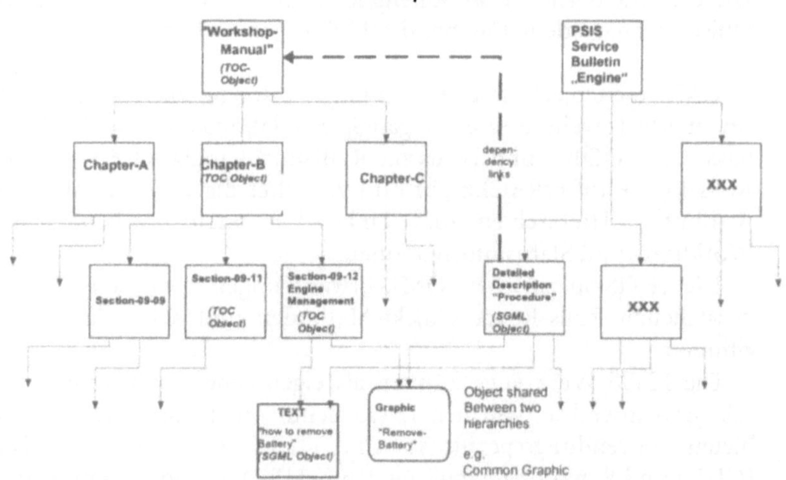

Abbildung 5
Objekt-Hierarchie

2.5 Übernahme von Alt-Daten (legacy data)

In der „Ära vor IETIS" wurden die meisten Daten für die älteren Fahrzeuge aus den Jahren 1991 bis 1997 manuell von einer externen Firma mittels eines einfachen Hyperttext-Kodier-Systems für den damaligen CD-Viewer aufbereitet. Alle diese Daten wurden im Herbst 1997 durch die von CSC Ploenzke entwickelten semi-intelligenten Werkzeuge analysiert und automatisch nach SGML sowie in Tabellen und Datenbank-Informationen konvertiert. Diese alten Informationen sind mit den IETIS-Autorenwerkzeugen aktualisierbar und daher jetzt auch Bestandteil der CDs.

automatische Konvertierung der Alt-Daten

3 IETIS Werkzeuge und Prozesse

3.1 Autoren-Vorgehen bei Textänderung

Will ein Autor einen Text ändern, setzt sich der Vorgang typischerweise aus den folgenden Schritten zusammen:

- Aussuchen des Fahrzeuges oder der Baureihe, für die eine Änderung zutrifft. Alle Rolls-Royce-Fahrzeuge sind nach Modell, Modelljahr und Serien-Nummer klassifiziert (Abbildung 6).

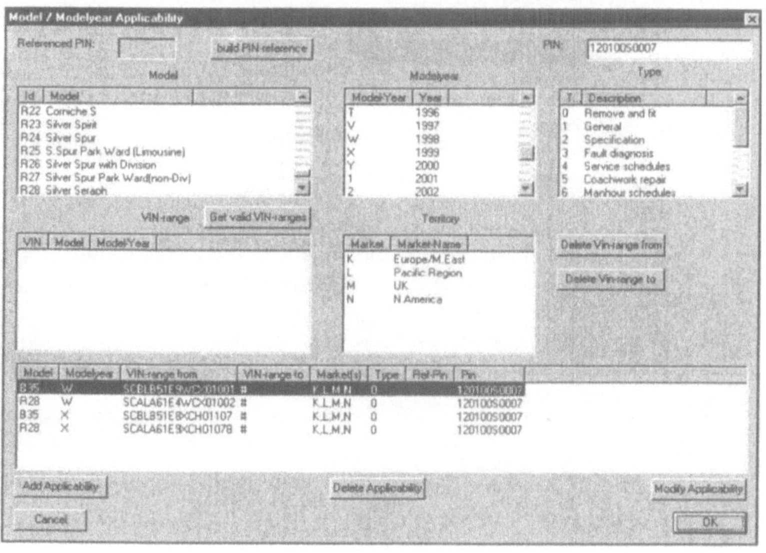

*Abbildung 6
Model, model-year und VIN builder*

- Aussuchen der Baugruppe und des Informationsbereiches, für die es eine Änderung gibt;

- Aufklappen der Hierarchie wie im Microsoft Explorer und Selektion des Text-Bausteins in der TOC-Informationshierarchie des Inhaltsverzeichnisses;

- Aufrufen des integrierten SGML-Editors durch Doppelklick auf den Textbaustein. Der Editor stellt auch die Links zu anderen IETIS-Objekten wie Graphiken, Tabellen dar (Abbildung 7).

- Modifikation des Textes oder der Hyperlinks zu anderen IETIS-Objekten. Auf dem Diagramm sind sowohl die Links zu Graphiken, wie auch Teile der IETIS-DTD zu sehen.

- Mit einem einfachen Verschieben (*Drag and Drop*) der Text-Dokumente in der Hierarchie-Anzeige können autorisierte Benutzer Struktur-Änderungen vornehmen (Abbildung 8).

- Mit der rechten Maustaste kann ein Menü aufgerufen werden, das kontext- und status-abhängig ist, z.B. kann ein noch nicht freigegebener (ausgecheckter) Textbaustein nicht editiert, sondern nur gelesen werden.

Abbildung 7
*Authoring:
Selektion und
Management
von SIEs*

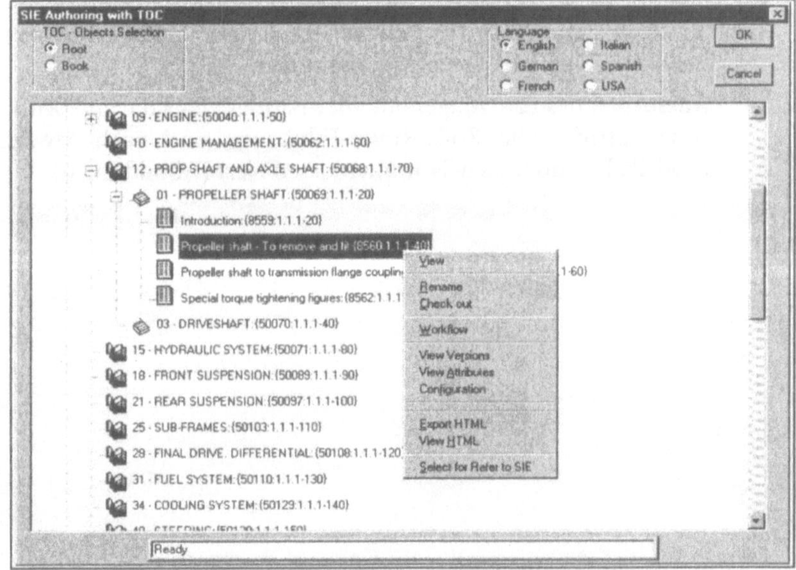

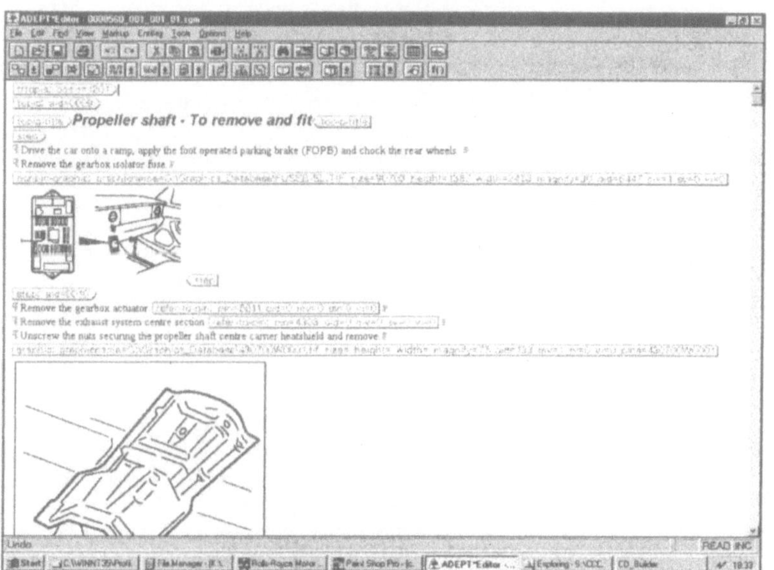

Abbildung 8
Typischer
SGML-Eintrag

3.2 Autoren-Vorgehen bei Änderung des Teilekatalogs

Das Vorgehen der Autoren bei Änderungen im Teilekatalog gestaltet sich analog zu den Textänderungen und ist ebenso einfach in der Bedienung (Abbildung 9). Zusätzlich können die Teileinformationen aus der Datenbank per *Drag and Drop* entsprechenden HotSpots auf den Graphiken zugeordnet werden.

einfache Bedienung

Die Ausführungen sollen zeigen, daß die Autorenwerkzeuge für die mit Rolls-Royce und mit der Automobil-Terminologie vertrauten technischen Autoren durchaus intuitiv und logisch ist.

Wie die Erfahrung der letzten Monate gezeigt hat, benötigt eine Person, die mit der Rolls-Royce-Terminologie und -Technik vertraut ist, weniger als zwei Tage, um die IETIS-Autorenwerkzeuge, auch einschließlich des SGML-Editors, anwenden zu können.

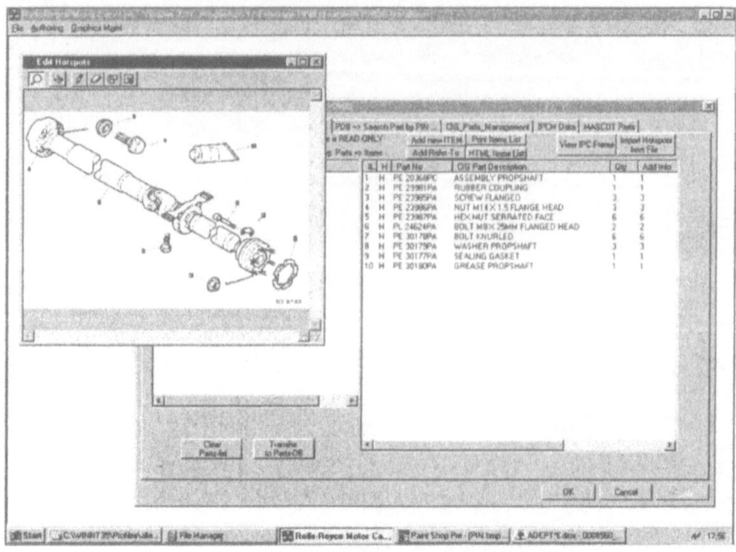

3.3 CD-ROM-Erstellung mit dem CD-Builder

Um eine neue CD-ROM mit aktuellen Service-Informationen zu produzieren, werden die von den Autoren freigegebenen Daten automatisch exportiert und mit Hilfe eines CD-Builders in eine virtuelle CD konvertiert. Diese virtuelle CD ist dann im Netzwerk für alle autorisierten Benutzer zum Suchen und Anzeigen verfügbar. Nach Beendigung der Testphase reicht es, die virtuelle CD auf eine physikalische CD zu brennen, mit herkömmlicher Kopiertechnik zu vervielfältigen und anschließend zu verteilen.

3.4 IETIS-Viewer

Im Verlauf des IETIS-Projektes erwies sich, daß der ursprünglich von Rolls-Royce eingesetzte, kommerzielle CD-Viewer seine Funktionalitätsgrenzen erreicht hatte. Infolge dessen hat Rolls-Royce entschieden, einen neuen, funktionsfähigen CD-Viewer zu entwickeln, der alle neuen Such- und Navigationsmöglichkeiten, die bereits in den IETIS-Daten vorhanden waren, unterstützt. Der neue IETIS-Viewer, wurde in Visual C++ für Windows NT, WIN 95 und Win-

Kundendienst-Information bei Rolls-Royce Motor Cars Ltd.

dows 3.11 implementiert und ist wie andere IETIS-Tools für Rolls-Royce-Mitarbeiter intuitiv bedienbar.

Der IETIS-Viewer unterstützt unter anderem

- *Hypertext-Navigation* über die Hierarchie des Inhaltsverzeichnisses (TOC-Hierarchie) und über direkte Links zwischen allen IETIS-Objekten wie Texten, Tabellen, Graphiken mit Hilfe von Hotspots;

- *intelligente kontextsensitive Suche* nach Fahrzeugtyp und Fahrzeuggestellnummer innerhalb aller von IETIS unterstützten Informations- und Dokumenttypen wie den Anleitungen zu Montage/Demontage und Reparatur, dem Teilekatalog mit Navigation über Hotspots, den Kundendienst-Tabellen, Arbeitszeit-Tabellen;

- *Volltextsuche* nach Einzelwörtern oder Ausdrücken bis zu fünf Worten;

- *automatisches Einbinden aktueller Informationen* in den CD-Kontext (inklusive Suche). Die Informationen können über das Rolls-Royce Intranet von der Zentrale heruntergeladen werden.

Einige dieser Funktionen sind in den folgenden Abbildungen illustriert.

Die Abbildung 10 zeigt die Eröffnungsseite des Viewers, und den Dialog für die Auswahl eines konkreten Fahrzeuges mittels einer Fahrzeuggestellnummer.

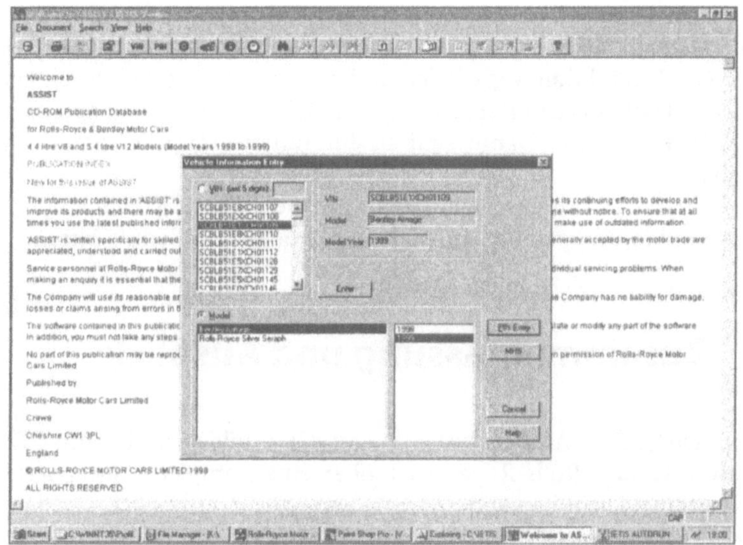

Abbildung 10
*Viewer Entry
Screen*

Die Abbildung 11 zeigt eine typische Bildtafel aus dem Teilekatalog.

Abbildung 11
Viewer:
Teilekatalog

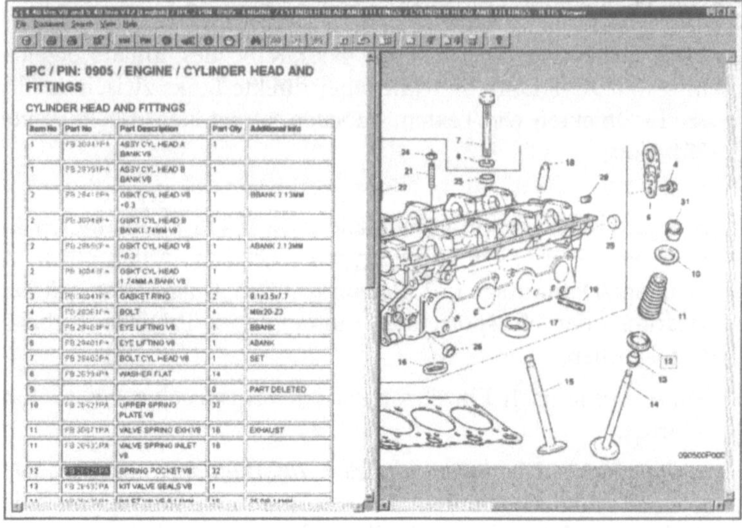

3.5 Intranet-/HTML-Unterstützung durch das IETIS

Alle Daten, einschließlich des *Table of Contents*, die in dem Prozeß der CD-Produktion verwendet und zuvor automatisch durch die Export-Tools aus den IETIS-Daten exportiert wurden, sind bereits in HTML vorhanden. Damit sind sie für Intranet-Zwecke sofort verfügbar.

Rolls-Royce begrenzt den Zugriff auf diese Daten jedoch zur Zeit aus Wettbewerbsgründen auf einen engen, internen Benutzerkreis.

4 Zusammenfassung und Ausblick

Mit dem IETIS-Autorensystem, dem CD-Builder und dem CD-Viewer verfügt Rolls-Royce jetzt über eine komplette, integrierte, konsistente, leicht bedienbare Umgebung, die es ermöglicht, kostengünstig und schnell

Kundendienst-Information bei Rolls-Royce Motor Cars Ltd.

- alle Kundendienst-Informationen einfach zu erstellen und zu verändern,

- Status und Fortschritt der Autoren-Aktivitäten zu kontrollieren,

- Status und Fortschritt der Sprach-Übersetzung zu kontrollieren,

- CDs einfach zu erstellen und zu aktualisieren,

- Informationen auf den CDs einfach zu suchen und zu betrachten,

- neben der CD auch Papierunterlagen automatisch zu produzieren sowie

- Service-Informationen im HTML-Format für Internet oder Intranet zu erstellen.

Die Akzeptanz des IETIS durch die Autoren ist sehr hoch, und die ursprünglichen Bedenken über die mögliche Komplexität und Benutzungsunfreundlichkeit von SGML stellten sich als nicht erwiesen heraus. Im Gegenteil, die Autoren und das Management sind einstimmig der Meinung, daß die Anwendung von SGML eine wichtige Basis des strukturierten Autorenprozesses ist. *hohe Akzeptanz*

Die durch IETIS ermöglichte Integration, die Wiederverwendbarkeit der Informationen und die bessere Kontrolle aller Autorenprozesse erspart der Firma Rolls-Royce bereits heute jährlich mehrere hunderttausend Pfund. Die Kosten für die Entwicklung des Systems haben sich bereits amortisiert. *große Einsparungen*

Der erfolgreiche Einsatz von IETIS hat Rolls-Royce dazu bewegt, einige Erweiterungspläne zu schmieden. Als Erweiterungen werden zur Zeit die direkte Übernahme der geometrischen Konstruktionsdaten aus dem CAD-System und der nicht geometrischen Daten aus dem konzernweiten Produktdaten-Managementsystem diskutiert. Weiterhin sollen die Dokumentation in japanischer Sprache und die Dokumentation für Autobesitzer, die bisher nur in Druckform vorliegt, unterstützt werden.

Ein Kundendienst-Informationssystem wie IETIS, die Autorenwerkzeuge sowie der Viewer, kann mit Sicherheit auch bei anderen Automobil-Herstellern eingesetzt werden. Ebenso kann es bei allen Firmen, die technische Information erstellen und an die vielen Vertreter, Verkäufer, Montage- und Wartungs-Werkstätten und nicht zuletzt den Endbenutzer verteilen müssen, Einsatz finden. *vielfältiger Einsatz möglich*

SGML/XML als Verbindungsschicht in Entwicklungsprozessen

Bernhard Weichel

Zusammenfassung

In modernen Entwicklungsprozessen gewinnt das Single-Source-Prinzip zunehmend an Bedeutung. SGML/XML kann als eine Integrationsplattform verwendet werden, da es ein einheitliches Ablage-, Austausch- und Archivierungsformat bietet. Der vorliegende Beitrag beschreibt eine mehrschichtige Architektur für Dokument- und Datenablage sowie die essentielle Rolle, die SGML/XML hierin übernehmen kann. Es werden mögliche Implementierungsstrategien sowie Anforderungen an Systeme diskutiert. Ein konkretes Fallbeispiel gibt praktische Erfahrungen weiter.

1 Entwicklungsprozeß für Motorsteuerungssysteme

Motormanagementsysteme für Verbrennungsmaschinen sind sehr komplex. Sie erfassen charakteristische Betriebsgrößen wie Drehzahl, Last, Temperaturen und steuern den Motor nach verschiedenen Optimierungskriterien. Über die grundlegenden Funktionen hinaus sind Aufgaben wie Diagnose oder Sicherheitsfunktionen zu erfüllen.

Jeder Automobilhersteller fertigt eine Vielzahl von Motortypen (Hubraum, Zylinderzahl, Füllungsverfahren usw.). Diese Motoren werden in verschiedenen Fahrzeugen eingesetzt, wodurch sich die Variantenvielfalt weiter erhöht. Hinzu kommen die spezifischen

Gesetzgebungen in der Welt. All dies führt zu hunderten verschiedener MOTRONIC-Programme (s. Abbildung 1).

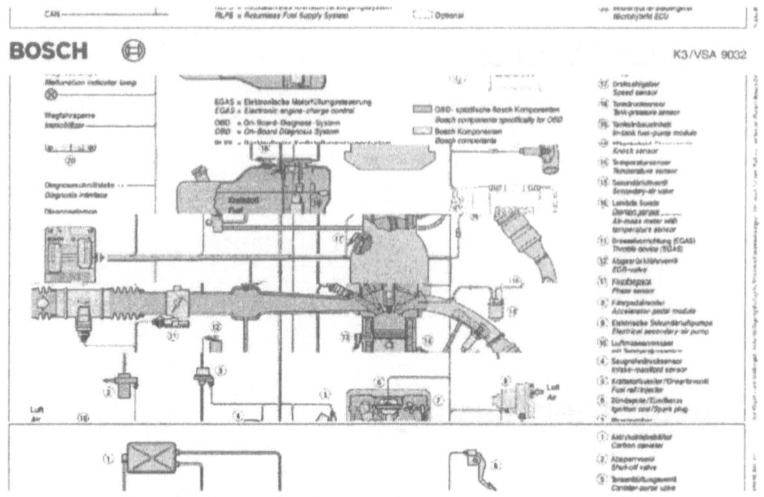

Abbildung 1
Motor-steuerungs-system

Der Entwicklungsprozeß für solche komplexen Systeme besteht aus mehreren Phasen, die von Personen mit unterschiedlichen Aufgaben abgewickelt werden. Die am Prozeß beteiligten Personen verwenden verschiedene Werkzeuge, um die in der jeweiligen Prozeßphase zu erstellenden Ergebnisse zu erzielen. Diese Ergebnisse werden im gesamten Prozeß wiederverwendet. Der Entwicklungsprozeß gliedert sich grob in folgende Phasen:

- *Systementwicklung*

  umfaßt die Entwicklung eines Systems mit vollständigen Programmen aus bereits existierenden Funktionen und aus neuen bzw. geänderten Funktionen. Letztere werden definiert als Anforderungen an die Funktionsentwicklung.

- *Funktionsentwicklung*

  definiert die Funktionen eines Steuergerätes zur Steuerung des Motors. Die Funktionsentwicklung konzentriert sich eher auf allgemeine physikalische Prinzipien als auf individuelle Anwendungsfälle (Motor oder auch Implementierung). Daher werden hier regelungstechnische Systemsimulatoren angewendet, die die Funktionen als Blockdiagramme oder Zustandsautomaten modellieren. Ein Beispiel hierfür findet sich in Abbildung 2. Im Rahmen der Funktionsentwicklung können auch physikalisch bedingte Implementierungsvorgaben anfallen.

- *Codierung*

  umfaßt die zielsystemspezifische Programmierung der entwickelten Funktionen. Bislang war diese Umsetzung manuell auszuführen. Inzwischen sind aber auch leistungsfähige Codegeneratoren verfügbar, so daß hier zumindest teilweise eine Automatisierung möglich ist.

- *Systemkonfiguration*

  stellt die verfügbaren Funktionen aus einer Bibliothek zu kompletten Systemen zusammen. Dies geschieht durch die Erstellung von Build Files, Projektkonfigurationslisten usw. Eine Systemkonfiguration besteht aus 250 bis zu 500 verschiedenen Funktionen.

- *Applikation*

  Ein komplettes System muß auf eine bestimmte Motorvariante angepaßt werden. In dieser Phase werden über 3000 Parameter im System eingestellt, um die geforderten Eigenschaften des Motors zu erreichen. Für diese Anpassung ist eine umfangreiche Dokumentation sowie die systemspezifische Konfiguration von Applikationswerkzeugen erforderlich. Diese Informationen entstehen in den früheren Phasen des Prozesses.

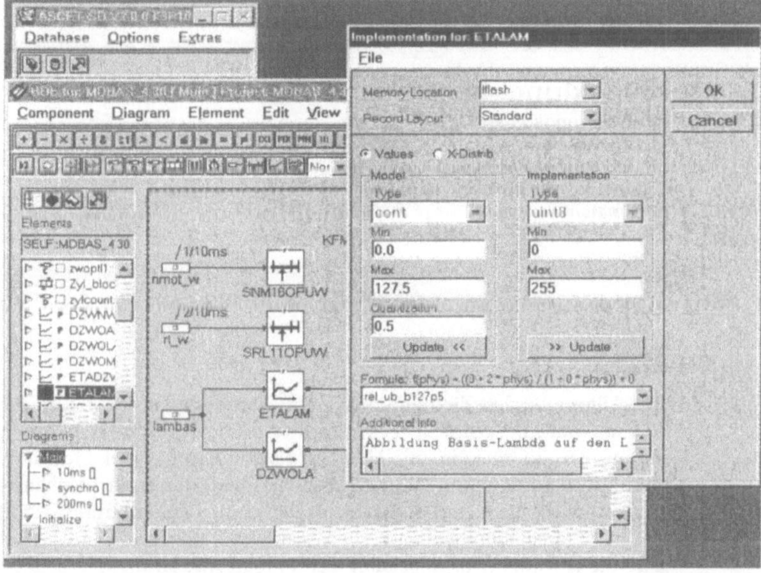

Abbildung 2
System-
entwicklung in
ASCET/SD

Jede Prozeßphase hat ihre spezifischen Daten und Dokumente, die nicht unbedingt allen Prozeßbeteiligten bekannt sind. Dies führt oft dazu, daß individuelle Dateninhalte und -formate definiert werden. Die fehlende Kompatibilität hat zur Folge, daß Daten mehrfach erfaßt werden.

2 Ein flexibles Schichtenmodell für Dokumentation

Im Umgang mit solchen komplexen Entwicklungsprozessen bleibt der Begriff *Dokument* oft unklar. Das Schichtenmodell in Abbildung 3 kann hier zur Klärung beitragen.

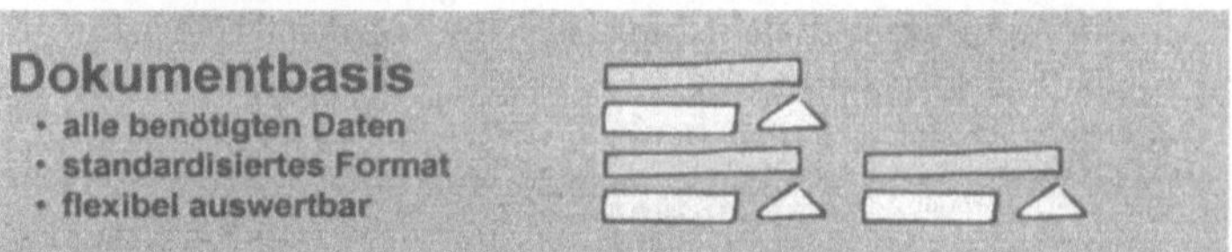

Abbildung 3
Schichtenmodell für Dokumentation

- *Präsentationsebene*

  Diese Ebene umfaßt die traditionelle Präsentationsweise von Information, etwa in Form eines gedruckten Dokumentes, bei dem die inhaltliche Strukturierung der Information mit Hilfe klassischer Layoutmittel (Schriftwahl, räumliche Anordnung usw.) und klassischer Navigationsmittel (Inhaltsverzeichnis, Index usw.) erschließbar wird. Der Einsatz von elektronischen Medien zur Präsentation bedingt keine wesentliche Veränderung und Erweiterung dieser Mittel (z.B. Anpassung der Typographie an die Gegebenheiten des Mediums, erweiterte Navigationsmöglichkeiten).

- *Entwicklungsbasis*

  Diese Ebene repräsentiert die Entwicklungsdaten in den Originalformaten der im Prozeß verwendeten Entwicklungswerkzeuge. Diese Dateien werden meist in EDMS (Engineering Data Management Systems) gehalten, welche keinen direkten Zugriff auf die verwalteten Inhalte besitzen.

Viele Entwicklungswerkzeuge besitzen Reportgeneratoren, um gewünschte Präsentationen zu erzeugen. Oft werden auch Exportfilter zu gängigen Textverarbeitungsprogrammen als Documentation Interface vermarktet.

Diese Ansätze bleiben jedoch auf einzelne Werkzeuge beschränkt. Eine werkzeugübergreifende Dokumentation kann nicht ohne Werkzeugkopplung oder manuelles Zusammenstellen gewonnen werden. Es besteht eine Lücke zwischen Entwicklungsbasis und Präsentationsebene.

- *Dokumentbasis*

  Die Lücke zwischen Präsentationsebene und Entwicklungsbasis kann durch Einführung einer Zwischenschicht, der Dokumentbasis geschlossen werden. Diese Ebene muß auf einem standardisierten Format basieren, welches alle Informationen aufnehmen kann, die zum Erzeugen der gewünschten Präsentationen erforderlich sind. Bis zu einem gewissen Grade muß die Semantik der Daten erhalten bleiben, um auch unvorhergesehene Präsentationen erzeugen zu können oder eine Kopplung von Entwicklungswerkzeugen zu gewährleisten.

  Die Dokumentbasis ist die Domäne von SGML/XML, einem Format, das vergleichsweise einfach zu erzeugen bzw. auszuwerten ist und gleichzeitig sehr komplexe Datenstrukturen abzubilden vermag.

3   Die Dokumentbasis als Verbindungsschicht im Entwicklungsprozeß

Die oben dargestellte Dokumentbasis kann zur Harmonisierung des Dokumentationsprozesses eingesetzt werden. Aber damit sind die Möglichkeiten noch nicht voll ausgeschöpft:

- Das standardisierte Datenformat ermöglicht es, die benötigten Präsentationen, Auswertungen und Ansichten mit Hilfe von standardisierten Werkzeugen zu erstellen, unabhängig von den ursprünglichen Datenquellen. Diese Möglichkeit besteht sogar über die Lebensdauer der Entwicklungswerkzeuge hinaus. Wenn neue Darstellungsanforderungen entstehen, können diese einfach bereitgestellt werden.

- Das standardisierte Datenformat kann zur Überwindung bidirektionaler Schnittstellen dienen. Derartige Schnittstellen sind meistens stark von den verwendeten Werkzeugen und den auszuführenden Prozeßschritten abhängig. Auf diese Weise wird nicht nur die Lücke zwischen Entwicklungsbasis und Präsentationsebene überbrückt, sondern auch Lücken in der Entwicklungsbasis selbst.

- Die Dokumentbasis kann als langfristiges Archivierungsformat dienen. Dadurch werden Investitionen in die Daten zuverlässig geschützt. Die Lebensdauer von Daten übersteigt die der Programme oft um ein mehrfaches. Die Dokumentbasis erlaubt einen Zugriff auf die Daten, auch wenn die ursprünglich eingesetzten Programme nicht mehr existieren.

- Die Dokumentbasis erlaubt die Integration von Entwicklungsergebnissen aus verschiedenen Entwicklungsgruppen, sogar dann, wenn diese unterschiedliche Werkzeuge verwenden. Damit lassen sich insbesondere firmenübergreifende Entwicklungsaktivitäten unterstützen (vgl. Abschnitt 5).

3.1 Die Rolle der DTD in der Dokumentbasis

DTD-Klassen Zum Aufbau der Dokumentbasis können alle Eigenschaften von SGML verwendet werden. Die Anwendungsbereiche der Dokumentbasis werden jedoch weitgehend von den semantischen Eigenschaften der eingesetzten Dokumenttyp-Definitionen (DTDs) bestimmt. Bezüglich der unterstützten Semantik gibt es im wesentlichen drei Klassen von DTDs:

- *layoutorientiert*

   Die Menge von Elementen und Attributen richtet sich nach den geforderten optischen Eigenschaften wie Schriftgrad oder Seitenlayout. Daher orientieren sich die Elemente und Attribute solcher DTDs meist an den Möglichkeiten vorhandener Textverarbeitungs- oder Layoutprogramme.

   Diese Art von DTD (z.B. die RAINBOW.DTD) eignet sich in der Regel nur zum Datenaustausch zwischen Layoutprogrammen und ist daher der Präsentationsebene zuzuordnen. Sie ist aus diesem Grund auch nicht angemessen für den Aufbau der Dokumentbasis.

- *präsentationsstrukturorientiert*

   Die Semantik dieser DTDs konzentriert sich auf die Struktur von Präsentationen (wie Kapitel, Listen, Tabellen) und weniger auf deren optische Darstellung. Daher können Instanzen dieser DTDs in verschiedenen Layouts auf unterschiedlichen Medien dargestellt werden.

   Solche DTDs sind geeignet für die Dokumentbasis, wenn sich die geforderten Präsentationen durch Layout, globale Informationsauswahl (z.B. unterschiedliche Sprachen oder Ein-/Ausblendungen von Kapiteln) und deren Anordnung unterscheiden.

   Eine Auswahl von Informationen aufgrund der Informationen selbst ist meist nicht möglich, da ihre Semantik selbst nicht mehr in der DTD modelliert ist.

- *datenbankorientiert*

   Diese Kategorie von DTDs ist notwendig, wenn die Möglichkeiten der Dokumentbasis nach Abschnitt 3 (flexible Präsentationserstellung, Datenaustausch zwischen Entwicklungswerkzeugen, Archivierung, Prozeßkopplung) genutzt werden sollen.

Diese DTDs konzentrieren sich auf die detaillierten Datenmodelle der Informationen ohne Rücksicht auf mögliche Darstellungen auf der Präsentationsebene. Daher gibt es hier z.B. Elemente wie <part-type> anstelle von <chapter> oder <interface-prms> anstelle von <table>.

3.2 Aufbau einer datenbankorientierten DTD

Für den Aufbau einer datenbankorientierten DTD stehen alle Verfahren der Datenanalyse zur Verfügung.

3.2.1 Relationale Datenmodelle

Das relationale Datenmodell definiert Tabellen gleichartiger Datensätze (Relationen), welche durch Verweise auf Fremdschlüssel zueinander in Beziehung gesetzt werden können. Die Tabellen werden im Rahmen einer Entity-Relationship-Analyse ermittelt, bei der auch die Beziehungen zwischen den Tabellen ermittelt werden. Um Daten redundanzfrei in den relationalen Tabellen abzulegen, muß das Datenmodell normalisiert werden. Es ist offensichtlich, daß relationale Datenmodelle sehr einfach in SGML/XML abgebildet werden können. Daher eignet sich SGML/XML als Archivierungs- und als Austauschformat für relationale Datenbankanwendungen.

Folgendes Beispiel mit zwei Relationen (Angestellte und Abteilungen) illustriert dies:

```
<company>
  <emps>
    <emp emp-no="4321"
         name="Bernhard Weichel"
         adress="Stuttgart"/>
    <emp emp-no="12345"
         name="Helmut Gengenbach"
         adress="Schwieberdingen"/>
  </emps>
  <depts>
    <dept name="Engineering" mgr="4321"/>
    <dept name="Research"    mgr="12345"/>
  </depts>
</company>
```

Abbildung 4
Beispiel für ein relationales Datenmodell in XML

Für Anwendungen im Entwicklungsprozeß ist das relationale Modell nur bedingt angebracht. Die Struktur der Informationen ist so komplex, daß die Normalisierung sehr aufwendig wird und sehr viele

Beziehungen explizit herzustellen sind. Dabei würde das Potential von SGML/XML nicht wirklich ausgeschöpft.

3.2.2 Objektorientierte Datenmodelle

SGML/XML hat das Potential, sehr komplexe Datenmodelle abzubilden. Dies ist im Wesentlichen dadurch begründet, daß es eine Baumstruktur repräsentiert, welche in intuitiver Weise die reale Welt modellieren kann. Im folgenden wird *objektorientiert* eher in dem Sinne verwendet, daß reale Objekte beschrieben werden als im klassischen Sinne der "objektorientierten Programmierung".

- Die Baumstruktur bildet sowohl die 1:1 als auch die 1:n Beziehungen des relationalen Datenmodells direkt ab. Die Möglichkeiten in SGML/XML gehen jedoch darüber hinaus, weil die Beziehungen beliebig tief verschachtelt werden und (wenn auch beschränkte) Möglichkeiten existieren, die Häufigkeit des Auftretens zu kontrollieren (Kardinalität). Daher besteht auch kein Bedarf zur Normalisierung.

- Die Objekte können in Behältern gruppiert werden. Dies drückt in den meisten Fällen die Objektbeziehungen direkt aus, so daß keine Verweise oder künstlichen Zugriffsschlüssel eingeführt werden müssen. Damit sind sowohl 1:1 als auch m:n Beziehungen abbildbar.

- Beziehungen können darüber hinaus über Verweise etabliert werden. Dazu sind meist existierende Daten (natürliche Schlüssel) verwendbar (vgl. 5.1, Verweismodell). Die spezifische Semantik dieser Beziehungen kann vom Kontext der Verweiselemente, den Verweiselementen selbst oder von Attributen im Verweiselement (Architekturen) abgeleitet werden.

- Die DTD stellt ein Datenmodell mit impliziten Zugriffspfaden dar. Dies ermöglicht eine sehr flexible Navigation und Datenabfrage.

- Der *occurrence indicator* ermöglicht ein Datenmodell, auf das viele Instanzen passen. Damit kann eine Klassenbildung (*subclassing*) vorgenommen werden. Diese kann über eigene Elemente (z.B. `<sw-param-class>` in Abbildung 5) oder über Attribute (*architectural forms*) gesteuert werden.

- Objektorientierung – im Sinne von Vererbung und Polymorphismus – kann mit SGML/XML dargestellt werden, indem man Elemente mit entsprechender Semantik einführt. Dies betrifft insbesondere die Vererbung von Dateninhalten (nicht von Datenstrukturen), wie auch die Möglichkeit, Abfragen in bestimmten Datenelementen zu halten. Allerdings existieren hierfür noch keine etablierten Standards.

Ein Beispiel für ein objektorientiertes Modell ist in Abbildung 5 zu finden. Es ist ein Auszug aus der MSR-Software-DTD (MSRSW DTD, s. Abschnitt 5, s. http:// www.msr-wg.de), welche für die Entwicklung von Software für Motormanagementsysteme verwendet wird. Die DTD repräsentiert u.a. das Datenmodell für die Applikationsparameter des Steuergerätes. Solche Parameter können in verschiedenen Ausprägungen wie Einzelwert, Kennlinie, Kennfeld auftreten (Polymorphismus). Dies zeigt sich in der DTD in verschiedenen z.T. alternativen Zweigen zur Unterstützung alternativer Details. Ein Einzelwert besitzt beispielsweise keine X- oder Y-Achse. Eine Kennlinie besitzt Werte und eine X-Achse, nicht jedoch eine Y-Achse. Diese tritt erst bei einem Kennfeld auf.

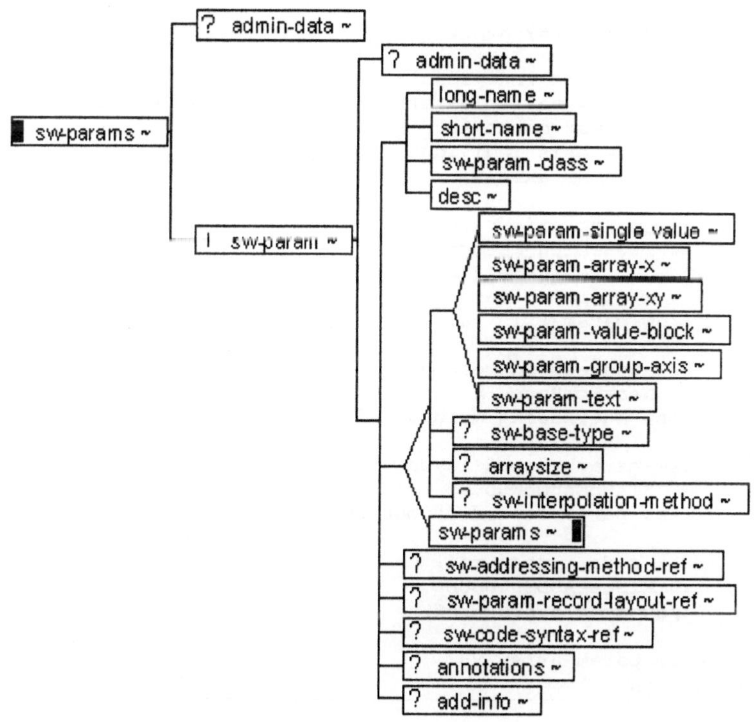

Abbildung 5
Beispiel für eine objektorientierte DTD

Das Element `<sw-param-class>` kennzeichnet die Ausprägung (Klasse) des Applikationsparameters und bestimmt damit, welche der o.g. Alternativen verwendet werden muß. Dies illustriert, wie

Subklassenbildung in objektorientierten DTDs realisiert werden kann.

Abbildung 6 zeigt eine Instanz zu dieser DTD. Es handelt sich um eine Kennlinie mit individuellen Stützstellen zur Applikation eines Motormanagementsystems. Das Beispiel entspricht dem Simulationsmodell in Abbildung 2.

Abbildung 6
Instanz einer objektorientierten DTD

```
<sw-param>
  <long-name>Lambda Wirkungsgrad</long-name>
  <short-name>etalam</short-name>
  <sw-param-class>curve_individual</sw-param-class>

  <desc>
    Abbildung Basis-Lambda
    auf den Lambda-Wirkungsgrad ohne Eingriff
    bezogen auf optimales Moment bei Lambda=1
  </desc>

  <sw-param-array-x>
    <sw-param-axis-x>
      <sw-axis-individual>
          <sw-variable-ref>lambas</sw-variable-ref>
          <max-count>10</max-count>
      </sw-axis-individual>
    </sw-param-axis-x>

    <sw-param-axis-values>
       <sw-compu-method-ref>
          rel_ub_b127b5
       </sw-compu-method-ref>
    </sw-param-axis-values>

    <sw-addressing-method-ref>
       NearRomByte
    </sw-addressing-method-ref>

    <sw-param-record-layout-ref>
       KlAUbSstUbWUb
    </sw-param-record-layout-ref>

    <sw-code-syntax-ref>
       KlNearAUbSstUbUb
    </sw-code-syntax-ref>

  </sw-param-array-x>
</sw-param>
```

4 Anwendung einer datenbankorientierten DTD

Für das Verständnis der später dargestellten Anwendungsfälle ist wichtig zu zeigen, wie eine datenbankorientierte DTD den gesamten Lebenszyklus im Entwicklungsprozeß unterstützen kann.

4.1 Unterstützung in allen Prozeßphasen

Wenn die DTDs der Dokumentbasis für alle Phasen im Prozeß verwendet werden soll, sind folgende Probleme zu beherrschen:

- In den meisten Phasen des Prozesses sind noch nicht alle Informationen verfügbar. Dadurch ist es nahezu unmöglich, in der DTD die korrekten *occurence indicators* einzustellen. Für den dargestellten Entwicklungsprozeß werden mehr als fünf unterschiedliche Ausprägungen von Instanzen verwendet. Hierfür müßten auch über fünf verschiedene DTDs verwendet werden.

- Die Daten entstehen in unterschiedlichen, teilweise parallel laufenden Prozeßschritten. So wird beispielsweise das Datenlexikon einer Steuerungsfunktion im Systemsimulator gebildet, während die verbale Funktionsbeschreibung mit einem SGML-Editor erfolgt. Würden unterschiedliche DTDs verwendet, wäre ein umfangreiches Konvertier- und Prozeßmanagement erforderlich.

- In den einzelnen Prozeßschritten existieren nicht alle Objekte des Gesamtsystems. Jedoch ist bekannt, welche Objekte später noch entstehen werden. Wenn z.B. eine Funktion definiert wird, ist bekannt, daß an anderer Stelle im Prozeß die notwendigen Variablen und Parameter entstehen, welche später in der Integrationsphase sichtbar werden. Daher sind offene Verweise möglicherweise kein Fehler, sondern eine prozeßbedingte Notwendigkeit. In der DTD muß daher ein prozeßorientiertes Verweiskonzept realisiert werden, welches auch zeitweilig offene Verweise beherrscht. Bei Übergabe der endgültigen Entwicklungsergebnisse kann dieses Verweiskonzept in eines der in SGML/XML definierten Verfahren (ID/IDREF, XLL, HyTime) überführt werden.

- Die verschiedenen Werkzeuge im Prozeß verwenden unterschiedliche globale Datenmodelle. Diese Modelle bestimmen auch die Eigenschaften der SGML/XML-Generatoren in diesen Werkzeugen, insbesondere hinsichtlich der vorhandenen Iteratoren. So kann es beispielsweise ein globales Datenlexikon geben, das alle Variablen aller Funktionen trägt, während ein anderes Werkzeug funktionslokale Datenlexika verwendet. In beiden Fällen ist also die Information vorhanden, jedoch mit unterschiedlicher Grobstruktur.

Auf den ersten Blick erscheint es sinnvoll, DTDs spezifisch für die einzelnen Prozeßschritte oder gar werkzeugspezifisch zu definieren. Damit könnten die Informationen je Prozeßschritt über die DTD exakt gefaßt werden. Auf der anderen Seite wären spezifische SGML-Anwendungen für jeden Prozeßschritt erforderlich, so daß der Vorteil der Dokumentbasis verloren ginge. Hinzu kommt, daß die dadurch entstehende Vielfalt von verwandten DTDs mit den derzeit in SGML/XML verwendeten Schemasprachen kaum beherrschbar ist.

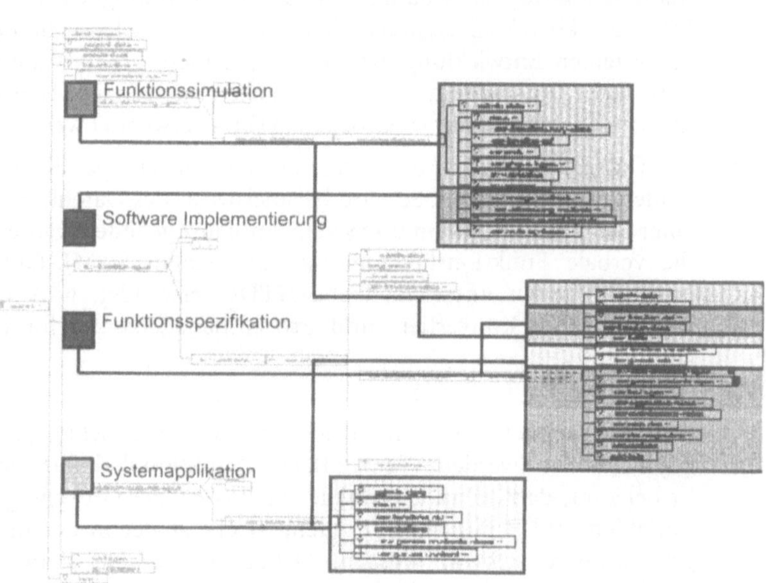

Abbildung 7
Eine DTD im gesamten Prozeß

Es hat sich als sinnvoll erwiesen, dieselbe DTD für alle Schritte und Informationsfragmente im Prozeß einzusetzen und keine spezifischen DTDs zu definieren. Dadurch können alle Anwendungen die gleichen Zugriffspfade zu den vorhandenen Informationen verwenden (s. Abbildung 7). Dieser Ansatz macht die Dokumentbasis wirklich universell einsetzbar:

- Wenn ein Formatierwerkzeug vorhanden ist, welches Papier- oder Hypertextdarstellungen für das Gesamtsystem erzeugen kann, ist dieses auch in den frühen Phasen verwendbar, in denen manche Information noch fehlt. Aber die vorhandenen Informationen können ohne weiteres bereits präsentiert werden. Bei Verwendung spezifischer DTDs wären spezifische Anwendungen erforderlich.

- Vorhandene Importfilter in Entwicklungswerkzeugen können Informationen aus allen Phasen des Prozesses verwenden. Exportfilter in den Werkzeugen sind unabhängig von den Prozeßphasen verwendbar.

- Wenn ein Werkzeug nicht in der Lage ist, die DTD in allen Details zu befüllen, können die erzeugten Dateien als *well-formed* XML behandelt und mit Hilfe von SGML-Werkzeugen zu einer validen SGML-Instanz aufgerüstet werden, ohne daß große Strukturanpassungen durchgeführt werden müssen.

Dieser Ansatz führt zu einer DTD, welche in allen Prozeßphasen verwendet werden kann. Allerdings muß alles, was in irgendeiner Prozeßphase fehlen kann, auch optional sein. In der Praxis bedeutet das, daß fast alle Elemente optional werden. Eine solche DTD ist noch immer sehr nützlich, weil sie eine endliche Menge von Zugriffspfaden zu den Informationen definiert. Dadurch können die entsprechenden Instanzen als abfragbare Datenbasen verwendet werden.

4.2 Ansätze zur Verarbeitung datenbankorientierter Instanzen

Der Einsatz datenbankorientierter DTDs erfordert beim Prozessieren der zugehörigen Instanzen die Verwendung von Verfahren, die der Struktur angemessen sind. Generell gilt, daß Dokumentinstanzen nur noch partiell als lineare Informationscontainer aufgefaßt werden (wie z.B. ein Buch oder ein Zeitschriftenartikel). Vielmehr wird das Dokument zur Informationsbasis mit den folgenden Eigenschaften:

- *nicht-lineare Informationszusammenhänge*

  Was sich dem Endnutzer als informationelle Einheit darstellt, kann aus Gründen der Allgemeinheit und Redundanzvermeidung diskontinuierlich abgelegt sein (z.B. die Mitarbeiterdaten und die zugehörigen Firmendaten).

- *weitgehende semantische Strukturierung*

  Die Funktion jedes relevanten Inhaltselementes ist durch Namen und Kontext eindeutig festgelegt; so werden z.B. Softwareparameter nicht als semantisch neutrale Tabelle kodiert, sondern, wie in Abbildung 5 und 6 gezeigt, in einer entsprechend expliziten semantischen Struktur.

- *definierte (semantische) Zugangspfade*

  Wenn eine bestimmte Information in der Informationsbasis vorhanden ist, ist auch klar, wo sie zu finden ist.

Solcherart beschaffene Instanzen erlauben eine Weiterverarbeitung in vielfältiger Weise:

- Konsistenz- und Plausibilitätsprüfung der Instanz

- Datenextraktion (z.B. für Kurzreports oder um Werkzeuge mit den extrahierten Daten zu beschicken)

- Erzeugung von partiellen oder vollständigen Präsentationen für Papier und Bildschirm

- Datenanreicherung, -mischung und -vervollständigung

Traditionelle Verfahren der Prozessierung sind in der Regel ungeeignet, um diese Prozesse effizient zu erstellen und durchzuführen. Werkzeuge, die für datenbankorientierte Dokumente der beschriebenen Art geeignet sind, unterscheiden sich insbesondere in den folgenden beiden Punkten von traditionellen Tools zur Dokumentbearbeitung:

- *Zugriffsart*

  Diese bestimmt, wie auf die Information im Quelldokument zugegriffen werden kann: nur sequentiell oder wahlfrei. SGML/XML-Dokumente sind baumartig strukturiert; ein wahlfreier Zugriff auf sie erfordert also immer, daß der komplette Baum im Zugriff ist.

- *Aufbau der Zielstruktur*

  Diese Strategie legt fest, ob die Zielstruktur direkt als Reaktion auf Ereignisse oder Objekte in der Quellstruktur definiert (quellgetrieben) aufgebaut wird, oder ob sie unabhängig von der Quellstruktur spezifiziert wird, welche als Datenbank dient, um die Zielstruktur mit den geforderten Inhalten zu beschicken (zielgetrieben).

In der Regel geht eine sequentielle Zugriffsart mit einem quellgetriebenen Aufbau der Zielstruktur einher. Traditionelle Konvertierwerkzeuge fallen in diese Kategorie. Beim baumorientierten Zugriff sind prinzipiell beide Arten des Aufbaus der Zielstruktur möglich.

4.2.1 Linearer vs. baumorientierter Zugriff

Traditionelle Werkzeuge (Konvertierer, Formatierer) operieren in der Regel sequentiell auf Dokumentinstanzen. Nicht-lineare Zugriffe

  SGML/XML als Verbindungsschicht in Entwicklungsprozessen

sind nur sehr beschränkt möglich, insbesondere eine Vorausschau
auf weiter „vorne" liegende Teile des Dokumentes verbietet sich. Ein
Rückblick auf weiter „hinten" liegende Dokumentteile ist ebenfalls
nur in beschränktem Umfang möglich.

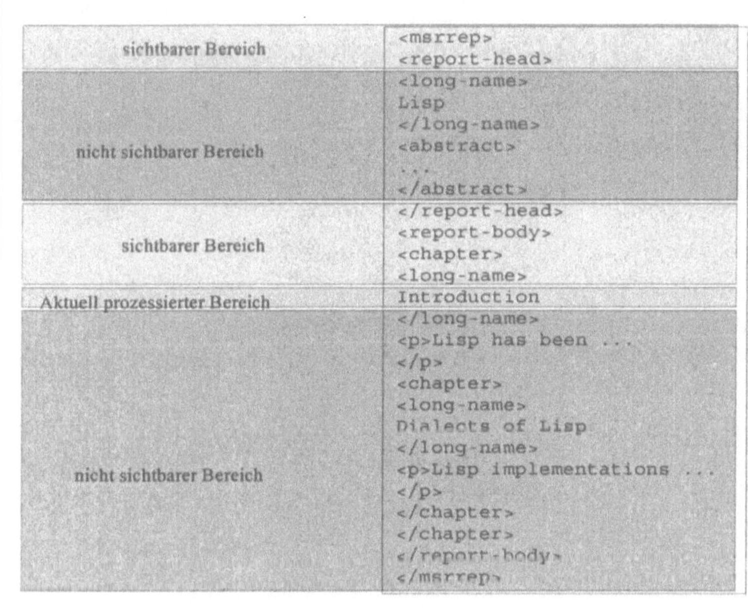

Abbildung 8
Linearer Zugriff
auf die Doku-
mentinhalte

Die lineare Bearbeitung (Abbildung 8) eignet sich daher nur für ein
sequentielles Prozessieren einer Instanz, bei dem nur lokale Operationen notwendig sind. Dies ist in der Regel gegeben bei der Um-
wandlung einer layout- oder präsentationsorientierten Instanz nach
z.B. HTML oder in ein beliebiges Satzformat. Allerdings kann es
auch hierbei zu massiven nicht-sequentiellen Operationen kommen,
z.B. bei der Erstellung eines Inhaltsverzeichnisses oder eines Indexes.
Diese werden dann in der Regel durch ein oder mehrere Durchgänge
durch das Dokument erzeugt.

Sequentielle Verfahren sind für datenbankorientierte Dokumentstrukturen prinzipiell ungeeignet, da diese grundsätzlich anders prozessiert werden: Die in Abbildung 6 und 7 vorgestellten Strukturen
können prinzipiell als Tabellen präsentiert werden. Dies wäre noch
mit einigem Aufwand mit einem sequentiell arbeitenden Prozessor
zu bewerkstelligen. Die Informationen, die in den Zellen enthalten
sind, stehen jedoch nicht in den Strukturen selbst, sondern in einem
Datenlexikon, das sich an anderer Stelle im Dokument befindet.

Ein baumorientierter Zugriff (Abbildung 9) gestattet es, das Dokument wie eine Datenbasis zu betrachten. Unabhängig davon, welche Stelle des Baumes gerade prozessiert wird, bleibt immer der gesamte Baum im Zugriff. Datenbankorientierte Strukturen lassen sich nur mit einem baumorientierten Ansatz adäquat prozessieren.

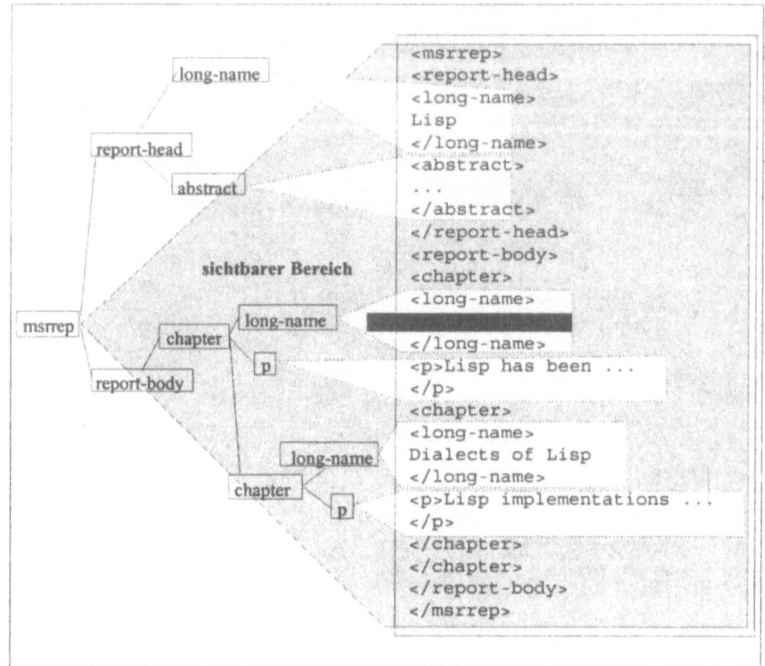

4.2.2 Quell- vs. zielgetriebener Aufbau des Zieldokuments

Beim quellgetriebenen Aufbau des Zieldokuments wird dessen Inhalt determiniert durch die Daten, die im Quelldokument enthalten sind. Dieses Verfahren ist geeignet für lineare Konvertierungen, bei denen z.B. Elementnamen umzubenennen sind, jedoch keine großen strukturellen Veränderungen vorgenommen werden müssen.

Bereits der Aufbau einer (CALS)-Tabelle aus einer semantischen Struktur stellt den quellgetriebenen Ansatz vor nicht-triviale Probleme, da ja für jedes Element in der Quelle zu spezifizieren ist, wo es in der Zielstruktur erscheinen soll (wenn überhaupt).

Relativ einfach ist dieses Problem mit dem zielgetriebenen Ansatz zu lösen: Die Tabellenstruktur wird erzeugt, ihre Inhalte werden durch Queries auf die Quellstruktur eingefügt. Diejenigen Teile der Quellstruktur, die nicht weiter von Interesse sind, werden gar nicht erst angefaßt.

Das folgende Beispiel verdeutlicht dies: Aus zwei datenbankorientierten Dokumenten soll eine Preisliste generiert werden. Das erste Dokument beinhaltet die jeweils aktuellen Umrechnungskurse, das zweite eine umfangreiche Teileliste, die sehr viel mehr Informationen enthält, als in der Preisliste abzudrucken sind.

1. Es wird eine Tabelle erzeugt.

2. Wenn nicht alle Teile in der Preisliste erscheinen sollen, werden die gewünschten Teile durch eine Query gesucht und entsprechend viele Zeilen erzeugt.

3. Es sollen nur zwei Preise (DM und $) ausgegeben werde, ferner die Kurzbeschreibung des Teils; es werden also pro Zeile drei Zellen erzeugt.

4. Es wird die Kopfzeile erzeugt, ihre Geometrie und ihr Inhalt ergibt sich aus der Art der Tabelle, die erzeugt werden soll (z.B. Preisliste für zwei Währungen).

In den Schritten 1 bis 4 wurde die Quellstruktur verwendet, um die Geometrie der Tabelle festzulegen. Erst in den folgenden Schritten wird die Tabellenstruktur durch Inhalt gefüllt.

5. Die jeweils erste Zelle einer Zeile wird mit dem Inhalt der zugehörigen Teilebeschreibung gefüllt.

6. Der Inhalt der jeweils zweiten Zelle einer Zeile wird dadurch generiert, daß beim zugehörigen `part` der Basispreis gesucht wird, dann wird die `conversion` gesucht, deren `currency` DM ist und der Basispreis mit dem dort gefundenen `factor` multipliziert.

7. Der Inhalt der jeweils dritten Zelle einer Zeile wird dadurch generiert, daß beim zugehörigen `part` der Basispreis gesucht wird, dann wird die `conversion` gesucht, deren `currency` $ ist und der Basispreis mit dem dort gefundenen `factor` multipliziert.

Der notwendige Code, um diese Struktur mit einem zielgetriebenen – und baumorientierten – Werkzeug zu erzeugen, ist tatsächlich erheblich kompakter und mit etwas Übung besser lesbar als diese informelle Beschreibung (Abbildung 10).

Abbildung 10
Zielgetriebener Dokumentaufbau

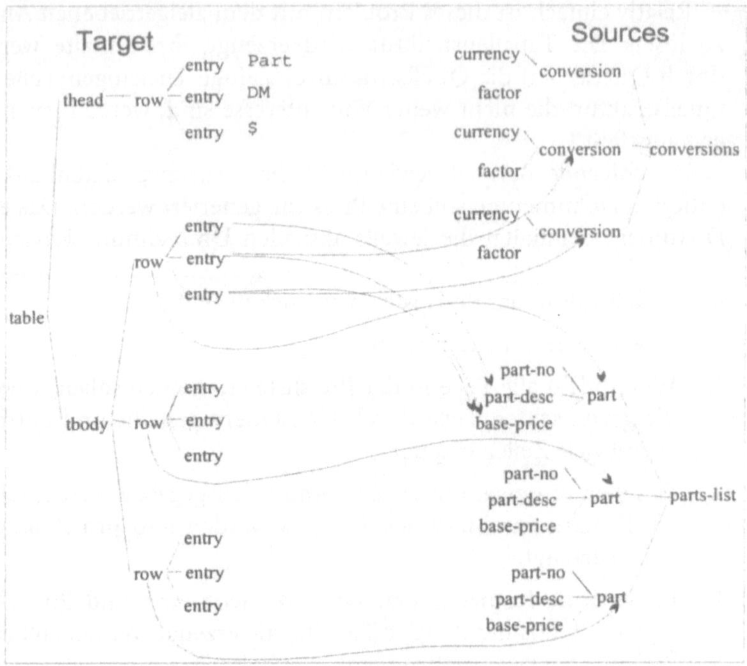

Wesentliche Eigenschaften des beschriebenen Verfahrens sind:

- Das Zieldokument wird als eine Art Template spezifiziert. Eigenschaften des Quelldokuments können seine generelle Struktur mitbestimmen.

- Werden Inhalte aus dem Quelldokument benötigt, so werden sie durch Abfragen aus diesem geholt.

- Nicht benötigte Inhalte werden nicht berührt.

Das folgende Codefragment (Abbildung 11) implementiert das oben beschriebene Beispiel nahezu vollständig. Es basiert auf der Query und Transformation Language des SGML/XML Toolkits MetaMorphosis (http://www.ovidius.com), das von der *Robert Bosch GmbH* und *Ovidius GmbH* gemeinsam entwickelt wird.

Strukturerzeugende Codeteile (auch Queries) sind fett gedruckt, inhaltsgenerierende Queries kursiv.

```
//Der Zugriff auf die Information zur Währungskonvertierung
//wird in einer Funktion gekapselt

!define \factor (*curr)
    source[?conversions].
    child[?conversion &
            child[?currency].data === *curr].
    child[?factor].data

table
      []

\\Eine Tabelle besteht aus thead und tbody.
\\Die row und entries innerhalb von thead
\\            werden direkt generiert.
        &lt;|thead|&gt;node
           {<row>node
                {<entry>node{"Part"},
                 <entry>node{"DM"},
                 <entry>node{"$"}
                 }
            },
\\für die parts-list wird der tbody generiert
\\es wird eine Zeile erzeugt für jedes part, dessen
\\part-no größer 1000 ist

&lt;|tbody|&gt;source[?parts-list]
        {<row>child[?part &
                    child[?part-no].data > "1000"]
          {<entry>child[?part-desc],
           <entry>child[?base-price]
               {data * \factor("DM")}
           <entry>child[?base-price]
               {child[?base-price * \factor("$")
          }
        }
```


An diesem Beispiel sieht man deutlich, wie die gewünschte Struktur direkt und ohne Umwege spezifiziert wird. Die Struktur des Codefragmentes ähnelt stark der tatsächlichen SGML-Struktur einer Tabelle. Dort wo die Inhalte der Zellen erscheinen, werden diese entweder direkt eingetragen oder durch eine Abfrage spezifiziert. Hierzu ist eine leistungsfähige Abfragesprache notwendig.

4.2.3 Abfragesprache

Linear arbeitende, quellgetriebene Prozessoren benötigen insbesondere Sprachelemente, die es gestatten,

quellgetriebene Prozessoren

- auf bestimmte Ereignisse (Elementanfang oder –ende, Entities usw.) zu reagieren und

- Strukturen zu verändern oder zu konstruieren.

Sie gehören strukturell in die Klasse der Stream-Editoren, wie z.B. awk, sed oder perl.

Zielgetriebene Baumprozessoren haben eine völlig andere Struktur. Sie besitzen im wesentlichen zwei Sprachkomponenten:

- Eine konstruktive Komponente, mit der Strukturen aufgebaut werden und

- eine mächtige Abfrage- und Navigationssprache.

An eine solche Sprache wird eine Reihe von Anforderungen gestellt:

- Sie muß optimiert sein für die Navigation in Bäumen, ein SQL-Derivat ist in der Regel wenig geeignet. D.h. sie muß spezielle Sprachelemente zur Verfügung stellen, die der Topologie von Bäumen angemessen ist (Zugriff auf Vaterknoten, Kinder, linke und rechte Nachbarn, alle Vorfahren, alle Nachkommen usw.).

- Sie muß optimiert sein für die Abfrage von SGML/XML-Dokumenten (Zugriff auf Elemente, Entities, PCDATA, Processing Instructions, Attribute).

- Als Resultat einer Query müssen neben den Standardobjekten wie Integers, Strings usw. auch Objekte wie Knoten und Bäume bzw. (heterogene) Listen oder Mengen zurückgegeben werden, die solche Objekte enthalten können.

- Das Resultat einer Query muß direkt als Input für die weitere Bearbeitung zur Verfügung stehen.

- Queries müssen zur mehrfachen Verwendung speicherbar sein.

- Ergebnisse von Queries müssen zur Weiterverwendung speicherbar sein.

- Es muß möglich sein, temporäre Hilfsstrukturen (Listen, Indexe usw.) anzulegen, um Queries zu optimieren.

- Von jedem Punkt eines Baumes muß jeder andere Punkt des Baumes erreichbar sein.

- Die Formulierung beliebig komplexer Bedingungen muß möglich sein.

- Die Sprache muß prinzipiell erweiterbar sein, entweder durch interne Sprachmittel oder durch externe Mittel oder durch beide.

4.2.4 MetaMorphosis – ein Beispiel für ein baumorientiertes System

Im Rahmen der Umsetzung der in diesem Artikel vorgestellten Strategien wurde das Werkzeug MetaMorphosis von der *Robert Bosch GmbH* und der *Ovidius GmbH* entwickelt, um die Anforderungen, die beim Prozessieren datenbankorientierter DTDs bestehen, zu erfüllen. MetaMorphosis, inzwischen auch als Produkt verfügbar, besteht im wesentlichen aus folgenden Komponenten (Abbildung 12):

- *Eingabeprozessoren*, welche die Dokumentbasis, aber auch nicht-SGML/XML-Daten in anderen Formaten in die MetaMorphosis-Baumstruktur überführen. Eingabeprozessoren können sowohl in „C" als auch in der MetaMorphosis-Sprache selbst implementiert werden.

- *MetaMorphosis-Baumrepräsentation*, eine mit dem Document Object Model (DOM) vergleichbare Struktur.

- *MetaMorphosis Kernel*, ein zielgetriebener Baumtransformierer, welcher die in den vorigen Abschnitten vorgestellten Abfragemoglichkeiten bietet. Die zielgetriebene Baumtransformation kann sowohl als Konstruktion eines neuen Baumes oder auch als Manipulation eines existierenden Baumes erfolgen.

- *Ausgabeprozessoren*, welche die MetaMorphosis-Baumrepräsentation in die gewünschten Ausgabeformate überführen. Diese Ausgabeprozessoren können sowohl in „C" als auch in der MetaMorphosis-Sprache selbst implementiert werden.

Die MetaMorphosis-Baumrepräsentation MMdb ist – wie oben erwähnt – in ihrem Aufbau mit dem Document Object Model (DOM) vergleichbar. Das MMdb-API ist weitgehend kompatibel mit dem DOM, es ist allerdings erweitert um MetaMorphosis-spezifische Funktionen. Mit dieser Architektur ist es z.B. möglich,

- mit beliebigen Prozessoren einen Dokumentbaum zu erzeugen, zu modifizieren oder auszulesen, solange dieser über das MMdb-API angesprochen wird. So kann z.B. ein Document Management System (DMS) direkt eine MMdb zur weiteren Verarbeitung durch MetaMorphosis erzeugen. Umgekehrt kann der Inhalt einer MMdb durch einen geeigneten Prozessor ohne Umweg über SGML in das gewünschte Zielformat und evtl. direkt in die Zielapplikation überführt werden.

- den Kernel direkt auf anderen Strukturen operieren zu lassen, sofern diese eine dem MMdb-API ähnliche Struktur besitzen. So kann der Kernel beispielsweise. in einen Editor eingebunden

werden, welcher ein DOM-API zu seiner internen Dokumentstruktur bereitstellt. Auf diese Weise können im Editor direkt
sehr mächtige Transformationsfunktionen (z.B. Umsetzung von
semantischen in präsentationsorientierte Strukturen) zur Verfügung gestellt werden.

Da alle Module als DLLs vorliegen, kann MetaMorphosis komplett
in eine bestehende Umgebung, z.B. in Entwicklungswerkzeuge, eine
Datenbank, einen SGML-Editor, ein Satzsystem, integriert werden.

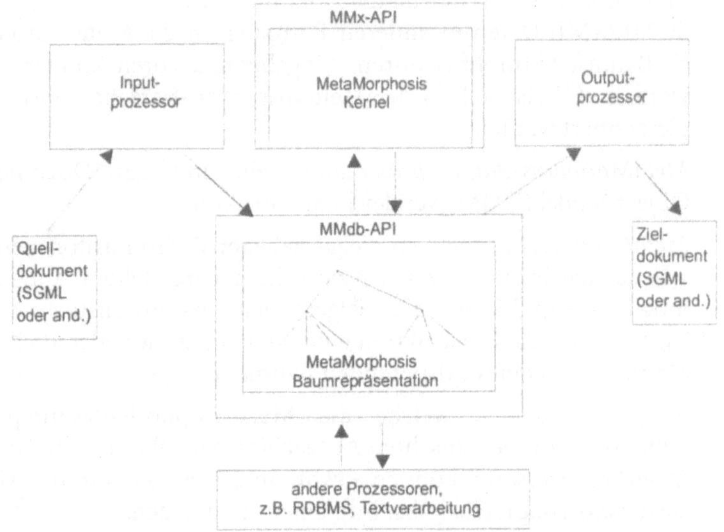

Was nach außen sichtbar wird, ist nur noch die erweiterte Funktionalität des Werkzeuges, nicht jedoch die Komplexität der integrierten Komponente.

Weiterführende Informationen wie Handbücher, Tutorials und
Demo-Versionen zu MetaMorphosis sind auf der Web Site des Herstellers (http://www.ovidius.com) zu finden.

4.3 Manuelle Bearbeitung datenbank-
orientierter SGML/XML-Instanzen

Es ist offensichtlich, daß datenbankorientierte SGML/XML-Instan-
zen vorzugsweise über Generatoren erzeugt werden, und daß eine

manuelle Bearbeitung schwierig ist. In bestimmten Fällen ist jedoch eine manuelle Bearbeitung notwendig (z.B. weil kein geeigneter Generator verfügbar ist, oder auch zur Erstellung von Testdaten). Diese manuelle Bearbeitung wird wesentlich erleichtert, wenn entsprechende Basisfunktionen im SGML-Editor verfügbar sind.

4.3.1   Verweismanager

Wie in Abschnitt 3.2 dargestellt, gibt es bei datenbankorientierten DTDs viele verschiedene Verweise mit definierter Semantik. Jede dieser Semantiken bildet also eine eigene Verweisklasse. Eine Steuergerätefunktion importiert beispielsweise Variablen. Ein Verweis, der dies ausdrückt, darf daher nicht auf ein Teammitglied oder auf eine Maßeinheit zeigen. Diese Verweisklassen müssen daher dem Benutzer für eine manuelle Bearbeitung in geeigneter Form präsentiert werden. Abbildung 13 zeigt ein Beispiel für einen solchen Verweismanager. Die linke Listbox zeigt alle möglichen Verweisklassen. Die Objekte einer Verweisklasse sind in der rechten Listbox dargestellt. Die Bedienungselemente erlauben das Aufbauen, Überprüfen und Manipulieren von Verweisen.

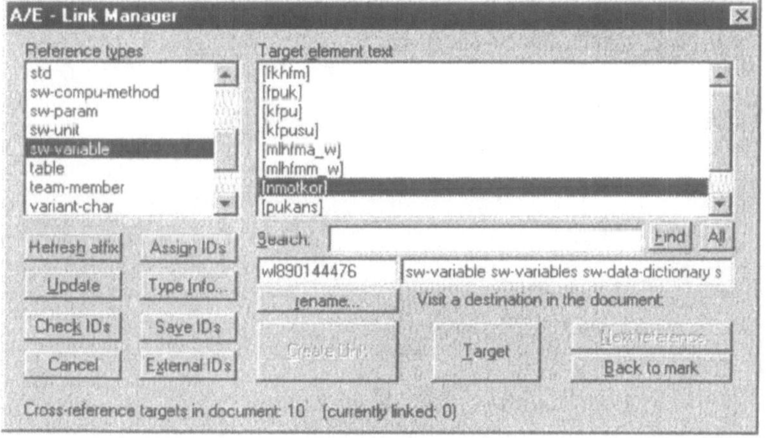

Abbildung 13
Beispiel für einen Verweismanager

Ein solcher Verweismanager ist hilfreich für das Einrichten von Verweisen wie auch zur Navigation in der Instanz, speziell zum schnellen Aufsuchen, Überprüfen und Bearbeiten von Objekten.

4.3.2   Templates

In datenbankorientierten DTDs gibt es sehr viele Elemente mit spezifischer Semantik, welche in einer wohldefinierten Struktur zusammengesetzt werden. Andererseits werden Subklassen gebildet (s. Abbildung 6). Die manuelle Bearbeitung solch komplexer Strukturen kann durch eine Template-Strategie wesentlich erleichtert werden.

Arbeitserleichterungen ergeben sich z.B. durch

- Anbieten der wesentlichen Strukturen und Subklassen als Templates, welche aus einem kontextabhängigen Menü ausgewählt werden können;

- automatisches Aufsuchen des geeigneten Einfügepunktes in der Instanz durch Analyse des Templates und der DTD. Dies ist ganz wesentlich, weil es den Benutzer davon entlastet, die DTD im Detail kennen zu müssen.

- die Möglichkeit, eigene Templates im Rahmen der laufenden Bearbeitung zu erstellen und sofort wieder zu verwenden. Dies erlaubt die Einführung weiterer Subklassen ohne vorherige Werkzeuganpassung.

Abbildung 14 zeigt ein Beispiel für die Implementierung solcher Templates.

4.4 Weitere Erfahrungen mit datenbankorientierten DTDs

Im folgenden sollen einige Erfahrungen im Umgang mit datenbank-orientierten DTDs gegeben werden. Diese Erfahrungen erheben keinen Anspruch auf Allgemeinheit und Vollständigkeit.

- Die Semantik der DTD muß so genau wie möglich definiert werden. Dies ist besonders schwierig, da SGML/XML kaum Mittel zur Spezifikation von Datentypen bereitstellt. Darüber hinaus gibt es kaum Verfahren zur formalen Definition von Semantik. In der Praxis wird daher die Semantik im Laufe der Pilotanwendungen definiert. Es ist jedoch essentiell, daß diese Definition wenigstens ausführlich dokumentiert wird.

- Beim derzeitigen Stand der Editoren und Viewer für SGML bzw. XML ist es besser, Elemente statt Attribute für die Ablage von Anwendungsdaten zu verwenden.

- SGML/XML-Dateien werden oft sehr groß. Beispielsweise ist das Datenlexikon eines Motormanagement-Systems (mit einer MSR-Software-DTD) etwa 10 MB groß, wobei etwa 80% auf Markup entfallen. Die Dateigröße kann wesentlich reduziert werden, wenn man *empty end tags* verwendet. Die Verwendung kurzer Elementnamen reduziert natürlich auch die Dateigröße, erschwert aber deutlich das Verständnis der DTD.

- Generell ist festzustellen, daß Speicherbedarf zum Problem werden kann, speziell bei rein baumorientierten Systemen.

- Wenn die Verarbeitung in speziell programmierten Werkzeugen erfolgt, ist es oft besser, Verweise aufgrund existierender Informationen zu etablieren, anstatt künstliche Zugriffsschlüssel (SGML ID/IDREF) einzuführen. In vielen Fällen ist es gar nicht erforderlich, den Verweis aufzulösen, wenn das Verweisziel z.B. über einen natürlichen Schlüssel spezifiziert wird.

- Das zugrundeliegende Datenmodell muß möglichst vollständig definiert und implementiert werden. Kompromisse müssen oft später mit wesentlich höherem Aufwand korrigiert werden.

- Es ist sinnvoll, die DTD hinsichtlich der globalen Container flexibel zu halten. Dadurch wird es für Entwicklungswerkzeuge deutlich einfacher, valide SGML-Instanzen zu erzeugen. Mit baumorientierten Verarbeitungswerkzeugen kann die Information bei Bedarf leicht umstrukturiert werden.

5 Die Dokumentbasis im MSR-Konsortium

Das Projekt MSR (Manufacturer Supplier Relationship) ist ein Entwicklungsvorhaben mehrerer deutscher Automobilhersteller und Elektrik/Elektronik-Zulieferer mit der Zielsetzung, die Zusammenarbeit zwischen Hersteller und Zulieferer zu verbessern und in der Effizienz zu steigern (Abbildung 15, s.a Beitrag von Jörg Schiller).

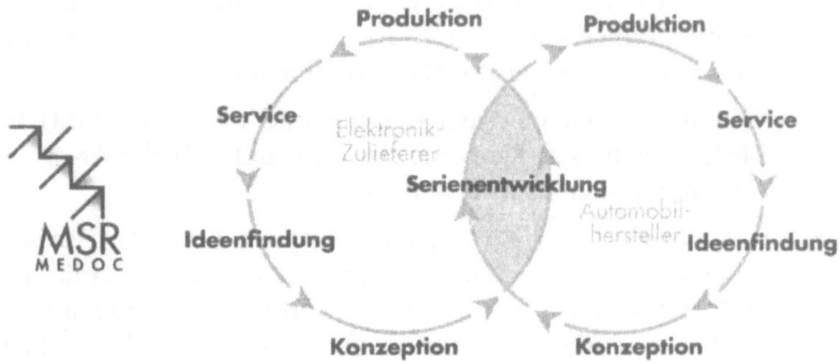

Abbildung 15
Kopplung von Entwicklungsprozessen bei MSR

Im Rahmen dieses Projektes wurde eine Reihe von DTDs definiert, welche für den Aufbau einer Dokumentbasis geeignet sind. Ein erster Schritt hierzu war die Definition von einheitlichen Grundsätzen und Regeln zum Umgang mit SGML/XML (MSR MEDOC Applikationsprofil). Ziel dabei ist die Interoperabilität der einzelnen entstehenden MSR-Standards sowie die Unterstützung der Wiederverwendung von Software, die die MSR-Standards implementiert, im Grunde genommen also die Definition einer Dokumentbasis.

Weitere Informationen finden sich auf der Web Site des MSR-Konsortiums: http://www.msr-wg.de.

5.1 Das SGML Applikationsprofil von MSR MEDOC

Alle MSR-DTDs haben die folgenden, im Applikationsprofil festgelegten und einheitlichen Prinzipien:

- *Verweismodell*

  Das MSR-Verweismodell unterstützt verschiedene Möglichkeiten, Hyperlinks innerhalb eines Dokuments oder auch zwischen unterschiedlichen Dokumenten zu definieren. Damit wird es ermöglicht, die Gesamtheit der verschiedenen Dokumente zu einem Steuergerät (System- und HW-Lastenheft, Softwaredokumentation, Vernetzungsbeschreibung usw.) als eine große, vernetzte „Steuergeräte-Datenbank" zu verwenden. Die unterstützten Verweismöglichkeiten sind:

  - HyTime
  - XLink
  - MSR-Verweismodell

  Dabei wird die natürliche Objekthierarchie benutzt, um durch Konkatenierung der im Entwicklungsprozeß vorhandenen natürlichen Objektkennungen (z.B. Kurznamen) einen Verweis aufzubauen. Beispielsweise würde der die Adresse "/SG1/MOTORPORT/ZUENDUNG" auf das Steuergerät „SG1", darin den Stecker „MOTORPORT" und darin auf den Anschluß „ZUENDUNG" verweisen.

- *Basiselemente*

  In allen DTDs werden dieselben Basiselemente verwendet. Diese Basiselemente umfassen u.a. alle Elemente zur reinen Textdarstellung (z.B. zahlreiche Listenformen, Tabellen), aber darüber hinaus auch einheitliche Modelle wie z.B. die Darstellung von Parametern oder die Behandlung von physikalischen Einheiten.

- *Konfigurierbarkeit*

  Zahlreiche Konfigurierungsmöglichkeiten in den DTDs dienen u.a. dazu, sich an unterschiedliche Prozeßschritte oder Werkzeugumgebungen anpassen zu können.

- *Klassifikationsmechanismen*

  Die DTDs beinhalten ein einheitliches Klassifikationskonzept, das über Namenserweiterungen der Datenelemente abgebildet ist (vgl. Abschnitt 3.2.2).

- *Administrative Daten*

  Die administrativen Daten umfassen Versions-, Änderungsinformationen sowie weitere Informationen ähnlicher Art. Sie erlauben so die Kopplung der MSR-Daten an Verwaltungssysteme wie Dokumentenmanagement-Systeme, Produktdatenmanagement-Systeme.

- *Konstruktionsmechanismen für die DTDs*

  Alle DTDs werden nach festgelegten Konstruktionsmechanismen gebildet (z.B. Namenskonventionen).

5.2 Die einzelnen MSR-DTDs

Im folgenden sind die derzeit festgelegten MSR-Standards aufgelistet und erläutert.

- *System (MSRSYS DTD)*

  Die MSRSYS DTD (früher MSRDOC) dient zur Spezifikation und Dokumentation kompletter Elektrik/Elektronik-Systeme. Sie erlaubt u.a. die folgenden Beschreibungen:

  - Projektdaten
  - Bauteile und ihr hierarchischer Aufbau
  - Verhalten
  - Architektur (Signale, Schnittstellen, Verbindungen)
  - Elektrische Eigenschaften
  - Mechanische Eigenschaften
  - Optische und akustische Eigenschaften
  - Umweltverträglichkeit

  Die DTD wurde in verschiedenen Autorenumgebungen implementiert und befindet sich in zahlreichen Projekten im Einsatz.

- *Software (MSRSW DTD)*

  Die MSRSW DTD dient zur Spezifikation und Dokumentation von Steuergerätesoftware und umfaßt die folgenden Bereiche:

  - Datenlexikon
  - Funktionale Spezifikation
  - Kenngrößeninhalte

  Erste Tool-Kopplungen für diese DTD sind am Markt verfügbar. Diese DTD befindet sich im produktiven Einsatz. Bei einem firmenübergreifenden Piloteinsatz wurde ein Motormanagementsystem bearbeitet mit 240 Funktionen. Die unterschiedlichen Entwicklungsdatenbanken in den beteiligten Häusern wurden über MSRSW DTD abgeglichen. Die Softwaredokumentation wurde als Papierdokument mit ca. 1800 Seiten sowie als Hypertextdokument mit reichhaltigen Verweisen aufbereitet.

- *Network (MSRNET DTD)*

  Die MSRNET DTD dient zur Spezifikation und Dokumentation der Fahrzeugvernetzung (mit dem aktuellen Fokus auf CAN-Netzwerke). Sie erlaubt u.a. die Beschreibung der Netzwerktopologie sowie der auf dem Netz ausgetauschten Signale und Botschaften. Erste Implementierungen der MSRNET DTD sind am Markt .

- *Report (MSRREP DTD)*

  Dies ist eine allgemein einsetzbare (präsentationsstrukturorientierte) DTD, die nur zu Publikationszwecken und zum Dokumentenaustausch, nicht aber zum Datenaustausch eingesetzt wird. Sie findet derzeit Anwendung für sämtliche Dokumentationen, die in den MSR MEDOC Arbeitsgruppen erstellt werden, sowie auch für Anwendungsgebiete, die noch nicht mit einer MSR DTD abgedeckt sind. Neben einem allgemeinen Dokumentmodell mit Kapiteln, Paragraphen etc. unterstützt die MSRREP DTD auch eine strukturierte Behandlung von Änderungsanforderungen, z.B. für den Änderungs- und Versionsplanungsprozeß.

6 Schluß

SGML/XML bietet viele Möglichkeiten, erforderliche Verbindungsschichten in komplexen Entwicklungsprozessen zu etablieren. Diese Schichten können dazu verwendet werden, Daten aus unterschiedlichen Quellen zu harmonisieren und zu integrieren und in einer langfristig tragfähigen Basis für Daten und Dokumente abzulegen. Um das zu erreichen, ist ein sorgfältiger Entwurf der DTDs sowie eine tragfähige Implementationsstrategie erforderlich. Im MSR-Projekt werden öffentlich verfügbar DTDs entwickelt, die für den Einsatz in einer Dokumentbasis konzipiert sind. Diese DTDs sind in Pilot- und auch in produktiven Projekten einsetzbar. Solche datenbankorientierten DTDs sind derzeit noch nicht im Fokus der SGML/XML-Welt, welche sich jedoch in diese Richtung bewegt. Der vorliegende Artikel soll einen Beitrag zu diesem Prozeß leisten und auch andere ermutigen, das Potential von SGML/XML besser auszuschöpfen.

6. Schluß

SGML in der Entwicklungsdokumentation elektronischer Komponenten

Jörg Schiller

1 Einleitung

Die technische Dokumentation elektronischer Komponenten ist ein lange Zeit stiefmütterlich behandelter Teil des Entwicklungsprozesses von Fahrzeugen in der Automobilindustrie. Pkw der neuesten Bauart weisen eine derartige Komplexität in ihrer Elektronik auf, daß die Beherrschbarkeit der Prozesse inzwischen eng mit der Qualität der Dokumentation zusammenhängt. Dies gilt nicht nur für die detaillierte Beschreibung der technischen Komponenten, sondern auch für die sie begleitenden Entwicklungsentscheidungen.

Qualität der Dokumentation

Die Dokumentation soll ihrem Wesen nach Informationen zwischen verschiedenen Personen oder Rollen transportieren. Dies gilt sowohl zwischen den verschiedenen Abteilungen innerhalb eines Betriebes als auch zwischen Auftraggebern und Auftragnehmern in verschiedenen Firmen.

Dieser Artikel soll die Erfahrungen wiedergeben, die beim Einsatz von SGML für die strukturierte Beschreibung dieser Information gemacht worden sind. Die Entwicklung solcher Strukturen war Teil der Arbeit, die sich ein Arbeitskreis unterschiedlicher Firmen im Umfeld des Automobilbaus zum Thema gemacht hat.

2 MSR

2.1 Zielsetzungen des Projekts

Ziele von MSR Inhalt und Ziel des Projekts *MSR (Meß-, Steuer- und Regelungstechnische Systeme)* ist die Verbesserung der Effizienz der Zusammenarbeit zwischen Automobilhersteller und Elektrik/Elektronik-Zulieferer (s.a. Beitrag von Bernhard Weichel).

- Durch verbesserten Informationsfluß und Austausch von Modelldaten soll eine Verkürzung der Entwicklungszyklen für die zu entwerfenden Systeme erreicht werden.

- Durch spezielle Spezifikationsmethoden und Dokumentationssysteme werden Fehleranfälligkeit und Fehlinterpretationen beim Entwurfsprozeß zwischen Hersteller und Zulieferer reduziert, was zu einer Erhöhung der Produktqualität wie auch zu deutlicher Kostenreduzierung führt.

- Durch Kostenreduzierung wie auch den Einsatz modernster Spezifikations- und Dokumentationsmethoden wird eine Stärkung der Wettbewerbsfähigkeit erzielt, die auch Auswirkungen auf die künftige Entwicklung haben wird.

2.2 Projektteilnehmer

Das MSR-Konsortium besteht aus den folgenden deutschen Automobilherstellern und Elektrik/Elektronik-Zulieferern:

- BMW AG
- Daimler-Benz AG
- HELLA KG
- Porsche AG
- Robert Bosch GmbH
- Siemens AG
- VDO A. Schindling AG
- Volkswagen AG

2.3 Strategie zur Erreichung der Ziele

Ein Entwicklungsmodell für die Zusammenarbeit zwischen Automobilhersteller und Zulieferer muß verschiedenen Anforderungen
genügen. Zum einen erfolgt die Entwicklung zumeist nicht streng
phasenorientiert, sondern in hohem Maße interaktiv zwischen den
beteiligten Entwicklungsfirmen. Zum anderen baut die Serienent-
wicklung in der Regel auf Vorgängerprodukten oder Vorserien-
Entwicklungen auf, d.h., es muß ein evolutionäres Entwickeln unterstützt werden. Um die Entwicklung von Produktfamilien zu unterstützen, werden außerdem hohe Anforderungen an die Wiederverwendbarkeit gestellt.

Daraus ergab sich als wichtiger Arbeitsinhalt die Festlegung ge-
meinsamer Vorgehensmodelle – also Prozesse und Methoden – für
Automobilhersteller und Zulieferer. Um den Datenaustausch und
die Kommunikation zwischen den beteiligten Entwicklungspartnern
zu gewährleisten, ist die Festlegung standardisierter Schnittstellen bei
Analyse, Entwurf sowie die Einführung einheitlicher (teil-)forma-
lisierter Beschreibungsformen bei Dokumentation und Datenhaltung von großer Bedeutung.

Eine Reduzierung der Kosten und Entwicklungszeiten sowie eine
Verbesserung der Qualität in der Entwicklung läßt sich durch die
Realisierung neuer Entwurfs- und Spezifikationsansätze herbeifüh-
ren, welche die Vermeidung von Spezifikations- und Entwurfsfeh-
lern in den frühen Entwicklungsphasen beinhalten und somit obso-
lete oder redundante Entwicklungsaktivitäten auf niedrigerer Ebene
vermeiden.

Zur Kostenreduzierung in der Systementwicklung gehört auch ein
Konzept zur Verwaltung solcher bereits entwickelter Teilkompo-
nenten bzw. Daten, die mit geringem Aufwand wiederverwendet
werden können. Eine Grundvoraussetzung für die Erreichung der
gesetzten Ziele ist die Integration der zu entwickelnden Werkzeuge
in bereits bestehende DV-Strukturen. Hierzu zählt auch die Berücksichtigung der Heterogenität derzeit im Einsatz befindlicher Ent-
wicklungsumgebungen bei Herstellern und Zulieferern. Um nicht
von speziellen Software-Produkten oder -Plattformen abhängig zu
sein, muß ein plattformübergreifendes Konzept entwickelt werden.

Die Anforderungsspezifikation in Form von Lastenheften sowie
die Produktspezifikation in Form von Pflichtenheften werden zur
Systemanalyse wie auch beim Entwurf herangezogen. Im MSR-
Projekt wurden Prozesse für den Einsatz von Methoden und Konzepten entwickelt und implementiert, die sich von der Anforde-
rungs- und Produktspezifikation bzw. Entwicklungsdokumentation

bis hin zum konkreten Entwurf und der Verifikation durch Simulation erstrecken.

Das Dokumentationssystem MEDOC umfaßt alle erwähnten Bereiche der Spezifikation und Entwicklungsdokumentation, wohingegen das Teilprojekt MESA/MERLAN die Systemanalyse und den Systementwurf mit Verifikation zum Inhalt hat. Auch Schnittstellen zwischen diesen beiden Teilsystemen werden berücksichtigt. Zur Erprobung und Verifikation der entwickelten Methoden und Konzepte wurden Prototypen in beiden Teilprojekten implementiert und eingesetzt.

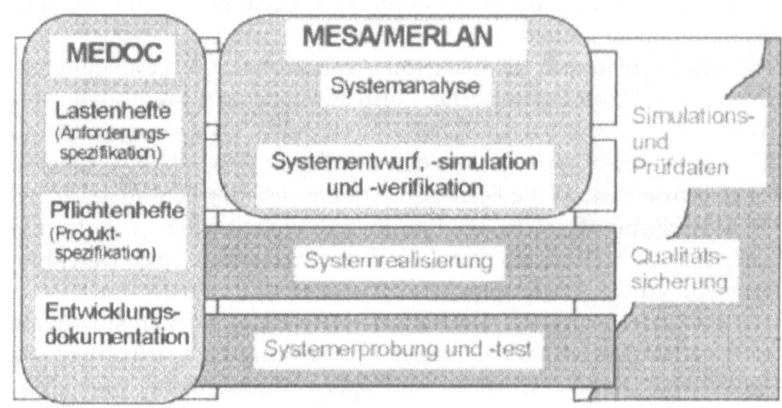

Abbildung 1
Die MSR-Teilprojekte MEDOC und MESA/MERLAN

Auf Basis der in dem Teilprojekt MEDOC definierten SGML-Dokumentenstruktur können Lasten- und Pflichtenheftdokumente erfaßt, verwaltet und ausgetauscht werden. Beim Software-Prototyp MESA des Teilprojekts MESA/MERLAN werden anhand von beispielhaft ausgewählten CASE-Entwurfstools Werkzeugkopplungen auf der Ebene des Systementwurfs und der Simulation durchgeführt. Weiterhin werden Schnittstellen für den Code- und Modellexport zu HiL- (Hardware-In-The-Loop) bzw. Rapid-Prototyping-Umgebungen bereitgestellt, die sich beide in produktivem Einsatz befinden.

standardisierte Schnittstellen

Sowohl interne Schnittstellen der Prototypen als auch der Datenaustausch zwischen den beiden Systemen benutzen international standardisierte Austauschformate und Beschreibungsmittel wie *CDIF (Case Data Interchange Format)* oder SGML.

SGML in der Entwicklungsdokumentation elektronischer Komponenten

2.4 Zusammenfassung des Teilprojekts MEDOC

2.4.1 Ausgangssituation

Herkömmliche Lasten- und Pflichtenhefte für elektronische Steuergeräte im Fahrzeug werden mit Hilfe von Textsystemen erstellt und umfassen informelle Texte zu Themen wie Steuergerätefunktionen, Schnittstellen des Steuergeräts, EMV-Verträglichkeit, klimatische Eigenschaften.

Lasten- und Pflichtenhefte

Durch fehlende Normierung kommt es dazu, daß diese Dokumente sehr uneinheitlich gegliedert sind. Lasten- und Pflichtenhefte für Entwicklungsdokumentationen enthalten deswegen mehrdeutige und redundante Beschreibungen und sind dadurch nicht eindeutig interpretierbar. Außerdem verteilen sich die Informationen auf zu viele Dokumente, wodurch bestehende inhaltliche Zusammenhänge oft nicht transparent sind. Systemzusammenhänge werden häufig ebenfalls nicht abgebildet.

Durch die getrennte Haltung von Dokumentation und Produktdaten existieren Informationen isoliert und redundant in unterschiedlichen Rollen. Dies gilt für die beiden Entwicklungspartner Zulieferer und Hersteller ebenso wie für die beiden Welten CAD und Publishing. Beispielsweise ist ein Parameterwert beim Zulieferer innerhalb eines CAD-Systems erfaßt und gleichzeitig, unabhängig davon, Bestandteil von verschiedenen Dokumenten.

Dokumentation und Produktdaten

Auf der Seite des Herstellers ist die Situation analog. Eine Unterstützung für die Rollen von Auftraggeber und Auftragnehmer fehlt gänzlich. Änderungsvorgänge während der Entwicklung können nur ungenügend dokumentiert werden. Darüber hinaus wird seitens der Entwickler unnötiger Aufwand in die Bearbeitung des Dokumentlayouts investiert.

Rolle von Auftraggeber und Auftragnehmer

2.4.2 Zielsetzung

Das Teilprojekt MEDOC verfolgt mehrere Ziele:

- Angestrebt wird eine einheitliche Struktur für die Dokumentation und für die in MSR betrachteten Produktdaten u.a. unter Berücksichtigung einer hierarchischen Produktstruktur und eines Konzepts zur Beschreibung von Prüfungen. Diese stellt die Grundlage sowohl für die Wiederverwendbarkeit von Dokumentteilen und Produktspezifikationsdaten als auch für die Etablierung eines Single-Source-Prinzips dar.

- Des weiteren muß der Daten- und Dokumentenaustausch standardisiert und werkzeugunabhängig gestaltet werden.

- Die Unterstützung der Rollen „Auftraggeber" und „Auftragnehmer" ist durch die Einführung eines Sichtenkonzepts zu realisieren, welches gleichzeitig die Trennung und die Korrelation von Lasten- und Pflichtenheftdokumentation ermöglicht.

- Darüber hinaus ist ein projekt- und versionsorientiertes Arbeiten zu ermöglichen, das ein zumindest teilautomatisiertes Änderungswesen, eine Statusverwaltung und Freigabeprozeduren für die Dokumente umfaßt.

- Der Entwickler ist durch eine inhaltsorientierte und Layoutunabhängige Dokumentbearbeitung zu unterstützen. Zusätzlich sind Mechanismen für ein geführtes Editieren (*guided editing*) vorzusehen.

Im folgenden werden die entwickelten DTDs kurz vorgestellt.

2.4.3 MSR-System

MSR-Sys-DTD

Die *MSR-Sys-DTD* beschreibt Steuergeräte mit all ihren mechanischen und elektrischen Komponenten. Insbesondere werden folgenden Informationen berücksichtigt:

- Projektdaten

- Teil- und Systemaufbau

- Architektur mit Signalen, Schnittstellen, Ausgängen und Verbindungsspezifikationen

- Verbindungen

- elektrische Eigenschaften

- mechanische Eigenschaften

- optische und akustische Eigenschaften

- Eigenschaften der Umgebung

2.4.4 MSR-Report

MSR-Report-DTD

Das MSR-Konsortium hat sich frühzeitig darauf verständigt, seine eigene Dokumentation ebenfalls in SGML abzulegen. Dazu war es nötigt, eine DTD für allgemeine Berichte zu entwickeln. Die *MSR-Report-DTD* kann dazu verwendet werden, Dokumentationen für solche Sachverhalte zu erstellen, die durch die anderen Strukturen nicht abgedeckt sind. MSR-Report bietet:

- eine allgemeine Dokumentstruktur (Kapitel, Absätze usw.)
- ein detailliertes Konzept für das Änderungsmanagement

2.4.5 MSR-Software

Für die Spezifikation und Dokumentation der Software von elektronischen Steuergeräten wurde die *MSR-Software-DTD* entwickelt. Die DTD wurde inzwischen erfolgreich eingesetzt bei firmenübergreifenden Projekten und bei der internen Verteilung der Informationen in unterschiedlichen Abteilungen einer Firma. Dabei kamen jeweils unterschiedliche Werkzeuge zur Erzeugung und Verwendung der Daten zum Einsatz. Diese DTD wird mehr und mehr von Software-Entwicklungswerkzeugen unterstützt. Die DTD deckt folgende Punkte ab:

MSR-Software-DTD

- Datenlexikon
- funktionale Spezifikation
- Kalibrierungsparameter

In einem einzelnen Projekt wurde damit ein Dokument mit ungefähr 1400 Seiten generiert und zwischen den Partnern ausgetauscht. Für die Erstellung des Dokumentes wurden sowohl mit einem Editor erfaßte Umfänge als auch mit Transformatoren erzeugte Daten zusammengeführt. Dabei wurde die Zusammenführung aus zwei Datenquellen (*Merge*) genauso wie das Übernehmen aus bestehenden Austauschdaten (*Update*) realisiert.

2.4.6 MSR-Netzwerk

Die *MSR-Net-DTD* wurde für die Beschreibung von Onboard-Netzen entwickelt. Der Schwerpunkt lag dabei auf dem CAN-Netzwerk. Sie gestattet die Dokumentation der Informationseinheiten, die über das Netzwerk transportiert werden. Ein Bestandteil der Dokumentation ist die Beschreibung der Netztopologie.

MSR-Net-DTD

2.4.7 FMEA

Im Bereich der *FMEA (Failure Mode and Effect Analysis)* wurde eine erste DTD entwickelt, die bislang noch nicht veröffentlicht wurde.

2.4.8 Diagnose

DTD für die Diagnose von Steuergeräten

Die aktuellste Aktivität beschäftigt sich mit der Dokumentation der Diagnose von Steuergeräten. Dies bezieht sich sowohl auf den On-board- als auch auf den Offboard-Bereich. Beschrieben werden alle Informationen, die über die reine Kommunikation zwischen einem Testsystem und dem Steuergerät hinaus gehen. Dazu gehören zum Beispiel Prüfanweisungen für die Tests des Steuergerätes in der Produktion wie auch Strategien für die Analyse von Fehlersymptomen in der Werkstatt.

2.4.9 SGML/XML Anwendungsprofile von MSR

Basiskonzepte der DTDs

Alle Datenstrukturen von MSR wurden durch SGML-DTDs beschrieben. Der Umgang mit den unterschiedlichen DTDs führte zu einer Reihe von Profilen, die in allen DTDs auf die gleiche Art angelegt werden. Zu diesen Basiskonzepten gehören:

- ein einheitliches Link-Konzept, das ID/IDREF, HyTime und eine MSR-spezifische semantische Adressierung unterstützt. Dieses Modell gestattet es, Instanzen von verschiedenen DTDs in einer gemeinsamen Datenbasis miteinander zu verbinden.

- Basismodelle (Parameter, Architekturen, usw.)

- Konfigurationinformationen

- Klassenstrukturen

- administrative Daten, um die Versionskontrolle innerhalb einer Instanz zu unterstützen. Dies ist insbesondere dann sinnvoll, wenn, wie in MSR konzipiert, eine Instanz aus mehreren Fragmenten besteht.

3 Erfahrungen

Die MSR-Strukturen sind seit einiger Zeit in unterschiedlichen Häusern zum Austausch von Informationen innerhalb einer Firma bzw. zwischen verschiedenen Firmen im Einsatz. Daraus ergeben sich auch unterschiedliche Systemkonzepte und Erfahrungen. Im folgenden wird ein kurzer Überblick über die Ergebnisse des Einsatzes gegeben.

3.1 Systemarchitektur

Die Systemarchitekturen sind in den einzelnen Firmen sehr unterschiedlich. Trotzdem ist es mit den MSR-Strukturen gelungen, einen Austausch mittels SGML zu bewerkstelligen. Dabei sind die beiden Seiten Erzeugung und Nutzung der Daten zu unterscheiden.

heterogene Systemarchitekturen

3.1.1 Erzeugung

In einigen Häusern werden SGML-Editoren zur Erfassung der Daten eingesetzt. Diese wurden in der Regel auf die besonderen Belange der Anwender angepaßt. Dabei waren organisatorische wie auch strategische Vorgaben zu berücksichtigen. Da eine Ablage der zahlreichen Instanzen ein Verwaltungsproblem darstellt, wurden die Editoren über Schnittstellen mit Datenbanken gekoppelt.

Erfassung

Eine andere Systemarchitektur sieht die automatische Erzeugung der SGML-Daten aus bestehenden Systemen (z.B. Spezifikationswerkzeugen) vor. Dabei ist mitunter ein nicht unerheblicher Anteil an Arbeit in die Angleichung der Datenstrukturen geflossen.

Generierung

3.1.2 Nutzung

Die Daten werden genutzt für

- die elektronische Darstellung,

- die Erstellung einer Printdokumentation,

- die Transformation in andere DTDs.

Die elektronische Darstellung geschieht i.d.R. mit marktüblichen SGML-Browsern wie Panorama Pro. Auch mit der Formatierung der Daten für die Erstellung von Printouts, z.B. über PDF oder Postscript, wurden gute Erfahrungen gemacht. Die Aufwände für diese Arbeiten sind allerdings nicht zu unterschätzen. Bei der Transformation werden als Zielformat zum Teil wiederum firmenspezifische DTDs verwendet. Die Erfahrungen damit sind meist recht gut.

3.2 Prozeßmodell / Arbeitsabläufe

Da es sich bei den MSR-DTDs um Austausch-DTDs handelt, kann auch hier, wie bei der Systemarchitektur, gesagt werden, daß ein sehr generisches Modell eine Schar von Prozessen unterstützen muß. Ziel von MSR ist es nicht, das Prozeßmodell der beteiligten Firmen zu

flexible Austausch-DTDs

standardisieren. Dazu sind die bestehenden Welten der Entwicklungsdokumentation noch viel zu divergent. Es wurde vielmehr versucht, über eine Strukturobermenge eine Angleichung der Prozesse zu erreichen. Dem wird zum Beispiel dadurch Rechnung getragen, daß MSR die Abbildung eines Rollenkonzepts in den Instanzen unterstützt. Die Definition der Rollen ist Aufgabe der beteiligten Firmen zum Zeitpunkt des Datenaustauschs.

Auf die Freigabeprozeduren wurde besonderes Augenmerk gelegt. Die Einzelfreigabe von Dokumenten mußte ebenso unterstützt werden wie die Freigabe von Informationen, die über mehrere SGML-Instanzen verteilt sind. Bei der Informationsfreigabe werden z.B. mehrere Rollen für die Abwicklung einer Freigabe benötigt.

Für die Unterstützung der Prozeßketten innerhalb einzelner Firmen hat sich der Einsatz von SGML-Datenbanken bewährt. Die für die Verwaltung einzelner Dokumente benötigten Metainformationen werden außerhalb der SGML-Instanzen ebenfalls in der Datenbank abgelegt.

Die Angleichung von Datenbanken über Firmengrenzen hinweg scheitert oftmals schon an Sicherheitsbestimmungen, obwohl sich eine Reihe von Vorteilen bei der gemeinsamen Nutzung von Datenbanken herausstellen könnten.

3.3 Linkkonzept

Da sich bei der Entwicklung der DTDs aufgrund ihrer Komplexität schnell herausstellte, daß eine DTD nicht genügte, um alle Informationen der Entwicklungsdokumentation zu beschreiben, tauchte schon sehr früh die Frage auf, wie die über mehrere DTDs verteilten Informationen zum Austauschzeitpunkt miteinander verbunden werden können. Zur Lösung dieses Problemen wurde ein ausgeprägtes Linkkonzept in den MSR-Strukturen entwickelt.

Das Konzept umfaßt drei durch unterschiedliche Technologien unterstützte Formen von Links:

- ID/IDREF

- HyTime

- semantische Links

Der ID/IDREF-Mechanismus ist Teil der SGML-Spezifikation. Dabei wird das Linkziel mit einer eindeutigen Adresse versehen (ID="4711"). Der Link selbst verwendet dann diese Adresse (IDREF="4711"), um die beiden Enden des Links miteinander zu verbinden. Die Bedeutung des Links wird über weitere Attribute des

Linkelementes angegeben. Nachteil dieses Mechanismus ist, daß er nur innerhalb eines Dokuments funktioniert und damit nicht für dokumentübergreifende Links verwendet werden kann. Ein Vorteil ist, daß er von vielen SGML-Editoren und -Browsern direkt bei der Eingabe bzw. beim Traversieren des Links unterstützt wird.

HyTime ist ein umfassender Standard zur Beschreibung von dokumentübergreifenden Links. Die Implementierung des kompletten Standard ist sehr komplex. Es wird in der Regel aber auch nur ein Teil der Funktionalität von HyTime wirklich benötigt (z.B `clink` mit eingeschränkten Adressierungsmethoden). Diese Form der Links wird nur von wenigen Werkzeugen unterstützt. Eine Reihe von Anwendungen haben allerdings gezeigt, daß dieses Subset erfolgreich eingesetzt werden kann.

HyTime

Das dritte Konzept beschreibt Verbindungen, deren Semantik erst aus der sie umgebenden Struktur abgeleitet werden kann. Die Adresse eines Ziels läßt sich dabei aus dem Kontext ableiten und stellt im Grunde genommen eine Suche dar. Dieser Mechanismus wird hauptsächlich *offline*, also nachträglich zur Eingabe der Daten durchgeführt und ist immer dann einzusetzen, wenn der Erstellungsprozeß der beiden Komponenten Verweis und Verweisziel parallel von verschiedenen Rollen durchgeführt wird. Dabei kann die Situation eintreten, daß bei der Erstellung des Verweises das Verweisziel im Detail noch gar nicht festgelegt ist, daß man aber ungefähr weiß, wo es sich befindet. Die referenzierende Stelle und ihr Kontext bestimmen, welche Ziele überhaupt sinnvoll sind. Zum Beispiel soll eine Schnittstelle auf die auszutauschenden Signale referenzieren. Welche Signale hierbei angeboten werden, ergibt sich aus der Stellung der Schnittstellenbeschreibung (Kommunikations- oder Hardwareschnittstelle) im Dokument, und aus der Angabe am Link ergibt sich, daß allgemein auf Signale gezeigt werden soll. Die benötigten Informationen für diese Referenzierung werden Semantik genannt. Dieser Prozeß ist wichtig bei der *online*-Unterstützung in Editoren und wurde erfolgreich umgesetzt.

semantische Links

3.4 Mehrwert durch Strukturierung

Der Einsatz von SGML und damit die Strukturierung von Informationen geht einher mit einer Reihe von Vorteilen, die sich in der Praxis eingestellt haben. Die Strukturinformation kann dafür genutzt werden, geführtes Editieren zu unterstützen und somit die Fehleranfälligkeit der Eingabe zu reduzieren. In den bisherigen Dokumentationen lag das am häufigsten genannte Problem in den fehler-

Fehlerreduktion bei der Eingabe

haften Verweise und Referenzen. In MSR-Anwendungen konnte nachgewiesen werden, daß sich diese Situation entscheidend verbessern läßt. Die geführte Eingabe kommt auch dem Wunsch des Anwenders nach einem intelligenten Eingabesystem entgegen, das ihm interaktiv Fragen nach der Bedeutung des einzugebenden Textes stellen kann, um dann die richtigen Strukturen einzusetzen. Dies geschieht durch eine kontextabhängige Anzeige von Menüs, aus deren Inhalt dann die benötigten Strukturen erzeugt werden. Aufbauend auf der Struktur kann ein solches System auch kontextsensitive Hilfen bei der Eingabe anbieten.

Prüf-
mechanismen

Da der SGML-Standard nur ein eingeschränktes Typkonzept für Elementinhalte anbietet, wurden in den DTDs Informationen selektiv für Elemente in Attributen hinterlegt, um so Prüfmechanismen auf Elementebene realisieren zu können.

Vermeidung von
Redundanzen

Das MSR-Konsortium hatte sich zum Ziel gesetzt, die Wiederverwendbarkeit von Informationen soweit wie möglich zu realisieren. Dieses Single-Source-Prinzip ist im Rahmen von Lasten- und Pflichtenheften für elektronische Steuergräte sehr wichtig, um beispielsweise den Toleranzbereich von Komponenten an genau einer Stelle beschreiben und prüfen zu können. Wenn dieses Ziel aus programmtechnischen Gründen vielleicht nicht hundertprozentig erreicht wurde, so können Redundanzen doch weitgehend vermieden werden. ·

3.5 Migration / Integration

Software

Es existieren für die Dokumentation bereits eine Reihe von Programmen, die zum Teil käuflich zu erwerben, zum Teil aber auch Eigenentwicklungen einzelner Firmen sind. Die Integration in diese Systeme ist natürlich ein vorrangiges Ziel aller Beteiligten. Wegen der unterschiedlichen Werkzeuge, die die einzelnen Firmen einsetzten, existiert keine gemeinsame Migrationsstrategie. Eine der umgesetzten Strategien besteht darin, den Zugriff auf SGML-Daten mit einheitlichen Bibliotheken in allen Anwendungen zu realisieren. An dieser Stelle sei auf die Aktivitäten im Umfeld von XML hingewiesen. Dort existieren bereits allgemein anerkannte, standardisierte Speicherdatenmodelle, welche die Integration in bestehende Systeme erheblich vereinfachen. Zudem wird XML von Software inzwischen besser unterstützt und dient somit der Integration.

3.6 Migration von Altdaten

Die Weiterverwendung bereits vorhandener Daten ist bei allen beteiligten Firmen sicherzustellen. Somit müssen neue Systeme mit den heterogenen Formaten der Altdaten umgehen können. Bei der Erstellung der SGML-Daten wird dies durch das Linkkonzept unterstützt. Wenn dabei auf Daten in anderen Formaten zugegriffen werden muß, wird über NOTATIONs hinterlegt, mit welchem Werkzeug die Darstellung der Daten ermöglicht werden kann.

Bei der automatischen Erzeugung der SGML-Daten etwa aus Spezifikationswerkzeugen kann im Umfeld von XML vermehrt auf die Unterstützung von bestehenden Systemen wie z.B. Oracle zugegriffen werden.

3.7 Akzeptanz

Die Akzeptanz von neuen SGML-Systemen hängt in starkem Maße von der Sichtbarkeit von SGML in den Anwendungen und von der Ausgangssituation ab. Bei der automatischen Erzeugung der SGML-Daten wird die SGML-Struktur in der Regel komplett vor dem Anwender versteckt. Sichtbar für den Anwender sind dann nur noch die Laufzeiten der Transformationsschritte. Diese können je nach Quell- bzw. Zielformat recht lang sein, so daß z.B. Batchprozeduren unterstützt werden müssen.

Beim Editierprozeß ist natürlich die SGML-Struktur klarer sichtbar. Mitarbeiter, die aus der WYSIWYG-Welt (z.B. Word) kommen, stellen hohe Ansprüche an die Präsentation von SGML-Daten auf dem Bildschirm. Eine anspruchsvolle Bildschirmformatierung ist aufgrund des hohen Aufwands immer erst dann vorzusehen, wenn die DTD-Struktur stabil geworden ist. Beim Einsatz von Standard-Editoren, die nur begrenzte Möglichkeiten zur Anpassung der Oberfläche des Editors an die Bedürfnisse der Anwender zur Verfügung stellen, dauert die Einarbeitung in das Arbeiten mit Strukturen relativ lang.

Heterogenität

Software-
Unterstützung

automatische
Erzeugung von
SGML-Daten

Editierprozeß

4 Ausblick

Erfahrungen   Die Erfahrungen aus den unterschiedlichen MSR-Anwendungen zeigen, daß die Einführung neuer SGML-Konzepte in die Dokumentation von Entwicklungsprozessen komplex, aber beherrschbar ist. Eine Reihe von Problemen entstehen dadurch, daß die Unterstützung von SGML durch die Standard-Werkzeuge relativ begrenzt ist und dadurch spezielle Werkzeuge eingesetzt werden müssen.

XML   Die derzeitigen Entwicklungen im Bereich von XML werden sich über kurz oder lang durchsetzen. Mit SGML-Systemen ist man damit auf der sicheren Seite. Eine Erzeugung von XML sollte immer möglich sein. Gerade hinsichtlich der Integration in bestehende Systeme gibt es derzeit eine Reihe von Ankündigungen, XML als Schnittstelle zu den Daten einzusetzen.

zukünftige Themen   Diesem Trend folgend wird sich auch die Strukturierung der Entwicklungsdokumentation durchsetzen. Neue Konzepte für den Umgang mit den entstehenden Datenpools müssen noch erarbeitet werden. Dazu zählen Themen wie Suchen in Datenpools, Verbinden von Informationen (Linken), Anzeigen (Browsen) und Editieren.

Praxis – morgen

SGML als Grundbaustein für das betriebliche Wissensmanagement

Eric Schoop und Katrin Strobel

1 Motivation

Ausgehend von der strategischen betriebswirtschaftlichen Zielsetzung, eine wissensbasierte Unternehmung aufzubauen, zeigt der vorliegende Beitrag die Potentiale des Einsatzes von SGML in der betrieblichen Dokumentation auf. Die sich aus der verstärkten Wissensorientierung ergebenden Anforderungen an ein strategisches Informationsmanagement führen zur Diskussion von Integrationspotentialen des Dokumentenstandards SGML. Der Bedarf an anwendungsorientierter, methodischer Vorgehensweise wird begründet und eine mögliche schrittweise Annäherung an das strategische Ziel am Beispiel mehrerer realisierter Projekte demonstriert.

2 Wissensmanagement als Führungsaufgabe

Bevor wir auf SGML als Dokumentenstandard im Rahmen der Unterstützungsfunktion des Informationsmanagements eingehen, halten wir es für sinnvoll, zunächst die sich in der betriebswirtschaftlichen Diskussion immer stärker abzeichnende Strategie einer wissensbasierten Unternehmensführung aufzugreifen und daraus Anforderungen an ein methodisches Wissensmanagement abzuleiten. Nach einer begrifflichen Abgrenzung werden daher die Interdependenzen zwischen Organisation und Wissen näher betrachtet.

Anforderungen

2.1 Daten, Dokumente, Informationen und Wissen

Informationen:
Definition

Nach betriebswirtschaftlichem Verständnis bilden *Daten* als digital gespeicherte Fakten und Regeln, wenn sie in den Kontext eines Problemzusammenhangs, in der Ökonomie in der Regel eine Entscheidungssituation, gestellt werden und damit Zweckbindung erfahren, *Informationen*. Informationen sind damit Kenntnis zur Vorbereitung wirkungsvollen Handelns.

Dokument:
Definition

Ein *Dokument* ist jede Art schriftlich fixierter Information, also aufbereitetes Ergebnis eines häufig arbeitsteiligen, anwendungsbezogenen, strukturierten Publikationsprozesses. Wir können Dokumente als Informationsträger auffassen, da sie Aggregationen unterschiedlicher Datentypen zur Befriedigung aufgabeninduzierter Informationsnachfragen darstellen. *Dokumentationen* fassen auf nächsthöherer Stufe die in Dokumenten vorgenommene zielorientierte Beschreibung betrieblicher Sachverhalte und Abläufe zusammen und bilden damit handlungsrelevante Bezugsnetze.

Wissen:
Definition

Diese zweckorientierte Vernetzung von Informationen stellt *Wissen* dar. Der Begriff spiegelt, über die reine Information hinausgehend, eine subjektive Überzeugung wider und beschreibt die begründete Kenntnis von strukturellen Zusammenhängen bestimmter Informationen und deren sinnvoller Verknüpfbarkeit zur Erreichung konkreter Ziele. Unterschieden wird zwischen *explizitem* (= dokumentiertem) und *implizitem* (= verinnerlichtem, schwer formalisierbarem) Wissen mit jeweils *individueller* oder *kollektiver* Verfügbarkeit (Schoop 1998b).

2.2 Wissen in der Organisation

Betriebswirtschaftliches Handeln vollzieht sich in Orientierung an langfristigen Plänen, die wiederum strategischen Zielvorgaben folgen. Im operativen Tagesgeschäft äußert es sich in Form vielfältiger, situationsabhängiger Entscheidungen einzelner oder von Personengruppen, die durch Wahrnehmung von Führungsfunktion koordiniert und mit den Planvorgaben abgestimmt werden müssen. Die operativen Entscheidungen beeinflussen die in den Plänen festgelegten Zielgrößen, die es zur Durchsetzung der übergeordneten Strategie langfristig zu erreichen gilt.

Was ist nun Inhalt einer Unternehmensstrategie? Sie ist zur Sicherung der Wettbewerbsfähigkeit marktorientiert, also unter Berück-

SGML als Grundbaustein für das betriebliche Wissensmanagement

sichtigung der Beziehungen zu Kunden, Lieferanten und Mitbewerbern, auszurichten, setzt eine einleitende Standortbestimmung im Rahmen einer Situationsanalyse mit Identifikation der Erfolgsfaktoren voraus und beschreibt die langfristig zu erreichende oder zu sichernde Marktposition der Unternehmung. Die als kritisch einzustufenden Wettbewerbsfaktoren werden festgestellt und Verbesserungsmaßnahmen vorgegeben.

Aufgrund der Globalisierung der Märkte und der Digitalisierung der darauf stattfindenden Transaktionen verändert sich die Wettbewerbsposition vieler Unternehmen in hochentwickelten Ländern rapide. Klassische Marktzutrittsschranken verschwinden, früher ausschließlich beherrschte Fertigkeiten und organisatorische Fähigkeiten stehen mittlerweile vielen internationalen Wettbewerbern zur Verfügung, gepaart mit mitunter erheblichen Kostenvorteilen. Somit wird zunehmend das Wissen in den Unternehmen zur entscheidenden Größe. Es manifestiert sich als eingehende Kenntnis über Märkte, Partner und Mitarbeiter, als langjährige Erfahrung aus Produkten, Prozessen und Projekten, aber auch als Fähigkeit zur flexiblen, innovativen Neugestaltung in Reaktion auf kurzfristige Umwelteinflüsse. *(schnelle Änderung der Wettbewerbsposition)*

Aus Managementsicht kann Wissen als strategischer *Erfolgsfaktor* betrachtet werden, der, richtig genutzt, zu einer langfristigen Erhöhung der Wertschöpfung beizutragen vermag, da er sich nicht so einfach kopieren läßt wie technische Prozesse oder organisatorische Verfahren. Alternativ wird Wissen auch als *Engpaßressource* aufgefaßt, die es hinsichtlich bestimmter Kernkompetenzen auszubauen gilt, oder als *Erklärungsgröße* für die Festlegung einer bestimmten Ausprägung der Organisation (Schneider 1996, S. 14ff.). *(Wissen als strategischer Erfolgsfaktor)*

2.3 Wissensorganisation und organisationales Lernen

Allen Sichten auf das Wissen der Unternehmung ist gemeinsam, daß seine Berücksichtigung als strategisches Ziel erhöhte Anforderungen an die organisatorische Gestaltung auf der operativen Ebene stellt. Wie lassen sich das Schaffen von Wissen, seine Modellierung, Speicherung, Nutzung und Substitution durch den Einsatz geeigneter Methoden und Werkzeuge unterstützen?

Rehäuser und Krcmar (1996, S. 7f.) fordern unter Rückgriff auf die in Abschnitt 2.1 wiedergegebene Charakterisierung von Wissen den gezielten Aufbau einer *organisationalen Wissensbasis*. Deren Aufgabe ist die Explikation bewußten Wissens, welches damit kollektiv *(Aufbau einer organisationalen Wissensbasis)* verfügbar gemacht wird, indem *Objektwissen*, z.B. eine Produktbeschreibung oder eine Verfahrensanweisung, und *Metawissen* (Wissen über Objektwissen) abgebildet werden. Jedoch lassen sich nur Teile des organisatorischen Wissens isolieren, auf Informationsinfrastrukturen abbilden und zugänglich machen. Andere Teile entziehen sich, da sie an Prozesse gebunden und/oder individueller Natur sind, einem unmittelbaren Zugriff und können erst über organisatorische Maßnahmen erschlossen werden (Schneider 1996, S. 22f.).

Als wichtige Aufgabe eines abgestimmten *Wissensmanagements* erkennen wir somit die Schaffung der infrastrukturellen und organisatorischen Voraussetzungen für eine *lernende Organisation*, deren Mitglieder sich der ökonomischen Relevanz von Wissen und der Notwendigkeit seiner zielorientierten Nutzung bewußt sind und permanent gemeinsam zur Verbreiterung der zugänglichen organisationalen Wissensbasis und zur Aktualisierung ihrer Inhalte beitragen. Dabei sind die Ergebnisse der kontinuierlich stattfindenden Lernprozesse zu dokumentieren und den Mitarbeitern und Partnern kollektiv zugänglich zu machen (Rehäuser und Krcmar 1996, S. 18ff.; Schneider 1996, S. 27f.). Diese Dokumentationsaufgabe kann durch die Integration strukturorientierter, computerunterstützter Lernumgebungen in das betriebliche Dokumentenmanagement – z.B. auf Basis von SGML – unterstützt werden. Die sich damit ergebenden Synergiemöglichkeiten werden in (Schoop 1998a) diskutiert.

3 Management des betrieblichen Informationssystems

Je nachdem, ob sich eine Unternehmung mehr auf Wissen als wettbewerbsorientiertem Erfolgsfaktor oder als Engpaßfaktor konzentriert, können wir die Unterstützungspotentiale durch ein an der jeweiligen Strategie ausgerichtetes *Informationsmanagement* einmal im Aufbau von *Metastrukturen* (Top-Down-Perspektive), zum anderen in der Bereitstellung zugreifbaren Objektwissens (Bottom-Up-Perspektive) sehen.

3.1 Strategisches Informationsmanagement

Die zuvor erwähnten betriebswirtschaftlichen Leitungs- und Entscheidungsprozesse werden von hierfür bestimmten Aufgabenträ-

gern wahrgenommen, die mit ihren zu lösenden Aufgaben und den
darauf anzuwendenden Methoden und Werkzeugen systematisch
aufbereitete, zielorientierte *Informationssysteme* bilden (Ferstl/Sinz
1993, S. 3). Diese Informationssysteme sind Gegenstand des Informationsmanagements als eines informationsbezogenen betriebswirtschaftlichen Leitungshandelns. Alle innerhalb und auch außerhalb des Unternehmens entlang der Wertekette anfallenden Infor-
mations- und Kommunikationsprozesse (betriebliche *Informations-
funktion*) werden identifiziert, zielorientiert koordiniert und durch
Bereitstellen geeigneter *Informationsinfrastruktur* (Hardware, Software, Personal, Regeln, Methoden und Werkzeuge) automatisiert.
Als Ergebnis entstehen funktions- oder prozeßorientierte Anwendungssysteme, deren Einsatz die innerbetriebliche Rationalisierung
und/oder die Differenzierung am Markt durch Beeinflussung kriti-
scher Wettbewerbsfaktoren zum Ziel hat (Heinrich 1996, S. 21). Auf
strategischer Ebene sorgt das Informationsmanagement für einen
Abgleich zwischen den Unternehmens- und den sie unterstützenden
Informatikzielen, auf administrativer Ebene plant es die benötigten
Architekturen, Methoden und Werkzeuge sowie die Systemumset-
zung, auf operativer Ebene wird der wirtschaftliche Ablauf der Informationsverarbeitung sichergestellt.

Die wettbewerbsorientierte betriebswirtschaftliche Bewertung von
Wissen als strategischer Erfolgsfaktor spiegelt sich somit wider in den
Anforderungen an das strategische Informationsmanagement. Aus
den marktorientierten Unternehmenszielen sind Sollstrukturen für
die organisationale Wissensbasis abzuleiten und für spätere Zugriffe
durch wissensverarbeitende Systeme zu modellieren. Sie beschreiben
als Metastrukturen das aus Sicht der Zielerreichung benötigte Wissen in der Unternehmung.

3.2 Bereitstellung von Informations-Ressourcen

Nachdem durch das strategische Informationsmanagement zielorientierte Wissensstrukturen vorgegeben wurden, besteht die anschließende Aufgabe ressourcenorientierter Ansätze darin, diese
Strukturen mit konkreten Inhalten zu füllen. Rehäuser und Krcmar
(1996, S. 15ff.) differenzieren als Trägerobjekte von Wissen zwischen
Dokumentationen, Daten-, Methoden- und Modellbanken, Exper-
tensystemen, dem Menschen als Experten und der dokumentierten
und/oder vorgelebten Unternehmenskultur. In diesen physischen
Wissensträgern sind die einzelnen Wissensobjekte der Unterneh-

mung als zugreifbare Ressourcen gespeichert. Sie bilden die Bausteine der organisationalen Wissensbasis.

Da der wichtigere, weil weniger leicht kopierbare, Teil der Wissensbasis kontextgebundenes Wissen darstellt, kommt den anwendungsbezogenen Methoden der Wirtschaftsinformatik für umfassende Organisations-, Prozeß- und Systemanalysen sowie für die daran anknüpfende Systemmodellierung an dieser Stelle entscheidende Bedeutung zu. Zur Bereitstellung von Datenbanken werden strukturierte Entity-Relationship-Modelle entwickelt, anwendungsbezogen normalisiert und in Form nutzerspezifischer externer Schemata (*views*) aufbereitet. Methoden- und Modellbanken enthalten prozedurales Wissen über Entscheidungs- und Problemlösungsverhalten in Form vorformulierter, modular gespeicherter und kombinierbarer Algorithmen. Expertensysteme geben eng begrenztes, zwischen Anwendungs- und Modellierungsexperten gemeinsam beschriebenes Domänenwissen wieder, z.B. in Form von Fakten und darauf basierenden Regeln oder als Frames explizit und unabhängig vom allgemeinen Problemlösungswissen (Ferstl/Sinz 1993, S. 85ff.).

Während sich die unmittelbare Abbildung individuellen und kollektiven impliziten menschlichen Wissens den Ansätzen eines an Informationsressourcen orientierten Informationsmanagements entzieht, halten die ebenfalls als Wissensträger identifizierten betrieblichen Dokumentationen ein reichhaltiges Reservoir expliziten organisatorischen Wissens über Produkte, Prozesse, Strukturen, Projekte, Aufgaben und Aufgabenträger bereit. Liegt dieses Wissen jedoch in herkömmlicher, linearer Weise auf Papiermedien oder in nicht weiter strukturierter elektronischer Form vor, ist es nur bedingt verfügbar und entzieht sich weitgehend unmittelbaren Zugriffen sowie der Verwaltung durch integrierte wissensverarbeitende Systeme. Es wird daher als latentes, durch Kommunikationsbarrieren blockiertes Wissen bezeichnet (Kirsch 1992, S. 317).

Wir sehen hier einen interessanten Ansatz zur effizienten Verbreiterung der organisationalen Wissensbasis, indem im Rahmen eines strukturorientierten Dokumentenmanagements unter Rückgriff auf den bewährten ISO-Dokumentenstandard SGML die Inhalte bereits vorliegender betriebswirtschaftlicher und technischer Dokumentationen modelliert, in einer elektronischen Dokumentenbasis verwaltet, untereinander anwendungsbezogen vernetzt und damit direkten, automatisierten Zugriffen zugänglich gemacht werden können.

3.3 SGML-basiertes Dokumenten-Management

Die Motivation für den Computereinsatz in Unternehmen hat sich in den letzten Jahrzehnten mehrfach gewandelt. Stand zunächst die Automatisierung einzelner, klar abgrenzbarer Funktionsbausteine im Vordergrund, später gefolgt von funktionalen Erweiterungen hin zu dedizierten betrieblichen Anwendungssystemen (z.B. Produktionsplanung und -steuerung, Finanzbuchhaltung), vollzog man später eine bereichsübergreifende Anwendungsintegration durch den Einsatz unternehmensweiter Datenmodelle und die verstärkte Funktionskoppelung durch Prozeß-Prozeß-Kommunikation wie z.B. CIM und EDI. Zu den bis dahin vorherrschenden datenbankbasierten Anwendungssystemen kamen durch den Auf- und Ausbau der Büroautomation und -kommunikation dokumentenverarbeitende Systeme. Heute wird nicht mehr von Daten-, sondern zunehmend von Informationsverarbeitung gesprochen. Spätestens seit der aktuellen Internet-Diskussion mit den daraus erwachsenden Fragestellungen der Integration betrieblicher Daten (z.B. multimediale Produktkataloge) und Funktionen (z.B. Warenwirtschaftssysteme) in Electronic-Commerce-Strukturen und der Unterstützung verteilter Organisationen durch CSCW auf Basis von Internet-, Intranet- oder Extranet-Architekturen hat sich der Fokus des betrieblichen Informationsmanagements von einer schwerpunktmäßigen Datenbankorientierung hin zu komplexen, multimedialen elektronischen Verbunddokumenten und zu darauf basierenden hypermedialen Anwendungssystemen gewandelt.

Ausgehend von der Tatsache, daß über 70% der in Unternehmen vorliegenden relevanten Information nicht in Datenbanken, sondern in aufbereiteter Form in Dokumenten vorliegt, muß das Informationsmanagement für die Explizierung organisatorischen Wissens viel stärker, als bisher üblich, auf ausgereifte Methoden des Dokumentenmanagements zurückgreifen. Betriebliche Dokumentationen, zum einen im Sinne von *Dokumentationsprozessen*, zum anderen im Sinne von *Dokumentationsprodukten*, sind in Form durchgängiger elektronischer Publikationsketten und durch die Integration einer mittels inhaltsbezogener Strukturierung zugänglich gemachten Dokumentenbasis in geeigneten Anwendungssystemen zu automatisieren (Schoop 1998b).

Diese Aufgabe setzt eine umfassende, anwendungsbezogene Methode in Analogie zur Datenmodellierung voraus. Wir bezeichnen sie als *Document Engineering* und verstehen darunter ein mehrstufiges Vorgehen auf Basis des Dokumentenstandards SGML. Zunächst

integrierte Informationsverarbeitung

Dokumentenbasis durch Strukturierung zugänglich

werden, ausgehend von Geschäftsprozeß-, Zielgruppen-, Nutzungs-, Restriktionen- und Dokumentenanalysen, potentielle semantische Komponenten isoliert und durch nachfolgende Bewertungen relativiert. Die verbleibenden Elemente und Elementbeziehungen bilden die Basis für die Modellierung von Dokumenttypdefinitionen (DTDs). Diese wiederum sind Grundlage der anschließenden Produktions- bzw. Redesign-Prozesse zur Bildung SGML-konformer Dokumentinstanzen. Im letzten Schritt werden zielmedienspezifische Layouts und/oder Funktionalitäten hinzugefügt (Schoop 1998b; zu SGML vgl. die in Schoop/Schraml 1996 diskutierte Literatur).

Integrationspotential durch SGML

Durch den Einsatz von SGML im betrieblichen Dokumenten-, Informations- und Wissensmanagement ergeben sich mehrfache Integrationspotentiale:

- *Medienintegration:* Die inhaltsbezogene, layout-unabhängige Speicherung der Dokumentbausteine ermöglicht die Kombination unterschiedlicher Daten- und Medientypen im Rahmen eines *electronic cross media publishing.*

- *Daten- und Dokumentenintegration:* Da sich bei Verfügbarkeit entsprechender Strukturbeschreibungen in Form von Entity-Relationship-Modellen (Datenbanken) bzw. Dokumenttypdefinitionen (Dokumente) die Inhalte von Datenbanken ebenso in Dokumente wie die Inhalte der Dokumente in Datenbanken überführen lassen, können die derzeit noch vorhandene weitgehende Trennung der Daten- und der Dokumentenbearbeitung schrittweise aufgehoben und die spezifischen Vorteile der jeweiligen Modelle besser genutzt werden.

- *Prozeßintegration:* Die Abbildung von Prozeß- und Objektwissen in Form von Metamodellen, die sich in Daten- und Dokumentenstrukturen überführen lassen, erlaubt das Zusammenführen bislang getrennter Geschäftsprozesse in daten- und in dokumentenverarbeitenden Bereichen im Rahmen integrierter Anwendungssysteme.

Interessant ist die Beantwortung der Frage, in welchen Bereichen, für welche Arten von Dokumentationen und unter Berücksichtigung welcher Einflußfaktoren sich der methodische Mehraufwand sorgfältiger Strukturmodellierung sowie der erhöhte Kostenaufwand auf Werkzeugebene durch den Einsatz von SGML-Systemen im redaktionellen und im Nutzungsbereich lohnt.

Untersuchungen zur Wirtschaftlichkeit

Strobel (1998) betont auf der Grundlage konkreter SGML-Projekte, in denen spezielle Wirtschaftlichkeitsuntersuchungen vorgenommen wurden, die Berücksichtigung strategischer Nutzenpotentiale durch eine bereichsübergreifende Integration der Dokumentenbasis, z.B. die Kombination der Dokumentationen im Qua-

SGML als Grundbaustein für das betriebliche Wissensmanagement

litätsmanagement und im Umweltschutzmanagement der Unternehmung, wodurch die Vorteile des SGML-Standards wie Austauschbarkeit der Elemente, Mehrfachnutzung oder Aufbau von Informationsnetzen durch das Einbringen von Hypertextstrukturen meist erst richtig zum Tragen kommen. Diese stufenweise Vergrößerung des lokalen Dokumentationsausschnittes führt letzlich zu der hier vorgeschlagenen, informationsressourcenorientierten Bottom-Up-Strategie zum Aufbau einer organisationalen Wissensbasis.

Weitere Argumente lassen sich aus der Tatsache, daß SGML-Dokumente die inhaltliche Grundlage für den Aufbau von Hypertext/Hypermedia-Systemen bilden können, ableiten. Hier sei auf die *three golden rules* nach Shneiderman (1989, S. 115ff.) verwiesen, wonach die Erstellung von Hypertexten insbesondere dann in Erwägung zu ziehen ist, wenn

- es sich um die Abbildung großer Informationsbereiche handelt, die sich stark fragmentieren lassen,

- diese gut abgrenzbaren Fragmente untereinander in enger, anwendungsbezogen begründeter Beziehung stehen und

- der Nutzer zu jedem Handlungszeitpunkt jeweils nur einen spezifischen Teilausschnitt aus dem gesamten Informationsnetz benötigt.

Diese Kriterien treffen auf viele betriebliche Dokumentationen zu, die damit die ideale Grundlage für eine elektronische organisationale Wissensbasis der Unternehmung bieten. Über das Intranet kann sie den Mitarbeitern die bereits vorhandenen Informationsressourcen für unmittelbare Zugriffe und eine flexible Weiterverarbeitung bereitstellen, über Extra- oder Internet können die Metastrukturen Kooperationspartnern, Lieferanten oder Kunden die Kernkompetenzen der Unternehmung verdeutlichen und damit ihre spezifischen Erfolgspotentiale herausstellen.

4 Aufbau einer organisationalen Wissensbasis mit Hilfe von SGML

Im Rahmen des Wissensmanagements sehen wir aus betriebs- und informationswirtschaftlicher Sicht somit ein sehr großes Anwendungspotential für SGML. Die nachfolgenden Beispiele stammen aus Projekten, die in den letzten Jahren am Lehrstuhl für Wirtschaftsinformatik, insbesondere Informationsmanagement, der *TU Dresden* in Zusammenarbeit mit dem *Steinbeis Transferzentrum Betriebliches*

*Dokumentation
betrieblicher
Abläufe*

Informationsmanagement Dresden in den Bereichen Software-Dokumentation, Produkt-Dokumentation, Normenverwaltung und Erstellung elektronischer Publikationen durchgeführt wurden. Sie sollen die – noch weitgehend theoretische – Vision eines ganzheitlichen, SGML-basierten Wissensmanagements der Unternehmung konkretisieren und einen praktikablen Weg zur schrittweisen Annäherung an diese Zielvorstellung weisen.

Neben Produkten sind in den Unternehmen auch betriebliche Abläufe zu dokumentieren. Da sich hier das eigentliche Know-How der Unternehmung (prozeßgebundenes Wissen) verbirgt, konzentrieren wir uns im weiteren Verlauf der Diskussion auf diesen Ausschnitt der betrieblichen Dokumentation.

Träger von Ablaufbeschreibungen sind (s. Ende 1997, S. 2; Erb 1998, S. 9; Riedel, et al. 1995, Kap. 11.2; Streib/Riemer 1993, S. 8):

- Organisationsanweisungen

- Verfahrensanweisungen

- Dienstanweisungen

- Geschäftsanweisungen

- Budgetierungsanweisungen

- Schulungsunterlagen

- Problemreports

- Projektmanagementhandbuch

- Qualitätssicherungshandbuch

- Umweltmanagementhandbuch

*Verteilte
Verwaltung des
Wissens*

Da diese betrieblichen Ablaufdokumentationen z.T. in unterschiedlichen Verantwortungsbereichen liegen, werden sie häufig separat und ohne inhaltlichen Zusammenhang erstellt und sind infolgedessen in der Regel nicht kompatibel. Darüberhinaus werden gleiche Informationen mehrfach in unterschiedlichen Kontexten erfaßt und verwaltet, was nicht im Sinne eines effizienten Wissensmanagements ist. Die verteilte Verwaltung des Wissens im Unternehmen bewirkt, daß einmal erarbeitetes, z.T. unter Zuhilfenahme externer Berater teuer erkauftes Wissen nicht optimal genutzt wird (vgl. Herterich 1998, S. 51). Die Lösung des Problems setzt eine einheitliche, aus den strategischen Unternehmenszielen abgeleitete Wissensbasis im Sinne von Metawissen voraus, um in Orientierung an diesen Strukturvorgaben die betrieblichen Abläufe in redundanzarmen, integrierbaren und mehrfachverwendbaren Bausteinen dokumentieren zu können.

4.1 Projekterfahrungen mit der Dokumentation betrieblicher Abläufe

Die Organisationsdokumentationen wurde im Rahmen der folgenden drei Projekte detailliert untersucht:

- Entwicklung einer Referenz-Struktur für ein Qualitätssicherungshandbuch auf Basis existierender Dokumentationen;

- Strukturierte Erstellung eines Organisationshandbuches für einen Energieversorger auf Basis von SGML;

- Konzeption einer SGML-basierten Normenerstellung für ein Unternehmen aus dem Maschinen- und Anlagenbau.

Dabei konnte festgestellt werden, daß die Dokumentationsarten sowohl strukturell als auch inhaltlich Ähnlichkeiten aufweisen. Weiterhin bestehen zwischen den einzelnen Dokumenten auch starke inhaltliche Bezüge.

4.1.1 Qualitätssicherungshandbuch

Ein Handbuch zur Qualitätssicherung (QS) besteht gemäß ISO 9000 ff. aus zwanzig vorgegebenen Qualitätssicherungselementen. Diese sind je nach Zertifizierungsvorhaben mehr oder weniger detailliert zu beschreiben. Die Beschreibung dieser QS-Elemente ist mit QS-Verfahrensanweisungen zu unterfüttern. Zudem werden weitere mitgeltende Unterlagen (Arbeitsanweisungen, Werknormen, Formulare) herangezogen.

Am Beispiel zweier bereits nach ISO 9001 zertifizierter Unternehmen aus den Branchen Edelstahl-Druckbehälter bzw. Rohrleitungsbau wurden im vorliegenden Projekt die jeweiligen Qualitätssicherungshandbücher einer eingehenden Analyse unterzogen, als deren Ergebnis ein weitgehend identischer Aufbau der Handbücher bei hoher inhaltlicher Fragmentierung sowie intensive Verweisstrukturen zwischen den Fragmenten identifiziert wurden.

Analyse

Ausgewählte Teile eines der Handbücher wurden als Referenzsystem exemplarisch mit Hilfe von SGML strukturiert. Mit den Werkzeugen Framemaker+SGML und Corel Word Perfect wurden Dokumenterfassungsapplikationen erstellt und deren Ergebnisse in den Umgebungen DynaText bzw. Panorama Publisher als elektronische Dokumente präsentiert.

Strukturierung mit SGML

4.1.2 Organisationshandbuch

Das Organisationshandbuch des untersuchten Energieversorgungs-
unternehmens besteht aus

- Organigrammen zur Darstellung der Aufbauorganisation,
- Funktionsbeschreibungen zur Aufbauorganisation im Sinne von
  Stellenbeschreibungen,
- Dienstanweisungen und
- Geschäftsanweisungen.

Zwischen den Dienst- und Geschäftsanweisungen, in die weitere
Dokumente eingebunden sind, bestehen inhaltliche Bezüge. Aus der
Aufbauorganisationsbeschreibung sollen künftig Verweise auf diese
beiden Texttypen möglich sein.

Modellierung von Prozessen und Anweisungen

    Ziel des Projektes war zunächst, die Dokumentationsprozesse so-
wie die Dienst- und Geschäftsanweisungen so zu strukturieren, daß
künftig eine verteilte und vor allem qualitätsgerechte Erstellung und
Pflege möglich wird. Den Nutzern sollten die für sie relevanten Anweisungen über entsprechende Suchalgorithmen im Unternehmens-
Intranet nach dem Holprinzip in zu jedem Abrufzeitpunkt garantiert
aktuellen Versionen zur Verfügung stehen. Zu diesem Zweck wurden die unterschiedlichen Zielgruppen bezüglich der inhaltlichen
Struktur der Dienst- und Geschäftsanweisungen intensiv befragt und
einzelne Vertreter aktiv am Modellierungsprozeß beteiligt.

Aufbereitung der Inhalte

    In einem ersten Pilotprojekt wurden neun Geschäfts- und zwölf
Dienstanweisungen nach der entwickelten DTD in SGML aufbereitet
und für die Redaktionsumgebung Framemaker+SGML Erfassungs-
Template entwickelt. Die abgebildeten Dienst- und Geschäftsanweisungen stehen in den SGML-Browsern DynaText und Panora-
ma-Viewer elektronisch zur Verfügung. Die Prototypen dienen als
Machbarkeitsstudie. Es ist geplant, die DTD im praktischen Einsatz
durch Mitarbeiter des Unternehmens auf Akzeptanz und Handhabbarkeit überprüfen zu lassen und ihre Struktur für die anschließende
Umsetzung der weiteren Bestandteile des Organisationshandbuches
gegebenenfalls zu verfeinern.

4.1.3 Normen

Die Werknormen des untersuchten Maschinenbauunternehmens
sind in drei Produktklassen zusammengefaßt:

- Produktnormen,
- Verfahrensanweisungen, wie beispielsweise Konstruktionsricht-
  linien, Toleranzen, Zeichnungserstellung, Konservierung, Kenn-

*SGML als Grundbaustein für das betriebliche
Wissensmanagement*

zeichnung, Verpackung, Kundensonderwünsche, dokumentationspflichtige Teile, QS-Verfahrensanweisungen und

- Lieferbedingungen.

Die Normenklassen unterscheiden sich nur geringfügig in ihrer Grundstruktur, jedoch wesentlich in ihren Inhalten. Im Rahmen des durchgeführten Projektes wurde eine umfassende Werknormen-DTD entwickelt, die die strukturellen und inhaltlichen Gemeinsamkeiten und Unterschiede der drei Einsatzkategorien in einer DTD vereint. Dafür wurde die vom Beuth-Verlag herausgegebene DIN-DTD den unternehmensspezifischen Belangen angepaßt. Für die inhaltliche Strukturierung der Normen wurde eine eingehende Befragung der Normennutzer durchgeführt, die so alternative Suchkriterien für die von ihnen benötigten Werknormen definieren konnten. Eine Framemaker+SGML-Applikation für die Erfassung der Werknormen wurde bereits umgesetzt (Pabst 1997).

Darüberhinaus wurde für die geplante Einführung der SGML-gestützten Werknormenerstellung im Unternehmen eine detaillierte Wirtschaftlichkeitsuntersuchung vorgenommen, wobei die potentiellen Nutzeneffekte der Integration weiterer Dokumentationsbereiche des Unternehmens in die SGML-Lösung besondere Berücksichtigung fanden (Schoop et al. 1997).

Entwicklung einer Werknormen-DTD

4.2 Konzeption einer organisationalen Wissensbasis

Die vorgestellten, in verschiedenen Unternehmen durchgeführten SGML-Projekte stellen Insellösungen im jeweiligen organisatorischen Unternehmensprozeß dar. Eine isolierte SGML-basierte Dokumentation birgt jedoch die wenigsten Einsatzpotentiale in sich. Sowohl aus wirtschaftlicher als auch aus Sicht des Wissensmanagements prädestiniert sind Anwendungsfälle, bei denen die Dokumente prozeßbezogen, bereichs- bzw. unternehmensübergreifend sowie anwendungssystem- und plattformunabhängig erstellt bzw. verteilt werden und verschiedene Ausgabeformate (Publikation auf Papier, CD-ROM, im WWW) aus einer Dokumentressource zu erzeugen sind.

Obwohl ein starker inhaltlicher Zusammenhang zwischen den zuvor beschriebenen Organisationsdokumentationen besteht (Abbildung 1), werden diese häufig isoliert voneinander erstellt und gepflegt bzw. sind unterschiedlichen Verantwortungsbereichen zugeordnet. Die Erstellung und Wartung des Qualitätssicherungs-

Insellösungen schöpfen das Potiential nicht aus

handbuches obliegt im allgemeinen dem Qualitätsbeauftragten des Unternehmens. Das Organisationshandbuch wurde im vorliegenden Untersuchungsbeispiel von der Abteilung Organisation erstellt, während im anderen Unternehmen die Normenabteilung für die Erstellung der Werknormen verantwortlich ist.

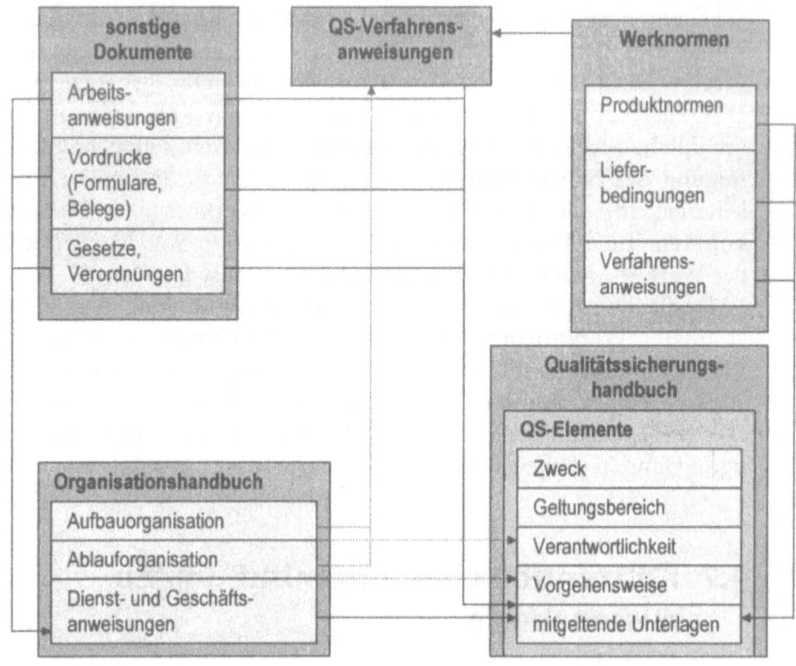

Die geteilten Verantwortlichkeiten bewirken, daß bei klassischer Vorgehensweise mit bereichsbezogener Dokumentation das jeweilige organisatorische Wissen innerhalb der einzelnen Verantwortungsbereiche verbleibt und nicht über die Bereichsgrenzen hinaus expliziert wird.

Zur Ausnutzung der strategischen Synergiepotentiale empfehlen wir daher eine frühzeitige Strukturentwicklung für eine gemeinsame Wissensbasis, die schrittweise von den einzelnen Bereichen durch Zurverfügungstellung ihrer jeweiligen explizierten Dokumente mit Inhalt gefüllt wird (Abbildung 2).Es ließen sich jederzeit die Dokumente weiterer Betriebsbereiche integrieren, wie die des betrieblichen Umweltbeauftragten, der Beschaffungs- oder Marketingabteilung mit kundenbezogenen Anweisungen oder der Serviceabteilung mit Reparaturmanualen.

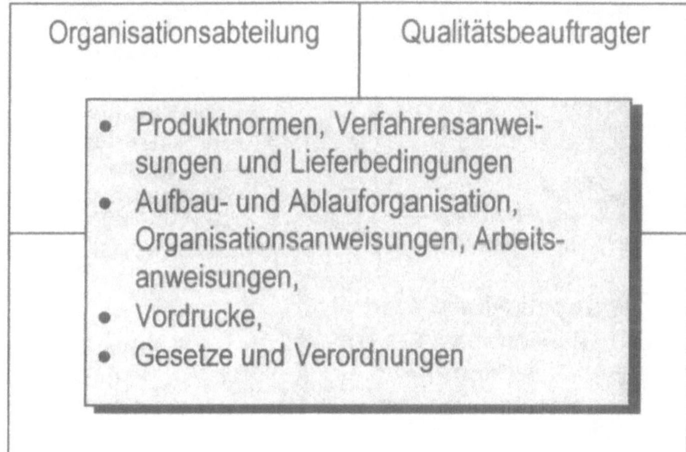

Abbildung 2
Ausschnitt aus einer organisationalen Wissensbasis

4.3 Einsatz von SGML zur Gestaltung der organisationalen Wissensbasis

In der Regel werden in den Unternehmen die Dokumente verteilt erstellt, d.h. mehrere Mitarbeiter wollen an unterschiedlichen Arbeitsplätzen zeitgleich dasselbe Dokument bearbeiten. Eine integrale Strukturierung der Dokumentklassen sollte daher nach Möglichkeit verschiedene Zugriffsbereiche berücksichtigen. Neben der nach wie vor erforderlichen Papierdokumention sollten die Dokumente den Nutzern auch elektronisch, z.B. über ein Unternehmensintranet, zur Verfügung stehen. Eine nutzerindividuelle Aufbereitung des Wissens, d.h. die beliebige Kombination der relevanten Wissenskomponenten, ist wünschenswert (Abbildung 3).

Grundsätzlich gilt, daß sich der Nutzen von Prozeßdokumentationen nur einstellt, wenn ihre Inhalte im Bedarfsfall garantiert aktuell, zielgenau und unmittelbar vom Arbeitsplatz aus zugänglich sind. Damit scheiden aktive Verteilsysteme nach dem Bringprinzip weitgehend aus. Da für die Organisationsdokumentationen neben den gesamten Dokumenten auch Dokumentteile benötigt werden, wie beispielsweise einzelne Ablaufdiagramme aus der Ablauforganisation für die Organisationsanweisungen und für das QS-Handbuch, ist eine strukturierte Dokumentablage erforderlich (s. Abbildung 4).

Aktualität, Zielgenauigkeit, unmittelbarer Zugriff

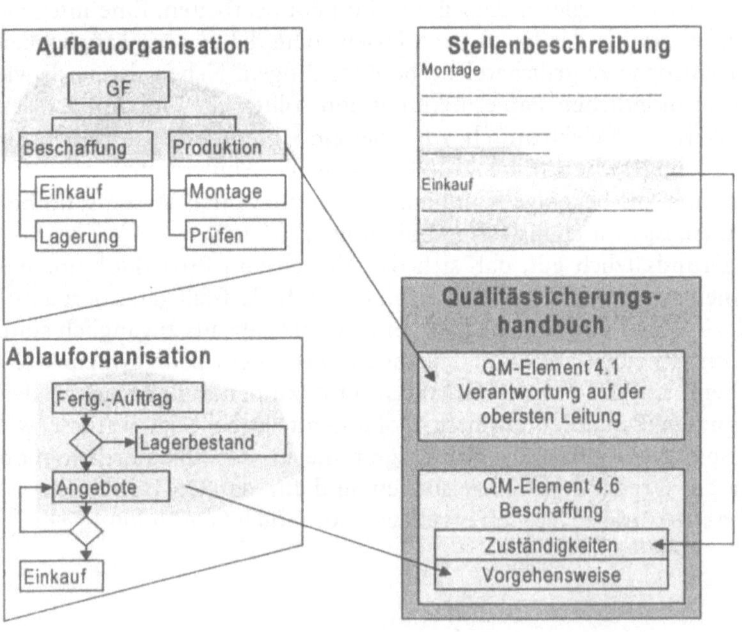

272   *SGML als Grundbaustein für das betriebliche*
Wissensmanagement

Aus den genannten Gründen empfehlen wir daher die zentrale Bereitstellung von in SGML strukturierten Dokumentationen und von den sie beschreibenden Wissensstrukturen in Form von DTDs, um eine modular gestaltete organisationale Wissensbasis aufzubauen.

Für die zuvor diskutierten Projekte liegen jeweils isoliert entwickelte Dokumenttypdefinitionen vor. Für die Integration in eine organisationale Wissensbasis sind sie auf ihre Eignung bezüglich des konkreten Anwendungsfalles zu überprüfen und in Metastrukturen zusammenzufügen, um so die doppelte Vergabe von Elementbezeichnungen und inhaltliche Unstimmigkeiten zu vermeiden und einen konsistenten Zugriff auf alle Organisationsdokumente zu ermöglichen (Abbildung 5).

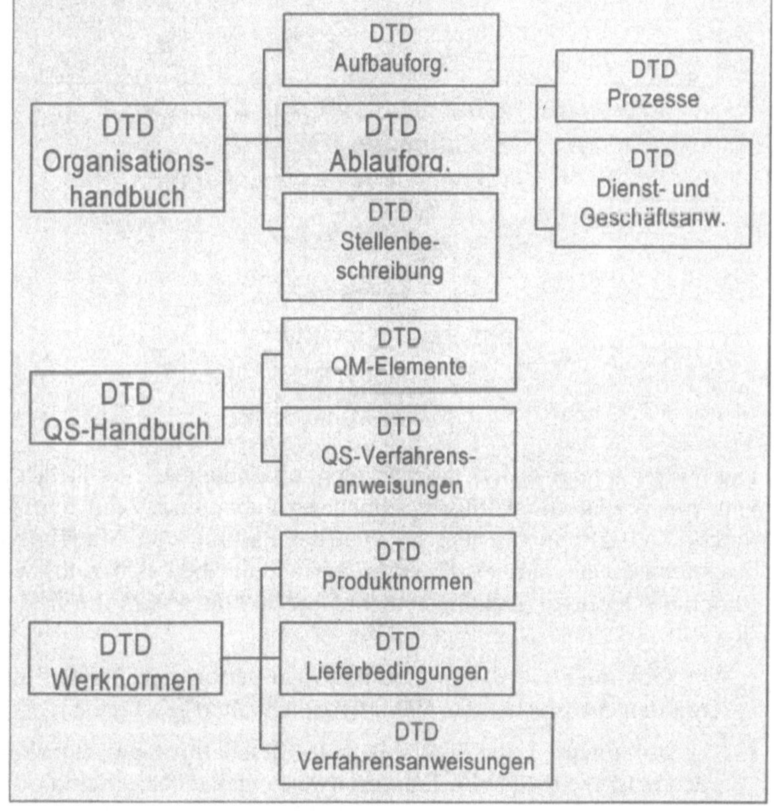

Abbildung 5
Metastruktur der Dokumente in einer Wissensbasis

Die Strukturierungstiefe der einzelnen Dokumentationsarten spiegelt sich in der jeweiligen DTD wider. Sie wird durch die Anforderungen der Dokumentnutzer und der Dokumentkonstrukteure bestimmt (Abbildung 6).

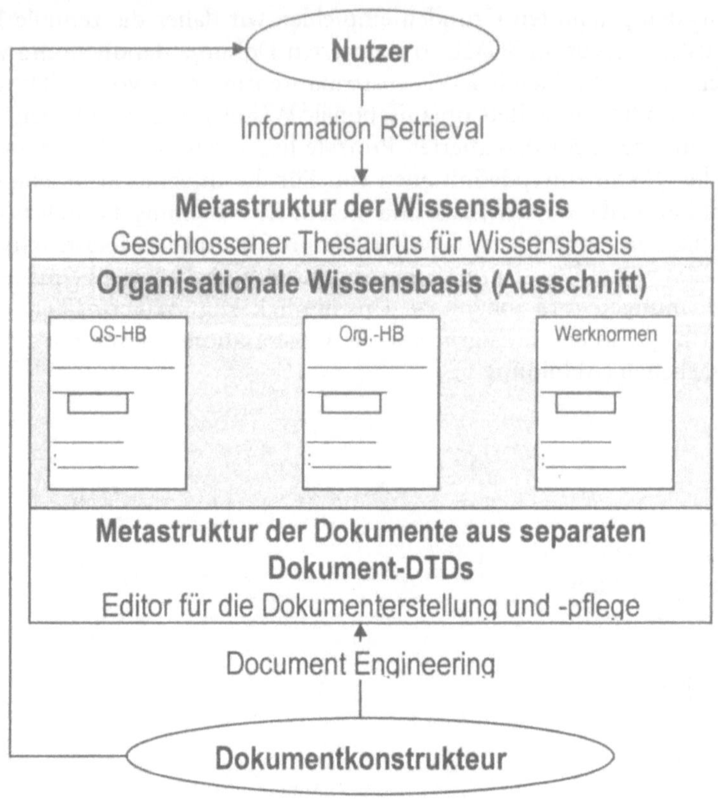

Der *Nutzer* hat das Ziel, herauszufinden, ob und an welcher Stelle die von ihm gewünschten Informationen verfügbar sind. Zum Beispiel möchte er wissen, was alles bei der Beschaffung von Material zu beachten ist. Dabei interessieren ihn u.a. alle für die Beschaffung von Material relevanten Zieladressen. Entsprechende Abschnitte finden sich z.B.

- in Dokumenten, die die Aufbauorganisation der Beschaffung mit den entsprechenden Verantwortlichkeiten beschreiben,

- in Dokumenten, die den Ablauf des Beschaffungsprozesses mit den entsprechenden Verfahrensanweisungen aufzeigen und

- in den Organisationsanweisungen, die die Unterschriftsberechtigungen und die Budgethandhabung regeln.

Das Ergebnis des Information-Retrieval-Prozesses sollte eine Liste aller relevanten Dokumente und Dokumentkomponenten sein, auch wenn der Begriff „Beschaffung" in den Dokumenten nicht direkt

SGML als Grundbaustein für das betriebliche Wissensmanagement

vorkommt. Somit erweist es sich als hilfreich, wenn die Dokumente und Dokumentkomponenten noch mit Zusatzwissen angereichert werden. Die Information-Retrieval-Funktionalität sollte daher

- eine gezielte Suche in Dokumentteilen ermöglichen,
- die Suchfunktionalitäten durch Deskriptoren auf Dokumentkomponentenebene unterstützen,
- synonyme Suchbegriffe, wie Beschaffung und Einkauf, einbinden,
- ähnliche Begriffe mit unterschiedlichen Bedeutungen von der Suche ausschließen sowie
- Groß-/Kleinschreibung und Schreibfehler bei der Suche wahlweise ignorieren.

Unser Lösungsansatz zeichnet sich daher durch die folgenden Merkmale aus:

- Realisierung der Suche in Dokumentbestandteilen durch die mit Hilfe von SGML strukturierte Ablage von Dokumenten und deren Indexierung, so daß eine genaue Zieladresse für die gewünschte Information angegeben werden kann,
- Zuordnung von Deskriptoren, die im Sinne von Schlagworten eine semantische Einordnung der Dokumente vornehmen, ohne jedoch zwingend als Stichworte in den Dokumenten und Dokumentkomponenten explizit vorkommen zu müssen, und
- Erstellung eines Thesaurus, der eine thematische Suche erlaubt sowie Homonyme, Synonyme usw. berücksichtigt.

Der *Dokumentkonstrukteur* betrachtet die Wissensbasis aus Sicht des Document-Engineering. Auch er muß auf die Dokumentteile zugreifen können. Dazu geht er in zwei Schritten vor:

1. Zunächst begibt er sich in die Position des Nutzers und sucht sich über die auf die Wissensbasis aufgesetzte Retrievalfunktionalität die relevanten Dokumente und Dokumentkomponenten heraus, bevor er
2. als Konstrukteur die herausgefilterten Dokumente und Dokumentkomponenten bearbeitet bzw. diese zu einem neuen Dokument zusammenfügt und es um weitere Informationen erweitert.

Für den zweiten Schritt benötigt er einen Editor, mit dem die herausgefilterten relevanten Dokumentkomponenten bearbeitet werden können, z.B. für die selektive Modifikation einzelner Dokumentkomponenten. Der Editor sollte auch das Zusammenfügen der Dokumentbestandteile unterstützen, d.h. die Überführung der Dokumentbestandteile aus Dokumenten einer DTD in Dokumente, die einer anderen DTD-Struktur unterliegen, sollte möglich sein.

5 Schlußfolgerung

SGML-Projekten eilt in der Praxis der Ruch eines extrem hohen, sich nur fraglich amortisierenden Vorabaufwandes voraus, so daß häufig wider besseren Wissens einfachere, weniger strukturexplizierende Lösungsansätze, i.d.R. HTML- oder auf proprietären Formaten bestimmter Textverarbeitungssysteme basierende Applikationen, gewählt werden.

SGML für die Modellierung organisatorischen Wissens

Wir vertreten aus theoretischer Überzeugung und auf Basis der in einer Reihe unterschiedlicher SGML-Projekte gewonnenen praktischen Erfahrungen die Meinung, daß eine rechtzeitige, ganzheitliche Erwägung diese Nachteile abbauen und langfristig die eigentlichen Erfolgsfaktoren der Unternehmung, ihr organisatorisches Wissen, überhaupt erst herausbilden kann. Dabei ist insbesondere von Bedeutung, daß eine die strategischen Ziele der Unternehmung berücksichtigende Strukturmodellierung einer organisationalen Wissensbasis „von oben" mit gegenläufiger Explikation konkreter Wissensträger, insbesondere Dokumente nach diesen Strukturvorgaben, „von unten" ergänzt wird.

Mit SGML steht ein probater Ansatz für den Aufbau strukturierter Dokumentenklassen zur Verfügung, dessen flexible Anwendung und schrittweise Erweiterbarkeit wir in den im vorliegenden Beitrag angesprochenen Projekten exemplarisch nachgewiesen haben.

Literatur

(Ende 1997)
Ende, A. vom: Die Integration der Produktdokumentationen in das Dokumentenmangement von Industrieunternehmen. Praxisseminar Wirtschaftsinformatik der TU Dresden, 1997

(Erb 1998)
Erb, H. G.: Die dritte Revolution in der Dokumentation. In: tekom nachrichten, 20 (1998), Nr. 1, S. 8-12

(Ferstl/Sinz 1993)
Ferstl, O. K.; Sinz, E. J.: Grundlagen der Wirtschaftsinformatik – Konzepte, Modelle und Methoden. München, 1993

(Heinrich 1996)
Heinrich, L.J.: Informationsmanagement. 5. Auflage. München, 1996

SGML als Grundbaustein für das betriebliche Wissensmanagement

(Herterich 1998)

Herterich, R: Organizational Memory Management für Industriebetriebe: Schritte zu erhöhter Unternehmenseffizienz. In: Information Management (1998), Nr. 1, S. 51-57

(Kirsch 1992)

Kirsch, W.: Kommunikatives Handeln, Autopoiese, Rationalität – Sondierungen zu einer evolutionären Führungslehre. München, 1992

(Pabst 1997)

Pabst, S.: Prototypischer Entwurf einer elektronischen Werknorm auf Basis von SGML unter besonderer Berücksichtigung ablauforganisatorischer und technischer Schnittstellen. Dresden, Technische Universität Dresden, Diplomarbeit, 1997

(Rehäuser/Krcmar 1996)

Rehäuser, J.; Krcmar, H: Wissensmanagement im Unternehmen. In: Schreyögg, G.; Conrad, P. (Hrsg.): Managementforschung 6. Berlin, 1996, S. 1-40

(Riedel et al. 1995)

Riedel, W.; Walter, K.-D.; Wallin-Felkner, C.: Praxishandbuch Technische Dokumentation: wirtschaftlich organisieren, systematisch erstellen, kundengerecht gestalten. Augsburg: WEKA Fachverlag für technische Führungskräfte, 1995

(Schneider 1996)

Schneider, U.: Management in der wissensbasierten Unternehmung: Das Wissensnetz in und zwischen Unternehmen knüpfen. In: Schneider, U. (Hrsg.): Wissensmanagement: Die Aktivierung des intellektuellen Kapitals. Frankfurt am Main, 1996, S. 13-48

(Schoop 1998a)

Schoop, E.: Structured Documentation: Defining Knowledge Components for Multimedia Learning Environments. In: Classification in the Information Age. Berlin, 1998 (Proceedings of the 22nd annual conference of the GfKl). In Begutachtung

(Schoop 1998b)

Schoop, E.: Strukturierung der betrieblichen Dokumentation als Grundbaustein für ein multimediales Wissensmanagement in der Unternehmung. In: Pribbenow, S.; Ohly, H. P., Czap, H. (Hrsg.): Wissensorganisation mit multimedialen Techniken. Würzburg, 1998 (Fortschritte in der Wissensorganisation Bd. 5). Im Druck

(Schoop et al. 1997)

Schoop, E.; Strobel, K.; Papenfuß S.; Sonntag, R: Projektdokumentation zum zweiten Abschnitt des Projektes „Konzeption einer SGML-gestützten Werknormenerstellung". Dresden, 1997

(Schoop/Schraml 1996)

Schoop, E.; Schraml, T.: Vergleichende Buchbesprechung: Dokumentenstandard SGML. In: Wirtschaftsinformatik 38 (1996) 2, S. 246-253

(Shneiderman 1989)

Shneiderman, B.: Reflections on Authoring, Editing, and Managing Hypertext. In: Barret, E. (Hrsg.): The Society of Text. Cambridge, 1989, S. 115-131

(Streib/Riemer 1993)

Streib, D.; Riemer, F.: Technische Dokumentation: Ein Leitfaden für den Technischen Redakteur. Gaildorf, 1993

(Strobel 1998)

Strobel, K.: Rechnet sich SGML in der Praxis? In: Proceedings der tekom Frühjahrstagung 14.-15.05.98 in Lübeck. o.O., 1998, S. 125-128

Semantisches Markup zur Inhaltserschließung von Agenturmeldungen

Gerhard Knorz und Wiebke Möhr

1 Einleitung und Motivation

Seit jeher gehört die inhaltliche Erschließung von Nachrichten zu den täglichen Aufgaben von Nachrichtenagenturen, Zeitungen und Magazinen, die für den internen Gebrauch in der Redaktion festhalten müssen, wann und wie über ein bestimmtes Ereignis berichtet wurde. Aber auch die Veröffentlichung eines nachrichtenerschließenden Index für den externen Gebrauch, für historische und sozialwissenschaftliche Forschungen zum Beispiel, hat eine lange, ehrwürdige Geschichte. Bis zum heutigen Tag wird etwa *The Times Index* einmal monatlich gedruckt oder auf Mikrofilm ausgeliefert. Er geht lückenlos bis auf das Jahr 1785 zurück, auf der Website in dürren Worten als *„Available 1785 forward"* vermerkt (http://www. thomson.com/psmedia/timesin.htm). In Deutschland bietet z.B. *Der Spiegel* seinen Lesern jährlich einen gedruckten Index zur besseren Nutzung zurückliegender Ausgaben an, und die *Frankfurter Allgemeine Zeitung* bringt seit einiger Zeit die Jahresausgaben der *FAZ*, inhaltlich sorgfältig erschlossen (Robertson 1995), als CD-ROM auf den Markt. Auch im Internet finden sich inzwischen zahlreiche Zugangshilfen (Online-Kataloge, spezielle Suchmaschinen) zu öffentlich angebotenen Nachrichtenarchiven.

Mit dem Anwachsen der Zahl elektronischer Dokumente haben sich die Methoden ihrer inhaltlichen Erschließung verändert: maschinengestützte und automatische Indexierungsverfahren verdrängen zunehmend die intellektuellen manuellen Methoden. Dagegen

inhaltliche Erschließung von Nachrichten

scheint sich der Zweck einer Indexierung, ob für den internen oder externen Gebrauch, nicht geändert zu haben. Er ist seit jeher das Wiederauffinden von Information gewesen, und heute wird Indexierung unter Berücksichtigung ihres elektronischen Charakters allgemein als „preprocessing of information in order to enable its effective, efficient and easy retrieval" (Ellis/Ford 1998, S. 28) verstanden.

Ausgehend von der kürzlichen Verabschiedung eines SGML-basierten Standards zum Austausch strukturierter Nachrichten, dem *News Industry Text Format* (*NITF*; IPTC-NAA 1998), möchten wir in diesem Artikel die Markierung semantischer, d.h. inhaltlich bedeutsamer Einheiten in Meldungstexten als eine besondere Art der inhaltlichen Erschließung diskutieren.

Definition einer semantischen Einheit

Der Begriff der *semantischen Einheit* kommt aus dem Bereich der Analyse natürlichsprachlicher Texte, die neben morphologischen, syntaktischen und pragmatischen Aspekten den semantischen kennt. Wir verstehen unter einer semantischen Einheit bedeutungstragende Wörter oder Wortfolgen in einem Text, die Individuen und Begriffe einer bestimmten Domäne repräsentieren. Sie können bei Bedarf mit den Indextermen in einem gegebenen kontrollierten Vokabular (Thesaurus, Ontologie) verbunden werden und je nach der Häufigkeit ihres Vorkommens in einem repräsentativen Corpus eines bestimmten Fachgebiets einen niedrigen oder hohen semantischen Stellenwert erhalten (vgl. Silvester/Genuardi 1994, S. 209). Im Rahmen dieses Papiers sprechen wir deshalb vom *semantischen Markup*. Es wird in anderen Kontexten auch als *content markup, intelligent markup* oder *deep encoding* bezeichnet.

Wir möchten dabei die Eigenarten und Probleme dieses semantischen Markup besprechen, die Parallelen und Unterschiede, die zu Indexierungen anderer Art bestehen, und wir behaupten, daß sich mit den neuen Methoden der inhaltlichen Erschließung auch die Nutzung der erschlossenen Nachrichten grundlegend ändern kann.

News Industry Text Format

Das NITF ist eine Antwort auf die Herausforderung der Nachrichtenindustrie durch die neuen Medien, insbesondere durch das Internet und das World Wide Web (s. Beitrag von Klaus Sprick). Es ist unter Beteiligung namhafter nationaler und internationaler Nachrichtenagenturen und Zeitungsverlage vom *IPTC* (*International Press Telecommunications Council*, http://www.iptc.org/iptc) und der *NAA* (*Newspaper Association of America*) entwickelt worden. Das NITF erlaubt neben der zuweisenden Indexierung durch Schlagwörter (*keywords*) und Klassifikationscodes (*subject categories*), die es auch in den alten Formaten (ANPA 1312, IPTC 7901) bereits gegeben hat, eine Kodierung semantischer Einheiten wie Organisationen, Personen, Ereignisse im fortlaufenden Text. Damit ist, wie wir zeigen wollen, eine für die Nachrichtenindustrie neue Art der inhaltlichen

Erschließung vorbereitet, die nicht nur dem Retrieval dient, sondern auch die ökonomische Mehrfachnutzung und Wiedernutzung von Nachrichteninhalten unterstützen kann und damit einen Wertezuwachs bedeutet. Dieser mag in der Veröffentlichung ein- und desselben Meldungstextes in unterschiedlichen Medien liegen oder in der Nutzung semantisch markierter Meldungen für kundenspezifische Angebote wie die *dpa-Selektion* der *Deutschen Presse-Agentur (dpa)* oder die *Target News* von *Reuters.* Durch semantisches Markup erschlossene Nachrichten lassen sich ebenfalls zur Faktenextraktion nutzen und damit zum Aufbau faktenbezogener Pressedatenbanken oder zur Wiedernutzung extrahierter Information in Hintergründen, Rückblicken und Chroniken.

Pilotprojekt
Markup-Server

Mehr noch als Zeitungen stehen Agenturen bei der Nachrichtenproduktion unter Zeitdruck. Die Berichterstattung erfolgt im Sekundentakt und rund um die Uhr. Daher kommt eine manuelle semantische Markierung von Nachrichten in einer Agenturredaktion nicht in Frage. Im deutschsprachigen Raum war es die *dpa*, die im Rahmen eines von der *DeTeBerkom* (heute: *Deutsche Telekom Berkom*) finanzierten Projekts den Auftrag vergab, durch die Pilotimplementierung eines Markup-Servers die Machbarkeit und das Potential einer automatischen semantischen Markierung von Agenturmeldungen im NITF-Format herauszufinden. Die *GMD – Forschungszentrum Informationstechnik mbH* hat diese Aufgabe durchgeführt und in einem weiteren Projekt mit der *dpa* die mögliche Realisierung dieses Markup-Servers in der Produktionsumgebung der *dpa* geprüft (s. Beiträge von Klaus Sprick und Lothar Rostek). Hier hat dieses Papier seinen Ursprung, und die folgenden Ausführungen beziehen sich daher im wesentlichen auf die Meldungstexte der *dpa*.

2 Die Agenturmeldung als Dokument- und Texttyp

2.1 Die verschiedenen Strukturebenen einer Meldung

Dokumenttyp
Nachricht

Agenturmeldungen können eine ganze Reihe unterschiedlicher journalistischer Darstellungsformen annehmen: Es gibt neben der Nachricht das Feature, den Korrespondentenbericht, das Porträt, den Hintergrund, das Interview, die Chronologie u.a.m. Die Meldungen können strukturell und sprachlich durchaus als unterschiedliche Dokumenttypen aufgefaßt und modelliert werden. Im Rahmen dieses Papiers konzentrieren wir uns allerdings auf die häufigste Form der Agenturmeldung, auf die Nachricht (Wilke/Rosenberger 1991, S. 175), und schreiben ihr archetypische Qualitäten zu (Zschunke 1994, S. 77).

Strukturebenen einer Nachricht

Bei der Analyse einer solchen Nachricht lassen sich – wie bei vielen anderen Dokumenttypen auch – vier unterschiedliche Strukturebenen unterscheiden:

1. die Ebene der sog. Metainformationen, die z.B. die Umstände der Entstehung einer Nachricht (Meldungsort, Meldungsdatum, Name des Reporters oder Redakteurs) oder Workflow-Informationen enthält;

2. die Ebene der sog. logischen (hierarchischen) Struktur, die formale Komponenten zum besseren Verständnis der Inhalte enthält wie Überschriften, Absätze, Listen;

3. die Ebene der Verweis- und Linkinformationen und

4. die Ebene für Informationen zur Inhaltserschließung, zu denen neben Schlagwörtern *(keywords)* und Klassifikationscodes *(subject categories)* auch die sog. Inline-Elemente *(inline elements)* zur Kodierung semantischer Einheiten gehören.

Die NITF-DTD repräsentiert alle diese Ebenen einer Meldung. Uns interessieren hier nur die Elemente, die für das semantische Markup definiert sind und zu denen beispielsweise Personennamen, Personenrollen, Orte und Ereignisse gehören.

2.2 Inhaltlicher Aufbau einer Meldung

Die typische Aufgabe einer Nachricht ist es, tatsachenorientiert und knapp in der sprachlichen Form über aktuelle Ereignisse zu informieren (z.B. Fischer Lexikon 1989, S. 69 ff.; La Roche 1992, S. 131).

die umgekehrte Pyramide

Die archetypische Nachricht nimmt – in der Anordnung ihrer Inhalte – die Form einer umgekehrten Pyramide an. Dieses, in der journalistischen Ausbildung beliebte Bild illustriert, daß die wichtigsten Inhalte einer Nachricht am Anfang und dort in zugespitzter Form stehen (z.B. Weischenberg 1990, S. 46; Zschunke 1994, S. 178). Dabei wird, notwendigerweise sprachlich verkürzt, in der Überschrift der wesentliche Kern einer Nachricht zum Ausdruck gebracht. In dem nachfolgenden ersten Satz oder Absatz, dem Einstieg oder *Lead*, wird dieser Kern um die wichtigsten Informationen, das aktuelle Ereignis betreffend, erweitert. Hier sind auch die berühmten journalistischen Ws (Wer?, Was?, Wann?, Wo?, Warum?, Wie?, Welche Quelle?) zu beantworten, und zwar so, daß der Lead für sich gelesen, eine knappe Zusammenfassung der gesamten Meldung ist (Wasson 1998). Zusatzinformationen und interessante Details folgen in der Reihenfolge abnehmender Bedeutungsschwere, so daß eine Meldung immer von hinten zu kürzen sein muß. Es ist selbstverständlich, daß hier nur ein Prinzip angesprochen wird, daß dieses aber, wenn es um eine eventuelle Gewichtung markierter semantischer Einheiten geht, bedeutungsvoll ist.

2.3 Meldungsspezifische semantische Strukturen

In der konkreten Instanz einer Meldung stehen semantische Einheiten, anders als lexikalisierte Begriffe in einem Wörterbuch, als Teil einer Aussage im Kontext eines laufenden Textes und damit in der mittelbaren oder unmittelbaren Nachbarschaft zu anderen semantischen Einheiten. Diese syntagmatischen Beziehungen zwischen den semantischen Einheiten entsprechen impliziten semantischen Relationen wie z.B. zwischen einem Personennamen und einer mit ihm verbundenen Personenrolle (*Ministerpräsidentin Heide Simonis*).

Einige dieser Relationen kommen häufig vor, sind typisch für Meldungstexte, bilden wiederkehrende semantische Strukturen, obwohl sie in ganz unterschiedlichen sprachlichen Realisierungen erscheinen. Damit die faktenbezogenen Aussagen, die sie repräsentieren, nicht im Text eingeschlossen bleiben, sondern für ein maschinelle Nutzung zugänglich werden, muß man sie durch eine semantische Markierung explizit machen.

Markierung: Explizitmachen semantischer Strukuren

Für eine formale Repräsentation der semantischen Strukturen in SGML oder XML, d.h. als Inhaltsmodelle bestimmter Elemente, ist es erforderlich, die Nachricht als Texttyp zu untersuchen, denn nur die semantischen Einheiten, die im laufenden Text benachbart sind, können auch als Einheit markiert werden. Der Entwurf eines Datenbankschemas, das etwa die Beschreibungsmerkmale einer Person festlegt, und keinerlei textliche Nähe zwischen einer Person und ihren Eigenschaften mitbedenken muß, ist dagegen relativ frei.

Inhaltsmodell: formale Repräsentation semantischer Strukturen

Journalisten und Nachrichtenredakteure bedienen sich einer Reihe sprachlicher Wendungen, Strukturen und Muster, die wegen ihrer Art, Inhalte in knapper Form anzubieten, nachrichtenspezifisch sind. Besonders die Schlagzeilen sind für ihre reduzierte

Form bekannt, aber auch der laufende Meldungstext enthält wiederkehrende semantisch kompakte Strukturen, die für diesen Dokumenttyp bezeichnend sind. Dies soll an einer kurzen dpa-Online-Meldung, die aus einer Schlagzeile und einem weiteren Absatz besteht, illustriert werden.

Christiane Schenk frauenpolitische Sprecherin im PDS-Vorstand

Frauenpolitische Sprecherin im Vorstand der PDS-Gruppe im
Bundestag wurde Christiane Schenk. Die Berlinerin komplettiert
den Vorstand, dem damit drei Frauen und zwei Männer angehören.

Die Verknappung der Schlagzeile besteht in der Regel darin, daß syntaktische Elemente, die für einen wohlgeformten korrekten deutschen Satz notwendig sind, ausgelassen werden. In dem zitierten Beispiel wurde das Prädikat unterdrückt. Dennoch ist die Bedeutung der Schlagzeile klar. Die semantische Struktur bildet sich hier aus zwei Elementen, einem Personennamen und einer Funktionsbezeichnung und der semantischen Relation, die beide verbindet. Diese ist zwar implizit, läßt sich über den fehlenden Relationszuweiser (das Prädikat) erschließen und folgendermaßen beschreiben:

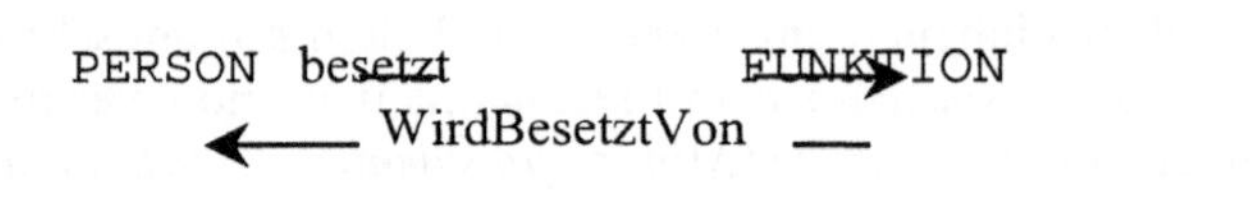

Andere, ebenfalls häufig eingesetzte, sprachliche Realisierungen demselben semantischen Gehalt, sind dann um aussagekräftige Satzbestandteile erweitert, um dem Leser schneller auf die Sprünge zu helfen. Hierzu gehören Formulierungen wie:

Christiane Schenk *neue* **frauenpolitische Sprecherin im PDS-Vorstand**

Christiane Schenk *als* **frauenpolitische Sprecherin im PDS-Vorstand
gewählt**

Untersuchungen haben ergeben, daß die semantische Struktur verkürzter Überschriften erhalten bleibt (Gerretz 1994, S. 59) und sich auch linguistisch formalisiert beschreiben läßt. Dies ist nicht unser Thema, wohl aber eine für solche Strukturen unzureichende, aber unter pragmatischen Gesichtspunkten sinnvolle SGML-Modellierung.

*Semantisches Markup zur Inhaltserschließung von
Agenturmeldungen*

3 Deklaration und Modellierung semantischer Strukturen im NITF

3.1 Die Inhaltselemente im NITF

Die Domäne der Nachrichtenindustrie, konkreter ausgedrückt, die Konzentration der Nachrichten auf Ereignisse und die damit verbundenen Informationen zu den Basisfragen *Wer? Was? Wo? Wann?* legen ein bestimmte Auswahl nachrichten-relevanter semantischer Einheiten zur Markierung nahe.

Die NITF-DTD (Version 2.01b, IPTC-NAA 1998) hat die folgenden Elemente zur Klassifizierung semantischer Einheiten in Meldungstexten deklariert: Ereignis (EVENT), Ort (LOCATION), Zeitangabe (CHRON), Person (PERSON), Funktion (FUNCTION) einer Person, Organisation (ORG), Welt-Objekt (OBJECT.TITLE), Währungseinheit (MONEY), Zahlenangabe (NUM). Weiterhin wird das Zitat (Q) spezifiziert, das wir als eine Sonderform einer semantischen Einheit ansehen möchten.

In der *Supporting Documentation* zum NITF werden diese Elemente als *non-structural elements* eingeführt, d.h. sie sind keine Komponenten der logischen Struktur und damit relativ frei in ihrer Position (IPTC-NAA 1998, 23.13). Wir werden sie als Inhaltselemente (*content elements*) oder semantische Einheiten ansprechen.

3.2 Modellierung komplexer Inhaltselemente im NITF

Das NITF hat ausgesuchte Inhaltselemente durch ein *content model* weiter spezifiziert. Dieses kann, SGML-typisch, eine semantische Struktur höchst unvollkommen nur durch die Schachtelung der Einzelkomponenten ausdrücken. Wir geben zwei Beispiele:

```
<!ELEMENT PERSON - - (#PCDATA | NAME.GIVEN |
                     NAME.FAMILY|FUNCTION)*>
```

```
<PERSON>
<FUNCTION>Brandenburgs Ministerpräsident</FUNCTION>
<NAME.GIVEN>Manfred</NAME.GIVEN>
<NAME.FAMILY>Stolpe</NAME.FAMILY></PERSON>
```



```
<!LOCATION - - (SUBLOCATION | CITY | STATE |
                REGION | COUNTRY | #PCDATA)*>
```



```
der Friedhof auf dem
<LOCATION><SUBLOCATION>Herzl-Berg</SUBLOCATION>
in <CITY>Jerusalem</CITY></LOCATION>
```

In beiden Beispielen bleiben die semantischen Relationen implizit. Die analoge Modellierung beider Strukturen läßt unbeachtet, daß sie ganz unterschiedlichen Typs sind. Während sich im PERSON-Beispiel Relationen wie *PERSON hat Name, hat FUNCTION* und ihre Inversen verstecken, orientiert sich das NITF-Modell LOCATION offensichtlich an einer Adresse. Wären die Elemente in aufsteigender Reihenfolge bezüglich der Größe der Orte angeordnet, könnte man partitive Relationen (*istTeilVon, hatTeil*) extrapolieren.

Sowohl das PERSON-Modell als auch das LOCATION-Modell lassen Stringenz vermissen: Im Personenmodell befindet sich FUNCTION zwar innerhalb von PERSON, ist aber gleichgeordnet mit den beiden NAMEs, deren Zusammengehörigkeit nicht formal ausgedrückt wird. Im LOCATION-Modell werden Elementtypen ganz unterschiedlicher Art und noch ungeklärter Bedeutung gleichgestellt: SUBLOCATION (= Untereinheit von LOCATION?), CITY (= administrative Einheit, definierbar über die Größe?), REGION (= eine geographische Einheit?), STATE (eine administrative Einheit auf der Ebene von Bundesstaaten/-ländern), COUNTRY (= nationale Einheit?). Auch die Rolle des Textes außerhalb der untergeordneten Elemente (PCDATA) bleibt unklar.

Es geht hier nicht darum, die eingeschränkten Möglichkeiten von SGML oder die NITF-Spezifikation zu kritisieren. Pragmatik ist hier sicherlich am Platze. Dennoch: Soll das Potential semantischer Mar-

kierung in Nachrichtentexten ausgeschöpft werden, brauchen wir für
eine anwendungsspezifische NITF-Version

- Erweiterungen und Konsistenz in der Modellierung der komplexen semantischen Strukturen und

- eindeutige Regeln für den Tagging-Prozeß.

Überlegungen zu diesen Punkten gelten die nächsten beiden Abschnitte.

4 Typische semantische Strukturen in der deutschsprachigen Nachricht

Die Beschäftigung mit semantischen Strukturen in Nachrichtentexten führt zu der Erkenntnis, daß die Entwickler des NITF sich bewußt auf nur wenige wichtige beschränkt haben. Das läßt sich aus einem Vergleich mit Versionen seines Vorgängers *UTF* (*Universal Text Format*) schließen.

Markierung für die Erkennung und Extraktion von Fakten

Markierung bedeutet Aufwand und rechtfertigt sich nur über Einsparungen oder Wertezuwachs in einer Gegenrechnung. Mit dem Ziel der Faktenerkennung und Faktenextraktion vor Augen entschloß sich die GMD in dem oben erwähnten Projekt mit der dpa, die NITF-Markierung um einige semantische Strukturen zu erweitern, von denen im folgenden nur einige herausgegriffen werden.

- *Typbezeichnung + Eigenname*
  Analog zu der Kombination *Funktionsbezeichnung* und *Personenname* werden auch andere Individuen mit typisierenden Bezeichnungen versehen. Beispiele hierfür sind: Marmeladenfabrik *Schwartau* (OrganisationsTyp + OrganisationsName), Narrenorden *Pälzer Krischer* (ObjektTyp + ObjektName), Mülheimer Theatertage *stücke 98* (EreignisTyp + Ereignisname), das tschetschenische Dorf Scholkowskaja (LokalModifikator + OrtsTyp + Ortsname).
  Das Vor- oder Nachschalten von Typbezeichnungen beim Nennen von Eigennamen gibt, entsprechend der Funktionsbezeichnung vor Personennamen, die Rolle an, in der ein Objekt im Text vorkommt. Diese kennzeichnenden Benennungen liegen in der Hierarchie zwischen den sehr abstrakten generischen Bezeichnungen der Elemente und ihren Instanzen, den Individualobjekten. Journalistisch gesehen, haben sie die Funktion der Orientierungshilfe für die Leser, wo nötig, werden sie auch zur Disambiguierung von homographen Ausdrücken eingesetzt.

- *Prämodifikator + Eigenname oder Begriffsbezeichnung*
  Es gibt eine Reihe von vorangestellten Modifikatoren z.B. geographischer oder temporaler Natur, die besonders vor Personen oder Funktionen, aber auch vor Organisationen für eine Faktenextraktion interessant sind. Hierher gehören Ausdrücke wie: der *hessische* Umweltminister (geographischer Prämodifikator + Funktion), der *zukünftige* Präsident (temporaler Prämodifikator + Funktion), der *gebürtige Hamburger* Ralf Hansen (qualifizierter geographischer Prämodifikator + Personenname), der *28jährige* Hansen (altersbezogener Prämodifikator + Personenname, der *grüne* Abgeordnete (politischer Prämodifikator + Funktion)
  Aus diesen Strukturen lassen sich Fakten ableiten. In den Beispielen oben etwa finden sich biographische Angaben zu Personen, die für die Aktualisierung einer Personendatenbank genutzt werden können.

- *Orts- und Zeitangaben*
  Orts- und Zeitangaben sind z.B. natürliche Ergänzungen zu Ereignissen und können diese vereindeutigen, auch wenn sie keinen Eigennamen haben oder dieser nicht genannt wird: Der Europäische Gipfel im *November* in *Essen* (EreignisTyp + Zeitangabe + Ortsname).
  Organisationen werden oft an einen Ort gebunden (Bundesanstalt für Arbeit in *Nürnberg*), bei staatlichen Organisationen etwa sind Orte sind sogar namensbildend (Staatstheater *München*, Oberlandesgericht *Bremen*).

- *Zitate*
  Zitate sind insofern Sonderformen, als sie sich nicht unbedingt in die logische (hierarchische) SGML-Struktur einer Nachricht einbetten lassen, sondern – wenn ein Zitat in einem Absatz anfängt und erst mit dem zweiten endet – durchaus orthogonal dazu liegen können. Um ein Zitat für das Retrieval oder die Faktenextraktion sinnvoll zu markieren, muß man Urheber oder Quelle eindeutig an dieses Zitat binden. Außerdem sollte man in die Struktur so erweitern, daß auch noch Verbreitungsmedium oder Quelle, Datum des Zitats, Thema, das Gegenüber und der Anlaß explizit werden.

  Beispiel: Wolf sagte in der ARD: „Wehner war ein Mann ...“ (Urheber + Quelle + Zitat + Thema).

5 Probleme bei der semantischen Markierung nach NITF

Die Markierung semantischer Einheiten im Text bedeutet, daß man ein bestimmtes Wort oder eine Wortfolge im laufenden Text abgrenzt, identifiziert und einer bestimmten semantischen Klasse, wie z.B. *Person, Funktion* oder *Organisation*, explizit zuordnet. In anderen Worten, die semantische Einheit wird als sprachliche Ausprägung (Instantiierung) eines bestimmten Begriffs kategorisiert und damit meistens auch vereindeutigt.

```
<PERSON><NAME.GIVEN>Christiane</NAME.GIVEN>
<NAME.FAMILY>Schenk</NAME.FAMILY></PERSON>als
<FUNCTION>frauenpolitische Sprecherin</FUNCTION>im
<ORG>PDS-Vorstand</ORG>gewählt
```

Die Kommentare des aktuellen NITF sagen wenig über die konkrete Füllung der Tags, d.h. über die Instantiierungen der definierten Elementklassen im Nachrichtentext. So heißt die Erläuterung zum EVENT: *An Event* und die zur LOCATION: *A significant location.*

Bereits das relativ harmlose Beispiel oben läßt weitere Möglichkeiten der Kodierung zu:

```
<PERSON><NAME.GIVEN>Christiane</NAME.GIVEN>     <NA-
ME.FAMILY>Schenk</NAME.FAMILY></PERSON>als    <FUNC-
TION>frauenpolitische Sprecherin im PDS-Vorstand
</FUNCTION>gewählt
```

```
<PERSON>><NAME.GIVEN>Christiane</NAME.GIVEN>
<NAME.FAMILY>Schenk</NAME.FAMILY>als<FUNCTION>
frauenpolitische Sprecherin im PDS-
Vorstand</FUNCTION></PERSON>gewählt
```

Hier werden Regeln benötigt, die eine Konsistenz in der semantischen Markierung möglich machen. Selbst wenn wir davon ausgehen, daß die semantischen Strukturen besser verstanden und stringenter modelliert wären, gibt es Markierungsprobleme, die ein konsistentes Markup gefährden und daher durch Markierungsregeln, über die man sich einigen muß, gelöst werden müssen. Es werden im folgenden einige Beispiele, insbesondere zur Kategorisierung und zur Spezifität gegeben (vgl. auch Allen/Möhr 1998).

5.1 Kategorisierung

Die Kategorisierung der in einer Meldung vorkommenden Ausdrücke durch die Markierung mit den in der NITF-DTD definierten Elementklassen hat, von der Texterschließung her gesehen, das Ziel, die Bedeutung dieser Ausdrücke in einem gegebenen Kontext festzulegen und sie damit zu disambiguieren. Die Mehrdeutigkeit der natürlichen Sprache, d.h. daß zwei oder mehr sprachliche Ausdrücke mit derselben Zeichenfolge auf unterschiedliche Begriffe oder Weltobjekte verweisen und damit von unterschiedlicher Bedeutung sind, ist das Grundübel, um das es hier geht: Kontextfrei läßt sich die Zeichenfolge *Washington*, zum Beispiel, als Stadt, als US-Bundesstaat, als Berg, als Vorname oder Nachname einordnen.

Die Tatsache, daß es in der Praxis, für Mensch und Maschine jeweils in unterschiedlicher Art, schwer ist, Korrektheit und Konsistenz bei dieser Kategorisierung in gegebenen Kontexten herzustellen, ist auf eine Reihe von Problemen zurückzuführen, die zum Teil grundsätzlicher Natur und zum Teil durch eine sorgfältige Modellierung zu beheben sind:

- mangelnde Trennschärfe etwa in einem Objekt oder in unserem Verständnis dieses Objektes: z.B. Theater als Organisation oder Ort;

- mangelnde Trennschärfe zwischen den definierten Elementklassen: z.B. STATE und REGION;

- unzureichende Differenzierung der definierten Markup-Elemente, so daß die Zuordnung zu einem konkreten Ausdruck ungeschickt oder falsch erscheint: z.B. der Name eines Dorfes in einem CITY-Tag;

- undefinierte Grenzen zwischen Begriff, Individualbegriff und Individualobjekt (Instanz eines Begriffs):
  Ist z.B. der Deutsche Bundestag eine Organisation oder eine Organisationstyp? Eindeutig wird ein Bundestag eigentlich erst,

wenn er mit Ordinalzahl auftritt, als 13. oder 14. Deutscher Bundestag etwa. Das kommt in Meldungstexten allerdings so gut wie nicht vor, da der Bezug zum aktuellen Bundestag unterstellt wird. Ähnlich gelagert sind etwa Preise und Orden, die zwar Namen tragen, die es denn aber in verschiedenen Ausführungen (Gold, Silber) und für verschiedene Leistungen gibt (für den besten Kurzfilm, Dokumentarfilm usw.)

- bildlicher Gebrauch der Sprache: *Er hörte Mozart,* wo *Mozart* ein Substitut für eines seiner Musikstücke ist, oder *Weißes Haus* für die *US-amerikanische Regierung.*

5.2 Spezifität: Abgrenzung der semantischen Einheiten im Text

Wo eine semantische Einheit im Text Anfang und Ende haben soll, ist auch nicht immer leicht zu entscheiden. Dies läßt sich einerseits über Markierungsprinzipien regeln, die wie Indexierungsregeln auch, die Spezifität des Markup von den Anforderungen her festlegen. Aber manchmal widersetzen sich auch Ausdrücke selbst einer klaren Entscheidung.

Das Kern- oder Basiswort eines Ausdrucks kann durch Prämodifikationen (linke Extensionen) oder durch Postmodifikationen (rechte Extensionen) erweitert werden. Jede Modifikation, die hinzugefügt wird, bedeutet eine Zunahme der Spezifität des Begriffs. Ein Grundbegriff wie *Ministerpräsident* wird so links erweitert zu *niedersächsischer Ministerpräsident* und rechts erweitert zu *Ministerpräsident von Niedersachsen.* In beiden Erweiterungen sind dabei zwei unterschiedliche Bezeichner (sprachliche Realisierungen) eines Begriffes, nämlich des (aktuellen) *Oberhauptes der niedersächsischen Landesregierung.* Modifikatoren haben aber durchaus unterschiedliche Qualität: Der *niedersächsische Ministerpräsident* könnte z.B. links einmal um das Attribut *populistisch,* ein anderes Mal um das Attribut *ehemalig* erweitert werden. Im Fall eins handelt es sich um denselben Begriff mit einer explizit zugewiesenen modifizierenden Eigenschaft (*populistisch*) und dem (default-mäßig) impliziten Merkmal „aktuell", im zweiten Fall verweist das Temporaladjektiv des Ausdrucks *ehemaliger niedersächsischer Ministerpräsident* auf einen anderen Begriff, nämlich auf eine Person, die in der Vergangenheit für eine bestimmte Zeit *Oberhaupt der niedersächsischen Landesregierung* war.

Kernausdrücke mit Modifikationen

Es läßt sich argumentieren, daß die differenzierte Auszeichnung möglichst spezifischer Bezeichner mit dem Ziel besserer Precision beim Retrieval anzustreben ist.

6 Das semantische Markup als Prozeß der inhaltlichen Erschließung

Vergleicht man Prozeß und Ergebnis des semantischen Markup mit der Inhaltserschließung im dokumentarischen Sinn, so wird unmittelbar deutlich, daß ersteres eine spezielle Form von Indexieren und Klassieren darstellt, allerdings durchaus mit eigenen und neuen Problemen.

Formalerfassung und inhaltliche Erschließung

Bevor wir uns an eine differenzierte Betrachtung wagen, sollte klargestellt sein, daß das Attribut *semantisch*, wie es zu Beginn dieses Artikels definiert wurde, im dokumentarischen Bereich anders aufgefaßt wird. Die dokumentarische Bearbeitung eines Dokumentes unterscheidet zwischen Formalerfassung, als der Erfassung der (formalen) bibliographischen Merkmale (Titel, Autor, Affiliation, Dokumentart, Seitenanzahl, Erscheinungsjahr usw.) und der Inhaltserschließung, also der Zuordnung inhaltskennzeichnender Merkmale in Form von formal- oder natürlichsprachigen Bezeichnungen, bis hin zur Erstellung von Kurzfassungen. Dieser Unterschied spiegelt sich in der benötigten Qualifikation wider: Formalerfassung erfordert bibliothekarisches Wissen, Inhaltserschließung erfordert zusätzlich und in erster Linie auch Wissen aus dem Fach, dem die Dokumente zuzuordnen sind. Die Auszeichnung etwa von Firmennamen, Zeiten oder Orten in Texten, die wir als *semantisches* Markup bezeichnen, gehört entsprechend dieser Betrachtungsweise aber im Regelfall eher in den Bereich der Formalerfassung. Wir werden deshalb im folgenden zwischen Formalerfassung und Inhaltserschließung nicht differenzieren.

Formalerfassung für die Normierung der Indexeinträge

Eine Anregung läßt sich aus dieser ersten Betrachtung bereits ableiten: Der Hauptaspekt formaler Erfassung ist die Normierung der resultierenden Indexeinträge. Bedenkt man, daß vor nur wenigen Jahren/Jahrzehnten gedruckte Register und alphabetische Sortierungen das ausschließliche Ziel waren, so kann man die Konzentration auf diesen Aspekt nachvollziehen: Eine Person, von der man nicht wissen kann, ob sie unter Bundeskanzler Helmut Kohl, Kohl, Helmut, Dr. Helmut Kohl, Dr. Kohl, Helmut, H. Kohl, Dr. oder in welcher Variante sonst in einem sortierten Personenregister zu finden ist, wird man nicht zielsicher finden können. Gegenwärtig, mit dem

Komfort elektronischer Suchfunktionen, bleiben die grundsätzlichen Argumente weiterhin gültig, wobei sich jedoch für viele Anwendungen das praktische Problem entschärft. Im Kontext strukturierter Informationsspeicherung durch relationale oder objektorientierte Datenbanken gewinnt Normierung zur Feststellung von Identität wieder seine ursprüngliche Bedeutung zurück. Die Normierung wird durch umfangreiche Regelwerke (beispielsweise *Anglo-American Cataloguing Rules, AACR2*; *Regeln für die alphabetische Katalogisierung, RAK*) und/oder durch erschöpfende Aufzählungen normierter (verbindlicher) Ansetzungen etwa von Institutionen (*authority lists*) im Sinne eines enumerativen Datentyps erreicht. Das gedruckte Verzeichnis aller weltweit tätigen physik-relevanten Institutionen entspricht im Volumen durchaus einem Telefonbuch. Wenn also Firmennamen, Branchen, Orte etc. in Agenturmeldungen entsprechend ausgezeichnet werden, so ist ein Attribut sehr sinnvoll, in dem eine normierte Bezeichnung des Objektes abgelegt werden kann. Das NITF z.B. bietet ein solches Attribut zur Identifizierung der Organisationen an: Die ORGID, in ORG geschachtelt, ist ein leeres Element mit zwei Attributen, das eine nennt die Quelle für den Identifikator, das andere seinen Wert. Die Übertragung dieser Möglichkeit auf alle Inhaltselemente ist nachdrücklich zu empfehlen.

Beschreibt man semantisches Markup mit der Terminologie von Inhaltserschließung, und speziell aus der Sicht intellektueller Indexierung, so handelt es sich um eine Stichwortindexierung: Indexiert wird das Dokument, und Wörter bzw. Wortgruppen werden als natürlichsprachige *Indexterme* unmittelbar dem Text entnommen. Was sich gegenüber „klassischer" Indexierung ändert ist die Tatsache, daß die Indexterme nicht wirklich „entnommen", also aus ihrem Kontext herausgelöst werden, sondern – im Dokument gekennzeichnet – verbleiben. Besteht die Möglichkeit, in Attributen analog zur ORGID normierte Bezeichner abzulegen, so kann grundsätzlich aus der Stichwortindexierung eine zuteilende (additive) Indexierung werden.

semantisches Markup = Stichwort-Indexierung

Dadurch, daß die Indexterme ihren Kontext beibehalten, haben sie auch weiterhin eine Reihenfolge. Noch weitergehend: Die Indexterme werden in ihrer Rolle gekennzeichnet, z.B. als <FUNCTION> und können auch ineinandergeschachtelt sein, beispielsweise <FUNCTION> in <PERSON>. Deshalb liegt zweifelsohne keine gleichordnende Indexierung (*coordinate indexing*) vor, sondern eine strukturierte Indexierung (Knorz 1996); die DIN-Norm nennt dies eine syntaktische Indexierung.

semantisches Markup = strukturierte Indexierung

Der letztgenannte Aspekt läßt sich auch anders deuten: Die Zuweisung von Textfragmenten zu NITF-Elementen kann als eine wohlbekannte Form der Inhaltserschließung aufgefaßt werden, und zwar als eine besonders einfache Variante: als Klassifikation auf der Basis einer sehr groben enumerativen Klassifikation. Objekte der klassifikatorischen Tätigkeit sind nun nicht die Dokumente, sondern die vorab selektierten Indexterme, die jeweils einer Klasse (dem NITF-Element) zugeordnet werden.

Welchen Gewinn kann es bringen, semantisches Markup als eine Form von Inhaltserschließung aufzufassen? In erster Linie wird klar, daß sich viele Überlegungen und Erfahrungen mit Indexieren und Klassieren auf einen Bereich übertragen lassen, der – was den praktischen Umgang anbetrifft – bisher Neuland ist. Darüber hinaus kann nun auch überprüft werden, inwieweit technische Lösungen für ein automatisiertes Markup bereits verfügbar sind und Anwendungsmöglichkeiten adaptiert werden können.

7 Kriterien zur Beurteilung von Indexierungen und Markup

Bei der Beurteilung von Markup läßt sich von der Indexierung lernen, daß sie kein Selbstzweck ist: Ein semantisches Markup M1 ist genau dann besser als eine konkurrierende Markup-Variante M2, wenn diejenigen Prozesse, die durch M1 unterstützt werden zu besseren Ergebnissen und zufriedeneren Nutzern führen, als die entsprechenden auf M2 basierenden Prozesse.

Diese Einsicht macht Qualität zu einer nur sehr schwer und aufwendig faßbaren und meßbaren Größe. Tatsächlich zieht sich diese Problematik von Anbeginn an durch die Geschichte des Gebietes Information Retrieval. Sie ist gegenwärtig mit den weltweit betriebenen und akzeptierten Evaluierungsaktivitäten im Rahmen von TREC zwar einen wichtigen Schritt weiter (Harman 1996), aber keineswegs endgültig überwunden.

7.1 Konsistenz

Im Gegensatz zu hinreichenden Bedingungen sind notwendige Bedingungen für die Qualität einer Indexierung bzw. eines semantischen Markups leichter zu operationalisieren.

Indexierungen und semantisches Markup vermitteln gleichermaßen zwischen Autoren (Dokumenten) und Informationssuchenden (Nutzern). Wenn eine Indexierung nicht vom Inhalt des Dokumentes, sondern von der Person des Indexierers funktional bestimmt wird, kann diese Vermittlung nicht gelingen, da der Nutzer im Einzelfall gar nicht wissen kann, *wer* die Indexierung produziert hat. Zwei verschiedene Indexierer müssen demnach – im Rahmen des praktisch Erreichbaren – einem vorgelegten Dokument dieselben Indexterme zuordnen. Diese Art der Konsistenz nennt man Inter-Indexerkonsistenz und mißt sie beispielsweise wie folgt:

$$\text{Konsistenz } q = \frac{\text{Anzahl gemeinsam zugeteilter Indexterme}}{\text{Anzahl insgesamt zugeteilter Indexterme}}$$

Richtwert für praktisch erreichte und erreichbare Konsistenzwerte ist q=0,5 = (z.B.) 7 + 5 Deskriptoren in zwei Indexierungen bei vier Übereinstimmungen. Da automatische Indexierungsverfahren in aller Regel absolut konsistent indexieren (d.h. ein zweimaliges Indexieren desselben Dokumentes führt zum selben Ergebnis; beim manuellen Indexieren entspricht dieser Test der Intra-Indexerkonsistenz) wird dieser Befund im Umkehrschluß unserer Argumentation als Beleg für Qualität herangezogen – unzulässigerweise, wie leicht einzusehen ist: Mangelnde Konsistenz verlangt sinnvolle konsistenzsteigernde Maßnahmen, um die Indexierung vorhersehbar und verläßlich zu machen. Dazu gehören Regelwerke, verbindliches Vokabular (Thesauri, Schlagwortlisten usw.), Fortbildung, Absprachen. Es sind aber leicht absolut unsinnige Maßnahmen denkbar, durch die sich perfekte Konsistenzwerte erreichen lassen, z.B. „Indexiere alle Wörter mit dem Anfangsbuchstaben *i*". Je einfacher und formaler demnach Indexierungsregeln sind, desto weniger Probleme löst eine entsprechende Indexierung – das Konsistenzproblem ausgenommen.

7.2 Präzision und Vollständigkeit

Fehler erster und zweiter Ordnung werden im Information Retrieval üblicherweise mittels Precision und Recall gemessen:

$$\text{Precision } p = \frac{\text{Anzahl gefundener relevanter Dokumente}}{\text{Anzahl gefundener Dokumente}}$$

$$\text{Recall } r = \frac{\text{Anzahl gefundener relevanter Dokumente}}{\text{Anzahl relevanter Dokumente}}$$

Die Precision ist als Trefferquote dem Nutzer unmittelbar zugänglich, der Recall ist in praktischen Situationen eine nur theoretische Größe, da er das Wissen um die Anzahl der relevanten Dokumente einer Datenbank voraussetzt, unabhängig davon, ob man diese Dokumente gefunden hat oder nicht. Die Folge ist, daß auch erfahrene Nutzer den erreichten Recall weit überschätzen.

Übertragen auf semantisches Markup läßt sich mittels Precision ausdrücken, inwieweit etwa ausgezeichnete Firmennamen korrekt sind, also mit einem normativ vorgegebenen Ergebnis übereinstimmen. Für die Festlegung dieses Qualitätsstandards gelten die Unsicherheiten und Probleme des letzten Abschnittes. Der Recall gibt entsprechend an, wie vollständig alle vorgegebenen Elemente im Text tatsächlich auch ausgezeichnet werden.

Die mittels Precision und Recall belegte Qualitätsaussage ist keineswegs absolut, sondern ausschließlich auf den zugrundegelegten vorgegebenen Qualitätsstandard bezogen. Er besteht in einem sorgfältig zusammengestellten Datenbestand mit manuell erstelltem Markup. Idealerweise basiert dieses Markup auf den abgeglichenen Arbeitsergebnissen mehrerer unabhängig arbeitender Personen. Ein wesentliches Ziel, das sich auf diesem Weg erreichen läßt, ist das Erarbeiten operationalisierbarer, empirisch überprüfter Regeln für das Auszeichnen der NITF-Elemente.

Das Niveau der Precision- und Recall-Werte hängt nun einerseits von dem Anspruch, der sich implizit im Qualitätsstandard manifestiert, von den Ressourcen, die der Analyse zur Verfügung stehen (Vollständigkeit spezialisierter Wörterbücher) und von dem Ausmaß, in dem typische einschlägige Probleme natürlicher Sprache gelöst werden:

- Auflösung von Homographie und Polysemie

- Analyse syntaktischer Strukturen

- Einbeziehung von Kontextinformation

Für die Extraktion von Firmennamen aus Wirtschaftsnachrichten durch das System CONSTRUE/TIS (s. Abschnitt 8.2) und für die Extraktion von Eigennamen aus Artikeln des *Wall Street Journal* durch den TextMiner (s. Abschnitt 8.3.1) werden p- und r-Werte über jeweils 90% genannt (Carnegie Group 1998; Göser 1997), wobei derartige Angaben ohne präzise Kenntnis der Randbedingungen schwer einzuschätzen sind.

8 Markup als Ergebnis automatischer Analysen

Zum automatischen Erkennen von semantischen NITF-Elementen kann auf eine Vielzahl von Ansätzen und Typen von Ressourcen zurückgegriffen werden, die in den Bereichen automatische Indexierung, Information Retrieval, Computerlinguistik, Data und Text Mining entwickelt und z.T. auch erfolgreich erprobt und eingesetzt wurden.

automatische Erkennung semantischer Einheiten

Wörterbücher mit Namen, typischem Vokabular und Wortfragmenten werden in jedem Fall eine zentrale Rolle spielen, ergänzt um Regeln zur Beschreibung syntaktischer Strukturen und zur Behandlung von Entscheidungssituationen.

8.1 Einfaches wörterbuchbasiertes Verfahren

PASSAT ist ein wörterbuchbasiertes kommerzielles Verfahren zur automatischen Stichwortindexierung, das einen Teil der benötigten Funktionalität bereitstellt. Es arbeitet mit einem manuell aufgebauten und kontrollierten Stammformen-Wörterbuch (einer sog. Vergleichswortliste), erkennt Wortformenvarianten der Wörterbucheinträge, kann Komposita erkennen (und zerlegen) und feste Syntagma (z.B. Deutscher Bundestag) erkennen. PASSAT ist ein System mit einer langen Geschichte, vergleichsweise vielen Anwendungen – gerade auch im Medienbereich – in mehreren Sprachen. PASSAT Fehlt, um sich für die Aufgabe *semantisches Markup* zu empfehlen, die nötige Flexibilität und Funktionalität bei der Behandlung von Wortgruppen sowie Kontextsensitivität.

8.2 Komplexes regelbasiertes Verfahren

CONSTRUE/TIS ist ein von der *Carnegie Group* für *Reuters Ltd.* entwickeltes Indexierungssystem, das die Nennung spezieller Klassen von Objekten (Firmen, Personen) erkennt und Agenturmeldungen mit kontrolliertem Vokabular (700 Deskriptoren) indexiert („kategorisiert"). Aus dieser Anwendung ist mit der Text Categorisation Shell (TCS) ein allgemeines Werkzeug zur Klassifikation von Texten entwickelt und vermarktet worden (Carnegie Group 1998). TCS arbeitet in drei Phasen (Knorz 1994):

1. *Begriffsidentifikation*
   In einer Regelbasis werden Begriffe (Lesarten von Wörtern) als komplexe Muster von Zeichen/Wörtern unter Einbeziehung des Wortkontextes definiert. Das Vorkommen eines erkannten Begriffes kann seiner Signifikanz entsprechend gewichtet werden.

2. *Deskriptor-Hypothesenbildung*
   Aufbauend auf den identifizierten Begriffen werden Deskriptoren durch Regeln als Indexierungshypothesen mit dem Dokument in Verbindung gebracht: Es wird spezifiziert, unter welchen Bedingungen (Vorkommen in einem bestimmten Kontext, zugewiesene Signifikanz) welche Kombination von Begriffen welchen Deskriptor (mit welcher Signifikanz) vorschlägt.

3. *Indexierungsentscheidung*
   In einem letzten Schritt werden die einzelnen, z.T. konkurrierenden Hypothesen durch eine weitere Klasse von Regeln verworfen oder bestätigt.

Mit TCS läßt sich ein semantisches Markup zweifellos bewerkstelligen, wobei vielfach die Verarbeitung der Phase 1 schon ausreichen wird, weil damit die lokale, textstellenorientierte Analyse ausgeführt wird. Was TCS allerdings kennzeichnet ist ein sehr mächtiger Formalismus zur Formulierung von Regeln verschiedener Art, der auf eine intellektuelle Bedienung und Optimierung bei der Systementwicklung zugeschnitten ist. Dies hat einerseits Auswirkungen auf das Ausmaß und die Anforderungen der Systempflege und läßt andererseits außer acht, daß die bereits bearbeiteten Dokumente eine unmittelbare Ressource für die Bearbeitung der neuen Dokumente sein können.

8.3 Data Mining

Die Verfügbarkeit von wachsend großen Datenmengen in Unternehmen hat das neue Gebiet und programmatische Schlagwort *Knowledge Discovery in Data Bases* hervorgebracht, das vielfach synonym mit dem entscheidenden Analyse-Teilschritt des *Data Mining* verwendet wird (Adriaans/Zantinge 1996). Ziel ist es, diese Datenmengen als Ressource zu nutzen, indem versucht wird, darin implizite Gesetzmäßigkeiten, Zusammenhänge und auffällige Tatbestände durch entsprechende Algorithmen auffinden zu lassen. Die Zielsetzung des Data Mining auf Textdokumente übertragen wird dann als *Text Mining* oder auch (anwendungsbezogen) als *Web Mining* bezeichnet.

Text Mining ist keineswegs nur die Ad-hoc-Übertragung einer aktuellen Entwicklung im Datenbankbereich, sondern führt direkt auf klassische Fragestellungen (und Lösungsansätze) des Information Retrieval und läuft parallel mit dem aktuellen Erfolg korpusbasierter Ansätze im Bereich Computerlinguistik (Erkennung gesprochener Sprache, korpusbasierte Übersetzungssysteme, statistisch basiertes Parsing).

Text Mining und korpusbasierte linguistische Ansätze

8.3.1 TextMiner von IBM

Ein aktuelles System, das auch kommerziell verfügbar ist, greift die neue Terminologie unmittelbar in seinem Namen auf: Das bisher noch auf das Englische beschränkte TextMiner-System (Göser 1997) extrahiert Eigennamen, Mehrwortausdrücke, deren regelhaft gebildete Abkürzungen und vordefinierte Faktentypen. Das System integriert verschiedene Extraktionsmethoden, die aus drei Verarbeitungsphasen bestehen:

TextMiner für englischsprachige Texte

1. Patternmatching auf der Grundlage regulärer Ausdrücke auf Zeichen und Wortklassen-Ebene;

2. dokumentbezogene Verarbeitung, in der mittels heuristischer Regeln versucht wird, verschiedene Vorkommensformen desselben Begriffes unter einer gemeinsamen Benennung zusammenzufassen;

3. Aggregierung über Dokumentmengen, die nicht bedeutungstragende Unterschiede zwischen oberflächlich verschiedenen Begriffsbenennungen durch Zusammenfassung eliminieren soll.

8.3.2 Automatisches Indexierungssystem AIR/X

Das neue Paradigma *Text Mining* wirft ein aktuelles Schlaglicht auf
einen Ansatz, der schon vor über zehn Jahren zur erfolgreichen und
umfänglichen Anwendung einer anspruchsvollen automatischen
Indexierung führte: Das System AIR/X (Lustig 1986) hat seit 1985 ca.
10.000 Dokumente/Monat für die Datenbasis PHYS auf der Basis
eines 20.000 Begriffe umfassenden Thesaurus indexiert. Grundlage
dafür sind die Ergebnisse dreier statistischer Lernprozesse:

1. In einem Indexierungswörterbuch verweisen Regeln (Relatio-
    nen) von Textwörtern auf die Deskriptoren des Thesaurus.
    Wenngleich die Quelle dieser Regeln prinzipiell beliebig ist, ist
    die tatsächlich entscheidende Quelle ein Verfahren, das aus
    Beispielen statistische Zusammenhänge zwischen Textphäno-
    menen und zugeteilten Deskriptoren bestimmt. Die Anwendung
    verwendete 300.000 gewichtete Regeln, die aus 400.000 manuell
    indexierten Dokumenten extrahiert wurden.

2. Das Indexierungssystem analysiert den Dokumententext (Iden-
    tifikation von Wörtern, Wortgruppen, weiterer Textphänomene
    wie auftretende Energiebereiche) und setzt das Dokument mit-
    tels der Regeln des Indexierungswörterbuchs mit Deskriptoren
    in Beziehung. Verfahren der Mustererkennung lernen an vorge-
    legten Beispielen, welche dieser Deskriptoren tatsächlich in-
    haltsbeschreibend sind.

3. Die daraus resultierende Indexierung ist in Einzelfällen in sich
    nicht stimmig. Die Aspekte, die bei einer solchen Einschätzung
    eine Rolle spielen, werden festgestellt und abermals einem Lern-
    prozeß unterworfen. Ergebnis ist eine abgestimmte Indexierung,
    bei der jedem zugeteilten Deskriptor ein Gewicht zugeordnet
    wird. Dieses Gewicht drückt die Wahrscheinlichkeit aus, daß ein
    unabhängiger Indexierer ebenfalls diesen Deskriptor zuteilen
    würde.

Mit diesem Verfahren wurden zu einer unabhängigen manuellen
Indexierung eine Konsistenz von ca. 0,5 erreicht (Knorz 1983), und
ein umfangreicher Retrievaltest mit 300 Fragen und 15.000 Dokumenten belegte die Konkurrenzfähigkeit der Indexierung auch beim
Retrieval (Fuhr/Knorz 1984).

*Semantisches Markup zur Inhaltserschließung von
Agenturmeldungen*

9 Fazit der neuen Sichtweise

Semantisches Markup muß grundsätzlich vorhersehbar und verläßlich und damit vom Bearbeiter weitgehend unabhängig sein. Dies bedeutet die Forderung nach einer akzeptablen Konsistenz zwischen verschiedenen Bearbeitern, die nur durch praxisgerechte und abgestimmte Verfahrens- und Entscheidungsregeln sachgerecht erreichbar ist. Diese Regeln müssen präzisieren, in welchen Fällen mit welchen Grenzen Textstellen wie auszuzeichnen sind.

Für die routinemäßige Produktion eines Markup wird ein intellektuelles Arbeiten entweder anspruchsvoll und gleichzeitig zu teuer und zeitaufwendig oder aber zu oberflächlich und gegenüber vollautomatischen Verfahren nicht konkurrenzfähig sein. Es kommen also tatsächlich für einen laufenden Betrieb im wesentlichen automatische Verfahren in Frage, für die allerdings z.T. erheblicher intellektueller Entwicklungsaufwand und weiterhin Anpassungs- und Pflegeaufwand anfällt. Automatische Verfahren für ein semantisches Markup lassen sich auf der Basis bekannter Techniken aus den Bereichen Computerlinguistik, Statistik, Information Retrieval, Künstliche Intelligenz, Mustererkennung adaptieren bzw. entwickeln.

Adaption automatischer Verfahren

Eine wesentliche Grundlage zur Entwicklung und Optimierung automatischer Markup-Verfahren werden qualitativ hochwertig intellektuell getaggte Korpora sein, aus denen automatisch oder zumindest maschinell unterstützt Regeln und Parameter für eine vollautomatische Verarbeitung abgeleitet werden.

Darüber hinaus wird es sinnvoll sein, auch die vollautomatisch bearbeiteten Dokumente in den Prozeß des Lernens einzubeziehen: Neue Dokumente werden also im Kontext allen bekannten maschinell repräsentierten Wissens analysiert und tragen anschließend selbst zum „Wissenszuwachs" bei.

Was NITF in einer Weiterentwicklung bieten sollte, um semantisches Markup möglichst effektiv nutzbar zu machen, sind Attribute, in denen sich normierte Bezeichnungen ablegen lassen. Dadurch kann aus der Stichwortindexierung eine additive, begriffsorientierte Indexierung werden. Auf diesem Weg läßt sich auch ein hier bisher nicht angesprochenes Problem angehen: das der Anaphora. Für viele Suchoperationen und sonstige Auswertungen ist es unmittelbar von Nutzen, wenn Textstellen mit Verweischarakter (*Der Vorsitzende des Langohrdackelvereins, Herr Otto Schmitt-Breugel, Vereinsvorsitzende, Schmitt-Breugel, der Vorsitzende, Er*) auf ein und dasselbe Objekt bezogen werden können.

Forderung: normierte Bezeichnungen

10 Anwendungen und Perspektiven

Data Mining bzw. Text Mining wird bisher als eine vielversprechende Technik bzw. Sichtweise genannt, um die Voraussetzungen für ein automatisches semantisches Markup zu schaffen. Gleichzeitig kann Text Mining auch als eine bedeutende Anwendungsperspektive des semantischen Markup angesehen werden. Marketingabteilungen in Unternehmen, Parteien und viele Institute beobachten publizierte Meinungen und Fakten mit großem Interesse, Aufwand und Kosten. Trenderkennung, Image- oder Konkurrenzanalysen auf der Basis ausgewerteter Agenturmeldungen (als Anwendungen von Text Mining) sind in ihrer Qualität unmittelbar von der Qualität des Ausgangsmaterials hinsichtlich Inhalt und Aufbereitung abhängig. Da Text Mining die Bearbeitung sehr großer Textmengen verlangt, ist eine zu aufwendige Analyse der Texte zur Identifikation elementarer Textphänomene problematisch. Hier kann ein semantisches Markup als „Vorleistung" entscheidend zur Verbesserung der Ausgangssituation für weitergehende Auswertungen beitragen.

Faktenextraktion

Als eine fortgeschrittene Form des Text Mining kann die Faktenextraktion angesehen werden: Vordefinierte Klassen von Fakten („Firma A kooperiert mit Firma B hinsichtlich C") werden aus entsprechenden Agenturmeldungen herausgefiltert und strukturiert in Datenbanken abgelegt (s. auch Artikel von Lothar Rostek). Die dazu notwendigen Analyse- und Umformungsprozesse können als direkte Fortsetzung der Herstellung des semantischen Markup angesehen werden und profitieren demnach von dessen Vorarbeit.

*Unterstützung
des Retrieval*

Die Unterstützung des Retrieval ist die besonders direkte Anwendung des semantischen Markup. Die Suche nach Ausprägungen der Objekttypen *Person*, *Organisation*, *Ereignis* kann für den Nutzer deutlich vereinfacht und hinsichtlich Recherchequalität verbessert werden. Viele Probleme der Polysemie und Formulierungsvarianten werden nicht mehr auftreten. Darüber hinaus ermöglicht semantisches Markup die Bereitstellung von Recherchehilfen zur Steigerung der Precision, etwa in Form strukturierter KWICs (*keywords in context*): Bei der Suche nach einer Person können beispielsweise Selektionslisten von Funktionsbezeichnungen angeboten werden, die in einer Datenbasis zusammen mit dieser Person vorzufinden sind. Dies geht in Richtung des Suchkomforts, den intellektuell aufbereitete Datenbestände wie etwa die FAZ-Datenbank durch eine strukturierte Indexierung bereitstellt, in der zu einer zu suchenden (indexierten) Person eine zusätzlich indexierte Facette (z.B. *privat*, *Ehrung*) mit selektiert werden kann.

Da beim Volltextretrieval die Verwendung des logischen Operators UND problematisch ist, kommt den Kontextoperationen eine besonders wichtige Rolle zu. Wenn semantisches Markup – wie vorgeschlagen – das Problem der Verweisungen, etwa über IDs, mit löst, kann in dieser Hinsicht eine deutlich effektivere Suchmöglichkeit angeboten werden: *Clinton NEAR Meineid* kann auch dort gefunden werden, wo der Text lautet: *<P> ... Bill Clinton, Präsident der USA ... </P> <P> ... wird der Präsident des Meineids verdächtigt ...</P>.*

Ein Service bei der Unterstützung von Recherchen, der absehbar an Bedeutung gewinnen wird, ist die Aufbereitung der Suchergebnisse: Unstrukturierte oder nach vermuteter Relevanz geordnete Dokumentmengen kosten den Bearbeiter oft viel Aufwand und Zeit, um an die gewünschte Information zu kommen. Effektiver sind verdichtete und vernetzte Darstellungen, die aus den gefundenen Dokumenten generiert werden und in denen der Nutzer je nach Bedarf navigieren und zoomen kann. Dazu müssen Kernsätze extrahiert, Reihenfolgen gefunden und Links in den Antwortdokumenten und zu weiterführender Hintergrundinformation in Text- oder Faktenform generiert werden. All dies kann durch semantisches Markup wirksam unterstützt werden.

Literatur

(Adriaans/ Zantinge 1996)
Adriaans, P.; Zantinge, D.: Data Mining. Harlow: Addison-Wesley, 1996

(Allen/Möhr 1998)
Allen, David; Möhr, Wiebke: Considerations for the Semantic Markup with the NITF: Supporting Documentation of the NITF. o.O., 1998. Erhältlich im Internet: http://www.iptc.org/iptc/orddocs.htm#nitf

(Carnegie Group 1998)
Carnegie Group (Hrsg.): Research and Technology: Language, Text and Voice Processing. o.O, 1998. Erhältlich im Internet: http://netra1.cgi.com/web2/govt/gov-text.html

(Ellis/Ford 1998)
Ellis, David; Ford, Nigel: In search of the unknown user: Indexing, Hypertext and the World Wide Web. In: Journal of Documentation, 54 (1998), Nr. 1

(Fischer 1998)
Fischer, Dietrich: From Thesauri towards Ontologies? In: International Society for Knowledge Organization (Hrsg.): Proceedings of the ISKO 5 Conference. o.O., 1998

(Fischer Lexikon 1989)
Noelle-Neumann, Elisabeth et al. (Hrsg.): Fischer Lexikon: Publizistik – Massenkommunikation. Frankfurt (Main): Fischer Taschenbuch Verlag, 1989

(Fuhr/Knorz 1984)

Fuhr, Norbert; Knorz, Gerhard: Retrieval Test Evaluation of a Rule-based Automatic Indexing. In: Van Rijsbergen, C.J. (Hrsg.): Research and Development in Information Retrieval. Cambridge: University Press, 1984, S. 391 – 408

(Gerretz 1994)

Gerretz, Michael: Semantische Relationen und kognitive Strukturen. Hildesheim, Universität Hildesheim, Dissertation, 1994

(Göser 1997)

Göser, S.: Inhaltsbasiertes Information Retrieval: Die TextMining-Technologie. In: LDV-Forum (1997), Nr. 1, S. 48-52

(Harman 1996)

Harman, D. K.: Overview of the Forth Text Retrieval Conference (TREC-4). In: D.K. Harman (Hrsg.): The Forth Text Retrieval Conference (TREC-4). Gaithersburg, MD: National Institute of Standards and Technology, 1996, S. 1- 23

(IPTC-NAA 1998)

IPTC-NAA (Hrsg): IPTC-NAA News Industry Text Format (NITF). Version 2.0b1, August 1998. o.O., 1998. Erhältlich im Internet: http://www.iptc.org/iptc

(Knight 1979)

Knight, G. Norman: Indexing, the Art of: a guide to the indexing of books and periodicals. Medford (N.J.): Learned Information, 1979, S. 139-153

(Knorz 1983)

Knorz, Gerhard: Automatisches Indexieren als Erkennen abstrakter Objekte. Tübingen: Niemeyer, 1983 (Sprache und Information, Bd. 8)

(Knorz 1994)

Knorz. Gerhard: Automatische Indexierung. In: Hennings; Knorz , G. et al. (Hrsg.): Wissensrepräsentation und Information Retrieval. Potsdam, Mai 1994. Universität Potsdam, Modellversuch BETID. Erhältlich im Internet: http://www.iud.fhdarmstadt.de/iud/wwwmeth/Publ/skript/AutInd94/ paper1.htm

(Knorz 1996)

Knorz, Gerhard: Indexieren, Klassieren, Extrahieren. In: Buder, M.; Rehfeld, W. et al. (Hrsg): Grundlagen der praktischen Information und Dokumentation. Bd. 1. 4. Ausg. München: Saur, 1996, S. 120-140

(La Roche 1992)

La Roche, Walter von: Einführung in den praktischen Journalismus. 13. Aufl. München: List, 1992

(Lustig 1986)

Lustig, G.: Automatische Indexierung zwischen Forschung und Anwendung. Hildesheim: Olms, 1986

(Robertson 1995)

Robertson, Michael: Software Reviews: Die FAZ auf CD-ROM. In: The Indexer 19 (1995), Nr. 4, S. 308-309

(Silvester/Genuardi 1994)

Silvester, June P.; Genuardi, Michael T.: Machine-Aided Indexing from the Analysis of Natural Language Text. In: Raya Fidel (Hrsg.): Challenges in Indexing Electronic Text and Images. Medford, N.J.: Learned Information, 1994

(Wasson 1998)

Wasson, Mark: Using Leading Text for News Summaries: Evaluation and Implications for Commercial Summarization Applications. o.O., 1998. Erscheint in den Proceedings zu COLING '98, Université de Montréal , August 10-14, 1998

(Weischenberg 1990)

Weischenberg, Siegfried: Nachrichtenschreiben: Journalistische Praxis zum Studium und Selbststudium. Opladen: Westdeutscher Verlag, 1990

(Wilke/Rosenberger 1991)

Wilke, Jürgen; Rosenberger, Bernhard: Die Nachrichten-Macher: Eine Untersuchung zu Strukturen und Arbeitsweisen von Nachrichtenagenturen am Beispiel von AP und dpa. Köln: Böhlau, 1991

(Zschunke 1994)

Zschunke, Peter: Agenturjournalismus: Nachrichtenschreiben im Sekundentakt. Konstanz: Ölschläger, 1994

Automatische Erzeugung von semantischem Markup in Agenturmeldungen

Lothar Rostek

1 Einleitung und Motivation

Neue Medienformen und Verbreitungstechnologien verändern auch das Angebots- und Aufgabenprofil von Nachrichtenanbietern. Die parallele Veröffentlichung einer Nachricht über unterschiedliche Medien oder die Wiedernutzung der einmal recherchierten und zusammengetragenen Information in unterschiedlichen Angebotsformen erfordern entsprechend aufbereitete Nachrichtenformate, aus denen sich der gewünschte Mehrwert ohne menschliches Eingreifen erzeugen läßt. Die Nachrichtenindustrie hat auf diese Herausforderungen u.a. mit der Entwicklung *des News Industry Text Format (NITF)* reagiert. Das NITF (IPTC-NAA 1998) ist ein SGML/XML-konformer Standard zur formalen (strukturellen) und inhaltsorientierten (semantischen) Auszeichnung von Nachrichtentexten, der unter der Federführung des *IPTC (International Press and Telecommunications Council)* und der *NAA (Newspaper Association of America)* und unter Beteiligung namhafter Nachrichtenagenturen und Zeitungen ausgearbeitet worden ist.

Das große Volumen an Nachrichten und der starke Zeitdruck, unter dem sie erzeugt werden, verbieten eine manuelle Auszeichnung von Nachrichten durch Reporter, Journalisten oder Redakteure. Die *Deutsche Presse-Agentur (dpa)* beauftragte daher das *GMD – Forschungszentrum Informationstechnik* mit der Pilotimplementierung eines Markup-Servers, der ein NITF-konformes semantisches

Erzeugung von Mehrwert

Generierung von Markup

Markup von Agenturmeldungen automatisch generieren sollte (s.a. Beiträge von Klaus Sprick; Gerhard Knorz und Wiebke Möhr).

Das Pilotprojekt von dpa und GMD sollte zunächst die technische Machbarkeit und den möglichen Leistungsumfang einer automatischen Erzeugung von semantisch markierten, d.h. inhaltlich erschlossenen, Nachrichten nachweisen. Es sollte darüber hinaus demonstriert werden, daß eine Verbindung des Markup-Servers mit den integrierten Informationsressourcen der dpa zusätzlichen Nutzen bringt und daß die Ergebnisse des Markup-Prozesses insbesondere für die kontrollierte und schnelle Aktualisierung einer dpa-Faktendatenbank eingesetzt werden können. Dieser Beitrag berichtet über ausgewählte Aspekte dieses Pilotprojekts.

2 Der Markup-Server

Die Pilotimplementierung eines Markup-Servers steht im Zusammenhang mit den Überlegungen der dpa, ihren Kunden eine Option auf neuartige SGML/XML-basierte Dienste zu bieten sowie intern aktuelle Nachrichten und Langzeitinformationen in einer Wissensbank zu integrieren, um dadurch vielfältige Funktionen in den Bereichen *Redaktion*, *Dokumentation* und *Selektion* zu unterstützen.

Abbildung 1 skizziert die mögliche Struktur einer solchen Wissensbank, die man sich als Netz stark verknüpfter Informationseinheiten (Informationsobjekte) vorstellen kann. Daher sprechen wir auch von einem *Objektnetz*.

Diese Informationsobjekte repräsentieren z.B. Personen, Organisationen, Ereignisse und Orte; Informationen zu diesen Objekten werden in Attributen und Relationen gespeichert. Die Nachrichten selbst mit ihren Texten und Metainformationen werden ebenfalls in dem Objektnetz abgelegt. Dazu kommen noch Objekte, die Begriffe, lexikalische Informationen oder Kategorien eines Klassifikationssystems repräsentieren. Dieses Objektnetz muß nicht als eine einzige Datenbank realisiert sein, sondern kann als verteiltes System die verschiedenen Ressourcen auch dynamisch integrieren.

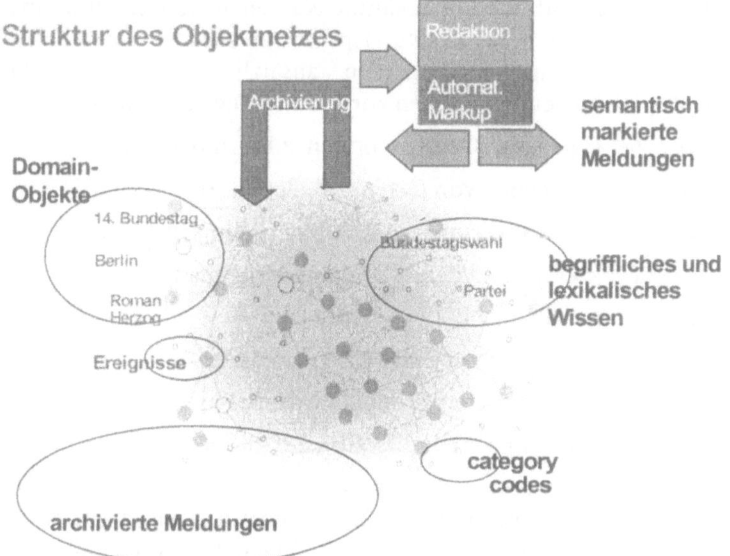

Die Kernfunktion des Markup-Servers ist die Analyse von Meldungstexten mit dem Zweck, die darin vorkommenden Einzelwörter oder Wortgruppen semantisch zu klassifizieren. Für die Analyse berücksichtigt der Markup-Server vornehmlich die im NITF-Standard spezifizierten semantischen Klassen:

- *Person*: Person mit Vor- und/oder Nachname. Das PERSON-Element kann ein FUNCTION-Element enthalten, das die Funktion oder Rolle der entsprechenden Person bezeichnet.

- *Function*: zur Markierung von Personenrollen oder –funktionen

- *ORG:* Namen von Organisationen oder Institutionen

- *Location, Sublocation, City, State, Region, Country*: Ortsbezeichnungen

- *Event*: Namen von Ereignissen

- *ObjectTitle*: Namen von Zeitungen, Büchern usw.

- *CHRON*: Zeitangaben, mit optionalem Attribut *NORM,* das eine normalisierte Form des Datums enthalten kann

- *NUM*: numerische Angaben, z.B. 40 Milliarden, 400 000, usw.

- *Money*: Geldangaben, z.B. 40 Millionen £

- *Quote*: Zitate

Um Indikatoren auf noch unbekannte Namen auswerten zu können und um den weiteren Verarbeitungsprozessen spezifischere Analyseergebnisse bereitzustellen, wurden zusätzlich zu den NITF-Elementen die folgenden Klassen zur Markierung verwendet:

- *OrgType*: Typen von Organisationen, z.B. Landgericht
- *LocationType*: Typen von Orten, z.B. Ferienort
- *EventType*: Ereignis-Typen, z.B. Fußballweltmeisterschaft
- *ObjectType*: Objekt-Typen, z.B. Nachrichtenmagazin
- *Age*: Altersangaben, z.B. der 49jährige
- *TempMod*: zeitlicher Modifikator, z.B. frühere
- *GeoMod*: geographischer Modifikator, z.B. Berliner
- *OrdMod*: numerischer Modifikator, z.B. der sechste

Hat der Markup-Server die entsprechenden Wörter oder Phrasen den semantischen Klassen zugeordnet, dann kann damit ein NITF-konformer Meldungstext automatisch erzeugt werden. Darüber hinaus kann der Markup-Server in vielen Fällen auch einfache Fakten, wie z.B. Funktionen, Altersangaben und Parteizugehörigkeit von Personen, mit Hilfe partieller Kontextanalysen erkennen. Die Liste der in einem Text erkannten und semantisch getypten Bezeichnungen und einfachen Beziehungen kann als Suchanforderung oder auch zur Überprüfung ihrer Korrektheit an eine Faktendatenbank gesendet werden.

In diesem Sinne verwendet man den Markup-Server als Instrument für den Zugriff auf die Inhalte einer Faktendatenbank (s. Abbildung 2) und erreicht damit eine – für den Benutzer einfache – Selektion auf die Teile der Datenbank, die mit den im Text erwähnten Objekten und Begriffen in Beziehung stehen. Dies wird nicht immer vollständig und korrekt möglich sein, aber selbst wenn nur ein wesentlicher Teil korrekt berücksichtigt wird, kann dies eine wertvolle Hilfe für den Dokumentar oder Redakteur sein, der die Faktendatenbank unter dem Aspekt einer gegebenen Agenturmeldung befragen möchte.

Im Prinzip geht es darum, daß der Markup-Server im Text vorhandene Informationen, die der Faktendatenbank bekannt sind, ausfiltert und dem Bearbeiter nur neue bzw. inkonsistente Fakten zur Überprüfung vorlegt. Dies ist sowohl für einen Redakteur nützlich, der gewissermaßen eine „semantische Rechtschreibprüfung" (*Außenminister Fescher*) erhält, als auch für einen Dokumentar, der zu entscheiden hat, welche Informationen in die Faktendatenbank übernommen werden sollen.

Um eine Demonstration dieses Vorgehens zu ermöglichen, hat dpa eine exemplarische biographische Faktendatenbank zur Verfügung gestellt, auf deren Inhalte der Markup-Server zugreifen konnte.

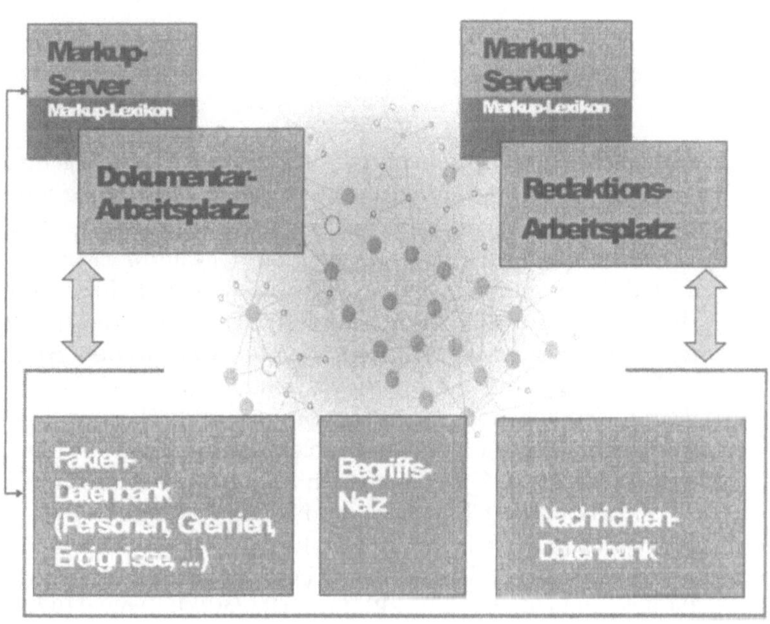

Neben dem Lexikon der semantisch klassifizierten Begriffe (in Abbildung 2 Markup-Lexikon genannt), auf das die Analyse-Algorithmen zugreifen, wurde zur Identifikation von personen-bezogenen Fakten in Agenturmeldungen ein *nachrichten-spezifisches Begriffsnetz* aufgebaut. In diesem Begriffsnetz wurden zunächst Funktions- und Organisationsbezeichnungen durch Oberbegriffs-/ Unterbegriffsrelationen sowie über Synonymbeziehungen miteinander verknüpft. Das hat den folgenden Sinn: Die Personen-Datenbank enthält die offiziellen Bezeichnungen von Funktionen und Organisationen; in den Meldungstexten dagegen werden offizielle Bezeichnungen häufig durch eine abstraktere, weil kürzere Form (*Minister* für *Bundesminister der Verteidigung*) oder durch journalistische Varianten (*Regierungschef* für z.B. den *Bundeskanzler der Bundesrepublik Deutschland* oder für den *Ministerpräsidenten* eines Bundeslandes) ersetzt. Das Begriffsnetz erlaubt dem System, die Formulierung *Regierungschef Gerhard Schröder* als bekannt einzustufen, selbst wenn Gerhard Schröder in der Personendatenbank als *Bundeskanzler der Bundesrepublik Deutschland* geführt wird. Des weiteren kann dieser Mechanismus zur Auflösung von Mehrdeutigkeiten eingesetzt werden, wenn z.B. in der Personendatenbank zwei Personen mit dem Namen *Gerhard Schröder* gespeichert sind, aber nur eine von ihnen in der Rolle des *Regierungschefs* auftritt.

3 Der Markup-Prozeß

Erkennung und Klassifikation von Eigennamen

Die Identifikation und semantische Klassifikation von Eigennamen gehört zu den wichtigen Aufgaben, die zur Unterstützung von Anwendungsprojekten der natürlichen Sprachverarbeitung und des Information Retrieval (z.B. McDonald 1996, Mani/MacMillan 1996, Paik et al. 1996) zu lösen sind. Auch geisteswissenschaftliche Projekte, die die Erzeugung semantisch kodierter Texte zum Ziel haben wie *Orlando* (Hockey et al. 1997), der *Thesaurus Linguarum Hiberniae* (Flanders 1997) und das *Analytical Onomasticon* (McCarty 1994 McCarty 1995), benötigen die Erkennung und Klassifikation von Eigennamen. Man hat sich dem Problem in verschiedenen Sprachen gestellt, Wakao et al. (1996) berichten z.B. über das Englische, Chen-Lee (1996) über das Chinesische und Kitani/Mitamura (1994) über das Japanische. Es gibt auch verschiedene nachrichten-bezogene Projekte, die sich mit diesem Thema beschäftigen. Zu ihnen gehören SCISOR (Jacobs/Rau 1990), PROFILE (Radev/McKeown 1997) und CONSTRUE/TIS (Carnegie Group 1998).

Vorgehen bei der Analyse

Da uns für das Deutsche kein allgemein verwendbares semantisches Analysesystem bekannt ist, haben wir einen pragmatischen Ansatz für das automatische semantische Markup von Agenturmeldungen gewählt: Für die Analyse benutzt der Markup-Server eine Menge texttyp-spezifischer lokaler Kontextregeln, die in erster Linie mit Hilfe des Markup-Lexikons aktiviert werden, in dem hauptsächlich – wie angesprochen – semantisch klassifizierte Begriffe gespeichert sind. In einem zweiten Schritt werden globale Regeln über die markierten Phrasen angewendet, um zusätzliche Informationen zu extrahieren, wie z.B. die Zuordnung von Altersangaben zu Personen.

Kontextregeln und Lexikon

Der erste Schritt im Parsing-Prozeß für das automatische semantische Markup ist die Zuordnung eines Wortes oder einer Wortfolge zu einer semantischen Kategorie. Entweder ist diese Zuordnung bereits im Markup-Lexikon vorhanden, oder das System versucht, sie durch Markup-Regeln algorithmisch zu ermitteln. Das Ergebnis dieser ersten Phase ist eine Menge von typisierten Textsegmenten.

In einer zweiten Phase werden globale Regeln, die sich auf den gesamten Meldungstext beziehen, auf diese Menge angewendet und können die vorläufigen Zuordnungen gegebenenfalls revidieren. Ein – im Lexikon geführter – potentieller Nachname wird beispielsweise erst als Personenname klassifiziert, wenn er mindestens einmal im Text nach einem Vornamen steht. Auf diese Weise wird vermieden, daß Allerweltsworte wie *Aller, Jäger, Kurz* als Personen markiert werden, wenn es sich in dem entsprechenden Text nicht um einen Nachnamen handelt. Die alternative Strategie wäre, solche nicht-eindeutigen Familiennamen grundsätzlich nicht als Personen zu markieren, das würde aber zu sehr unvollständigen Ergebnissen führen. Für die Entwicklung der Markup-Regeln wurden XGrammar, ein interaktives Parsing-Tool, und das Textanalyse-Werkzeug TATOE (Alexa/Rostek 1996) eingesetzt; zur Methodologie der Regelentwicklung siehe Rostek/Alexa (1998).

Abbildung 3
Ergebnis eines Markup-Prozesses im NITF-Format

Die vom Parser identifizierten Ausdrücke sind die Basis zur Berechnung des NITF-konformen Textes (Beispiel s. Abbildung 3). Dazu wird ein Inklusionsverband dieser Ausdrücke berechnet, um die überlappenden Elemente zu ordnen und die Positionen für das Einfügen der SGML-Elemente festzulegen. Schließlich müssen noch die SGML-Tags in den Originaltext eingefügt werden. Dieser Prozeß muß auch die Abhängigkeiten beachten, die zwischen den Elementen bestehen. In einem komplexen Ausdruck wie *(der) Parlamentarische Geschäftsführer Heiner Bartling* besteht eine Abhängigkeit zwischen dem ersten *(Parlamentarische Geschäftsführer)* und dem zweiten Teil *(Heiner Bartling)*. Aus diesem Grunde muß das semantische Element FUNCTION innerhalb des Elements PERSON erscheinen.

Zur Markierung zeitlicher Information (CHRON) wird – der NITF-DTD gemäß – ein Attribut (NORM) erzeugt, das als Wert das konkrete Datum des Zeitausdrucks in seiner normalisierten Form hat. So bedeutet beispielsweise der NITF-markierte Text

```
<CHRON NORM="19931022">Freitag</CHRON>,
```

daß der Freitag, um den es hier geht, der 22. Oktober 1993 war. Diese Berechnung beruht auf dem Meldungsdatum, mit dem jede Nachricht versehen ist. Da der Wert des CHRON-Attributs nicht notwendigerweise mit dem Meldungsdatum übereinstimmt, muß der Markup-Server für das obige Beispiel herausfinden, ob es um den vergangenen oder den kommenden Freitag geht, um den korrekten Attributwert zu setzen. Natürlich müssen auch alle Elemente zur Markierung der Dokumentstruktur (BODY, HEDLINE, H1 usw.) eingebettet werden.

4 Lexikonaufbau und -bearbeitung

Um einen Grundbestand des Markup-Lexikons aufzubauen, wurde zunächst die Klassifikation festgelegt, nach der das Vokabular aus einem Ursprungskorpus von ca. 500 personen-relevanten Meldungstexten kategorisiert werden sollte. Im wesentlichen entsprechen die ausgewählten Klassen den gewünschten semantischen Einheiten.

Für die manuelle Zuordnung der Wörter zu diesen Klassen wurde ein spezielles Werkzeug entwickelt und in die TATOE-Umgebung integriert (Abbildung 4). Es kann sowohl zur Eingabe von Lexikoneinträgen als auch zur Nachbereitung von vorklassifiziertem Wortmaterial eingesetzt werden. Der Markup-Server arbeitet zur Zeit mit einem Bestand von ca. 35.000 Einträgen.

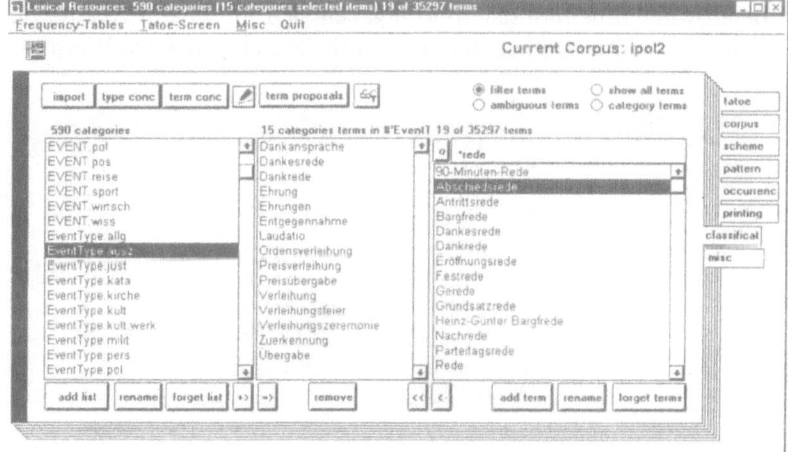

Um den Aufwand einer manuellen Zuordnung der Wörter zu den ausgewählten Klassen zu reduzieren, und für die Klassifikation der im Lexikon noch nicht vorhandenen Wörter wurde ein Verfahren zur automatischen Klassifikation implementiert. Dieses Verfahren berechnet einen Entscheidungsbaum aus den bereits kategorisierten Wörtern und nutzt die Tatsache, daß im Deutschen semantische Klassen häufig durch das Wortende erkennbar sind: Die Zeichenkette *chef* am Ende von *Fraktionschef* oder *Küchenchef* ist z.B. ein Indikator für eine Funktion. Nach einer späteren Bearbeitung der Klassifikationsvorschläge kann der Entscheidungsbaum mit der nun verbesserten Basis neu berechnet werden.

Vorklassifikation der Wörterbuch-Einträge

5   Bewertung des Markup

Zur Bewertung der Markup-Ergebnisse wurde das Textanalysesystem TATOE eingesetzt, mit dem unterschiedliche Referenzkorpora manuell nach vorher festgelegten Markup-Regeln kodiert wurden. Der Korrektheitsgrad einer automatischen Markierung wird durch einen Vergleich mit der manuellen Kodierung des entsprechenden Referenzkorpus ermittelt. Dafür wird die Überlappung zwischen den beiden Auszeichnungsergebnissen berechnet.

Das Maß der Überlappung kann sowohl für alle Kategorien gemeinsam als auch für jede Kategorie einzeln berechnet werden. Für einen Korpus von 175 personen-relevanten Meldungen aus dem

Referenzkorpora zur Berechnung der Korrektheit

Bereich der Innenpolitik (ipol) ergaben sich mit einem (nicht vollständig) optimierten Lexikon die in Tabelle 1 abgebildeten Werte.

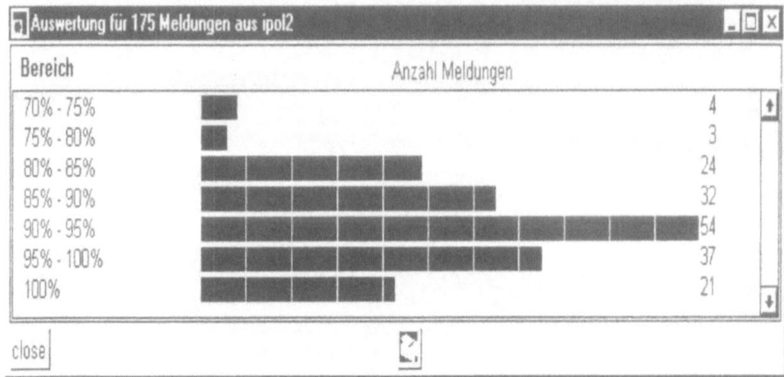

Tabelle 1
Meldungstexte nach Überlappungsmaß geordnet

Berechnen der Überlappung

Die Tabelle 2 zeigt die Überlappungsmaße für die einzelnen semantischen Kategorien, berechnet über die 175 Meldungen des ipol-Referenzkorpus. Das Überlappungsmaß ist der Quotient aus der *Anzahl der korrekten Markierungen* und der *Gesamtanzahl der Markierungen* und liegt damit zwischen 0 und 1. Die *Gesamtanzahl der Markierungen* ergibt sich aus der Vereinigung der automatischen Markierungen mit den manuellen Referenzmarkierungen. Als korrekt wird eine Markierung angesehen, wenn dieselbe Wortfolge manuell und automatisch mit denselben Kategorien ausgezeichnet wurde; in allen anderen Fällen wird sie als falsch gezählt. Eine Markierung wurde als nicht vorhanden (*missed*) eingestuft, wenn sie im Referenzkorpus existierte, aber keines der Wörter in diesem Textsegment automatisch markiert wurde. Diese Anzahl ist ein Indikator für Lücken im Wörterbuch.

Die Titelleiste der Tabelle 2 nennt das globale Überlappungsmaß für alle Kategorien gemeinsam (0.909141). Außerdem wird die Gesamtanzahl der Markierungen (10962) sowie die Anzahl der fehlerhaften Markierungen (996) angezeigt.

formale Ermittlung – guter Indikator

Diese Werte sind, wie beschrieben, formal ermittelt, und sie stellen einen guten Indikator für die generelle Machbarkeit der automatischen semantischen Markierung von Meldungstexten dar. Sie geben keine Auskunft darüber, wie gravierend sich die Fehler auswirken. Je nach Anwendungsfall sind die Fehler unterschiedlich zu bewerten.

■
■
■ *Automatische Erzeugung von semantischem Markup in Agenturmeldungen*

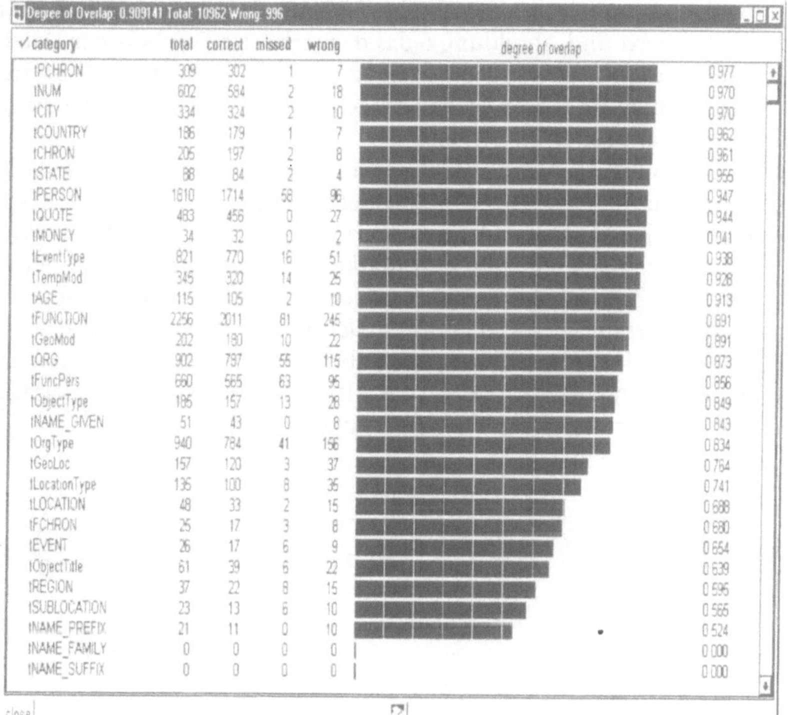

✓ category	total	correct	missed	wrong	degree of overlap
tPCHRON	309	302	1	7	0.977
tNUM	602	584	2	18	0.970
tCITY	334	324	2	10	0.970
tCOUNTRY	186	179	1	7	0.962
tCHRON	205	197	2	8	0.961
tSTATE	88	84	2	4	0.955
tPERSON	1810	1714	58	96	0.947
tQUOTE	483	456	0	27	0.944
tMONEY	34	32	0	2	0.941
tEventType	821	770	16	51	0.938
tTempMod	345	320	14	25	0.928
tAGE	115	105	2	10	0.913
tFUNCTION	2256	2011	81	245	0.891
tGeoMod	202	180	10	22	0.891
tORG	902	737	55	115	0.873
tFuncPers	660	565	63	95	0.856
tObjectType	185	157	13	28	0.849
tNAME_GIVEN	51	43	0	8	0.843
tOrgType	940	784	41	156	0.834
tGeoLoc	157	120	3	37	0.764
tLocationType	135	100	8	35	0.741
tLOCATION	48	33	2	15	0.688
tFCHRON	25	17	3	8	0.680
tEVENT	26	17	6	9	0.654
tObjectTitle	61	39	6	22	0.639
tREGION	37	22	8	15	0.595
tSUBLOCATION	23	13	6	10	0.565
tNAME_PREFIX	21	11	0	10	0.524
tNAME_FAMILY	0	0	0	0	0.000
tNAME_SUFFIX	0	0	0	0	0.000

Tabelle 2
Überlappungs-maße für die verschiedenen Kategorien

Unser Ziel war es, die obere Grenze für die Qualität des Markup abzuschätzen. Wie Tabelle 2 zeigt, liegt diese oberhalb von 90%. Eine genaue Fehleranalyse läßt erwarten, daß man nicht wesentlich über 95% erzielen kann, da der gewählte pragmatische Ansatz seine inhärenten Grenzen hat. Die z.Z. erreichte Qualität – bei unbekannten Texten und ohne Wörterbuchbearbeitung – bewegt sich, abhängig von Ressort und Texttyp, durchschnittlich zwischen 70% und 85%.

6 Anbindung einer Faktendatenbank

Damit Aussagen zur Anbindung einer Faktendatenbank an den Markup-Server gemacht werden können, hat die dpa eine exemplarische Personendatenbank als MS-ACCESS-Datei zur Verfügung gestellt. Die Inhalte dieser Datenbank wurden in ein Objektnetz importiert, das mit den Analyse-Ergebnissen des Markup-Prozesses, d.h. mit der Menge der getypten Textsegmente, befragt werden kann.

Personen-Datenbank

Zu diesem Zweck werden alle Informationen, die zu einer Person im Text gefunden wurden, gebündelt und mit den Inhalten der Faktendatenbank verglichen. Abbildung 5 zeigt einen semantisch markierten Text und Abbildung 6 das dazugehörige Ergebnis der Datenbankabfrage. Dieses Ergebnis zeigt zuerst alle im Text identifizierten Personen an und zwar geordnet nach der Häufigkeit, mit der sie im Text erwähnt sind.

Das Wort *Aller* in der Schlagzeile wird als Person erkannt, da im ersten Absatz *Heinrich Aller* mit dem Vornamen als Person eingeführt worden ist. Der Markup-Server versucht mit Hilfe heuristischer Regeln auch die als AGE markierten Elemente bestimmten im Text erwähnten Personen zuzuordnen und beim Datenbankabgleich diese Altersangabe (Abbildung 5: *Der 49 Jahre alte gelernte Polizist*) zu prüfen. Hierfür wird aus dem Geburtsdatum dieser Person, sofern in der Datenbank vorhanden, das Alter zum Zeitpunkt der Meldung berechnet und dieses mit der Altersangabe im Text verglichen.

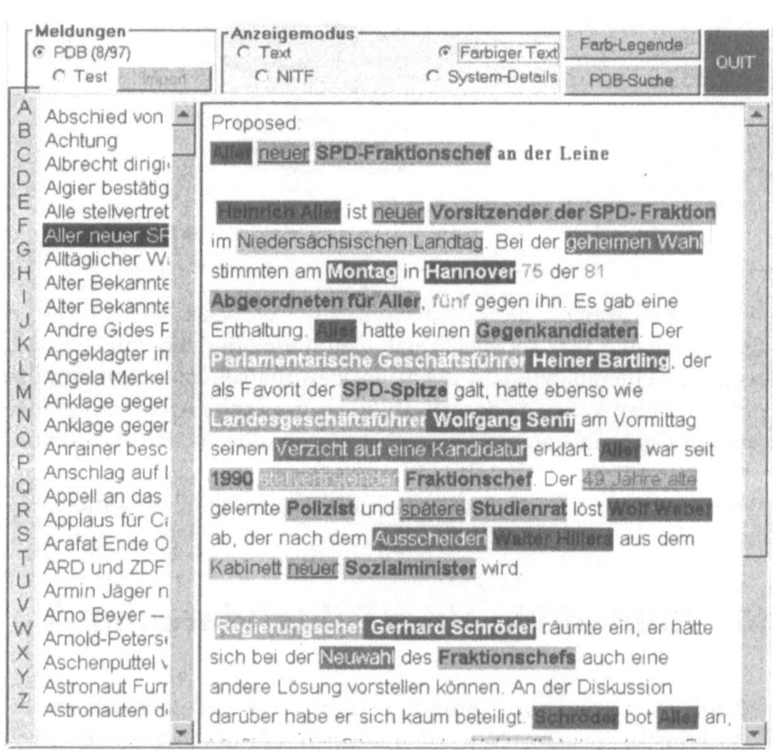

Abbildung 5
Semantisch markierte Meldung

Das Textbeispiel zeigt auch die weiter oben erwähnte Vereindeutigung von *Gerhard Schröder* mit Hilfe der identifizierten Rolle *Regierungschef*. Tatsächlich sind in der Datenbank Informationen zu zwei verschiedene Personen *Gerhard Schröder* gespeichert.

Informationen zu 6 Personen:

Heinrich Aller[<#PIN->58>]

Alter: **49** (geb.30. September 1947)

(6 mal im Text erwähnt)

Gerhard Schröder[1] (Ministerpräsident)[<#PIN->71>]

Funktionen: Regierungschef

(2 mal im Text erwähnt)

Wolfgang Senff

Funktionen: Landesgeschäftsführer

Heiner Bartling

Funktionen: Parlamentarische Geschäftsführer

Wolf Weber

Walter Hillers

Weitere Funktionen:

Vorsitzender der SPD- Fraktion

Sozialminister

SPD Fraktionschef

Fraktionschef

Abbildung 6
Abgleich mit der
Fakten-
Datenbank

7 Zusammenfassung

Die technische Machbarkeit eines Markup-Servers mit zufriedenstellender Fehlerrate der Ergebnisse ist durch die Pilotimplementierung nachgewiesen worden. Es hat sich dabei gezeigt, daß auch auf heutigen handelsüblichen Arbeitsplatzrechnern (Pentium II, 300MHz, Windows NT 4.0) die durchschnittliche Zeit für das Markup im Bereich von ein bis zwei Sekunden liegt. Daraus folgt auch, daß der gewählte pragmatische Ansatz für den Markup-Prozeß, ein semantisch klassifiziertes Lexikon mit lokalen Kontextregeln zu verbinden, sich im Prinzip bewährt hat.

Die Qualität des Markup hängt wesentlich von zwei Faktoren ab: von den Kontextregeln und von dem Abdeckungsgrad des Lexikons.

Machbarkeit und
Geschwindigkeit

stabile
Markup-Regeln

Wir erwarten, daß die Markup-Regeln für den gegebenen Texttyp und nach einer Anpassungsphase – recht stabil sind und keinen nennenswerten Pflegeaufwand mehr erfordern. Da aus aktuellen Meldungen ständig neues Vokabular hinzukommt, wird das Markup-Lexikon hingegen dauernd gepflegt werden müssen. Die Fehlertypen im Markup zu bewerten und daraufhin abzuschätzen, wie tolerierbar sie sind, bzw. wie hoch der Korrekturaufwand sein wird, kann natürlich nur im Kontext konkreter Einsatzszenarien durchgeführt werden. Es wurde weiterhin demonstriert, daß sich die Ergebnisse des Markup für einen Abgleich mit den Daten einer Faktendatenbank nutzen lassen und daß sie in analoger Weise eine effiziente Aktualisierung einer solchen Faktendatenbank unterstützen können.

NITF-Service

Damit ist es grundsätzlich möglich, mit Hilfe eines Markup-Servers einen NITF-Service von insbesondere semantisch markierten Agenturmeldungen aufzubauen. Für ein Online-Angebot könnten automatisch Links zur Faktendatenbank mit Hintergrundinformationen in eine entsprechende HTML-Seite eingebettet werden. Darüber hinaus kann der Markup-Server eine Nachricht analysieren und automatisch die Liste der semantisch getypten Ausdrücke als Frage an die Faktendatenbank senden. Dies kann den Zugriff und die Nutzung einer Archivdatenbank im Redaktions- und im Dokumentationsprozeß vereinfachen.

Literatur

(Alexa/Rostek 1996)
Alexa, M.; Rostek, L.: Computer-assisted, corpus-based text analysis with TATOE. In: ALLC-ACH 96, Book of Abstracts (Bergen, Norway). o.O., 1996, S. 11-17

(Carnegie Group 1998)
Carnegie Group: Research and Technology: Language, Text and Voice Processing. o.O., 1998. Erhältlich im Internet:
http://netra1.cgi.com/web2/govt/gov-text.html

(Chen/Lee 1996)
Chen, Hsin-Hsi; Lee. J.-L.: Identification and classification of proper nouns in Chinese Texts. In: Proceedings of COLING-96 (Copenhagen, Denmark). Bd. 1. o.O., 1996, S. 222-229

(Flanders et al. 1997)
Flanders, J.; Bauman, S.; Caton, P.; Cournane, M.; McCarty, W.; Bradley, J.: Applying the TEI: Problems in the classification of proper nouns. In: Queens University (Veranst.): ACH-ALLC Conference Abstracts (Kingston, Canada, June 3-7, 1997). o. O., 1997, S. 53-58

(Hockey et al. 1997)
Hockey, S.; Butler, T.; Brown, S.; Fischer, S.: The Orlando Project: Humanities Computing in Conversation with Literary History In: Queens University

(Veranst.): ACH-ALLC Conference Abstracts (Kingston, Canada, June 3-7, 1997). o.O., 1997, S. 83-89

(IPTC-NAA 1998)
IPTC-NAA (Hrsg): IPTC-NAA News Industry Text Format (NITF). Version 2.0b1. o.O., 1998. Erhältlich im Internet: http://www.iptc.org/iptc

(Jacobs/Rau 1990)
Jacobs, Paul S.; Rau, Lisa S.: SCISOR: Extracting Information from On-line News. Communications of the ACM 33 (1990) Nr. 11, S. 88-97

(Kitani/Mitamura 1994)
Kitani, T.; Mitamura, T.: An accurate morphological analysis and proper noun identification for Japanese text processing. In: Transactions of Information Processing Society of Japan 35 (1994), Nr. 3, S. 404-413

(Lingsoft 1996)
Lingsoft - GERTWOL: German Morphological Analyzer. Helsinki (Finnland), 1996. Erhältlich im Internet: http://www.lingsoft.fi.

(Mani/MacMillan 1996)
Mani, I.; MacMillan, R. T.: Identifying Unknown Proper Names in Newswire Text. In: Boguraev, B.; Pustejovsky, J. (Hrsg.): Corpus Processing for Lexical Acquisition. Cambridge, MA: MIT Press, 1996, S. 41-59

(McCarty 1994)
McCarty, W.: Encoding Persons and Places in the Metamorphoses of Ovid. Part 1: Engineering the Text. o.O., 1994 (Texte 13/14), S. 121-172

(McCarty 1995)
McCarty, W: Peering Through the Skylight. Part 2: Towards an Electronic Edition of Ovid's Metamorphoses. o.O. , 1995 (Texte 15/16), S. 261-305

(McDonald 1996)
McDonald, D.: Internal and External Evidence in the Identification and Semantic Categorization of Proper Names. In: Boguraev, B.; Pustejovsky, J. (Hrsg.): Corpus Processing for Lexical Acquisition. Cambridge, MA: MIT Press, 1996, S. 21-39

(Paik et al. 1996)
Paik, W.; Liddy, E. D.; Yu, E; McKenna, M.: Categorizing and Standardizing Proper Nouns for Efficient Information Retrieval. In: Boguraev, B.; Pustejovsky, J. (Hrsg.): Corpus Processing for Lexical Acquisition. Cambridge (MA): MIT Press, 1996, S. 61-73

(Radev/McKeown 1997)
Radev, D. R.; McKeown, K.: Building a Generation Knowledge Source using Internet-Accessible Newswire. In: Proceedings of the Fifth Conference on Applied Natural Language Processing, Washington, DC, 1997, S. 221-228

(Rostek/Alexa 1998)
Rostek, L.; Alexa, M.: Marking up in TATOE and exporting to SGML – Rule development for identifying NITF categories. In: Computer and the Humanities 31 (1998), S. 311-326

(Rostek et al. 1993)
Rostek, L.; Möhr, W.; Fischer, D.: Weaving a web: The structure and creation of an object network representing an electronic reference work. In: Electronic Publishing 6 (1994), 4, S. 495-505

(Wakao et al. 1996)
Wakao, T.; Gaizauskas, R.; Wilks, Y.: Evaluation of an Algorithm for the Recognition and Classification of Proper Nouns. In: Proceedings of COLING-96 (Copenhagen, Denmark). Bd. 1. o.O., 1996, S. 418-423

Modell einer mehrschichtigen Textannotation für die computerunterstützte Textanalyse

Melina Alexa und Ingrid Schmidt

1 Motivation

Die computerunterstützte Textanalyse überführt einen Text, dessen hierarchische Struktur markiert sein kann, in einen Text mit inhaltsorientierten Auszeichnungen. Diese können beispielsweise den Interpretationsrahmen oder den spezifischen Zweck der Analyse widerspiegeln oder linguistisch motiviert sein und somit die Kategorien der Morphologie, der Syntax, der Semantik oder der Diskursanalyse abdecken. Darüber hinaus können Texte aus der Nachrichtenindustrie, den Geisteswissenschaften oder den Sozialwissenschaften, um nur einige mögliche Anwendungsbereiche zu nennen, mit fachgebietsbezogenen, studienspezifischen und anderen inhaltlich motivierten Kategorien annotiert werden. Sobald mehrere Analyseaspekte auf einen Text angewendet werden, spricht man von *mehrschichtiger Textannotation*. Die Textanalyse befaßt sich mit drei Hauptaufgaben:

1. der automatischen oder manuellen Auszeichnung einer Textsammlung, eines einzelnen Textes oder von Textteilen nach mindestens einem Kategorienschema;

2. dem Durchsuchen oder Befragen einer Textsammlung, eines einzelnen Textes oder von Textteilen, nicht nur nach speziellen strukturellen Einheiten wie Titel, Wörter oder Wortfolgen in einem Absatz, sondern auch nach inhaltlichen Auszeichnungen;

computerunterstützte Textanalyse

Hauptaufgaben der Textanalyse

3. der Anreicherung einer bereits ausgezeichneten Textsammlung, eines einzelnen Textes oder von Textteilen mit zusätzlichen Kodierungen nach einem weiteren Kategorienschema.

Ein inhaltsorientiert ausgezeichneter Text kann auch für Textanalysen, die ein vollkommen anderes Ziel verfolgen, genutzt werden, indem diese von den bereits existierenden Auszeichnungen profitieren oder auf ihnen aufbauend weitergehende Analysen durchführen. Beispielsweise können nach linguistischen Kategorien ausgezeichnete Leitartikel als Grundlage für eine computerunterstützte Textanalyse dienen, die sich entweder mit der Textstruktur des Texttyps „Leitartikel" befaßt oder die spezifische Sichtweise von Leitartikeln auf ein spezielles Thema untersucht, wie etwa die Außenpolitik eines Landes. Die bereits existierenden Auszeichnungen helfen bei dieser weiteren Analyse, da sie zusätzliche Abfragen ermöglichen. Außerdem können sie für die Entwicklung und die Validierung eines Kategorienschemas zu diesem neuen Analyseaspekt genutzt werden. Auf diese Weise entstehen mehrschichtig und *reichhaltig annotierte Texte*.

SGML und Textanalyse   Der Einsatz von SGML für die Textanalyse erweist sich als vorteilhaft,

- um reichhaltig annotierte Texte zu erstellen,

- die wiederum für verschiedene weitergehende Analysen genutzt und

- problemlos und ohne Informationsverlust zwischen unterschiedlichen Anwendungen ausgetauscht werden können.

Wir stellen in unserem Beitrag die oben genannten Punkte in den Rahmen einer Machbarkeitsstudie, die darauf abzielt, mehrschichtig ausgezeichnete Texte zu erstellen und zu nutzen. Dabei gehen wir zunächst auf die Richtlinien der *Text Encoding Initiative (TEI)* ein sowie auf deren Rolle bei der Auszeichnung struktureller und inhaltsorientierter Informationen und fahren fort mit einer Skizze des derzeitigen Forschungsstandes in bezug auf mehrschichtige Textauszeichnung. Anschließend beschreiben wir das im Rahmen dieser Studie realisierte DTD-Konzept, um daran beispielhaft die Prozesse und komplexen Strukturen zu verdeutlichen, die für die Erstellung und Analyse mehrschichtig annotierter Texte relevant sind. Abschließend diskutieren wir projektbezogene Themen im Hinblick auf ihre Perspektiven.

■ *Modell einer mehrschichtigen Textannotation für die*
■ *computerunterstützte Textanalyse*

2 Die Text Encoding Initiative

2.1 Die TEI-Richtlinien

Die TEI-Richtlinien (Sperberg-McQueen/Burnard 1994), eine Anwendung von SGML, stellen wir in diesen Zusammenhang, da

Textanalyse und
TEI-Richtlinien

- ihre frei verfügbaren DTDs für die unterschiedlichsten Aus-
  zeichnungsaufgaben herangezogen werden können, und

- sie somit ein Instrumentarium für die Aufgabe der Textannotation zur Verfügung stellen.

Die Richtlinien empfehlen Auszeichnungen, die die Weiterverarbeitung von Texten vereinfachen, indem sie die verschiedenen Zwecke
und Zielsetzungen einer Analyse berücksichtigen.

Die TEI-Richtlinien stellen ein modular aufeinander abgestimm-
tes Set von DTDs zur Verfügung, die unverändert übernommen
oder anwendungsbezogen modifiziert werden können. Dieses sogenannte *pizza model* der TEI schreibt vor, daß zunächst die Kern-
DTD (*Teig*) mit einem auf die Textgattung, beispielsweise Drama
oder Lexikon, ausgerichteten DTD-Modul (*Grundbelag*) ergänzt
werden muß. Auf diese Textgattung können dann rein textbezogene
Strukturen, wie linguistische Annotation (*zusätzlicher Belag*), als
weiteres DTD-Modul aufgesetzt werden. Individuelle Modifikationen der TEI-DTDs werden in einer separaten DTD gehalten, die
problemlos in dieses Modulkonzept eingehangt werden kann.

Modularität

Die TEI-Richtlinien schlagen für die unterschiedlichen Texttypen
und Analysezwecke eine Reihe inhaltsorientierter Auszeichnungen
vor, die sich auf einer hierarchischen Ebene befinden und optional
verwendet werden können, nach dem Motto „if you want to encode
this feature, do it this way" (Sperberg-McQueen/Burnard 1994, S. 6).
Mit diesem Mechanismus kann eine Vielzahl von Phänomenen bis
zu jedem gewünschten Detaillierungsgrad und jeder erforderlichen
Komplexität ausgezeichnet werden. Die Verwendung derselben TEI-
DTD kann dadurch, je nach Analyseschwerpunkt und -ziel, zu unterschiedlichen Auszeichungen führen, die die verschiedenen Sicht-
weisen auf den Text reflektieren.

inhaltsorientierte
Auszeichnungen

Die Richtlinien sind so angelegt, daß sie generell anwendbar sind,
unabhängig von Sprache, Texttyp und Inhalt (Sperberg-McQueen/
Burnard 1994, S. 1). Sie finden in zahlreichen Projekten der unterschiedlichsten Fachgebiete Verwendung: im Museumsbereich, in

Universalität

den Literaturwissenschaften, in der Lexikographie, im Bereich des Elektronischen Publizierens, um nur einige zu nennen. Eine ausführliche Auflistung findet sich unter http://www-tei.uic.edu/orgs /tei/app/topics.html.

2.2 Überlappende Informationsstrukturen

Definition   Die TEI-Richtlinien gehen davon aus, daß ein Text über eine einzig gültige hierarchische Struktur verfügt, die durch inhaltsorientierte Strukturen ergänzt werden kann. Sobald Informationsstrukturen abzubilden sind, die quer zu einer dieser Ebenen liegen, d.h. deren Grenzen nicht innerhalb der oben genannten Strukturen liegen, sind die Möglichkeiten der TEI erschöpft. Beispiele hierfür sind:

- *Texttyp „Gespräch"*
  Bei der Transkription von Gesprächen ist es oft notwendig, bestimmte Textstellen mit einem Kommentar zu versehen. Dazu müssen Textteile ausgezeichnet werden, die unabhängig von der hierarchischen Struktur des Dokuments sind. Dies ist beispielsweise dann der Fall, wenn festgehalten werden soll, über welche Gesprächspassagen der Befragte am Fenster stand.

- *Morpho-Syntax*
  Die Grenzen morpho-syntaktischer Einheiten sind nicht immer klar zu definieren. In dem Satz „She takes care of him" kann das Wort „of" als Teil der Verbphrase „to take care of" angesehen werden, oder es kann Teil der Präpositionalphrase „of him" sein. Um diese beiden Interpretationsmöglichkeiten explizit repräsentieren zu können, müssen im Auszeichnungsschema Überschneidungen möglich sein.

- *Ambiguität*
  Für eine bestimmte Texteinheit ist mehr als eine Interpretation möglich. So kommt in dem Satz „Der Flughafen Frankfurt ist einer der größten Flughäfen der Welt", eine semantische Ambiguität für „Flughafen Frankfurt" vor, da er sowohl als Ortsbezeichnung wie auch als Organisation ausgezeichnet werden kann (vgl. Beitrag von Gerhard Knorz und Wiebke Möhr).

CONCUR   Barnard et al. (1995) erläutern, wie durch das SGML-Feature CONCUR diese Probleme umgangen werden können. Es ermöglicht, für ein und denselben Text zwei oder mehr voneinander getrennte Auszeichnungsschemata zu entwickeln, die in einer jeweils separaten DTD definiert werden. Dabei können die Auszeichnungen der einen DTD mit denen der anderen DTD überlappen. Dies wäre bei dem

Modell einer mehrschichtigen Textannotation für die computerunterstützte Textanalyse

obigen Gesprächsbeispiel dann der Fall, wenn die Struktur des Gesprächs in einer DTD modelliert wird und der Kommentartext einer anderen DTD angehört. Da derzeit keine SGML-Software CONCUR unterstützt, wird es in der Regel nicht bei der DTD-Entwicklung berücksichtigt.

CONCUR löst jedoch nicht das Problem der Überlappung, wenn die sich überschneidenden Strukturen demselben Auszeichnungsschema und damit derselben DTD angehören, wie das sowohl bei dem oben angeführten Beispiel zur Morpho-Syntax der Fall ist, als auch auf die Auszeichnung von Hyperlinks zutreffen kann.

Eine anderer Lösungsansatz ist die Entkopplung von Anfangs- und Endetag. Bei diesem Ansatz, der nichts anderes als eine Notlösung darstellt, müssen zwei Elemente als EMPTY definiert und über den ID-IDREF-Mechanismus aufeinander bezogen werden. Aus SGML-Sicht ist daran problematisch, daß nicht sichergestellt werden kann, daß das Anfangselement vor dem Endelement steht oder daß es zu jedem Anfangselement nur ein Endelement gibt. Eine konsistente Anwendung ist nur mit spezieller Softwareunterstützung vorstellbar.

Notlösung

2.3 Mehrschichtige Informationsstrukturen

Die TEI-Richtlinien ermöglichen es zwar, verschiedene Sichten auf einen Text auszuzeichnen, berücksichtigen aber nicht die Anforderungen einer mehrschichtigen Textannotation. Hierfür scheint das Textmodell des *Corpus Encoding Standard (CES)* ein geeignetes Konzept anzubieten. Der CES ist eine TEI-kompatible SGML-Applikation. Allgemeines Projektziel ist „the identification of a minimal encoding level that text corpora must achieve to be considered standardised in terms of descriptive representation (marking of structural and linguistic information) as well as general architecture" (CES 1998). Der CES hält den Originaltext und die Annotationen voneinander getrennt. Die Annotationen werden somit nicht, wie allgemein üblich, direkt in den Text eingebracht, sondern sind in einer separaten Datei gespeichert. Annotation und Originaltext werden mittels eines HyTime-basierten, von der TEI entwickelten Adressierungsmechanismus miteinander verknüpft. So kann ein Text mit beliebig vielen verschiedenen Annotationsdateien verknüpft werden.

Corpus Encoding Standard (CES)

3 Computerunterstützte Textanalyse und SGML

Die Frage einer reichhaltigen SGML-basierten Textannotation ist unmittelbar verknüpft mit der Frage nach der Verfügbarkeit von Werkzeugen, die diese in allen Bearbeitungsstufen und Nutzungsmöglichkeiten unterstützen. Dabei sollte die Benutzerschnittstelle so beschaffen sein,

- daß der Anwender das zugrundegelegte Auszeichnungsschema ausnutzen kann, ohne detaillierte Kenntnis davon haben zu müssen, und

- daß er bestehende Auszeichnungsschemata erweitern sowie neue Auszeichnungsschemata entwickeln und auf die schon existierenden Texte anwenden kann.

Funktionalität

Hauptaspekte bei der Funktionalität solcher Werkzeuge sind:

- der Import und Export von SGML-Instanzen;

- die Manipulation der Elemente und Attribute;

- die Repräsentation der DTD als „Wissen" über die Struktur;

- der Export einer modifizierten DTD bei einer Ausweitung des Kategorienschemas;

- der Export einer neuen DTD bei der Erstellung eines neuen Kategorienschemas.

*Projekt-
beschreibungen*

Wir beschreiben im folgenden kurz einige wichtige Arbeiten, die sich mit einzelnen der oben aufgeführten Aspekte befassen.

SARA

SARA (SGML Aware Retrieval Application) wurde speziell als Zugangssystem zum British National Corpus (BNC) entwickelt (Burnard 1995). Das BNC ist ein großes Korpus der zeitgenössischen gesprochenen und geschriebenen englischen Sprache mit mehr als 100 Millionen Wörtern. Es entstand in einer Zusammenarbeit von Wissenschaft und Industrie. Unter der Leitung der Oxford University Press beteiligten sich Longman UK Ltd., Chambers/Larousse, Oxford University Computing Services, die Universität Lancaster und die British Library. Das BNC ist TEI-konform ausgezeichnet. Dabei werden automatisch die einzelnen Sätze markiert und jedem Wort wird vom CLAWS-Tagger der Universität Lancaster eine Wortart-Kategorie zugewiesen. SARA steht allen BNC-Lizenzinhabern kostenlos zur Verfügung und ermöglicht dem Benutzer, ohne Kenntnis der zugrundegelegten TEI-Struktur, eine schnelle Suche auf dem gesamten Datenbestand durchzuführen, etwa nach morpho-syntaktischen Merkmalen. Die Suche kann auf bestimmte

Modell einer mehrschichtigen Textannotation für die computerunterstützte Textanalyse

Kontexte begrenzt werden, beispielsweise auf Zeitungsschlagzeilen oder gesprochene Äußerungen, und sie kann ausschließlich bestimmte, mitunter sehr spezifische Textsorten berücksichtigen, wie wissenschaftliche Publikationen oder gesprochene Sprache von Frauen mittleren Alters aus Südengland. Es kann mit Jokern und regulären Ausdrücken gesucht werden sowie nach dem Inhalt von Wortart-Kategorien, um so z.B. alle Vorkommen von *can* als Nomen zu finden. Darüber hinaus werden komplexe Suchanfragen unterstützt. Die gefundenen Treffer können dann auf vielfältige Art sortiert und in unterschiedlichen Formaten dargestellt werden.

Simons (1997) befaßt sich mit dem Problem, TEI-konform ausgezeichnete Texte in eine objektorientierte Datenbank zu importieren, ohne daß dabei die TEI-Dokumente oder das Datenbankschema geändert werden müssen. Er schlägt vor, die SGML-Daten auf *architectural forms* (DeRose/Durand 1994) abzubilden. Diese können dann von CELLAR (Computing Environment for Linguistic, Literary, and Anthropological Research) in Datenbankobjekte überführt werden. Dabei hängt die Qualität des Resultats vom Grad der Kongruenz zwischen dem konzeptuellen DTD-Modell und dem Zielschema der Objektdatenbank ab.

Ide et al. (1997) berichten von Versuchen, die TEI-DTD zusammen mit den dazugehörigen Dokumentinstanzen in dem framebasierten Wissensrepräsentationssystem CLASSIC (Brachman et al. 1989) abzubilden, um das Retrieval auf TEI-konformen Texten, gemessen an den bisher verfügbaren Möglichkeiten, zu verbessern. Ihr Fokus liegt dabei auf der Repräsentation des Markup, um mächtigere Suchanfragen zu ermöglichen. Dieser Ansatz ist insofern vielversprechend, als er versucht, den Zugang zu den Texten über ihre semantischen statt über ihre strukturellen Eigenschaften zu ermöglichen.

Rostek und Alexa (1998) beschreiben die Entwicklung einer „Grammatik", die dazu dient, in TATOE (Text Analysis Tool with Object Encoding), einem Werkzeug für die computerunterstützte Textanalyse (Alexa/Rostek 1996), deutschsprachige Nachrichtentexte automatisch semantisch auszuzeichnen. Dabei werden die Annotationen getrennt von den Textdaten gespeichert. So wird ein flexibler Im- und Export von Texten nach unterschiedlichen DTDs möglich. In ihrer Arbeit definieren Rostek und Alexa dann eine Export-Prozedur nach SGML für Texte, die in TATOE mit zusätzlichem Markup angereichert wurden. Sie ist jedoch speziell auf das Projekt abgestellt, über das sie berichten. Eine generelle Lösung für den Export von SGML-Daten wird als allgemein beschreibender Formalismus skizziert. Dieser würde, in TATOE implementiert, ermöglichen, die TATOE-Auszeichnungen eines beliebigen Textes auf SGML-Markup abzubilden.

4 Das TECA-Projekt als Modell mehrschichtiger Textannotation

Arbeitsgruppe „Sozialwissenschaftliche Textanalyse"

Seit Anfang 1997 besteht beim *Zentrum für Umfragen, Methoden und Analysen (ZUMA)* in Mannheim die Arbeitsgruppe „Sozialwissenschaftliche Textanalyse", die an einem neuen Konzept für die computerunterstützte Textanalyse in den Sozialwissenschaften arbeitet. Einer ihrer Arbeitsbereiche ist die Konzeption eines neuen, auf die Sozialwissenschaften zugeschnittenen Analyseprogramms, das u.a. die Kombination von qualitativer Textdaten-Analyse und computerunterstützer Inhaltsanalyse sowie die Bearbeitung und Erstellung mit Information angereicherter (*information rich*) Textbanken ermöglichen soll.

TECA-Projekt

In diesem Zusammenhang steht das ZUMA-Grundlagenforschungsprojekt *Towards Extending Content Analysis (TECA)*. Dieses als Pilotstudie angelegte Projekt soll das Methodenspektrum für die Analyse sozialwissenschaftlicher Texten erweitern. Dabei werden die Erfahrungen und Techniken aus der Linguistik, insbesondere der Computerlinguistik, aus dem Anwendungsbereich standardisierter Textformate, insbesondere SGML, sowie der angrenzenden Wissenschaften einbezogen und für die Sozialwissenschaften nutzbar gemacht.

Antworten auf offene Fragen

Als Untersuchungsmaterial wurde ein Texttyp gewählt, der typisch für die Auswertungen von Umfragen ist und der in der Alltagspraxis von ZUMA am häufigsten vorkommt, *Antworten auf offene Fragen*, wie sie in einem Fragebogen erscheinen. Im Gegensatz zu den geschlossenen Fragen, die von den Befragten nach dem Multiple-Choice-Prinzip beantwortet werden, handelt es sich bei den Antworten auf offene Fragen um frei formulierte Texte, die von dem Interviewer handschriftlich im Fragebogen festgehalten werden. Diese werden bei der Verschriftung in elektronischer Form erfaßt, wodurch sie zu einer Textsammlung zusammengeführt werden, die anschließend inhaltlich analysiert wird.

Projektszenario

Das TECA-Projekt arbeitet mit Antworten auf offene Fragen aus zwei repräsentativen Stichproben. Für jede Stichprobe liegt eine Textsammlung vor, in die die Antworten auf die jeweiligen folgenden Fragen zusammengeführt sind.

- *Die „Stolz-Texte":*
  „Wenn Sie an die ehemalige DDR zurückdenken, gibt es Dinge, auf die die Menschen dort/Sie (West-/Ostversion) stolz sein können?" Wenn mit ja geantwortet wurde, kam die Nachfrage: „Und auf was sind die/Sie stolz?"

- *Die „Links/Rechts-Texte":*
  „Können Sie mir bitte nun noch sagen, was Sie persönlich unter
  den Begriffen LINKS und RECHTS verstehen, wenn es um Poli-
  tik geht?
  Links bedeutet:
  Rechts bedeutet:"

Die zwei Textsammlungen werden mit Hilfe eines linguistischen
Analysesystems (Parser) bearbeitet. Dadurch wird jedes Textkorpus
mit linguistischen Angaben angereichert, wie z.B. Wortstämmen,
Wortartkategorien und syntaktischen Komponenten wie Verbphra-
sen, Nominalphrasen etc.

Im weiteren werden drei Analyse-Ansätze angewendet: die konventionelle Inhaltsanalyse, die computerunterstützte Inhaltsanalyse
und die interaktive Kodierung, die mehrschichtige Analysen ermöglicht. Die drei Ansätze werden miteinander verglichen und bewertet.
In Abbildung 1 wird der Analyseablauf für das TECA-Projekt skizziert.

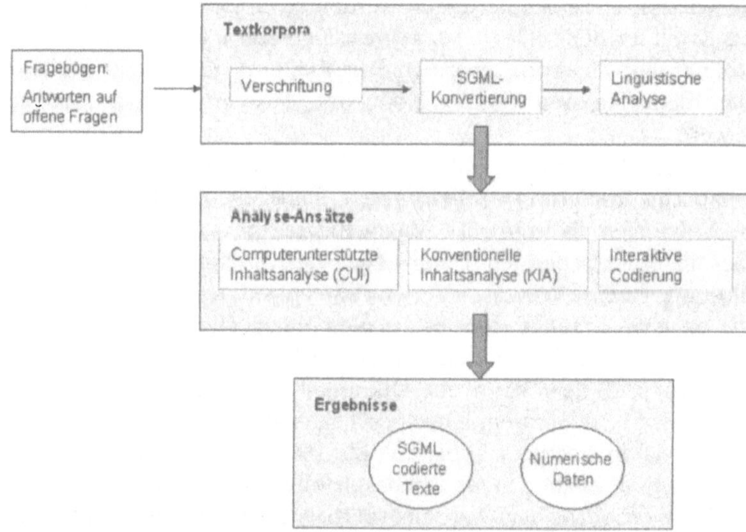

Abbildung 1
*Analyseablauf im
TECA-Projekt*

4.1 Verschriftung und Inhaltsanalyse

Verschriftung

Die *Verschriftung* der Antworten auf offene Fragen geschieht auf der Basis von Verschriftungsregeln, die für jedes Umfrageprojekt neu erstellt werden. Die Erfassung der Antworten erfolgt in einem gängigen Texteditor.

Inhaltsanalyse

Der Inhaltsanalyse wird ein Kategoriensystem zugrunde gelegt. Es wird für jede Umfrage entweder neu entwickelt oder ein schon vorhandenes wird übernommen und gegebenenfalls modifiziert. Das gewählte Kategoriensystem macht es möglich, die Antworten hinsichtlich einer bestimmten Hypothese zu interpretieren. Die inhaltliche Analyse hat zwei Ausprägungen: die *konventionelle Inhaltsanalyse (KIA)* und die *computerunterstützte Inhaltsanalyse (CUI)*, die durchaus beide auf die Texte einer Umfrage angewandt werden können. Weder bei der KIA noch bei der CUI gibt es eine Standardisierung für die Darstellung und Archivierung von kodierten Texten.

KIA – konventionelle Inhaltsanalyse

Bei der KIA findet das Kategoriensystem als Kategorienschema Anwendung. Jeder Antwort werden die darin zutreffenden Kodes zugewiesen. Diese Kodierungen werden manuell von einem einzelnen Kodierer oder einer Gruppe von Kodierern vorgenommen. Sie erfolgten entweder auf separaten Formblättern oder direkt im Text; über Identifikatoren können Kode und Text einander zugeordnet werden.

CUI – computerunterstützte Inhaltsanalyse

Bei der CUI wird mit Hilfe eines Textanalyseprogramms eine automatische Kodierung vorgenommen. Dabei dienen die verschrifteten Antworten als Input für eine Software, die Kodes auf der Basis eines in einer separaten Datei abgelegten *Diktionärs* vergibt. Das Diktionär ist eine Wortliste, der ein Kategoriensystem zugrundeliegt, d.h., es verzeichnet zu den festgelegten Kategorien alle Wörter und Wortstämme, die als Indikatoren gelten können. Je nach Kategoriensystem und Text kann ein Diktionär mehrere tausend Wörter umfassen. Meist kann ein einzelnes Textanalyseprogramm nicht alle erforderlichen Features anbieten. Ein Wechsel zu einem anderen Programm setzt aber meist ein bestimmtes Textformat voraus, das eine Konvertierung der Texte erforderlich macht, bei der nicht selten Informationen verloren gehen (Alexa/Züll 1998). Eine Schwäche der gegenwärtigen CUI-Methode ist, daß die Analyse überwiegend auf Einwort-Kodierungen basiert und den Kontext nicht berücksichtigt. Diese fehlende Kontextsensitivität führt zu ungenauen Ergebnissen bzw. beschränkt die Anwendung der Methode der computerunterstützten Inhaltsanalyse auf bestimmte Themen und Textsorten.

Modell einer mehrschichtigen Textannotation für die computerunterstützte Textanalyse

Die Vorgehensweise bei der Inhaltsanalyse soll im folgenden bei- *Beispiele*
spielhaft verdeutlicht werden. Bei der manuellen Kodierung der
„Links/Rechts-Texte" sollte herausgefunden werden, was derzeit in
Deutschland „die inhaltliche Bedeutung der Begriffe links und
rechts" ist (Bauer-Kaase 1998). Zu diesem Zweck wurde ein existie-
rendes Kategorienschema (Fuchs/Klingemann 1990) von Bauer-
Kaase erweitert und modifiziert, so daß seine nun in Gruppen zu-
sammengefaßten 180 Kategorien den *semantischen Raum* von links
und rechts rekonstruieren. Bei der Kodierung werden einer Antwort
keine, eine oder mehrere Kategorien zugewiesen. Wenn sich ein
Befragter beispielsweise in seiner Antwort auf politische Parteien
bezieht, dann entnimmt der Kodierer dem Kategorienschema eine
zutreffende Kategorie aus der Kategoriengruppe „Politische Partei-
en" und weist den Kode manuell der ganzen Antwort zu. Anders bei
der automatischen Inhaltsanalyse der „Stolz-Texte": Enthält eine
Antwort das Wort „Sportleistungen", dann wird im Diktionär dieses
Wort gesucht und, wenn es vorhanden ist, mit dem Kode verknüpft,
in diesem Falle mit dem der Kategorie „Sport". Da bei dieser Methode alle Instanzen eines Wortes unabhängig von ihrem Kontext kodiert werden, erfolgt die gleiche Zuordnung auch in der Phrase „keine großen Sportleistungen". Die Kodierung wird dabei direkt an den
Ausdruck „Sportleistungen" angehängt und nicht wie bei der manuellen Kodierung der Antwort als Ganzes zugewiesen.

4.2 Linguistische Analyse

Im Rahmen des TECA-Projekts sollte ebenfalls untersucht werden, *Parser-*
inwieweit linguistische Information die computerunterstützte In- *Output*
haltsanalyse unterstützen und verbessern kann. Um solche Informationen zu bekommen, werden die verschrifteten Antworten von
einem deutschsprachigen morpho-syntaktischen Analysesystem
(Parser) verarbeitet. Der Output des Parsers ist ein linguistisch markierter Text. Jedem Wort wird dabei ein Lemma und eine Wortart-
kategorie zugewiesen. Zusätzlich wird ihm, soweit möglich, eine
syntaktische Kategorie, wie Nominal- oder Verbphrase, zugeordnet.
Für ein Wort, eine syntaktische Gruppe oder einen ganzen Satz ist
häufig mehr als eine linguistische Analyse möglich; in diesem Fall
spricht man von ambigen Analysen. Zu Forschungs- und Testzwek-
ken sollen alle ambigen Strukturen explizit repräsentiert werden.

*Nutzen für die
Inhaltsanalyse*

Diese gewonnenen linguistischen Informationen könnten für die verschiedenen Methoden der Inhaltsanalyse genutzt werden: Bei der KIA könnten sie die Erstellung und Validierung des Kategorienschemas unterstützen, bei der CUI zur Entwicklung und Validierung des Diktionärs und zur Überprüfung und Präzisierung der bisherigen Kodierung im Hinblick auf den Kontext beitragen (s. Abschnitt 4.1).

4.3 Interaktive Kodierung

*interaktive
Kodierung,
KIA, CUI*

Die interaktive Kodierung nutzt, neben der Kombination der Verfahren von KIA und CUI, das mit allen verfügbaren Informationen angereicherte Textkorpus. Damit werden *mehrschichtige Analysen* möglich, d.h. es können parallel verschiedene Informationsebenen ausgewertet werden. Mögliche Vorteile, die bei dieser Methode gerade aus der Auswertung der linguistischen Analyseergebnisse entstehen, sind:

- Hilfsmittel zur Entwicklung von Kodierregeln;

- Flexibilität bei der Entwicklung von Kategorien;

- Kontrolle der Kodierung;

- Nachvollziehbarkeit und Transparenz bei der heuristischen Vorgehensweise.

*Kodierung
mit TATOE*

Ein Werkzeug für die computerunterstützte Textanalyse, insbesondere für die interaktive Kodierung, ist die Software TATOE. TATOE hält die Kodierung getrennt vom Textinhalt und ermöglicht so mehrere unterschiedliche Sichten auf den Text. Dabei können die Texte nach einem bestehenden Kategoriensystem weiter kodiert werden, oder ein bereits vorhandenes Kategoriensystem kann um zusätzliche Kategorien ergänzt werden. Es ist auch möglich eine weitere Annotationsschicht hinzuzufügen, indem ein neues Kategoriensystem in TATOE entwickelt und auf die eingelesenen Texte angewandt wird (Alexa/Rostek 1996; Rostek/Alexa 1998; s. auch Beitrag von Lothar Rostek).

4.4 Entwicklung eines modularen Konzepts

Die Anreicherung eines Textes mit umfassender Information und
seine Verwendung für die oben angeführten unterschiedlichen Ansätze erfordern ein Textformat, das es erlaubt, neben dem eigentlichen Text alle vorhandenen und generierten Informationen verfügbar zu haben und wahlweise abrufen zu können. Das Textformat
muß den Ansprüchen eines Standards genügen; nur so ist es über
das derzeitige Projekt hinaus verwendbar. Daher fiel die Entscheidung für SGML. Ein weiteres Augenmerk gilt der mehrschichtigen
Annotation ein und derselben Textsammlung (Alexa/Geis, in Vorbereitung).

SGML

Diese Problemstellung legte es nahe, ein modulares DTD-
Konzept für die Antworten auf offene Fragen zu entwickeln. Dabei
haben sich fünf inhaltlich motivierte Module herauskristallisiert, in
denen fünf verschiedene Stufen in der Bearbeitung der Antworten
auf offene Fragen zum Ausdruck kommen: die Verschriftung, bei der
nun zusätzlich alle projektrelevanten Daten miterfaßt und damit an
einer Stelle zusammengeführt werden sollten, die linguistische Analyse, die konventionelle Inhaltsanalyse (KIA), die computerunterstützte Inhaltsanalyse (CUI) und die Archivierung.

modulares
DTD-Konzept

SGML-technisch sah die Lösung vor, für jedes der fünf inhaltlich
verankerten Module eine Dokumenttypdefinition (DTD) zu erstellen. Dabei zeigte sich, daß jede dieser Haupt-DTDs im wesentlichen
aus derselben Grundstruktur bestand, die an bestimmten Stellen
variierte. Das bedeutet, daß eine eventuell anfallende Änderung an
dieser Grundstruktur in allen fünf Haupt-DTDs durchgeführt werden müßte, damit die Struktur für alle Module über die Zeit konsistent bleibt. Die Wahrscheinlichkeit von Inkonsistenzen ist in einem
solchen Modell sehr hoch. Um dem entgegenzuwirken, wurde die
Grundstruktur aus den fünf Haupt-DTDs extrahiert und in einer
separaten Datei als Rahmenstruktur-DTD abgelegt. Diese Rahmenstruktur ist nun nicht mehr physischer Bestandteil der einzelnen
Haupt-DTDs, sondern sie wird als sogenanntes DTD-Subset von
den Haupt-DTDs aus referenziert. Damit man die modulspezifi-
schen Modifikationen berücksichtigen kann, besteht die Rahmenstruktur-DTD neben den festen Definitionen aus veränderbaren
Platzhaltern. Ein solches Modell bewirkt einerseits, daß die Rahmenstruktur nur an einer Stelle gepflegt werden muß, um eine konsistente Grundstruktur in allen Modulen sicherzustellen, andererseits
erlaubt es, daß sich die Struktur innerhalb der Module an bestimmten Stellen unterscheiden kann.

DTDs

Dieses Prinzip der DTD-Organisation wurde für die linguistische Analyse ausgeweitet. Da die linguistische Annotation auf den TEI-Richtlinien basiert, entstand ein weiteres DTD-Subset für die TEI-Definitionen und ein zweites für die TECA-Modifikationen der TEI-Definitionen. Diese beiden DTD-Subsets werden – neben dem DTD-Subset für die Rahmenstruktur – in der Haupt-DTD für die linguistische Annotation und für die Archivierung referenziert.

Das modulare Konzept bezieht sich somit auf zwei unterschiedliche, miteinander verschränkte Ebenen: Inhaltlich werden fünf Module unterschieden. Diese fünf Module sind SGML-technisch als fünf Haupt-DTDs organisiert, die alle das Rahmenstruktur-DTD-Subset referenzieren. Die Haupt-DTD für die linguistische Annotation und die für die Archivierung referenzieren außerdem noch die beiden anderen DTD-Subsets.

Die Module/Haupt-DTDs sind:

- Modul 1: Verschriftung

- Modul 2: Linguistische Annotation

- Modul 3a: Konventionelle Inhaltsanalyse (KIA)

- Modul 3b: Computerunterstützte Inhaltsanalyse (CUI)

- Modul 4: Archivierung

Die DTD-Subsets sind:

- Subset 1: Rahmenstruktur für Antworten auf offene Fragen

- Subset 2: TECA-spezifische Elemente und Attribute für die linguistische Analyse

- Subset 3: Modifizierte Version der TEI-DTD teiana2.dtd

Bei der Entwicklung dieses modularen Konzepts wurde im Vorfeld das Textmodell des *Corpus Encoding Standards (CES)* (Abschnitt 2.3) in die Überlegungen mit einbezogen. Das darin vorgestellte Textmodell wäre durchaus auf das TECA-Projekt übertragbar. Es hätte den Vorteil, daß neben KIA, CUI und Linguistik problemlos und flexibel weitere Annotationsschichten hinzugefügt und wieder weggenommen werden könnten, indem Annotationsdateien entweder berücksichtigt werden oder entfallen. Im Gegensatz dazu führt bei direkt im Originaltext vorgenommenen Annotationen das Hinzufügen immer weiterer Aspekte auf der Ebene der SGML-Instanz zu einer „Überladenheit" des Originaltextes, häufig auch zu Überschneidungen der Kodierungen und damit zu großer Unübersichtlichkeit, sofern keine geeignete Software zur Verfügung steht, die es dem Benutzer ermöglicht, die verschiedenen Auszeichnungsaspekte voneinander zu trennen. Ebenso ist die Adaption des CES-Modells für die Praxis nur mit

Softwareunterstützung vorstellbar. Für das TECA-Projekt scheitert die Verwendbarkeit genau daran, daß wir bislang keine Software ausfindig machen konnten, die die Handhabung dieses Textmodells unterstützen würde.

4.5 Linguistische Annotation

Bei der Prüfung der linguistischen Annotationsmöglichkeiten in SGML stellte sich heraus, daß von der TEI nicht vorgesehen ist, morpho-syntaktische Ambiguitäten abzubilden. Daher wurden zwei weitere einschlägige linguistische Projekte mit in Betracht gezogen, von denen jedoch keines einen geeigneten Lösungsvorschlag für dieses Problem bot.

Ambiguität und TEI

Bei der *Expert Advisory Group on Language Engineering Standards (EAGLES)* heißt es: „The encoding of ambiguity in morphosyntactic annotation has so far received little attention, and we make no recommendations except to propose that in principle, all the kinds of ambiguity listed above should be distinguishable by different mark-up." (EAGLES 1996)

Ambiguität und EAGLES

Der *Corpus Encoding Standard (CES)* – einerseits TEI-basiert, andererseits an den Ergebnissen des EAGLES-Projekts orientiert – schien auf den ersten Blick über die Möglichkeiten der TEI hinauszugehen und einen Vorschlag zur Auszeichnung ambiger Strukturen zu machen. Bei näherem Hinsehen wurde jedoch deutlich, daß es dabei nicht um Ambiguität geht, die auf den Satzkontext bezogen ist. Es werden vielmehr alle lexikalisch verzeichneten Lesarten eines Wortes gelistet und eine davon als die für den Satz relevante herausgestellt. Ambiguität auf syntaktischer Ebene wird dabei nicht berücksichtigt.

Ambiguität und CES

Diese Ergebnisse führten dazu, daß der linguistischen Annotation im TECA-Projekt die TEI-Richtlinien zugrundegelegt und projektbezogen modifiziert wurden. Die inhaltlichen Modifikationen wurden nach den Regeln der TEI durchgeführt und bestehen im wesentlichen darin, daß zwar nur eine Untermenge der von der TEI vorgeschlagenen Annotationen verwendet wird, die allerdings durch die Möglichkeit ambige Strukturen abzubilden erweitert wurde. Darüber hinaus wurden die einzelnen Strukturelemente in der Regel spezifischer definiert als in der TEI und tragen damit den softwarespezifischen Ausgaben des Syntaxparsers Rechnung. In technischer Hinsicht wurden die Regeln der TEI nicht eingehalten. Im TEI-Modell (s. Abschnitt 2.1) ist die linguistische Annotation quasi die dritte Schicht in einem eng miteinander verwobenen Verbund von Modu-

Adaption der TEI-Richtlinien

len. Für das TECA-Projekt sollte jedoch nur die linguistische Annotation der TEI verwendet werden. Dazu mußte die entsprechende DTD aus diesem Verbund herausgelöst und in die Struktur der Antworten auf offene Fragen eingebunden werden. Um das tun zu können, mußte das TEI-Modul für die linguistische Annotation formal soweit verändert werden, daß es als eigenständige Einheit fungieren kann. Diese Vorgehensweise weicht von den Benutzungsvorgaben der TEI ab, jedoch konnte im Rahmen dieser Projektstufe keine befriedigendere, d.h. vollständig TEI-konforme Lösung gefunden werden. Ein weiterführendes Projekt sollte eine erneute Auseinandersetzung mit diesem Aspekt vorsehen.

5   Beispiel eines Analyseablaufs

Um den Analyseablauf zu verdeutlichen und ein Beispiel für die verschiedenen Annotationsschichten zu geben, haben wir aus den „Stolz-Texten" eine einzelne Antwort aus der Gesamtheit der Antworten auf offene Fragen herausgegriffen. Sie soll exemplarisch für das gesamte Textkorpus stehen. Das Beispiel zeigt das Verhältnis von Markup und Text sowie die hohe Dichte des Markups. Es gibt eine Vorstellung davon, was es bedeuten würde, alle Annotationsschichten in einer einzigen DTD abbilden zu wollen, und warum wir uns daher für einen modularen Aufbau entschieden haben.

Die für jeden Bearbeitungsschritt neuen Teile sind fett herausgehoben; Kürzungen sind durch Auslassungsmarkierungen gekennzeichnet.

Verschriftung   Die in einem gängigen Texteditor verschriftete Antwort umfaßt die Fragebogennummer und den Antworttext des Fragebogens.

```
0196 Gutes Gesundheitssystem , alles kostenlos ;
     Kindergärten waren kostenlos .
```

Konvertierung nach SGML   Bei der Konvertierung nach SGML werden die Antworttexte um die Projektdaten und den Namen des Verschrifters ergänzt.

```
<!DOCTYPE OFFENEFRAGEN SYSTEM "O-FRAGE.DTD">
<offeneFragen>
 <projektdaten>
  <titel>Stolz-Texte</titel>
  <umfragezeitraum von="1.4.98" bis="30.4.98">
  <betreuer>A.G.</betreuer>
  <sprache sprache="DE">
```

   ■   *Modell einer mehrschichtigen Textannotation für die*
■   *computerunterstützte Textanalyse*

```
<fragetxt id-frage="f1">Wenn Sie an die ehemalige DDR
   zur&uuml;ckdenken, gibt es Dinge, auf die Menschen
   dort/Sie (West-/Ostversion) stolz sein k&ouml;nnen?
   Wenn mit ja geantwortet wurde, kam die Nachfrage:
   Und auf was sind die/Sie stolz?</fragetxt>
 </projektdaten>
 <vschrifter>P.L.</vschrifter>

<frageboegen><eineFrage>
<fragebogen ref-fragebogen="0196">
   <antwort ref-frage="f1">Gutes Gesundheitssystem ,
    alles kostenlos ; Kinderg&auml;rten waren kostenlos .
   </antwort>
  </fragebogen>
 </eineFrage></frageboegen>
</offeneFragen>
```

Für die konventionelle Inhaltsanalyse (KIA) werden die Projektdaten um das Kategorienschema erweitert und neben dem Verschrifter
wird auch der Kodierer genannt. Den Antworten als Ganzes werden
dann die aus dem Kategorienschema zutreffenden Kodes zugewiesen.

KIA

```
<!DOCTYPE OFFENEFRAGEN SYSTEM "O-FRAGE.DTD">
<offeneFragen>
 <projektdaten>
  <titel>Stolz-Texte</titel>
  <umfragezeitraum von="1.4.98" bis="30.4.98">
  <betreuer>A.G.</betreuer>
  <sprache sprache="DE">
  <fragetxt id-frage="f1">Wenn Sie an die ehemalige DDR
   zur&uuml;ckdenken, gibt es Dinge, auf die Menschen
   dort/Sie (West-/Ostversion) stolz sein k&ouml;nnen?
   Wenn mit ja geantwortet wurde, kam die Nachfrage:
   Und auf was sind die/Sie stolz?</fragetxt>
  <kategorienschema><kschema-ja>
   <kategorie schluessel="00">trifft nicht zu</kategorie>
   <kategorie schluessel="1">soziale Sicherheit (allgemein)
     </kategorie>
   <kategorie schluessel="10">Ruhe/Friede</kategorie>
   <kategorie schluessel="11">soziale Dienste</kategorie>
   <kategorie schluessel="12">soziale Betreuung
     (medizinisch)</kategorie>
   <kategorie schluessel="2">Kosten und Preise</kategorie>
   <kategorie schluessel="3">Sport</kategorie>
[...]
   <kategorie schluessel="98">weiß nicht</kategorie>
   <kategorie schluessel="99">keine Angabe/kein Text
     </kategorie>
  </kschema-ja></kategorienschema>
 </projektdaten>
 <vschrifter>P.L.</vschrifter>
 <kodierer>A.R.</kodierer>
 <frageboegen><eineFrage>
```

Melina Alexa und Ingrid Schmidt   339

```
   <fragebogen ref-fragebogen="0196">
    <antwort ref-frage="f1" kategorien="12 02 11">
      Gutes Gesundheitssystem , alles kostenlos ;
      Kinderg&auml;rten waren kostenlos .
    </antwort>
   </fragebogen>
  </eineFrage></frageboegen>
 </offeneFragen>
```


Die linguistische Analyse fügt zu den Projektdaten den Namen der
Analysesoftware hinzu. Das Beispiel zeigt die von uns modifizierten
TEI-Annotationen, weist aber weder auf der Lemmaebene noch auf
der syntaktischen Ebene Ambiguität auf.

```
<!DOCTYPE OFFENEFRAGEN SYSTEM "O-FRAGE.DTD">
<offeneFragen>
[...]
 <vschrifter> P.L.</vschrifter>
 <ling-software>TextWorks</ling-software>
 <frageboegen><eineFrage>
  <fragebogen ref-fragebogen="0196">
   <antwort ref-frage="f1">
    <s>
    <phr ana="np">
     <phr ana="attr">
      <w ana="adje" lemma1="gut" lemma-anzahl="1">
        Gutes</w>
     </phr>
     <w ana="nomen" lemma1="Gesundheitssystem"
       lemma-anzahl="1">Gesundheitssystem</w>
    </phr>
    <w ana="sz" lemma1="," lemma-anzahl="1">,</w>
    <phr ana="np">
     <w ana="quantor" lemma1="all" lemma-anzahl="1">
       alles</w>
    </phr>
    <w ana="adje" lemma1="kostenlos" lemma-anzahl="1">
      kostenlos</w>
    <w ana="sz" lemma1=";" lemma-anzahl="1">;</w>
    <phr ana="np">
     <w ana="nomen" lemma1="Kindergarten"
       lemma-anzahl="1">Kinderg&auml;rten</w>
    </phr>
    <phr ana="k-verbp">
     <w ana="k-verb" lemma1="sein" lemma-anzahl="1">
       waren</w>
    </phr>
    <w ana="adje" lemma1="kostenlos" lemma-anzahl="1">
      kostenlos</w>
    <w ana="sz" lemma1="." lemma-anzahl="1">.</w>
    </s>
   </antwort>
  </fragebogen>
 </eineFrage></frageboegen>
</offeneFragen>
```


*Modell einer mehrschichtigen Textannotation für die
computerunterstützte Textanalyse*

6 Diskussionspunkte

Im Projektverlauf haben sich folgende Problemfelder herauskristallisiert:

- *Arbeitsprozesse*
  Dadurch, daß die Strukturierung der Antworten auf offene Fragen nicht nur an den inhaltlichen Anforderungen ausgerichtet war, sondern auch die bei ZUMA bislang üblichen Vorgehensweisen mitberücksichtigte, konnten nicht alle Möglichkeiten der SGML-basierten Strukturkontrolle ausgeschöpft werden. Dies wurde im Rahmen des Projektes bei der KIA deutlich: Die manuell vergebenen Kategorien können in der derzeitigen Modellierung nicht automatisch mit denen des Kategorienschemas abgeglichen werden. Würden bei der Strukturierung konsequent nur die inhaltlichen Aspekte berücksichtigt, ergäben sich möglicherweise noch andere, bislang nicht bedachte Informationen aus der Struktur. Würde man beispielsweise bei der KIA festhalten, wieviele und eventuell auch welche Anhaltspunkte in der Antwort zur Vergabe einer Kategorie geführt haben, könnte man die einer Antwort zugeordneten Kategorien im Verhältnis zueinander gewichten.

- *Konformität mit schon bestehenden Richtlinien/Standards*
  Gerade bei der linguistischen Annotation gibt es eine Reihe von Vorarbeiten, auf die – zumindest auf den ersten Blick – zurückgegriffen werden konnte (TEI, EAGLES, CES). Dabei erwies sich, daß bei keiner dieser Arbeiten die Darstellung ambiger Strukturen vorgesehen war. Durch eine im Sinne der TEI vorgenommene Modifikation konnte die inhaltliche Konformität mit den TEI-Richtlinien sichergestellt werden. Die technische Einbindung des in der TEI unselbständigen Moduls für die linguistische Annotation mußte aus dem gesamten Verband herausgelöst und nicht-TEI-konform modifiziert werden, damit es im Sinne des TECA-Projekts eingesetzt werden konnte.

- *Software*
  Bei der für das Projekt ausgewählten SGML-Software der Firma Softquad Inc. erwies sich der Einsatz des SGML-Editors Author/Editor insofern als problematisch, als der Author/Editor Sonderzeichen in den Attributwerten nicht als Entity-Referenzen exportiert, sondern als Sonderzeichen stehen läßt. Daher muß ein nachgeschalteter Konvertierungsprozeß diese Aufgabe übernehmen. Diese Schwierigkeit besteht jedoch ebenso bei anderen in Augenschein genommenen SGML-Editoren. Darüber hinaus

verlangt die mehrschichtige Textannotation ein Werkzeug, das über die normale Editorfunktionalität hinausgeht und als Textanalyse-Software charakteristiert werden kann. Erforderlich ist dabei eine Schnittstelle zu SGML, wie sie beispielsweise in TATOE realisiert ist.

Als Perspektiven für das TECA-Projekt wären anzustreben:

- *XML-Kompatibilität*
  Die vorliegenden SGML-DTDs sollten auf ihre XML-Kompatibilität geprüft und gegebenenfalls modifiziert werden, damit die Textbasis künftig in einer internettauglichen Form zur Verfügung steht.

- *Textmodel des Corpus Encoding Standard (CES)*
  Die Adaption des CES-Modells für das TECA-Projekt, die im Moment noch daran scheitert, daß am Markt keine Software verfügbar ist, die die Handhabung dieses Textmodells unterstützt, sollte im Auge behalten werden. Damit könnte Annotationen ein flexibel ausbaubares Konzept zugrundegelegt werden, das auch in der Zukunft tragfähig sein kann.

7 Perspektiven

Grundsätzlich gilt, daß je mehr ein Analysesystem über die Texte „weiß", desto

- komplexere Fragen kann der Benutzer stellen;

- genauer kann kodiert werden;

- größer ist die Unterstützung des Benutzers während der Operationalisierung des Schemas, z.B. von Merkmalen zu Kategorien;

- besser kann die Validierung eines Schemas unterstützt werden;

- vielfältiger sind die Textexplorationsmöglichkeiten.

Für das TECA-Projekt werden der Text, seine inhaltliche Kodierung, die linguistische Information und die zugehörige Textbeschreibung (Projektdaten) auf Basis des oben vorgestellten Modells für die mehrschichtige Textannotation explizit repräsentiert und in einer Datei bzw. in entsprechenden getrennten Dateien abgespeichert. Nach dem bisherigen Verfahren wurde die Textbeschreibung separat erstellt und abgelegt, dabei war die elektronische Form nicht unbedingt vorgeschrieben. Die Vorteile des neuen Vorgehens sind:

- die Textbeschreibung kann nicht verloren gehen;

- für die Analyse stehen alle vorhandenen Informationen gleichzeitig zur Verfügung;

- die verschiedenen inhaltlichen Sichten auf einen Text werden getrennt voneinander gehalten;

- die Texte können für unterschiedliche Analysezwecke genutzt werden, dadurch daß die verschiedenen Analyseschichten unabhängig voneinander herausgegriffen werden;

- durch eine flexible Kombination der verschiedenen Analyseergebnisse, und damit auch der unterschiedlichen Analysemethoden, entstehen neue Zugangsmöglichkeiten zu den Texten;

- die Analyse und die daraus resultierenden Auszeichnungen sind jederzeit nachvollziehbar;

- die annotierten Textdaten und die Textbeschreibung können in einem einheitlichen Format archiviert werden und sind als Gesamtheit für weitere Nutzungen greifbar.

Das in Abschnitt 4 beschriebene Modell hat Konsequenzen für das Datenmodell der Textanalyse-Software: Um mehrschichtig annotierte Texte und komplexe Fragestellungen analysieren zu können, um unterschiedliche Darstellungsformen der Daten zu ermöglichen und um genauer kodieren und gezielter validieren zu können, müssen Textanalyse-Systeme mit einem entsprechend komplexen Datenmodell arbeiten. Ein solches Datenmodell muß mindestens die folgenden Informationstypen berücksichtigen:

- Korpus – Subkorpus – Text (Bild – Ton) – Absatz – Satz – Wortgruppe;

- Wort – Grundform (Lemma) – Stamm;

- Kategorienschema(ta) – Kategorien – Diktionäre;

- kodierte Einheiten;

- Relationen zwischen den Kategorien, den Wortformen und den Benennungen.

Mehrschichtige Textannotation sollte man als eine *Option* verstehen. Dabei gilt es, das Verhältnis von Aufwand und Nutzen im Hinblick auf die Analyseziele abzuwägen, also beispielsweise zu hinterfragen, inwiefern eine Trennung der unterschiedlichen Informationsschichten einen Mehrwert darstellen kann. Im TECA-Projekt ermöglichte sie, die verschiedenen Analyse-Ansätze zu testen. Einerseits ist die Tauglichkeit und der Verwendungswert komplexer, mehrschichtiger Auszeichnungen abhängig von der Verfügbarkeit angemessener Werkzeuge, die mit diesen reichhaltig annotierten Texten umgehen können (s. Abschnitt 4.4); in der Praxis bedeutet das, je weniger anspruchsvoll die Auszeichnungen, desto größer die Chance, ein angemessenes Werkzeug zu finden. Auf der anderen Seite beeinflußt der Detaillierungsgrad der Auszeichnungen, wie komfortabel ein System unterschiedliche Analyseaufgaben unterstützen kann; d.h., je detaillierter die Auszeichnung, desto flexibler können die Unterstützungsmöglichkeiten durch die Software sein.

Textanalyse als Aufbau einer Wissensbasis

Durch mehrschichtig SGML-konform annotierte Texte gewinnt man einen anderen Zugang zur computerunterstützten Textanalyse: Man kann sie als Aufbau einer *Wissensbasis* betrachten. Dabei ist unter einer Wissensbasis ein zusammenhängendes Netz von unterschiedlichen Informationstypen zu verstehen. Je nach Interesse und Textanalysezweck des Benutzers könnte eine solche Wissensbasis dann gezielt durchsucht und mit neuen Analyseaspekten angereichert werden.

Mehrschichtigkeit als added value

Der *Verwendungswert (added value)* eines Texts oder einer Textsammlung erhöht sich durch die mehrschichtige Textannotation, da so bearbeitete Texte einem erweiterten Kreis von Nutzern angeboten werden können. Dies wird dadurch möglich, daß die kumulierten Kodierungen in standardisiertem Format flexibel auseinandergezogen werden können, wodurch unterschiedlich annotierte Texte für unterschiedliche Zwecke der Textanalyse entstehen.

Literatur

(Alexa/Geis, in Vorbereitung)
Alexa, Melina; Geis, Alfred: Das TECA-Projekt. Mannheim: ZUMA (ZUMA Arbeitsbericht). In Vorbereitung

(Alexa/Rostek 1996)
Alexa, M.; Rostek, L.: Computer-assisted, corpus-based text analysis with TATOE. In: ALLC-ACH 96, Book of Abstracts (Bergen, Norway). o.O., 1996, S. 11-17

(Alexa/Züll 1998)
Alexa, Melina; Züll, Cornelia: Software for computer-assisted textanalysis: a review. Mannheim: ZUMA, 1998

(Barnard et al. 1995)
Barnard, David T.; Burnard, Lou; Gaspart, Jean-Pierre; Price, Lynne A.; Sperberg-McQueen, Michael C.; Varile, Giovanni Battista: Hierarchical encoding of text: technical problems and SGML solutions. In: Computers and the Humanities 29 (1995), S. 211-231

(Bauer-Kaase 1998)
Bauer-Kaase, Petra: Die Bedeutung der politischen Richtungsbegriffe „links" und „rechts" seit 1974. o.O., 1998. Unveröffentlichtes Projektpapier

(Brachman et al. 1989)
Brachman, R.; Borgida, A.; McGuiness, D.; Resnick, L.: The CLASSIC knowledge representation system. In: Proceedings of the 11th IJCAI. o.O., August 1989

Modell einer mehrschichtigen Textannotation für die computerunterstützte Textanalyse

(Burnard 1995)

Burnard, Lou (Hrsg.): User's reference guide: British National corpus. Version 1.0. Oxford: Oxford University Computing Services, May 1995. Erhältlich im Internet: http://info.ox.ac.uk/bnc/getting/bncman.html

(CES 1998)

Corpus Encoding Standard (CES). o.O., 1998. Erhältlich im Internet: http://www.cs.vassar.edu/~ide/CES

(DeRose/Durand 1994)

DeRose, Steven J.; Durand, David G.: Making Hypermedia Work: A User's Guide to HyTime. Boston: Kluwer Academic Publishers, 1994

(Fuchs/Klingemann 1990)

Fuchs, Dieter; Klingemann, Hans-Dieter: The „Left-Right-Schema". In: Kent Jennings, M.; van Deth, Jan et al. (Hrsg.): Continuities in Political Action: A Longitudinal Study of Political Orientations in Three Western Democracies. Berlin: Walter de Gruyter, S. 203-234

(EAGLES 1996)

Expert Advisory Group on Language Engineering standards (EAGLES): Index of EAGLES96. o.O., 1996. Erhältlich im Internet: http://www.ilc.pi.cnr.it/EAGLES96.

Zu Ambiguität. Erhältlich im Internet: http://www.ilc.pi.cnr.it/EAGLES96/annotate/node23.html

(Ide et al. 1997)

Ide, Nancy; McGraw, Tim; Welty, Chris: Representing TEI Documents in the CLASSIC Knowledge representation system. o.O., 1997. Paper presented at the Text Encoding Initiative Tenth Anniversary User Conference, 1997

(Rostek/Alexa 1998)

Rostek, Lothar; Alexa, Melina: Marking up in TATOE and exporting to SGML. In: Computers and the Humanities 31 (1998), S. 311-326

(Simons 1997)

Simons, Gary: Using architectural forms to map TEI data into an object-oriented database. o.O., 1997. Paper presented at the Text Encoding Initiative Tenth Anniversary User Conference, 1997

(Sperberg-McQueen/Burnard 1994)

Sperberg-McQueen, Michael C.; Burnard, Lou (Hrsg.): Guidelines for the encoding and interchange of machine-readable texts (TEI P3). Chicago, April 1994

Anhang

Verzeichnis der Autoren

Dr. Melina Alexa

Melina Alexa received her Ph.D. in computational linguistics from the University of Manchester, Institute of Science and Technology (UMIST), U.K., where she worked afterwards as Research Associate. She is a Research Associate at ZUMA and has been a member of the Text Analysis group for the last two years. Before that, Melina was a Research Associate at the Integrated Publication and Information Systems Institute (IPSI) of the German National Research Center for Information Technology, Darmstadt, where she worked on corpus-based text type analysis (cross-linguistically) for multilingual text generation purposes. She has co-designed and co-developed (with Lothar Rostek) TATOE, a tool for computer-assisted general text analysis. Her main research focus and current research interests are in computer-assisted text analysis methodology and tools, semantic mark up, computational support for combining quantitative and qualitative text analysis, transfer of corpus linguistics techniques with computer-assisted text analysis methodology, and (standard) markup languages.

Dr. Melina Alexa
ZUMA - Centre for Survey Research and Methodology
B2, 1
D-68072 Mannheim
Tel: +49 (0)621 1246-222, Fax: +49 (0)621 1246-100
alexa@zuma-mannheim.de
http://www.zuma-mannheim.de/research/methods/en/textanalysis/

Angelika Binding

Angelika Binding arbeitete nach Abschluß ihres Mathematikstudiums zunächst einige Jahre als wissenschaftliche Angestellte an der Universität Heidelberg. Beim Springer-Verlag in Heidelberg leitete sie die Abteilung Neue Techniken/Produktentwicklung, und bei der Verlagsgruppe Georg von Holtzbrinck war sie Leiterin des Competency Centre for Content Management, bevor sie in die neu gegründete Holtzbrinck Tochter Activ Publishing, Gesellschaft für medienneutrale redaktionsdienstleistungen mbH, wechselte.

Angelika Binding
Activ Publishing GmbH
Q1/15
D-68161 Mannheim
Tel: +49 (0)621 17 809-23, Fax: +49 (0)621 17 809-28
angelika.binding@activ-publishing.de

Privat: Kaiserstr. 3, D-69115 Heidelberg
Tel: +49 (0)6221 20955, Fax: +49 (0)6221 181846
angelika.binding@gmx.de

Pamela Gennusa

Pamela is Managing Director of Database Publishing Systems Ltd where she has led the consultancy, development, and conversion service activities since 1990. During that time, she has served as consultant for a number of SGML-related applications in the oil, pharmaceutical, telecommunications, and defence industries. Prior to joining DPSL, Pamela worked for Datalogics, Inc. in the U.S. Her last role there was Director of Marketing. She has participated on both the ANSI and ISO committees responsible for the creation of ISO 8879. Until 1992, she served as Co-Chair of the CALS committee responsible for MIL-M-28001. Pamela is a recipient of the GCA Tekkie Award. Each Spring since 1991, Pamela has chaired the GCA's SGML/XML Europe Conference. She has served as President of the International SGML Users' Group since 1992. She also served as Chief Marketing Officer and President on the first SGML Open (now known as OASIS) Board of Directors (1993-1995). In 1992, she became a member of the Graphic Communications Association (GCA) Board of Directors, and serves as Chairperson of that Board in 1997-98.

Pamela Gennusa
Managing Director
Database Publishing Systems Ltd
608 Delta Business Park, Great Western Way
Swindon, Wiltshire SN5 7XF
United Kingdom
Tel: +44 (0)1793 512-515; Fax: +44 (0)1793 512-516
pam.gennusa@dpsl.co.uk
http://www.dpsl.co.uk

Dr. Charles F. Goldfarb

Dr. Goldfarb invented the SGML language in 1974 and later led the team that developed it into the International Standard on which both HTML and XML are based. He serves as Editor of the *SGML Standard (ISO 8879)* and as a consultant to developers of SGML and XML applications and products.

While at IBM Dr. Goldfarb led the project that invented SGML's precursor, GML, in 1969, for which he coined the term markup language. He designed and coded the first and – with its derivatives, notably SGMLS – the most widely-used SGML parser, ARCSGML. He also helped develop IBM's multi-site multi-national GML (now SGML) publishing system, producing 11 million master pages, and served as a market planner for information systems products.

He edits Prentice-Hall's *Definitive XML Series from Charles F. Goldfarb* and co-authored *The XML Handbook* and the *SGML Buyer's Guide*. He has been profiled in Forbes and other publications, and the Seybold Report cited *his SGML Handbook* as the definitive reference on SGML.

Dr. Goldfarb holds the first GCA International SGML Award and the PIA Gutenberg Award. He is a graduate of Harvard Law School and Columbia College.

Dr. Charles F. Goldfarb
Principal Consultant and CEO
Information Management Consulting
13075 Paramount Court, Saratoga, CA 95070
U.S.A.
Charles@SGMLsource.com
http://www.SGMLsource.com

ascha Höning

Sascha Höning, geb. 1963, absolvierte nach dem Wirtschaftsabitur ein Studium an der Fachhochschule für Bibliothekswesen Stuttgart (heute Fachhochschule Stuttgart – Hochschule für Bibliotheks- und Informationswesen – University of Applied Sciences), im Studiengang Wissenschaftliche Bibliotheken und Dokumentationseinrichtungen. Seit 1987 arbeitet er beim Verlag Bibliographisches Institut & F. A. Brockhaus AG. Er wurde dort Leiter der Arbeitsgruppe „Bibliographie" und Redakteur der Brockhaus-Enzyklopädie und zahlreicher anderer Werke des Hauses. 1993 arbeitete er an Konzeption und Aufbau der Bibliographischen Datenbank auf SGML-Basis, die seit 1994 im Routinebetrieb läuft. Seit 1998 ist Sascha Höning Leiter des Servicebereichs „Bibliographie, Information und Dokumentation".

Sascha Höning
Bibliographisches Institut & F. A. Brockhaus AG
Bibliographie, Information und Dokumentation
Dudenstraße 6
D-68167 Mannheim
Tel: +49 (0)621 3901-654, Fax: +49 (0)621 3901-324/406
sascha.hoening@bifab.de

Dr. Thomas Kamps

Dr. Thomas Kamps erhielt 1991 ein Diplom im Fach Mathematik von der Technischen Universität Darmstadt. Danach arbeitete er am Institut für Integrierte Publikations- und Informationssysteme der GMD in Darmstadt. Der Hauptschwerpunkt seiner Forschungstätigkeit lag im Bereich Elektronische Publikationsysteme mit besonderem Fokus auf Informationsvisualisierungsverfahren. Als Resultat seiner Forschungstätigkeit schloß er 1997 seine Promotion über automatische Diagrammgenerierung ab. Ende 1997 gründete er zusammen mit ehemaligen Forscherkollegen die Firma Intelligent Views, welche im Bereich wissensbasiertes Publizieren und Informationsvisualisierung ihre Hauptaufgabenfelder sieht.

Dr. Thomas Kamps
Intelligent Views Software und Consulting GmbH
Eisenbahnstr. 2
D-65347 Eltville
Tel: +49 (0)6723 999-044, Fax: +49 (0)6723) 999-045
kamps@i-views.de
http://www.i-views.de

Prof. Dr. Gerhard Knorz

Prof. Dr. Gerhard Knorz schloß sein Studium der Informatik an der TH Darmstadt 1983 mit einer Dissertation über das Thema „Automatische Indexierung" ab. Seit 1986 ist er Professor am Fachbereich Information und Dokumentation der Fachhochschule Darmstadt.

Gerhard Knorz hat die folgenden Gastprofessuren/Vertretungsprofessuren innegehabt: Computerlinguistik (Universität Konstanz, 1985), Datenbanken (TH Darmstadt, 1989/90), Information Retrieval (TH Darmstadt, 1992). Er vertritt das Gebiet Dokumentationssprachen mit den Lehrveranstaltungen des Faches Informationsmethodik. Sein fachliches Profil umfaßt: Information Retrieval, Wissensrepräsentation, Datenbanksysteme, Text Mining, Mensch-Maschine-Interaktion.

Neben seiner Lehrtätigkeit und den wissenschaftlichen Aufgaben nimmt Gerhard Knorz die folgenden Funktionen wahr: Er ist Herausgeber des *LDV-Forum*, dem Organ der Gesellschaft für Linguistische Datenverarbeitung (GLDV); weiterhin ist er im Editorial Board von *Information Processing and Management* (Pergamon Press), von *RIS (Review of Information Science)* sowie der Schriftenreihe *Schriften zur Informationswissenschaft* (Universitätsverlag Konstanz). Er ist Vorstandsmitglied der GI-Fachgruppe Information Retrieval und des Hochschulverbandes Informationswissenschaft (HI), im wissenschaftlichen Beirat der GLDV, Mitglied des Verwaltungsrates des IZ Sozialwissenschaften, im Beirat des Verbandes Optische Informationssysteme (VOI) und stellvertretender Koordinator für das Gebiet Informationswesen des BMBF-Förderprogramms aFuE.

Prof. Dr. Gerhard Knorz
Fachhochschule Darmstadt
Fachbereich Information und Dokumentation
Schöfferstr. 3, Hochhaus Raum 714
(Postadresse: Haardtring 100)
D-64295 Darmstadt
Tel: +49 (0)6151 16-8499, Fax: +49 (0)6151 16-8980
knorz@iud.fh-darmstadt.de
http://www.iud.fh-darmstadt.de/methodik/index.htm

Dr. Manfred Krüger

Dr. Manfred Krüger (58) ist Geschäftsführer der MID/Information Logistics Group GmbH in Heidelberg, Deutschland. Er lernte und arbeitete in wissenschaftlichen Verlagen und studierte Wirtschaftswissenschaften in Berlin und Mannheim. 1984 machte er sich als Berater und Systementwickler für integrierte Publikationssysteme auf der Grundlage von SGML selbständig. Er beschäftigt sich mit Technologien zur Erstellung, Pflege und Verwaltung umfangreicher technischer Dokumentationen und wissenschaftlicher Publikationen für multiple Medien. Er arbeitet an Projekten in unterschiedlichen Industrien: Normung, Wissenschafts- und Fachverlage, Computer-Software, Telekommunikation, Flugzeugbau, Luftfahrt, Automobilbau und Versicherungen.

Dr. Manfred Krüger
Geschäftsführer
MID/Information Logistics Group GmbH
Ringstraße 19
D-69115 Heidelberg
Tel: +49 (0)6221 14870 Fax: +49 (0)6221 23921
krueger@mid-heidelberg.de
http://www.mid-heidelberg.de/index.html

Lucky Kuffer

Lucky Kuffer arbeitet freiberuflich als Consultant für Internetentwicklung und SGML – hauptsächlich für die Süddeutsche Zeitung. Er ist 35 Jahre, lebt in München und arbeitet seit Mitte 1994 bei der Süddeutschen Zeitung als freier SGML-Consultant; zudem ist er u.a. für Bertelsmann, Burda, Computerwoche und Cybernet als Berater tätig gewesen.

Lucky Kuffer
c/o Süddeutsche Zeitung
Sendlinger Strasse 8
D-80331 München
Tel: +49 (0)89 2183-9381
Lucky.Kuffer@sueddeutsche.de

Dr. Renate Mayer

Renate Mayer hat bis 1986 in Stuttgart Informatik und Computerlinguistik studiert. Seit 1989 beschäftigt sie sich mit dem Thema Dokumentenmanagement und technische Dokumentation, das sie in ihrer Dissertation (1991) beleuchtete. Von 1992 bis 1995 war sie am Fraunhofer Institut für Arbeitswirtschaft und Organisation (IAO) beschäftigt. Seit 1995 ist sie als Management Beraterin bei der CSC Ploenzke AG tätig. Dort widmet sie sich den Themen Dokumentenmanagement und Knowledge Management. Renate Mayer hat sich mit vielen Fragestellungen des Dokumentenhandlings auseinandergesetzt und ihre Erfahrungen in die entsprechenden Projekte in den unterschiedlichsten Branchen eingebracht.

Dr. Renate Mayer
CSC Ploenzke AG
Zettachring 2
D-70567 Stuttgart
Tel: +49 (0)711 72583-43, Fax: +49 (0)711 72583-83
rmayer@csc.com

Dr. Wiebke Möhr

Wiebke Möhr ist wissenschaftliche Mitarbeiterin des Instituts für Integrierte Publikations- und Informationssysteme der GMD in Darmstadt. In den letzten Jahren hat sie an verschiedenen Projekten mitgewirkt, in denen objektorientierte und wissensbasierte Ansätze für den Publikationsprozeß von Multimedia-Publikationen prototypisch realisiert und untersucht wurden. Zu ihnen gehören eine Individuelle Elektronische Zeitung, eine Kunstenzyklopädie, Agenturmeldungen und ein persönlicher historischer Atlas. SGML spielte in allen Anwendungen eine große Rolle. Wiebke Möhr war im Rahmen dieser Projekte für die Dokumentanalyse und die Entwicklung der Dokumenttypdefinitionen verantwortlich.
Bevor Wiebke Möhr zum GMD-IPSI kam, war sie als Redakteurin für wissenschaftliche Publikationen tätig. Sie hat ebenfalls einige Jahre als Dozentin für Deutsche Literatur und Sprache gearbeitet und besitzt einen Ph.D. for Germanic Languages and Literatures der Harvard University.

Dr. Wiebke Möhr
Institut für Integrierte Publikations- und Informationssysteme (IPSI)
GMD-IPSI, Dolivostr. 15
D-64293 Darmstadt
Tel: +49 (0)6151 869-908, Fax: +49 (0)6151 869-818
moehr@darmstadt.gmd.de
http://www.darmstadt.gmd.de/~moehr

Christoph Josef Obermeier

Christoph Josef Obermeier (geb. 18.10.1960 in Pfarrkirchen) studierte Informationswissenschaft/Geschichte an den Universitäten München und Regensburg. 1992/93 war er Wissenschaftlicher Mitarbeiter am Umweltbundesamt Berlin (MONUFAKT-Projekt), 1994-97 Wissenschaflicher Mitarbeiter am

Brandenburgischen Landesamt für Denkmalpflege, Berlin. Seit 1998 ist er Produktmanager Lexika beim Systhema Verlag, München.

Christoph Obermeier
Systhema Verlag GmbH
Produktmanagement Lexika
Frankfurter Ring 224
D-80807 München
Tel: +49 (0)89 32473-149, Fax: +49 (0)89 32473-112
christoph.obermeier@systhema.de

Klaus Reichenberger

Klaus Reichenberger (geb. 1965) erhielt seine Ausbildung als Gestalter unter anderem an der Hochschule für Gestaltung in Offenbach. Anschließend arbeitete er am Institut für Integrierte Publikations- und Informationssysteme der GMD am Thema Interaktionstechniken für elektronische Publikationen, sowie an automatischen Visualisierungs- und Seitenlayoutverfahren. Seit 1997 ist er creative director der Firma Intelligent Views und betreut dort das user interface design für die elektronische Version des Fischer Weltalmanach.

Klaus Reichenberger
Intelligent Views Software und Consulting GmbH
Eisenbahnstr. 2
D-65347 Eltville
Tel: +49 (0)6723 999-044, Fax: +49 (0)6723) 999-045
reichen@i-views.de
http://www.i-views.de

Lothar Rostek

Lothar Rostek arbeitet am Institut für Integrierte Publikations- und Informationssysteme (IPSI) der GMD, in Darmstadt. Nach Abschluß seines Mathematikstudiums trat er 1975 der GMD (damals: Gesellschaft für Mathematik und Datenverarbeitung) bei und beschäftigte sich seitdem mit Information Retrieval, Automatischem Indexieren, Wissensrepräsentation, partiellem Parsing und Faktenextraktion. Seit 1985 ist er an der Entwicklung objektorientierter Systeme beteiligt, wie z.B. das Smalltalk Frame Kit (SFK), ein objekt-orientiertes Modellierungswerkzeug; das XGrammarTool, ein allgemeines Parsing-Tool; die Editor's Workbench sowie TATOE (Text Analysis Tool with Object Encoding).

Lothar Rostek
Institut für Integrierte Publikations- und Informationssysteme (IPSI)
GMD-IPSI, Dolivostr. 15
D-64293 Darmstadt
Tel: +49 (0)6151 869-904, Fax: +49 (0)6151 869-818
rostek@darmstadt.gmd.de
http://www.darmstadt.gmd.de/~rostek

Jörg Schiller

Jörg Schiller hat seinen Abschluß als Diplom-Informatiker 1989 an der TU Berlin erlangt. Seitdem arbeitet er beim debis Systemhaus in Ulm. Durch die verantwortliche Mitarbeit als Leiter von Projekten, die sich mit der Realisierung von Diagnosewerkzeugen für elektronische Steuergeräte befaßten, kam er 1994 mit der Technologie SGML erstmals in Berührung. Heute ist er verantwortlich für eine Gruppe von 15 Mitarbeitern, welche die Themen Diagnoseprojekte und SGML/XML betreibt.

Jörg Schiller
Leiter Diagnose Projekte / SGML-Technologie
debis Systemhaus GEI
Kfz-Elektronik
Magirusstraße 43
D-89077 Ulm
Tel: +49 (0)731 9344-1818, Fax: +49 (0)731 9344-100
joerg.schiller@debis.com

Ingrid Schmidt

Ingrid Schmidt arbeitet seit 1993 freiberuflich als Beraterin für SGML-basiertes elektronisches Publizieren, entwickelt DTD-Konzepte und DTDs und führt Schulungen durch. Seit 1992 war sie an verschiedenen Forschungsprojekten des GMD-IPSI beteiligt. Davor war sie von 1991 bis 1993 für die Texcel Software GmbH tätig, wo sie neben geschäftsführenden Aufgaben auch für die Konzeption und Entwicklung von SGML-Anwendungen zuständig war. Zwischen 1986 und 1991 arbeitete sie bei der MID/Information Logistics Group GmbH in den Bereichen Anwendungsentwicklung und SGML-Beratung.

Ingrid Schmidt
Parkstr. 7
D-69126 Heidelberg
Tel: +49 (0)6221 373266, Fax: +49 (0)6221 374679
schmidt@epc.de

Klaus-Dirk Schmitz

Prof. Dr. Klaus-Dirk Schmitz, Diplom in Informatik und Mathematik an der Universität des Saarlandes (1978), Promotion zum Dr. phil. in Angewandter Sprachwissenschaft und Informationswissenschaft an der Universität des Saarlandes (1985). Von 1978 bis 1992 wissenschaftlicher Mitarbeiter und ausführender Projektleiter in verschiedenen Forschungsprojekten zur maschinellen Übersetzung, zum Übersetzerarbeitsplatz und zur Erprobung einer Studienkomponente Sprachdatenverarbeitung. Seit 1992 Professor für übersetzungsbezogene Terminologielehre am Fachbereich Sprachen der Fachhochschule Köln. Geschäftsführender Leiter des Instituts für Informationsmanagement der FH Köln und des Deutschen Informations- und Dokumentationszentrums für Terminologie (DEUTERM) an der FH Köln. 1. Vorsitzender des Rates für Deutschsprachige Terminologie (RaDT), Vizepräsident des International Network for Terminology (TermNet), stellvertretender Vorsitzender des Deutschen Terminologie-Tag e.V. (DTT), Generalsekretär der Gesellschaft für Terminologie und Wissenstransfer e.V. (GTW), Beiratsmitglied verschiedener Organisationen (Infoterm, DIT, EAFT, Normenausschusses Terminologie im DIN), Mitarbeit im DIN-Normenausschuß „Datenverarbeitungsgerechte Terminologie und Lexikographie" und im ISO Technical Committee 37 „Terminology – Computer applications". Herausgeber, Autor und Mitautor zahlreicher wissenschaftlicher Publikationen.

Prof. Dr. Klaus-Dirk Schmitz
Fachhochschule Köln, Fachbereich Sprachen
Mainzer Straße 5
D-50678 Köln
Tel: +49 (0)221 8275-3272 Fax: +49 (0)221 8275-3312
klaus.schmitz@fh-koeln.de
http://www.fh-koeln.de/fb-spr/su/kdshome.htm

Prof. Dr. Eric Schoop

Prof. Dr. Eric Schoop, Jahrgang 1958, ist seit 1993 Inhaber des Lehrstuhls für Wirtschaftsinformatik, insbesondere Informationsmanagement, an der Fakultät Wirtschaftswissenschaften der Technischen Universität Dresden. 1977 bis 1983 studierte er Volkswirtschaftslehre an der Universität Heidelberg, 1987 erfolgte die Promotion zum Dr. rer. pol. mit einer Arbeit über dezentrale Fertigungsinformationssysteme an der Universität Bamberg, 1993 die Habilitation zum Dr. rer. pol. habil. an der Universität Würzburg mit einer Arbeit über entscheidungsorientierte Informationsverarbeitung mit Hypertext.

Aktuelle Arbeitsschwerpunkte sind prozeß- und strukturorientiertes Dokumentenmanagement in der betrieblichen Dokumentation, Konzeption und Umsetzung von Hypertextsystemen, Informationsmanagement in kooperativen Arbeitsumgebungen, Wissensmanagement und organisationales Lernen sowie die Entwicklung hypermedialer Lernumgebungen für die Neugestaltung der universitären Lehre.

Prof. Dr. Eric Schoop ist u. a. aktiv in mehreren Fachgruppen der Gesellschaft für Informatik und stellvertretender Leiter des Arbeitskreises Hypermedia in der Aus- und Weiterbildung der Gesellschaft für Informatik.

Prof. Dr. Eric Schoop
Lehrstuhl für Wirtschaftsinformatik, insbes. Informationsmanagement
TU Dresden
Mommsenstr. 13
D-01062 Dresden
Tel: +49 (0)351 463-2845, Fax +49 (0)351 463-2171
schoop@wiim.wiwi.tu-dresden.de
http://wiim.wiwi.tu-dresden.de/

Marion Spengler

Marion Spengler (Dipl. Informationswirtin) ist seit Anfang 1996 bei der Verlagsgruppe Handelsblatt im Bereich Elektronische Medien tätig. Dort ist sie vor allem verantwortlich für die Einführung von SGML in der Produktion von Fachzeitschriften. Ihre Arbeit umfaßt dabei die Dokument- und Prozeßanalyse, DTD Entwicklung sowie Systemauswahl und -einführung.

Neben diesen Aufgaben ist sie mit der Entwicklung diverser CD-ROM- und Online-Publikationen betraut. In den Jahren 1994 und 1995 hat Marion Spengler bei Pira International in England als SGML- und Electronic-Publishing-Beraterin für verschiedene Verlage und Institutionen gearbeitet. Dort hat sie auch an mehreren Forschungsprojekten in diesem Bereich mitgewirkt.

Ihre Kenntnisse in SGML hatte Marion Spengler zuvor überwiegend im Rahmen freier Mitarbeit am GMD-IPSI und während ihres Studiums der Information und Dokumentation an der FH Darmstadt erworben.

Marion Spengler
Projektleiterin Elektronische Medien
Verlagsgruppe Handelsblatt GmbH
Kasernenstr. 67
D-40213 Düsseldorf
Tel: +49 (0)211 887-1094 Fax: +49 (0)211 887-1090
m.spengler@vhb.de

Klaus Sprick

Klaus Sprick, Jahrgang 1941, ist bei der dpa Deutsche Presse-Agentur GmbH, Hamburg, Technischer Leiter und Geschäftsführer.

Mit Ingenieur-Diplomen in Elektrotechnik und Kerntechnik kam er nach einer Tätigkeit im Kernforschungszentrum Jülich 1968 zu dpa, wurde dort 1970 Technischer Leiter und 1985 Geschäftsführer. Unter seiner Leitung wurde bei dpa schon 1973 die computergestützte Nachrichtenverarbeitung eingeführt und seitdem ständig weiterentwickelt. In der Agentur sieht er auf effiziente Informationsverarbeitung unter Einsatz moderner Technologien inklusive der Verarbeitungskette bis zum Kunden. Die vollständige Digitalisierung der Produktionsprozesse und die multimediale Darbietung der dpa-Produkte sind Schwerpunkte seiner heutigen Arbeit.

In nationalen und internationalen Gremien förderte Sprick schon früh die Standardisierung der Nachrichtenverarbeitung der Presse. Als Vorsitzender des IPTC Technical Committee schuf er 1979 den ersten internationalen Standard für Nachrichtenformate. In den achtziger Jahren wirkte er als Vorsitzender des Standards Committee des IPTC maßgeblich an dem neuen, heute von vielen Agenturen verwendeten Standard *IPTC/NAA Information Interchange Model (IIM)* mit. Er ist einer der Väter des auf SGML basierenden neuen Nachrichtenformats *NITF News Industry Text Format*, das er bei dpa 1996 in einem Entwicklungsprojekt verifiziert hat.

Sprick war von 1990 bis 1993 auch Verbands-Vorsitzender des IPTC, des International Press Telecommunication Council, und fördert dort heute als Vorstandsmitglied u.a. den Fortschritt der internationalen Normung für Agenturdienste.

Klaus Sprick
Geschäftsführer Technik
dpa Deutsche Presse-Agentur GmbH
Mittelweg 38
D-20148 Hamburg
Tel: +49 (0)40 4113-2400 Fax: +49 (0)40 4113-2407
sprick@hbg.dpa.de

Katrin Strobel

Dipl.-Wirtsch.-Inf. Katrin Strobel, Jahrgang 1971, ist seit Januar 1996 wissenschaftliche Mitarbeiterin am Lehrstuhl für Wirtschaftsinformatik, insbes. Informationsmanagement, von Prof. Dr. Eric Schoop an der Fakultät Wirtschaftswissenschaften der Technischen Universität Dresden. Sie ist verantwortlich für den Projektbereich Dokumentenmanagement auf Basis des Dokumentenstandards SGML und führt im Rahmen ihrer wissenschaftlichen Aufgabenstellung Untersuchungen zur Dokumentationsprozeßunterstützung mit SGML durch.

Nach Schule und Berufsausbildung zum Verkehrskaufmann mit Abitur studierte Frau Strobel von 1990 bis 1995 an der Technischen Universität Dresden Wirtschaftsinformatik und schloß als Diplomwirtschaftsinformatikerin ab.

Dipl.-Wirtsch.-Inf. Katrin Strobel
Lehrstuhl für Wirtschaftsinformatik, insbes. Informationsmanagement
TU Dresden
Mommsenstr. 13
D-01062 Dresden
Tel: +49 (0)351 463-2845, Fax +49 (0)351 463-2171
stro@Rcs1.urz.tu-dresden.de
http://wiim.wiwi.tu-dresden.de/

Dipl.Ing. Leszek Wawryzniak

Leszek Wawrzyniak beschäftigt sich mit dem Thema Dokumentenmanagement und Technische Dokumentation in der Industrie seit 1976 (Implementierung eines Zentralen Zeichnung-Verwaltungs-Systems auf IBM-Mainframes und PDP-11/70 der Polnischen Baumaschinen Industrie). In den Jahren 1978-1993 war er bei Digital als Consultant und Manager tätig und war u.a. an Implementierungen von Engineering Data Managementsystemen bei VW, Bosch, Renault und Ericson beteiligt.

Seit 1994 arbeitet er als Senior Management Berater bei CSC Ploenzke und hat die Implementierung von SGML-basierenden Redaktionssystemen bei Ford Motor Company in USA und Europe geleitet. Außerdem war er an den Implementierungen von JCALS (SGML-Verwaltungssystem für das US-

Verteidigungsministerium) und ECALS (Caterpilar) beteiligt.

Leszek Wawrzyniak beschäftigt sich seit 1986 mit SGML und hat u.a. einen Vortrag auf der SGML Europe 1996 gehalten

Leszek Wawrzyniak
Senior Management Berater
CSC Ploenzke AG
München
Tel: +49 (0)89 54491-316 Mob: 0172-620-7606
lwawrzyn@csc.com

Bernhard Weichel

Bernhard Weichel wurde 1952 in Göppingen geboren. Er studierte Elektrotechnik an der Universität Stuttgart. Im Jahr 1978 trat er in die zur Robert Bosch GmbH ein und entwickelte Software für Motorsteuerungssysteme. Schon bald begann er den Entwicklungsprozeß zu optimieren und auch benötigte Werkzeuge zu implementieren. Bernhard Weichel ist heute Gruppenleiter für technische Informationsverarbeitung. Seit 1995 ist er auch aktiv im MSR-Projekt (Manufacturer Supplier Relationship, eine Initiative in der Deutschen Automobilindustrie), wo er den Einsatz von SGML/XML als Austauschmedium für Dokumentation und technische Daten vorantreibt.

Bernhard Weichel ist verheiratet und hat drei Kinder. Mit seiner Familie ist er engagiert in seiner Kirchengemeinde sowie im Christlichen Verein Junger Menschen in Stuttgart.

Bernhard Weichel
Robert Bosch GmbH
Abt. K3/EES4
Postfach 30 02 40
D-70442 Stuttgart
Bernhard.weichel@pcm.bosch.de

Literaturauswahl

Alschuler, Liora
ABCD . . . SGML: A User's Guide to Structured Information. International
Thomson Computer Press, 1995

Behme, Henning; Mintert, Stefan
XML in der Praxis. Professionelles Web-Publishing mit der Extensible Markup
Language. Addison-Wesley Longman, 1998

Bradley, Neil
The Concise SGML Companion. Addison-Wesley Longman, 1997

Bryan, Martin
SGML: An Author's Guide to the Standard Generalized Markup Language.
Addison-Wesley, 1988

Bryan, Martin
HTML and SGML Explained. Second Edition. Addison Wesley
Developers' Press, 1997

Connolly, Dan (Editor)
XML: Principles, Tools, and Techniques. O'Reilly & Associates, Inc., 1997

DeRose, Steven J.; Durand, David G.
Making Hypermedia Work: A User's Guide to HyTime. Second Edition.
Kluwer Academic Publishers, 1995

DeRose, Steven J.
The SGML FAQ Book: Understanding the Foundation of HTML and XML.
Kluwer Academic Publishers, 1997

Donavan, Truly
Industrial-strengh SGML: An Introduction to Enterprise Publishing.
Prentice Hall, 1997

Ensign, Chet
  SGML: The Billion Dollar Secret. Prentice Hall, 1997

Flynn, Peter
  Understanding SGML and XML Tools: Practical Programs for Handling
  Structured Text. Kluwer Academic Publishers, 1998

Goldfarb, Charles F.
  The SGML Handbook. Clarendon Press, 1990

Goldfarb, Charles F.; Pepper, Steve; Ensign, Chet
  SGML Buyer's Guide: A Unique Guide to Determining Your Requirements
  and Choosing the Right SGML and XML Products and Services.
  Prentice Hall, 1998

Goldfarb, Charles F.; Prescod, Paul
  The XML Handbook. Prentice Hall, 1998

Herwijnen, Eric van
  Practical SGML. Second Edition. Kluwer Academic Publishers, 1994

Ide, Nancy; Véronis, Jean (Editors)
  Text Encoding Initiative: Background and Context. Kluwer Academic
  Publishers, 1995

ISO 8879:1986
  Information Processing – Text and Office Systems – Standard Generalized
  Markup Language (SGML). International Organization for Standardization
  (ed.), 1986

ISO/IEC 10744:1992
  Information technology – Hypermedia/Time-based Structuring Language
  (HyTime). International Organization for Standardization/International Elec-
  tronic Commission (eds.), 1992

ISO/IEC 10179:1996
  Information technology – Text and office systems – Document Style Semantics and Specification Language (DSSSL). International Organization for Stan-
  dardization/International Electronic Commission (eds.), 1996

Maler, Eve; El Andaloussi, Jeanne
  Developing SGML DTDs: From Text to Model to Markup. Prentice Hall, 1996

Rieger, Wolfgang
  SGML für die Praxis. Ansatz und Einsatz von ISO 8879. Springer-Verlag, 1995

Turner, Ronald C.; Douglass, Timothy A.; Turner, Audrey J.
  Readme.1st: SGML for Writers and Editors. Prentice Hall, 1996

Travis, Brian E.; Waldt, Dale C.
  The SGML Implementation Guide: A Blueprint for SGML Migration.
  Springer-Verlag, 1995

Zeitschriften
  <TAG> Newsletter. Architag International Corporation.
  http://tagnewsletter.com

  <ISUG> Interchange: The Newsletter of the International SGML Users'
  Group. http://www.isgmlug.org

  Markup Languages: Theory & Practice. MIT Press.
  http://mitpress.mit.edu/MLANG

Web-Seiten
  GCA Web Page
  http://www.gca.org

  OASIS Web Page
  http://www.oasis-open.org

  The SGML/XML Web Page (Robin Cover)
  http://www.oasis-open.org/cover/sgml-xml.html

  XML FAQ Web Page
  http://www.ucc.ie/xml

  W3C Web Page
  http://www.w3.org

  (Stand der Web-Seiten: Dezember 1998)

Abkürzungen

AACR2
Anglo-American Cataloguing Rules

AAP
Association of American Publishers

AIR/X
Automatisches Indexierungssystem

ANPA
American Newspaper Publishers Association (heute NAA)

ANSI
American National Standards Institute

AP
Associated Press

ARCSGML
SGML-Parser

API
Application Programming Interface

ASCII
American Standard Coder for Information Interchange

ASME
American Society of Mechanical Engineers

ASSIST
After-Sales Service Information SysTem

ATA
Air Transport Association

AVI
Audio Visual Interleave (Videoformat)

BGA
Bundesgesundheitsamt

BNC
British National Corpus

CAD
Computer Aided Design

CALS
Computer Aided Logistic Support; Computer-aided Acquisition and Logistic Support; Continuous Acquisiton and Life-Cycle Support; Commerce At Lightening Speed

CAN
Controller Area Network

CASE
Computer-aided Software Engineering

CDIF
Case Data Interchange Format

CELLAR
Computing Environment for Linguistic, Literary, and Anthropological Research

CERN
Conseil Européen pour la Recherche Nucléaire

CES
Corpus Encoding Standard

CGM
Computer Graphics Metafile

CIM
Common Information Model

CIM
Computer Integrated Manufacturing

CLASSIC
Framebasiertes Wissensrepräsentationssystem

CLIP-ING
Projekt für die Produktion multimedialer Agenturmeldungen

CONSTRUE/TIS
Automatisches Indexierungssystem

CSCW
Computer-Supported Cooperative Work

CSS
Cascading Style Sheets

DAPHNE
Document Application Processing in a Heterogeneous Environment

DBMS
Database Management System

DFN
Deutsches Forschungsnetz

DLL
Dynamic Link Library

DIN
Deutsches Institut für Normung

DMTF
Desktop Management Task Force

DoD
US Department of Defense

DOM
Document Object Model

dpa
Deutsche Presse-Agentur

DSSSL
Document Style Semantics and Specification Language

DTD
Document Type Definition

DTP
Desktop Publishing

EAGLES
Expert Advisory Group on Language Engineering Standards

EDI
Electronic Data Interchange

EMV
Elektromagnetische Verträglichkeit

EPS
Encapsulated PostScript

E-TIF
Electronic Terminology Interchange Format

EURODICAUTOM
Terminologiedatenbank der Kommission der EU

FMEA
Failure Mode and Effect Analysis

FORMEX
Formalized Exchange of Electronic Publications

FOSI
Formatting Output Specification Instance

GCA
Graphic Communications Association

GI
Generic Identifier

GID
Gesellschaft für Information und Dokumentation

GIF
Graphics Interchange Format

GML
Generalized Markup Language

HiL
Hardware-In-The-Loop

HTML
Hypertext Markup Language

HTTP
Hypertext Transfer Protocol

HyTime
Hypermedia/Time-based Structuring Language

IETIS
Integrated Electronic Technical Information System

IETM
Interactive Electronic Technical Manual

IETP
Interactive Electronic Technical Publication

IGES
Initial Graphics Exchange Specification

IIM
Information Interchange Model

IPSI
Institut für Integrierte Publikations- und Informationssysteme der GMD - Forschungszentrum Informationstechnik mbH

IPTC
International Press Telecommunications Council

ISBD
International Standard Bibliographic Description

ISO
International Organization for Standardization

IT
Informationstechnologie

JSML
Java Speech Markup Language

KWIC
Keyword in Context

LAN
Local Area Network

LISA
Localization Industry Standards Association

MARTIF
Machine-Readable Terminology Interchange Format

MATER
Magnetic tape exchange format for terminological/lexicographical records

MEDOC
MSR-Entwicklungs-dokumentationssystem

MESA/MERLAN
MSR-Entwurfs-, Simulations- und Analyseumgebung/MSR-Echtzeitsystem für Rapid Verification in Labor und Applikation

MOM
Message-Oriented Middleware

MPEG
Motion Picture Experts Group (Videoformat)

MSR
Manufacturer Supplier Relationship; Meß-, Steuer- und Regelungstechnische Systeme

NAA
Newspaper Association of America

NITF
News Industry Text Format

OASIS
Organization for the Advancement of Structured Information Standards (früher SGML Open)

ODBC
Open Database Connectivity

OLIF
Open Lexicon Interchange Format

OME
Object Management Engine

OS
Output Specification

OSCAR
Open Standards for Container
/Content Allowing Re-use

OSD
Open Software Description

P3P
Platform for Privacy Preferences

PASSAT
Verfahren zur automatischen Stichwort-Indexierung

PDF
Portable Document Format

POP
Presentation-Oriented Publishing

PROFILE
System zur Informationsextraktion

QS
Qualitätssicherung

RAK
Regeln für die alphabetische Katalogisierung

RDB
Relationales Datenbanksystem

RDF
Resource Description Framework

RTF
Rich Text Format

SAE J2008
Amerikanisches Standard-
Austauschformat für unabhängige
Auto-Händler

SARA
SGML Aware Retrieval Application

SCISOR
System for Conceptual Information
Summarization, Organization, and
Retrieval

SGML
Standard Generalized Markup
Language

strukTEXT
Strukturierung von Text
(SGML-Anwendung)

SQL
Structured Query Language

SZonNet
Online-Ausgabe der Süddeutschen
Zeitung

TATOE
Text Analysis Tool with Object
Encoding

TBX
TermBase eXchange

TCS
Text Categorisation Shell

TEAM
Terminologiedatenbank der
Siemens AG

TECA
Towards Extending Content
Analysis (Projekt)

TEI
Text Encoding Initiative

TIFF
Tagged Image File Format

TMX
Translation Memory eXchange

TREC
Text Retrieval Conference

UML
Unified Modeling Language

URL
Universal Resource Indicator

VIN
Vehicle Identification Number

W3C
World-Wide Web Consortium

WebSGML
WWW Adaption to ISO 8879

WIDL
Web Interface Definition Language

WWW
World-Wide Web

WYSIWYG
What You See Is What You Get

XLink
XML Linking Language

XLL
Extensible Linking Language

XML
Extensible Markup Language

XPointer
XML Pointer Language

XSL
Extensible Style Language

ZGDV
Zentrum für Graphische Datenverarbeitung

ZUMA
Zentrum für Umfragen, Methoden
und Analysen

Register

T

Druck: Mercedesdruck, Berlin
Verarbeitung: Buchbinderei Lüderitz & Bauer, Berlin